Domination, Resistance, and Social Change in South Africa

Domination, Resistance, and Social Change in South Africa

The Local Effects of Global Power

Kathryn A. Manzo

Westport, Connecticut
London

Library of Congress Cataloging-in-Publication Data

Manzo, Kathryn A.
   Domination, resistance, and social change in South Africa : the
local effects of global power / Kathryn A. Manzo.
      p. cm.
   Includes bibliographical references and index.
   ISBN 0–275–94364–X (alk. paper)
      1. South Africa—Race relations. 2. South Africa—Politics and
government. I. Title.
DT1756.M37   1992
305.8′00968—dc20   92–9116

British Library Cataloguing in Publication Data is available.

Library of Congress Catalog Card Number: 92–9116
ISBN: 0–275–94364–X

First published in 1992

Praeger Publishers, 88 Post Road West, Westport, CT 06881
An imprint of Greenwood Publishing Group, Inc.

Printed in the United States of America

The paper used in this book complies with the
Permanent Paper Standard issued by the National
Information Standards Organization (Z39.48–1984).

10 9 8 7 6 5 4 3 2 1

Contents

Preface

During a research trip to South Africa in 1988 I attended a wedding, a "crossover" marriage uniting an Afrikaans speaker named Johannes and an English speaker named Wendy. Although struggling to follow conversations largely in Afrikaans, I was struck nonetheless by the familiarity of the scene; I could have been in England where I was reared or in the United States where I was born and now live. My hosts even referred to themselves and their community as "European." And yet the fleeting glimpse of a black person passing the reception hall window was a reminder that we were indeed in Africa. One word sprung to mind which seemed most aptly to capture my sense of the occasion; that word was *colonial*.

From that moment on I was unable to accept that the politics of South Africa are historically a product of isolationism—that is, to accept the notion that Boers beyond the frontier of British liberal influence articulated a theory of racial difference drawn straight from the Bible and left untouched by any of the ideas of the European Enlightenment. Whatever it was that had shaped modern South Africa, it seemed to me, was intimately bound up with the history of its relations with the West. Investigating what those relations have been, and how they have shaped both the practices of domination in South Africa and the struggles of the oppressed to overcome them, was the research project that resulted in this book.

This book seeks to make sense of South Africa, but it is not a narrow country study intended to expose historians to new archival material. Informed by the critical social theory of Michel Foucault and drawing upon published works and documents, the book examines the effects of global power relations in one particular locale; as such, it goes to the heart of the sorts of questions usually asked by scholars of international relations and comparative politics alike. What is power? How does it operate? How are relations of domination effected and reproduced? How do changing global power relations affect local struggle and modes of resistance? Why are open defiance and mass unity relatively rare; that is, why do oppressed peoples fight among themselves instead of at all times against the dominant elite? What are they fighting about? These questions are the stuff of politics, not of straightforward historical narrative.

Although this book answers the above questions through a historical analysis of the South African case, it is as much about the West as it is about Africa. The ongoing appeal of the concept of civilization to those wanting to justify domination in South Africa, as well as the historical similarities between the methods employed there and elsewhere in the Western world to control people of color, means that white South Africans at their worst (as well as at their best) are rather more like us than we might care to admit. Constituting the country as a pariah governed by alien others in white masks merely obscures the extent to which those others represent the dark side of the Western self. In demonstrating how South African politics are an effect of global power relations, this book will cast a light on contemporary South Africa that illuminates the less noble practices associated with Western civilization.

Deciding whom to thank for their contributions to one's scholarly work is no mean task, for every project bears the mark to some extent of the intellectual interactions that preceded it. First, I must acknowledge the lasting influence of Pat McGowan and Richard K. Ashley, my mentors at Arizona State University. Without Pat, I would never have become interested in South Africa or the Third World, while it was Rick who introduced me to Foucault and critical theory. Neither may care for the use to which I have put their ideas, but I want to point out their contributions all the same.

Since being at Williams College I have benefited enormously from conversations about South Africa with my colleague Michael MacDonald, who also gave me valuable feedback on portions of the final manuscript. We may not agree about much theoretically, but the intellectual exchange has forced me to sharpen and clarify my own thinking on many important points.

Norma Kriger read the entire manuscript, despite being enormously busy finishing conference papers and planning a trip to Zimbabwe. Her careful analysis of the argument and her valuable suggestions for additional reading are greatly appreciated.

Parts of this manuscript were completed after I returned from South Africa in early 1991. The research assistance of Janis van der Westhuizen and the hospitality and conversation of Yolanda Kleynhans enabled me to devote valuable time to assessing F. W. de Klerk's reforms. They also enabled me to spend more time than might otherwise have been possible with Colin and

Nomsa Matlala, without whose friendship I would never have experienced South African life through the eyes of township residents.

Above all, I want to thank David Campbell, for without his professional encouragement, academic insights (not to mention library), and personal support I would not have had the wherewithal to complete this project.

A NOTE ON TERMINOLOGY

It is commonplace now for writings on South Africa to classify the population as either black or white, and when differentiating within the former group to refer to Africans, "Indians," and "Coloreds." If the use of quotation marks is intended to convey a problematization of the enclosed classification—that is, to convey that the identity is constructed and thus contested—then it seems to me that "black" and "white" need to be rendered in that way as well. No racial identity in South Africa is unproblematically given, as the historical material in later chapters will demonstrate. Having said this, I recognize that continuous quotation marks become quickly tedious for the reader. For this reason, I have decided to omit them altogether and will trust to the text to convey the necessary problematizations.

Introduction: Global Power and South African Politics

In February 1990, State President F. W. de Klerk unbanned all major opposition groups and committed his government to the release of Nelson Mandela and other famous political prisoners. Since then, a new word has entered popular discourse to describe the process of change occurring in South Africa: *normalization.* Mandela and others have been released, the National party has expressed an intention to negotiate with "genuine black leaders," National party discourse has shifted from groups and minorities to community rights, the pillars of apartheid—the Land Acts, Population Registration, and Group Areas—have been abolished, universal franchise for the country's black majority has been promised, and a new, mutually acceptable constitution for the country supposedly will emerge from all-party negotiations. All in all, the National party has committed South Africa's white minority regime to a politics of negotiation for a new South Africa.

President de Klerk told Parliament in 1990 that actions to be taken by his cabinet were "in accordance with the Government's declared intention to normalise the political process in South Africa without jeopardising the maintenance of the good order."[1] His speech to Parliament was interpreted a year later by one South African newspaper as an appeal for the maintenance of "Christian values and universally accepted civilized norms and standards."[2] But exactly what does "normalization" mean or, more precisely, what are its intended effects for the millions of ordinary South Africans who have been apartheid's victims? Does normalization involve, as the National party proclaims and so many hope, the movement toward a new, nonracial, democratic South Africa in which real progress away from material deprivation and human indignities can be discerned? In other words, is normalization synonymous with nonracialism and democracy? Are nonracialism and democracy the essence of "civilization"? Or is the maintenance of "civilized norms and standards" a euphemism for the perpetuation of white domination via mechanisms more normal to the capitalist democracies of the West? Finally, should the scrapping of apartheid legislation be considered analogous to the tearing down of an entire social edifice or only to the removal of scaffolding around an edifice strong enough to stand without it?

In order to answer the above questions and make sense of the politics of South Africa today, it is necessary to demonstrate how South African politics historically are an effect of global power relations. Networks of power constitute subjects (or agents) whose struggles and conflicts frequently involve questions of identity and relations between the self and others. Power normalizes relations of domination while disseminating ideas about what constitutes "normality" in dealing with the various types of resistance that domination inevitably generates. What form resistance takes, its magnitude, and struggles among the subjugated themselves over how best to resist are also, in South Africa as elsewhere, a local effect of global power relations.

I use the term *global* instead of the more conventional term *international* for three reasons: (1) South Africa was for centuries several colonies and republics and not a *nation-state* as that term is conventionally understood, (2) many of the external factors shaping subjectivity and social practice have been located within the boundaries of what is now South African territory and not in some other state, and (3) many of the relationships that have shaped the South African situation involve groups and individuals and not the entire nation. *Global*, then, refers to a broad range of entanglements involving the people of South Africa and citizens of other countries.

Although it seeks to interpret the political present in South Africa, this book is not simply a lengthy explanation of the practices of de Klerk's National party. Nor is it, despite its historicization of domination and resistance, a "new" history of South Africa. This book is about the local effects of global power relations involving Western white people and African/Asian black people and about how the relations of power have normalized certain social practices but not others, how they have conditioned the nature of resistance to domination, and how they have produced multiple and often overlapping identities—Western, Christian, African, civilized, barbaric, white, black, and so on. Explaining political change over time requires historical analysis of the effects of power.

The attitude toward power, resistance, struggle, and social change adopted here has been inspired by the work of Michel Foucault. The rest of this chapter, therefore, summarizes briefly what that attitude is and how its adoption leads away from more conventional interpretations of the South African situation.

RESISTING AN ECONOMISM OF POWER

Foucault wants to resist what he calls an economism in the theory of power which links, despite innumerable and enormous differences between them, both liberal and Marxist conceptions of political power.[3] He argues that power is not given, exchanged, or recovered, but is exercised and exists only in action. Power is not primarily the maintenance and reproduction of economic relations but is, above all, a relation of force. As such, power should not be analyzed in terms of cession, contract, or alienation, or functionally in terms of its maintenance of the relations of production; it should be analyzed primarily in terms of struggle, conflict, and war.

Perhaps most important, Foucault insists that power is productive and is not simply a negative force, the sole function of which is repression. He treats power as a netlike organization, or web of relationships, running through the whole social body, which constitutes subjects and endows them with capabilities. The subjects of struggle which power relationships have constituted are always in the position of simultaneously undergoing and exercising their power. This is what Foucault means when he says that individuals are not inert material on which power comes to fasten; instead, they are one of the prime effects of power relationships.[4]

Resisting the view of power as a commodity to be exchanged means overcoming the notion that change in South Africa occurs only when power is handed over from white to black. The tendency to consider South Africa as a problem because whites have power that they refuse to cede to blacks is so deeply ingrained in the shared understanding of most of us that it will not be easy to dislodge. But from a Foucaultian perspective, two difficulties exist with the conventional formulation. One difficulty is that it treats the categories of white and black as static and natural, rather than as identities constituted through social practices and whose meaning, over time, has been ever-changing.

A second difficulty resides with the presumption that blacks are powerless because they lack rights. If they have no power, then they cannot be agents of social change. Thus, non-Marxist writers in recent years have tended to explain progressive change in terms of either the maintenance needs of a capitalist mode of production or the changed material interests of a dominant elite or class. The first argument tends to stress the contradictions between economic realities and white domination caused by skilled labor shortages in an expanding economy,[5] while the second focuses on the behavior over time of an Afrikaner or British capitalist bourgeoisie.[6] In either case, economic development within a capitalist framework is the ultimate determinant of social change in South Africa.

Yet precisely because blacks have exercised power in their relations with whites and others, they have forced changes in both the mechanisms of domination and in the discourses of normalization deployed to sustain them. As Stanley Greenberg has argued,[7] the elaboration of state structures in South Africa is a symptom of insufficient state capacity to direct black lives and not of effective state control. In other words, the extension of the repressive apparatuses of the state (via the expansion of courts, prisons, the police force, the army, and so on) reflects the failure, and not the success, of the state to suppress illegal acts. While Greenberg argues that the dawning realization of this incapacity is behind the present "discourse on legitimacy" and search by some whites for an alternative to apartheid, this book will demonstrate that such a realization is not new. Much of the postwar legislation issued by the National party, for example, was no more than a reissuing or restating of laws already on the books. As with all previous influx control laws and other measures designed to regulate labor, this legislation represented ongoing attempts by the state to exercise power over blacks in the face of an evident failure to do so; new measures of control would not have been necessary had the existing ones been working effectively. The more that white civil society has failed to control blacks, the more it has turned to the state for assistance. The greater the failure of the state's own efforts to control blacks, the higher the number of laws promulgated and structures elaborated in an effort to succeed. Processes of change in South Africa are thus a reflection of black activism and resistance to domination and are not, as liberal understandings of power would suggest, a manifestation of black passivity and powerlessness.

Marxist conceptions of power as class domination attribute South African state policies over time to capitalist influences (be they foreign or domestic) while investing total responsibility for meaningful change in the future to an organized black proletariat.[8] This book draws upon some neo-Marxist or "dependency" writings to demonstrate in later chapters the local effects of global capital relations. Nonetheless, it needs to be emphasized that the attribution of social change to a single, organized class or social actor—be it the white bourgeoisie, the black proletariat, or an enlightened National party—is highly problematic. Such attribution freezes out of the picture a whole range of political practices that often in combination, though frequently unorchestrated, have contributed to change in the past—the behavior of black South African peasants, women, the United Nations, Western investors, and so on.

Another problem with the economism of Marxist analyses of change is the prime importance attached to a static understanding of "class." A number of South African historians a few years ago began to "look at how state forms, identities, consciousness, and structures took many different forms, only coalescing into larger entities (such as 'races') at particular moments."[9] Driven by a desire to reconcile structure and agency and to develop a "decolonized" scholarship which questions imported categories and paradigms, this literature has demonstrated convincingly the simplistic nature of earlier "radical" attempts to correlate class, culture, and consciousness.[10]

In its emphasis on oral tradition, local-level processes, and detailed description, the new social history from South Africa is self-consciously atheoretical and as such has been accused of failing to concern itself with questions about power.[11] In spite of this weakness, however, the work of the social historians shows how identities are socially constructed, not given, and has uncovered a whole range of black political practices of resistance to domination. As such, it can provide a material base for more creative theorizing about change in South Africa.

GLOBAL POWER AND THE CONSTITUTION OF SUBJECTS

The territorial space called South Africa has been part of a global political economy that has shaped its internal politics since 1652 when Jan van Riebeeck established an outpost of the Dutch East India Company at the Cape of Good Hope. Thus, the netlike organization, or web of relations, that has constituted subjects in South Africa is global rather than national in scope. The social whole within which South African subjectivities have been constituted is the global political economy and not the domestic state, for the state is itself an effect of power relations. In other words, the way in which the state variously has been constituted as white (for example, through a 1909 constitution that limits the franchise to whites only), as Western or European, and as African has been made possible by the larger network of power within which the South African state is embedded.

The Age of Colonialism

It is important to recognize that power is global in order to understand how it is that individual South Africans may have multiple subjectivities (or identities) and that struggles not only between whites and blacks but among whites and blacks as well often take the form of conflict over which particular subjectivity to privilege. Take first the notion of multiple subjectivities. Major struggles during the colonial era (i.e., prior to 1945) in South Africa involved Dutch settlers in their relations with colonial administrators (both Dutch and British), with European capitalists, and with missionary and antislavery societies. It was out of these struggles that Afrikaner nationalism emerged. Drawing upon a fairly rich literature that examines the creation of Afrikaner identity and historical contests over its meaning, chapter 1 explains how the nationalist movement constituted those of European/non-British heritage *as* Afrikaners as much as it fought on their behalf. Chapter 1 also demonstrates how blacks began to forge connections with other oppressed and subjugated peoples in their struggles against colonial powers and how, through global social movements such as Pan-Africanism and Ethiopianism, an African or black subjectivity began to subsume the old tribal affiliations.

Carriers of a discourse that constructed European settlers everywhere as "Christian/civilized" and natives as "pagan/barbaric," missionary societies had a number of effects on those who were to become the dominant white group in South Africa. Perhaps most important, they made possible the constitution and regeneration of the identity of the European self; if one was not a European, then one had to be a native and thus barbaric. Almost all settlers felt themselves superior to the indigenous peoples. This is one reason why South African social practices under the guise of such principles as trusteeship so often have claimed to mimic those of other colonial powers, for European identity in Africa implies aligning behavior with that of other Europeans on the African continent.

In contrast to the amount of literature detailing the impact of local struggle on competing nationalisms, little attention has been paid to the effects on racial identity itself of global institutions such as the League of Nations. South Africa's entry into the league brought South African politicians more fully in contact with Europeans who were subjugating colored races on a global scale—not only colonial powers but also white settlers in the United States and Australia. This reinforced European identity by bringing South Africa into the club of "civilized nations" and provided a diplomatic forum within which contested social practices could be justified in standard Western terms—that is, by appeal to the principle of trusteeship. But the League of Nations was not important only because it brought whites together. As a catalyst for demands for racial equality from both within and without its chambers, the league helped to distance the concept of race from its association with nation and align it more closely with the idea of skin color. Chapter 1 demonstrates how polarization between those peoples who demanded equality and those who refused it turned the struggle for racial justice into a fight between two opposing camps—white and black.

As the example of the League of Nations demonstrates, changing relations of power may undermine or reinforce the subjectivities that already exist. After World War II, the rise to global economic hegemony of the United States, in tandem with the concerted efforts of antiapartheid activists around the world to isolate South Africa; the Cold War between the United States and the Soviet Union; and the decolonization of the African continent all had effects on the different identities of South Africa's various peoples.

American Hegemony, the Cold War, and Decolonization

As neo-Marxist and dependency writers have argued, direct foreign investment by American companies in South Africa served to strengthen the ties that already bound South Africa to the West and thus kept Western powers to the fore as a point of identification.[12] Signaling the triumph of private property relations and private enterprise after National party flirtations with the idea of nationalization and socialism in the 1930s, direct foreign investment served to align the South African state more fully with the West against the Soviet Union and its East European allies. But foreign investment also aligned the state more fully against emergent Afro-socialist states on the rest of the continent, the local effects of which have been less considered by the "radical" school. Chapter 2 discusses the way in which capital relations helped strengthen the identification of whites with the West and of blacks with the African experience.

Radical scholars writing about South Africa in the 1970s were influenced greatly by Andre Gunder Frank's dependency theory and thus tended to assume an essential harmony of interests among all of the various fractions of foreign and domestic capital.[13] Analyses of the supposed "alliance of merchants and farmers"[14] or of the alliance of "gold and maize"[15] were commonplace. This type of analysis (preoccupied as it is with exposing the conscious underdevelopment of African peasant societies by capital and the state) has tended not only to overlook the way in which peasant resistance to proletarianization has shaped state policy but also to pay insufficient attention to the effect of struggles among the dominant.

Although it is true that the South African economy remains highly dependent on external sources of capital and technology, capital relations have not constituted merely a "comprador bourgeoisie"; they also have forced private business and state capital during times of social upheaval (as Greenberg demonstrated in his earlier work)[16] to demand meaningful change as a way to retain business confidence. In this way, capital relations have engendered struggle with those who wish to persist with apartheid as a model of race relations for the rest of the world to follow. What exactly constitutes meaningful change is open to interpretation, but F. W. de Klerk's recent moves to scrap apartheid legislation can be read as prompted in part by a desire to break South Africa's isolation and return it to a place within the international community of nations.

While the Cold War stimulated the United States to act more forcefully against racial discrimination at home and abroad in order to win friends in an emerging Third World, it precluded serious hostility toward any state—like South Africa—claiming to represent a bastion of Western civilization in the fight against global communism. Three important points should be noted about the post-1948 era in this regard. First, at the height of the civil rights movement in the United States, the National party went on the offensive, consistently drawing attention to its policy of "separate development" as the solution to race problems in the entire Western world.

Second, the National party justified all policies, including segregation, in terms of a Christian-National Protestant ethic. Intended to appeal to those like former U.S. President John F. Kennedy, who described the U.S.-Soviet conflict as one of freedom under God versus godless, ruthless tyranny, this discourse was part of an ongoing effort to retain South Africa's membership in the club of civilized nations.

Third, the association of communism with demands for racial equality in South Africa's panoply of security laws was another indication of the larger effort to retain Western support for the regime by playing up the country's Western character and anticommunist orientation. The U.S. government busily was labeling any domestic subversive group in the United States as "communist"; by doing the same in South Africa, the National party could claim to be fighting the global Cold War locally and so shift the discursive terrain from racism to anticommunism. The Cold War provided a ready-made discourse, a shorthand language through which South Africa could be upheld as Western at a time when pressures for racial equality were mounting. The success of the South African strategy can be seen in the historical prevalence of "constructive engagement" in U.S. foreign policy. As with the movement to end slavery in the 1800s, Western governments have had to be pushed by their own domestic publics to oppose apartheid with anything stronger than loud words.

A more subtle effect of the Cold War on subjectivity in South Africa was the way it reinforced the historical equations of white with civilization and of black with barbarism. Christianity, economic productivity, and private property were defined as hallmarks of civilization by Western thinkers in the nineteenth century. In theory, if not always in practice, a communist state espouses barbarous traits as virtues and, in seeking to spread its message abroad, plays on historical fears of barbarism overwhelming civilization. The defense of European civilization in South Africa during the Cold War era meant resisting any social change long equated with barbarism and advocated by communists, such as communal ownership of land and absence of the concept of private property. Preserving civilization, in short, has meant defending capitalism.

The U.S.-dominated United Nations kept South Africa tied diplomatically to the West, but it also brought South Africa and colonial powers more fully into confrontation with colonized peoples demanding self-determination. Anticolonial struggle revived historical fears of rape and pillage at the hands of barbarians, prompting Prime Minister H. F. Verwoerd to hold a referendum on whether or not South Africa should become a republic. This referendum seemed to indicate a "circling of the wagons," or defiant celebration of white unity, in the face of mounting pressure for change from the West, from Africa, and from local resistance movements. Yet white South Africans historically are too implicated in global relations to relish isolationism or to succumb to a "laager" mentality. Chapter 2 argues that it was not for any inherent economic reason (such as the need for cheap labor) that the idea of homelands as independent sovereign entities took hold of the National party. In order not to be seen as out of step with the march of history, the National party advocated a policy of separate development on the basis of the reality of incipient nations within South Africa itself. African peoples everywhere were demanding independence; by "decolonizing" the "nations" under its protection, the National party reckoned that it could fend off impending international ostracism and domestic upheaval. A good deal was at stake in selling the neocolonial project of separate development, so much so that the National party continued trying to sell it to Africa long after it had abandoned hope that the West would buy it.

Separate development could not appeal to blacks because it was built upon the notion of South Africa as a state belonging to only one nation, a white nation. Another reason it could not appeal to blacks was not that it appealed to the principle of self-determination, but that it privileged the wrong self. As African National Congress (ANC) activist Govan Mbeki argued at the time, "there is no similarity at all between what the people of Kenya or Sierra Leone have and what the Nationalist Party is imposing on Africans."[17] Had the homelands system actually granted a genuine form of political autonomy, it might have been more accepted, particularly by rural people who had struggled for local control of their own affairs. But, even then, acceptance would have been contingent upon an idea of regional autonomy within a united entity and not upon national autonomy within a South African constellation of states. African nationalism for blacks did not mean breaking Africans down into sovereign units for the Zulu, Xhosa, and so on; what was desired was freedom for the African people as a whole, not for each tribe.

At the same time, African decolonization brought to the surface struggles over African identity in the same way that earlier struggles with the British had highlighted contested understandings of Afrikaner identity. Chapter 2 points out how the differences between the Pan-Africanists, associated currently with the Pan Africanist Congress (PAC), and the Africanists, as represented by the existing African National Congress, replicate historical conflicts within Afrikanerdom as well.

Whatever the differences between them, neither the ANC nor the PAC has granted legitimacy to the idea of homelands. Faced with ongoing global and local opposition to separate development, the National party in office has responded in two quite different ways to South Africa's pariah status.

One reaction reflects the influence in the National party of P. W. Botha, first as defense minister under B. J. Vorster and then as state president. Looking for a way out of trouble in the lessons of a heroic and mythical Boer past, Botha set about symbolically reenacting the 1838 Battle of Blood River between Boers and Zulus. Brought into a new tricameral parliament in 1983 as junior partners to whites, the Coloreds and Indians were symbolically the servants who fought with the Boers inside the wagons. Africans were the enemy—communists—who must be excluded by force rather than assimilated by negotiation.

This strategy was bound to fail, not only because the "servants" were not loyal and the "enemy" refused to be defeated, but because it could not appeal to the majority of Afrikaners who did not relish isolation and whose sense of national identity was expanding to incorporate other South African citizens. Exemplified by editorials in the Afrikaans press in 1980, it was evident that there were still Afrikaners who refused to consider whiteness the hallmark of their identity. Even while the Botha government was "circling the wagons," Afrikaans-speaking whites began casting about for an alternative to neocolonial solutions to domestic problems and to policies built upon a privileging of a mythical heroic subject.

The decolonization of Zimbabwe in 1980—that is, the experience of another settler society—set in motion a debate about whether the National party should negotiate power sharing with the black majority and *not* about domestic factors such as township unrest and the accession to power of F. W. de Klerk. Local factors undoubtedly strengthened the "let's negotiate" forces against the "fight-at-all-costs" supporters, but the onset of the debate was nonetheless much earlier than the outbreak of mass protest in 1984, as the final part of chapter 2 will show.

The lesson of Zimbabwe suggested to many Afrikaans-speaking whites the folly of trying to retain all power and privilege in the teeth of widespread opposition—everything would be lost in the attempt. To negotiate from a position of strength, retaining most of what had been won, was viewed as the better course of action. Underpinning de Klerk's willingness to negotiate a "new" South Africa was not a desire to negotiate a transition to a nonracial democracy but was the perception that, with the end of the Cold War, the regime's major adversaries had been weakened.

As the conflicts engendered by separate development highlight, an understanding of how power relations have constituted subjectivity in South Africa is necessary to understand what motivates political struggles. It is tempting to explain struggle by saying that blacks want to be represented in parliament and whites will not let them. At one level, this is undoubtedly the case. But what the notion of multiple subjectivities illuminates is how the identity of the subject to be represented or privileged is by no means fixed and given; it is itself an object of struggle. The drawing of boundaries between subjects is a political act, one usually contested by many of the subjects themselves who then seek to redraw the boundaries in various ways.

These conflicts are illustrated throughout this book by reference to the ways in which identifying terms are used. The term *Afrikaner* has been used to refer to the descendants of Dutch settlers only, to both Dutch and English settlers, and to both Dutch settlers and people of mixed race. *Native* has been used to refer to indigenous peoples only as well as to both indigenous peoples and those of mixed race. *African* has included indigenous peoples only, both indigenous peoples and those of mixed race, and all peoples who profess their loyalty to Africa. The meanings of the terms black and colored/Colored have also been contested and thus shifted over time. Often these differences have turned on whether identity is presumed to be something that can be freely chosen or is taken to be fixed and given by nature or heritage; questions of identity thus have been central to political struggle, in South Africa as elsewhere.

NORMALIZING DOMINATION: THE EXERCISE OF POWER THROUGH DISCIPLINE

Analysis of how power is exercised from a Foucaultian perspective necessarily extends beyond the limits of the state apparatus. The state, for all its omnipotence, does not occupy the whole range of actual power relations and can only operate on the basis of other, already existing power relations. The state consists, in other words, "in the codification of a whole number of power relations which render its functioning possible."[18] More central to the exercise of power than state institutions, for Foucault, is the production of truth.

Foucault uses the term *discipline* to refer to a type of power that is exercised by means of both continuous surveillance and the workings of knowledge-producing apparatuses, or disciplines (such as schools, universities, and the media), which present mechanisms of domination as normal, natural, and even desirable. These disciplines may be the carriers of a discourse that speaks of a rule, but the rule is not a juridical one deriving from sovereignty; it is a natural rule, a norm. The code that the disciplines come to define is not that of law but that of normalization. By normalizing mechanisms of domination—such as differentiation, hierarchization, and exclusion—discipline renders repression unnecessary. Discipline engenders in everyday existence the widespread acceptance of and compliance with norms, thereby containing possible resistance within narrow and tolerable bounds. The weakness of disciplinary power, as a consequence, often manifests itself in overt and widespread repression.[19]

In colonial societies, the key knowledge-producing apparatuses were the schools and churches affiliated with various European missionary societies. Through discourse, they effectively normalized certain practices and ways of thinking about the world, thereby delimiting the range of possibilities for both dominant and subordinate alike.

As already mentioned, missionary influence made possible the constitution and regeneration of European identity in Africa. But it also explains why South African social practices to this day so often have been justified in terms of a "civilizing mission," or the defense of European/Western civilization on a "barbarous" continent. As chapter 1 discusses in more detail, what has been played out in this context are different European understandings of identity/difference and clashing perspectives on what constitutes appropriate strategy when encountering the alien, foreign, and potentially dangerous "other."

In a seminal work on the conquest of America by the Spaniards, Tzvetan Todorov showed how debates between the administrators Las Casas and Sepulveda over how to treat the Indians were a confrontation between the two major hierarchies of identity/difference at work in medieval Europe: that of Christian/pagan and civilized/barbarian. These categories obviously overlapped to a considerable extent because Christianity was often considered a hallmark of "civilization"; this view certainly was present in African mission schools and churches. But an important distinction was drawn in terms of the presumed ease of movement from one condition to the other. The civilized/barbarian dichotomy was more fixed in the sense that differences were thought to represent entrenched and natural characteristics. The Christian/pagan dichotomy was less fixed. Christianity was not a "natural" condition; it was voluntary in that it required only the freely chosen adoption of faith.

Beginning from a postulate of innate difference, the civilized/barbarian dichotomy invoked by Sepulveda treated enslavement (or worse, extermination) as an appropriate strategy for dealing with the barbarian other. In contrast, the Christian/pagan distinction made by Las Casas began from the postulate of identity and presupposed that the pagan other could be taught to resemble (and eventually be assimilated with) the Christian self. Neither orientation seeks to end dominion over other peoples or escapes the presumption that other peoples are inferior to the self. The primary question is whether that dominion entails violent conquest or "peaceful" colonialism and religious conversion.[20]

Beginning from the postulate of innate difference, the early European settlers at the Cape of Good Hope enslaved the indigenous Khoikhoi peoples and exterminated the San peoples. As the Cape colony expanded eastward in the 1800s, there clearly existed those who wanted to exterminate the troublesome Xhosa as well. But they were constrained by the influence of missionary societies operating from the presupposition that the alien other could be taught to resemble the civilized European self and eventually become assimilated (the postulate of identity). In response to the claim that colonizers had a duty to bring Christianity to the indigenous peoples, European settlers began to invoke a "civilizing mission" to justify a wide range of social practices that entailed domination of the other but nonetheless fell short of extermination and enslavement.

The defense of Christian civilization has been the most consistent justification for white rule in South Africa, deployed by the National party even more often than the defense of Afrikaner self-determination. The ongoing availability of the appeal to civilization is due to the essential plasticity of the concept—that is, to a continual rewriting of what the essence of civilization is. With missionary successes in converting blacks to Christian religions and educating them in mission schools, along with the necessity to justify land dispossession and colonial expansion, settlers in South Africa, as elsewhere, began to emphasize economic productivity and private property relations as factors distinguishing civilized from barbarous society. The fact that the same discourse was deployed to justify domination from the Americas to the Cape demonstrates the global nature of the power relations that constituted and regenerated the European identity of settler societies.

Mission schools and churches worked against the unifying thrust of global social movements, such as Pan-Africanism and Ethiopianism, to stifle the emergence of a united front among the oppressed. Considering themselves inferior to Europeans yet superior to the largely uneducated mass of their fellow countrymen in the rural areas, the African elite received support from neither social group and was despised by both. Struggling to defend existing rights via petitions, deputations, and education of the Bantu people, formal organizations such as the African National Congress did not reject the premise of white superiority until the 1940s.

The policies that the United party (UP) began to espouse in 1946 and those that the National party (NP) initiated in 1948 reflected again a confrontation between the postulate of identity and the postulate of difference. Defending the UP's plan to extend limited rights to blacks, Jan Smuts argued that it was consistent with the idea and practice of "guardianship" to give these people, as they "developed," a certain measure of political rights and, in so doing, to ensure the position of the European in South African society.[21] Guardianship itself is consistent with the postulate of identity because it is built upon the notion that the other, although inferior to the self, can eventually come to resemble the self ("develop," like a child into an adult) and be assimilated into one's own society. Apartheid, on the other hand, is based on the premise that each culture must develop in its own sphere because the capacities for development are racially determined. Rejecting integration and assimilation as legitimate ways to perpetuate "civilization, culture, and way of life," the NP operated from the postulate of difference. The diversity it detected everywhere was taken to be the product of entrenched and natural characteristics.[22]

The notions that capacity for civilization is fixed by race—that is, genetically determined—and that the object to be civilized is a nation and not an individual flowered in the 1930s in South Africa as a result of academic contact with European schools and universities, particularly those attended by Afrikaans speakers. The French Revolution, German romanticism, Kuyperian (Dutch) theology, and National-Socialism all are "modern" European intellectual currents that underpinned National party policy after World War II and that came to fruition in the 1960s with "homelands" and the policy of separate development. Consistent with the postulate of difference, blacks were considered inherently alien; therefore, it was believed that any attempt to assimilate them would lead only to trouble and strife. What the world now knows as apartheid may well represent the failure of the Enlightenment to permeate southern Africa; as a way of life based on the postulate of innate difference, apartheid is, nonetheless, a product of contact with modern Europe, not of African isolation.

In insisting that its policies were consistent with the principle of guardianship and that they formally recognized innate cultural differences among the black people themselves, as well as their incipient "nationhood," the NP claimed to be much more closely in tune with Western colonial practices than its predecessors had been. It also sought to refigure the conventional way in which the "problem" of South Africa was understood, by shifting the terms of political debate from the question of how to empower a majority to how to guarantee and protect the rights and freedoms of each minority.

The National party scheme required acceptance of arbitrarily drawn boundaries between whites, Coloreds, Africans, and Indians. A major problem was that many of the people so constituted (in particular, Coloreds, who considered themselves variously as Afrikaans, colored, Malay, Griqua, or African, but rarely Colored) did not identify themselves in such terms and did not recognize the supposed cultural divisions separating them from others in a different category. This problem in itself was certain to generate struggle. But the NP went further and designated these groups as races. The designation scheme was innovative not because it separated races, whose existence could be unproblematically assumed, but because of the way that it constituted racial identity and separated people on that basis. This racialization of identity was aimed primarily at Africans and equated race with tribe—the Xhosa became a race, the Tswana became a race, and so on—but under National party initiative the Colored and Indian groups were to be considered different races as well.

To succeed, multiracialism (i.e., the constitution of multiple racial identities) had to overcome three obstacles. First, it needed to negate the influence of global social movements such as Pan-Africanism, which had put an end to the race equals tribe equation that opposition movements such as the ANC had once considered normal.[23] Second, it had to break the association of race with skin color, which the League of Nations had helped to render normal. Third, it had to overcome more localized affinities; the tribes identified by the National party and others as incipient nations bore little relationship to many people's self-understanding or even to the "scientific" evidence on which the NP supposedly based its policies. The journal *Bantu Studies*, for instance, was devoted in the 1930s to articles on such tribes as the Lamba, Aba-Mbo, Zulu, Thonga, Balobedu, BaMasemola, Lovedu, and Phalaborwa, only one of which—the Zulu—is recognizable as a tribe today.[24] Obviously, these tribes were incorporated for classification purposes into larger entities, but the incorporation often was done in a manner that made little sense to the people involved. The Tshidi people, for example, were from an area now incorporated into BophuthaTswana; when homeland acts were promulgated, they protested that the sinking of their identity into a generic Tswana nationality had no basis in either history or contemporary political reality.[25] The Mfengu of the Cape are considered members of the Xhosa nation (and citizens of the Ciskei), yet they fought alongside the British against other Xhosa-speaking Africans in 1934.[26] The Griqua, a largely autonomous community in the nineteenth and early twentieth centuries, were categorized as Colored, a classification that had little meaning to them.

The arbitrary, vague, and often inconsistent way in which the NP constructed difference among blacks (discussed in chapter 4) was reflective of the lack of systematic criteria by which to differentiate blacks from each other and from whites. Whatever measure was chosen—Christianity, private property, religion, culture, language, even skin color—would have resulted in an inability to differentiate many of the black others from the white self. Multiracialism thus was fraught with political problems. The National party's next innovation, which was national independence for the African races, appeared to hold out more promise because the NP strove to work with global trends, like African nationalism, and not against them. Hitting upon the idea of "decolonizing" its own African "nations" (an idea vehemently rejected by the NP in the late 1940s), the National party intended to "make foreign" a large percentage of the domestic South African population.

Long-term social stability in South Africa required more than repression to contain dissent. Putting beyond question, or treating as natural and normal, that which was socially constructed and open to contestation was also required. In this regard, the NP turned to knowledge-producing apparatuses to normalize its new practices of domination. One form of knowledge-producing apparatus was the government-appointed fact-finding commission. Like the Tomlinson Commission in the 1950s (which provided "scientific" proof for the claim that Africans are not a homogeneous national group), these commissions throughout the history of South Africa have used so-called experts to disseminate a particular truth about South Africa, its history, and its peoples.[27] Others in the business of naturalizing the notion of social heterogeneity during the National party's first term in office were affiliated with the Afrikaner Broederbond and thus were aimed at the Afrikaans-speaking community itself. The most important of these were the Institute for Christian-National Education (ICNE) and the South African Bureau for Racial Affairs (SABRA), formed to counter the influence of the more "liberal" South African Institute for Race Relations (SAIRR).

Undoubtedly, it was the state's own schools and universities, through the mechanism of "Bantu education," that were the key knowledge-producing apparatuses of the National party era; as stated previously, such apparatuses in earlier periods of South African history were mission schools and churches. The plan to tie black identity to the race or tribe, rather than to the common society, required removing education from the hands of so-called liberals. Bantu education was the other side of the coin of homelands creation; the latter could not succeed unless the former was able to naturalize tribal identity.

RESISTANCE AND THE UNEVEN EFFECTS OF NORMALIZATION

In thinking about how disciplinary power has affected struggle and change in South Africa, it becomes clear that the dissemination and acceptance of a norm are bound to be uneven, like the spread of capitalism. The norm may be accepted only by the dominant and thus may generate mass resistance from the subjugated in a two-way struggle.[28] Or the norm may filter only partially among the oppressed, so that some groups but not others accept certain practices as normal, while the same groups accept some norms and reject others. The second part of this book attempts to demonstrate how this latter situation, despite the simple black/white dichotomy usually invoked, is more typical of South Africa.

The differential effects of mission schools and churches is one important factor in accounting for differences among the subjugated, for those most removed from white society and the discourse of the civilizing mission— such as peasant members of independent African churches—have been least acceptant of particular practices of domination. Inevitably, the oppressed peoples will struggle among themselves over questions of identity and relations between self and other; as a result, a united front of mass resistance to domination has been relatively rare. This situation also accounts for such phenomena as black-on-black violence and more generally, political conflicts among the subjugated; they are an effect of normalization, not of inherited genetic predispositions toward aggression or inherent tribal instincts.

The uneven effects of normalization can be detected even where resistance operates overtly. Early struggles by the formal black political organizations, for example, often were built around acceptance of a civilized/uncivilized dichotomy and of the normality of considering certain people, supposedly in need of "upliftment," as unqualified to vote. At the same time, these groups rejected many of the practices supposedly consistent with a civilizing mission. As chapter 3 demonstrates, the notion that blacks would be better off laboring for whites than leading idle lives on their own land has never been accepted by the majority in South Africa; their rejection of such an idea explains why demands for economic justice, autonomy, and dignity have been more central to political struggle than demands for the franchise. Any negotiated settlement in South Africa in the future that fails to take these factors into account is doomed to fail.

Because disciplinary power seeks to engender in everyday existence the widespread acceptance of and compliance with a norm, mass demonstrations in protest against specific laws are not the only form that political struggle may take. Rather than focusing on the state, resistance may focus on those knowledge-producing apparatuses, such as schools, that cast certain mechanisms of domination as normal. In South Africa, it is not incidental that black education has been a focus and township schools a locus of ongoing resistance or that a major movement like Black Consciousness emerged out of the universities. Bantu education usually is condemned for being discriminatory because facilities for blacks are clearly inferior to those for whites. But this criticism is not the only reason that schools and universities so often have been the sites as well as the object of struggle in the postwar era. The ANC's founding of its own alternative schools in the 1950s, the people's education movement started in Colored schools in 1980, and the more recent slogan of "education for liberation" suggest that black opposition to apartheid has been as much about the rejection of a particular truth about South Africa's people, their history, and their identity as it has been a demand for better facilities or representation in the state. As Black Consciousness leader Steve Biko insisted, blacks must rewrite their history and produce in it the heroes that form the core of resistance to domination.[29] That other demands also have been prevalent is not disputed, but they could not have been made at all if the notion of national diversity among African people had been completely normalized.

Localized resistance also has involved ignoring laws that are unfair and unjust, boycotting shops that do not treat black people with respect (i.e., by calling blacks "Kaffir," forcing blacks to wait until whites have been served first, or making blacks use separate entrances), and countering strategies of differentiation with a celebration of identity (such as using the term *black* to embrace all the victims of white domination). These are all examples of widespread political strategies of resistance to domination, even though they do not take place within or against the central institutions of the state.[30]

Resistance, in short, frequently is localized and focused on the conditions of everyday life, precisely where normalization seeks its greatest effect. Localized resistance in South Africa frequently has been unorganized, but lack of organization does not mean that localized resistance has no effect on the practice of domination. James Scott suggests that each realm of open resistance to domination is shadowed by a "hidden transcript" which aims at the same strategic goals but whose low profile is better adapted to resisting an opponent who probably could win any open political confrontation. Enabled by the inability of the dominant to destroy entirely the autonomous social life of subordinate groups—their churches, social clubs, coffee houses, and so on—this transcript contains not only speech acts but a whole range of practices, which in peasant societies often take the form of poaching, pilfering, clandestine tax evasion, and intentionally shoddy work for landlords. Scott suggests that the offstage discursive practices, at a minimum, sustain resistance until the time is ripe for more overt action, although the aggregation of petty acts of resistance may have dramatic economic and political effects in their own right.[31] The importance of autonomous social spaces also explains why struggles to retain autonomy often have been as central to political resistance as demands for representation in the state.

It is not possible to account for a wide range of social practices by the dominant economic elite, by the state, and by mass opposition movements in later eras without considering aspects of a hidden transcript of resistance such as strikes, breaches of labor contracts, diamond smuggling, illicit alcohol trafficking, tax evasion, economic boycotts, and so on. Most scholarly explanations for why farmers, mineowners, and white workers demanded racially discriminatory legislation from the state point to the nature of class antagonisms among whites. Yet such legislation was as much the product of resistance to enforced proletarianization and land dispossession as it was the product of struggles within white society. Chapter 3 shows how the demands of mineowners for hut taxes, for the compound system for mineworkers, for alcohol prohibition, for increased police surveillance in urban areas, and for prohibitions on the right to strike were driven by resistance to domination rather than by class struggle among competing white groups.

As for the state, the promulgation both of increasingly onerous legislation and of the odd "progressive" law before 1948 is indicative less of enormous state power than it is a symptom of insufficient state capacity to exercise power over black lives. When black South Africans have resisted domination by ignoring the edicts of the state, they have exercised power and have not been its victims. The more that white civil society has failed to control blacks, the more it has turned to the state for assistance. The greater the failure of the state's own efforts to control blacks, the higher the number of laws promulgated and structures elaborated in an effort to succeed. This correlation explains the proliferation over time of discriminatory legislation, much of which takes the form of amendments to earlier laws to try to improve their efficacy. Progressive legislation—such as the bill introduced in 1947 to recognize trade unions for blacks—merely codified existing (if illegal) practices rather than instantiated something new; trade unions were alive and active despite government laws banning their existence. By the same token, the recent relaxation of pass laws codifies the failure of the state to exercise control over the rate of African urbanization. Specific practices of the state as it has operated over time are thus a reflection of black activism and resistance to domination.

Localized forms of resistance to domination also hold the key to understanding modes of mass resistance that much of the literature on South Africa treats as peculiarly "modern," namely, consumer boycotts, nonpayment of taxes, boycotts of puppet political structures, strikes, and armed rebellion. As the work of the new social historians has shown, it was workers and peasants, many of whom lived in rural areas and broke away from the paternalistic control of missionaries to join African separatist churches, who initiated such forms of resistance. If these practices eventually were to become widespread in urban areas, it was because they "migrated" with rural peasants and were used again in a different context; more typically urban practices, such as the formation of trade unions, attracted support in rural areas as well. In this sense, the forms of resistance now prevalent on a mass scale are an effect of domination, not of modernization, because they have been made possible by the constant recycling of people between urban and rural areas which migratory labor policies have entailed.

Struggles against an education designed to normalize the notion of national diversity among the African people have been central to political struggle since 1948. Chapter 4 shows that between 1948 and 1973 (when the National party began to reform apartheid) an ongoing hidden transcript of resistance existed that involved such practices as nonpayment of taxes, illegal entry to the towns, and illicit beer brewing and sale.[32] Numerous pieces of legislation issued by the state during this period can be understood only as attempts to stamp out such practices. The dissemination of Black Consciousness philosophy throughout schools, universities, and other community groups was in some sense a hidden transcript of resistance to domination that enabled later mass protests.

At the same time, the tendency of the oppressed to engage in practices that involved open confrontation and defiance increased.[33] By closing off to "civilized blacks" every avenue of incorporation into a common society, the NP forced elite blacks to throw in their lot with the oppressed masses in a way that the old liberal system never had. The NP's acceptance of the postulate of difference and, by implication, the notion that blacks would *never* be assimilated into white society brought home the futility of organizing political action around the demonstration of just how far "civilization" had spread among the "natives." Consequently, forms of resistance prevalent in rural areas in an earlier era came to be the dominant modes of struggle everywhere after 1948.

Apartheid paradoxically provided the conditions for mass struggle, of which the nurturing of a common black identity was one ingredient, at the same time as the National party tried to wipe out the notion of a single oppressed people by constituting national identities. But this does not mean that struggles among the oppressed themselves were nonexistent or that the effects of normalization were not evident. Even where resistance operated overtly, indications existed of the absence of the sort of common identity that the concept of blackness entails. This absence was most evident in the famed Freedom Charter drawn up by the Congress of the People in 1955. From a discourse of equal rights for all "civilized men," organized opposition to domination shifted after 1948 to one of equal rights for all "national groups." The shift may have been purely strategic and tactical and not a reflection of deeply held convictions, but it demonstrated nonetheless the normality of speaking of South Africa as a country of nationalities as opposed to a single nation comprised of peoples of different origins.

In order to resist this "normal" view of South Africa, several members of the ANC broke with the organization and founded the rival PAC. After initially insisting that Coloreds were Africans, the PAC came gradually to the view that anyone who subscribed to majority rule and was fully loyal to Africa, and nowhere else, was an African; in principle, the notion of a "white African" was not precluded. This voluntarist understanding of identity as something freely chosen was at odds with the dominant understandings of the era, which stressed "blood and heritage," but it was to inform the later understandings adopted by the Black Consciousness movement in its various guises.

The latest phase of "reform" in South Africa—the process of normalization referred to at the beginning of this chapter—was prompted by the massive rejection of apartheid evident over the past few years; in this regard, it is important to emphasize not only such indicators of rejection as mass riots and demonstrations but also the struggles against Bantu education that have wracked South Africa since 1976. This point is illustrated more fully in chapter 5. These struggles are indicative of the failure of schools and universities to normalize multiracialism and national separation. They reflect the success of Black Consciousness as a counter-discourse or hidden transcript of resistance to differentiation that spread rapidly throughout South Africa in the 1970s.

Even had commitment to national separation persisted in the face of widespread international and domestic opposition to homelands, the demands in recent months by most homeland leaders for reincorporation of their territories into South Africa, and the massive display of support for the ANC and other nontribal organizations within the homelands themselves, seem to have put to rest separate development once and for all.

Yet the uneven effects of normalization were apparent in South Africa even while the appeals for political action on the basis of a common black identity were being disseminated. Now renamed the Inkatha Freedom party (IFP), the Inkatha movement revived by Chief Gatsha Buthelezi in 1975 organized political action around appeal to an exclusive Zulu identity, one frozen through time and given by such fixed inherited traits as "warrior blood." This organization is evidence of collusion with the project of separate development, even while the idea of KwaZulu independence has been consistently rejected, and explains why Buthelezi is despised by many as a "stooge" and a collaborator.

There is no denying that Zulu identity is in some sense "real"—as is Xhosa, Swazi, Tswana, Shangaan, or any other tribal identity—but no other "genuine black leader" has sought to mobilize his own tribe only.[34] Nelson Mandela may be Xhosa (as may the entire ANC leadership), but he stands nonetheless for a long ANC tradition of constituting a common, as opposed to exclusive, African identity and mobilizing political opposition on that basis. The black-on-black violence engendered by struggles between Inkatha and its opponents is due to the uneven effects of normalization, not to the inability of blacks to get along with each other or to suppress their tribal instincts.

The most important point to make about the demise of separate development is that it is indicative of the abandonment of the postulate of difference on which National party policy since 1948 has rested. This point is discussed more fully in chapter 5. However exclusionary a new South Africa may be, the incorporation of blacks into a common society, the recognition of the legitimacy of their claims to rights therein, and the political importance attached by de Klerk and others to the concept of nation building all are indicative of a move away from the assumption that all blacks are inherently alien, unassimilable, and foreign. The boundaries between the national self and alien other have shifted due to the failure of attempts to normalize among black South Africans the idea that they are really different nations and thus foreigners in a white country. The new South Africa will no longer be a country of nationalities, but a country of minorities and local communities.

Due to the widespread tendency to consider the problem of South Africa as solved once certain laws are removed from the statute books, a distinction needs to be drawn between white domination and apartheid.[35] White domination describes an enduring, structural characteristic of the South African situation; whites have forcibly dispossessed people of their land, proletarianized them against their will, passed laws intended to restrict their movements, and denied their representatives access to the central institutions of the state, all in the name of civilization. What have changed continually over time, due to a combination of black resistance and changing global power relations, are the particular social practices by which that same domination has been effected and preserved. Apartheid is one such historically contingent set of political practices, which differed from its predecessors by being based on the postulate of difference rather than on the postulate of identity.

In order to determine whether de Klerk's reforms signal the end of white domination or only of apartheid, one needs to remember that the defense of civilization has been a far more prevalent justification for white domination in South Africa than Afrikaner self-determination. Various mechanisms now are being invoked—from attempts to maintain higher standards of living for the white community, to protect private property, to maintain a private enterprise economy, and to keep land in white hands, all by appeal to concepts such as reason—to preserve a boundary between a civilized self and a barbarous other. The privatization of the economy and the National party's refusal to redistribute land guarantee that South Africa's most important economic assets, and thus the country's wealth, will remain in white hands. High standards of living, without some sort of redistributive commitment by the state, no longer require the cover of a civilized labor policy. The various liberation movements know this, which is why struggles over issues of political economy are bound to be at the heart of organized politics for the next several years.

While scrapping apartheid legislation and promising a universal franchise for the black majority, the latest phase of reform seems intended to enable white control over the economy, schools, neighborhoods, and hospitals via a commitment to private enterprise and the discourse of community rights and standards. The onus for control will shift to white civil society and away from the state because the defense of white domination will be the responsibility of each community and the private (largely white) business sector. Chapter

5 illustrates how this phase can be dated from 1990 and the occasion of President de Klerk's address at the opening of the South African Parliament.[36]

The implementation of all these plans for a new South Africa inevitably will be shaped by the process of transition itself, by the way in which blacks either accept or resist the National party's initiatives. Despite attempts by de Klerk in 1991 to constitute highly successful strategies of resistance such as rent and consumer boycotts as undemocratic and abnormal,[37] such actions are more likely to increase rather than disappear in the future. The localization of domination will require the localization of struggle—that is, the enactment of punitive measures against schools, neighborhoods, businesses, and so on that refuse to admit blacks on the grounds that their standards (of education, hygiene, job qualifications, or whatever else) are not sufficiently high. Just as apartheid enabled the sort of mass action it was designed to prevent by making common oppression the stimulus to a common black identity, community rights may keep alive the mass-based struggles that de Klerk has insisted must cease. Localized struggles have always been prevalent anyway, but they probably will continue to be as vital an element in the struggle against white domination as the actions of such formal political organizations as the ANC.

At the same time, the future of South African politics cannot be considered independently of shifting and ongoing global relations of power. Whether apartheid ends or not, it is necessary to consider the possible implications of three important power relations for future struggle and change in South Africa: (1) the decline of communism in Eastern Europe and the reassertion of American hegemony internationally, (2) the ongoing interventions into the lives of Third World peoples by Western powers in the name of development, and (3) the multiracialism of Western states during the last few years. Whether the current exercise of global power enlarges or diminishes the prospects for an end to white domination in South Africa is a major political concern that is discussed in chapter 6.

NOTES

1. For a full text of the speech, see *Southern Africa Report*, February 9, 1990, pp. 7–16.

2. See *The Star* (Johannesburg), February 1, 1991, p. 2.

3. This overview of Foucault's thinking is drawn from his "Two Lectures," in Foucault, *Power/Knowledge: Selected Interviews and Other Writings, 1972–1977*, pp. 78–108.

4. Foucault, *Power/Knowledge: Selected Interviews and Other Writings, 1972–1977*, p. 98.

5. See Houghton, *The South African Economy*; Leftwich, "The Constitution and Continuity of South African Inequality: Some Conceptual Questions"; Nattrass, "Economic Development and Political Change—A Suggested Theoretical Framework."

6. See Adam and Giliomee, *Ethnic Power Mobilized: Can South Africa Change?*; and Lipton, *Capitalism and Apartheid: South Africa, 1910–1984*.

7. Greenberg, *Legitimating the Illegitimate: State, Markets and Resistance in South Africa.*

8. See, for example, Johnstone, "White Prosperity and White Supremacy in South Africa Today," pp. 124–40; Trapido, "South Africa in a Comparative Study of Industrialization," pp. 309–20; Harold Wolpe, "Capitalism and Cheap Labor Power in South Africa: From Segregation to Apartheid," pp. 425–56; Legassick, "South Africa: Forced Labor, Industrialization, and Racial Differentiation"; and Magubane, *The Political Economy of Race and Class in South Africa.*

9. Bozzoli and Delius, "Radical History and South African Society," p. 30.

10. Ibid.

11. The absence of theorizing in most social histories on South Africa, according to historian Colin Bundy, has invited the charge that the new social history concerns itself with the idiosyncratic, the unique, and the subjective to the point of estrangement from broader processes and structures. See his article "An Image of Its Own Past? Toward a Comparison of American and South African Historiography," pp. 117–43. On the new social history, see Van Onselen, *Studies in the Social and Economic History of the Witwatersrand, 1886–1914.* Vol.1, *New Babylon*; Marks and Rathbone, eds., *Industrialization and Social Change in South Africa: African Class Formation, Culture, and Consciousness, 1870–1930*; Bozzoli, ed., *Class, Community and Conflict: South African Perspectives*; Beinart and Bundy, *Hidden Struggles in Rural South Africa: Politics and Popular Movements in the Transkei and Eastern Cape, 1890–1930*; and the special feature "History from South Africa," *Radical History Review* 46/47, 1990.

12. On Western (mainly British) economic ties to South Africa, see First, Steele, and Gurney, *The South African Connection: Western Investment in Apartheid*; for a good overview of the role played by American corporations in the South African economy, see Seidman and Seidman, *South Africa and U.S. Multinational Corporations*; and for an analysis of the connections among the South African state, domestic capital, and foreign multinationals (a "dependent development" approach), see Seidman and Seidman, *Outposts of Monopoly Capitalism: Southern Africa in the Changing Global Economy.*

13. According to Bozzoli and Delius, "a variety of left-wing academics, teachers, and students came together in London, Oxford and Sussex where a recasting of entire periods and explanations took place—all in terms of the strident and confident neo-Marxism of the time" ("Radical History and South African Society," p. 19). The most cited example (in South African literature as elsewhere) of this "strident and confident neo-Marxism" remains Frank's *Capitalism and Underdevelopment in Latin America.*

14. Legassick, "South Africa: Forced Labor, Industrialization, and Racial Differentiation."

15. Trapido, "South Africa in a Comparative Study of Industrialization."

16. See, in particular, Greenberg, "Economic Growth and Political Change: The South African Case," pp. 667–704.

17. Mbeki, *South Africa: The Peasants' Revolt*, p. 47.

18. See Rabinow, ed., *The Foucault Reader*, pp. 51–75.

19. For a fuller discussion of discipline, see Foucault, *Discipline and Punish*, especially "The Means of Correct Training," pp. 170–94.

20. See Todorov, *The Conquest of America*, especially chapter 3. I am indebted to David Campbell for this reference; for a discussion of the ways that difference has been represented historically in the United States, see his *Writing Security: U.S. Foreign Policy and the Politics of Identity.*

21. See the speech by Smuts to Parliament in April 1946, reprinted in Lewsen, ed., *Voices of Protest: From Segregation to Apartheid, 1938–1948*, pp. 210–12.

22. See the speech on apartheid policy delivered to Parliament by Paul Sauer on January 22, 1948. Reprinted in Lewsen, *Voices of Protest*, pp. 281–84.

23. See, for example, the 1919 constitution of the ANC, which equates race with tribe throughout. In Karis and Carter, eds., *From Protest to Challenge: A Documentary History of African Politics in South Africa, 1822–1964*, vol. 1, pp. 76–82.

24. See Rheinallt-Jones, ed., *Bantu Studies: A Journal Devoted to the Scientific Study of Bantu, Hottentot, and Bushman.*

25. See Comaroff, *Body of Power, Spirit of Resistance,* chapter 2.

26. See Wren, "For a Dispossessed Tribe, a Time of Reckoning," p. 4.

27. For an in-depth textual analysis of the reports of government commissions issued since 1903, see Ashforth, *The Politics of Official Discourse in Twentieth Century South Africa.*

28. For similar arguments along these lines, see Abercrombie, Hill, and Turner, *The Dominant Ideology Thesis*; and Scott, *Domination and the Arts of Resistance: Hidden Transcripts.*

29. See Biko, "Black Consciousness and the Quest for a True Humanity," in his book *I Write What I Like.*

30. For a good overview of such strategies, see Motlhabi, *The Theory and Practice of Black Resistance to Apartheid.*

31. See, generally, Scott, *Domination and the Arts of Resistance.*

32. Resistance to the state's attempts to monopolize the brewing of beer has brought black women (for whom beer brewing has been traditionally an important source of revenue) into frequent, and often violent, confrontations with the police. This situation reinforces the notion of the hidden transcript as a series of political, not merely social, practices. See Bradford, "We Are Now the Men: Women's Beer Protests in the Natal Countryside, 1929," pp. 292–323.

33. After the banning of organized political protest movements, the late 1960s was a period of relative quiescence. But it was also a time when Black Consciousness as a "hidden transcript" of resistance began to emerge. Absence of open confrontation and defiance does not mean the absence of resistance per se.

34. Why the Zulu alone should be so susceptible to ethnic mobilization is a question that has not been posed, let alone answered. The charismatic figure of Buthelezi, with his ability to invoke a heroic precolonial Zulu past, is one possibility. Equally plausible, however, is the notion that the Zulus, as a group, are the most downtrodden and marginalized members of African society and thus are more alienated from it. I am indebted to Norma Kriger for this suggestion.

35. The two terms are often treated as synonymous. Stanley Greenberg, for example, describes apartheid as "patterns of racial and ethnic domination." See his *Race and State in Capitalist Development,* p. 7. Outside of academic circles, Howard Wolpe, the chairman of the Senate Foreign Relations Subcommittee on Africa, has spoken of the "apartheid system of white domination" in South Africa. See *Southern Africa Report,* January 12, 1990, p. 12.

36. See the transcript of the speech in *Southern Africa Report,* February 9, 1990, pp. 7–16.

37. Ibid., pp. 11–12, 16.

I

Subjectivity and the "Normal" Practice of Domination

1

Constituting the Civilized Self: South Africa in the Age of Colonialism

This chapter begins the analysis (to be completed in chapter 2) of how global relations have constituted particular subjectivities and shaped understandings in South Africa of what are normal social practices. Although the African continent remained colonized until the late 1950s, the process of decolonization began on a global scale in 1946, with the granting of independence to the Philippines. This chapter takes the end of the colonial age to be roughly coterminous with the end of World War II.

Given that what is now called the Republic of South Africa consisted of two British colonies and two independent Afrikaner Republics for most of its history until 1910, assigning the territory the name "South Africa" prior to 1910 is anachronistic; it is, nonetheless, convenient to do so. The early history of what was to become South Africa is so important that this chapter begins in 1652, with the landing of the first Dutch East India Company employees at the Cape of Good Hope.

To reiterate what was said in the introductory chapter, from a Foucaultian perspective, power relations constitute subjects through struggle. In the South African case prior to 1945, the major struggles clearly involved Dutch settlers in their relations with colonial administrators (both Dutch and British), with European capitalists, and with missionary and antislavery societies. It was out of these struggles that Afrikaner nationalism emerged, a movement that constituted a particular subjectivity for those of European/non-British heritage as much as it fought on their behalf. The rise of "Afrikanerdom" has had enormous implications for the country of South Africa particularly since World War II, but this chapter will demonstrate how the boundaries of that particular subjectivity historically have been fluid and often contested by the so-called Afrikaners themselves. This point will be reiterated in later chapters, when prospects for the building of a "new South African nation" under President de Klerk's stewardship are considered.

The identities of South Africa's English- and Afrikaans-speaking whites are not the only ones to have been forged through various entanglements with the West. In the course of their contacts with colonial administrators and missionary societies, blacks were constituted as *natives*, a term with a wide range of derogatory connotations but which nonetheless implied "of that place" (particularly when it was used interchangeably with *aborigine*). When blacks began to forge connections with other oppressed and subjugated peoples in their struggles against colonial powers, through global social movements such as Pan-Africanism, an African subjectivity began to subsume the old tribal affiliations. As a consequence, African nationalism did not embrace the "tribe equals incipient nation" equation that undergirded the National party's homelands policy.

Even prior to World War II, a nascent black subjectivity was emerging, although it was not until the Black Consciousness movement in South Africa in the 1970s that that subjectivity acquired real strength. Its early awakenings stemmed from three sources: (1) global social movements such as Pan-Africanism, which brought South African intellectuals into contact with oppressed coloreds or "Negroes" from the United States and elsewhere; (2) global social movements such as Ethiopianism (a religious movement with links to the United States which drew support away from missionary churches) and Rastafarianism (a cultural movement founded in Jamaica); and (3) the founding of the short-lived League of Nations, in which all peoples not of European heritage, such as the Japanese, were described as "colored races." The realization that domination of people of color existed on a global scale was an important factor in the development of black subjectivity in South Africa.

Struggle with citizens of other countries thus has constituted multiple and overlapping subjectivities in South Africa. Although power relations always involve struggle, they constrain what the struggles between socially constituted subjects will concern. To paraphrase Foucault again, the production of truth is central to the exercise of power, so knowledge-producing apparatuses, which through discourse effectively normalize certain practices and ways of thinking about the world, delimit the range of possibilities for dominant and subordinated alike.

The major knowledge-producing apparatuses to affect early South Africa were the schools and churches affiliated with various European missionary societies, as well as the individual clergy and teachers who came from different parts of Europe to minister to the needs of the Boers in the interior. As mentioned in the introductory chapter, these apparatuses made possible the constitution and regeneration of European identity in Africa and explain why South African social practices so often have claimed to mimic those of other Europeans on the African continent.

Missionary influence also explains why South African social practices to this day have been justified in terms of a civilizing mission, or the defense of European/Western civilization on a barbarous continent. What has been played out in this context are different European understandings of identity/difference and clashing perspectives on what constitutes appropriate strategy when encountering the alien, foreign, and potentially dangerous other.

Like the Spanish administrator Sepulveda, who argued for the violent conquest of American Indians on the basis of their supposedly innate and ineradicable difference from Europeans, early settlers at the Cape colony were not interested in peaceful colonialism and religious conversion of the other. They enslaved the indigenous Khoikhoi peoples and exterminated the San. As the colony expanded eastward in the 1800s, many settlers advocated exterminating the troublesome Xhosa as well. But as missionary societies became active in antislavery movements in Europe in the 1800s, they became increasingly vocal in their criticisms of a wide range of inhumane practices, including not only the extermination of indigenous peoples but also land dispossession and enforced servitude. Reminiscent of Las Casas's debates with Sepulveda,[1] missionary societies argued that colonizers had a duty to bring Christian light to the people in pagan darkness—that is, to teach those who were different to become like the European self. The effect of these critiques was not insubstantial in that they challenged the norms of extermination and slavery as appropriate responses to otherness and contributed to the outlawing of such practices. They did not eliminate the postulate of innate difference, but they forced those who held to it to devise a different response. As white South Africans so often emphasize, they (unlike settlers in the Americas) did not exterminate most of their country's indigenous people, but written out of the collective memory is the fact that many of their ancestors would have liked to try.

Humanitarian critiques also helped to break down the medieval European distinction between Christian/pagan and civilized/barbarian in the sense that European settlers began to invoke a civilizing mission to justify a wide range of social practices, from colonial expansion and land dispossession to enforced proletarianization. With the influence of Christian-National doctrine in South Africa in the 1930s and the Cold War between the United States and "Godless communism," the defense of Christian civilization became a prevalent justification for white rule, but its very appeal lies in part because the justification is of long standing.

Over time, the dominant came to associate civilized with European and white, while gradually equating noncivilized with native and black. But it needs to be stressed that no *necessary* correlation existed in the discourse between skin color and presumed degree of civilization. For the missionary societies and their institutional carriers, anyone who became Christian, literate, and so on was civilized, natives included. Differences were thought not to be given by nature. It was theoretically possible for whites to be considered uncivilized, as in fact many of them were. Afrikaners in the interior were often described as barbarous by Afrikaners at the Cape. This way of thinking reinforces the notion that, through struggle, nationalist discourse has constructed a particular Afrikaner subject and has not brought a given and unproblematic Afrikaner nation to consciousness. It also explains how the requirement to constitute the self as civilized in order to justify domination over the other has entailed a continual rewriting of what the essence of civilization is.

Christianity and literacy were long stressed as the hallmarks of civilization, although other factors such as the ability to control one's passions were mentioned as well. With missionary successes in converting blacks and educating them in mission schools, along with the necessity to justify land dispossession and colonial expansion, settlers in South Africa as elsewhere began to emphasize economic productivity and private property as factors distinguishing civilized from barbarous society. This shift in emphasis demonstrates again the global nature of the power relations that constituted and regenerated the European identity of settlers everywhere, for the claim that Indians in the Americas were "not industrious, neither have art, science, skill or faculty to use either the land or the commodities of it"[2] was used by European settlers as a justification for their subjugation of the indigenous peoples.

World War I brought severe economic hardship to whites in South Africa, and the fear that Europeans had "sunk to the level of the Kaffir" prompted an emphasis on standard of living as a necessary if not sufficient condition of civilization. Maintaining Christian civilization on a barbarous continent, then, required ensuring, through such mechanisms as the so-called civilized labor policy (i.e., job reservation for whites and Coloreds), that the economic privileges of the dominant group would never be threatened. In terms of contemporary practices, when F. W. de Klerk's National party speaks of maintaining civilized norms and standards, it is not too difficult to believe that it may be referring euphemistically to white privilege and private enterprise.

James Scott has argued that one of the effects of domination on the dominant is that elites come to attribute the behavior of subordinates not to the effect of power relationships but to the inborn characteristics of the subordinate group itself.[3] Steve Biko made a similar point in the early 1970s when he argued that people who have tasted the fruits of wealth, security, and prestige find it more comfortable to believe in the obvious lie and to accept it as normal that they alone are entitled to privilege.[4] In South Africa, the notion that Europeans are the bearers of civilization and thus culturally superior to blacks was supplemented in the 1930s by the notion that they are genetically superior as well; European race theory provided "scientific" justifications for perpetual white privilege and crushed the hopes of blacks that they would ever be considered worthy enough to merit equal treatment.

As for the subordinated groups in early South Africa, mission schools and churches worked against the unifying thrust of global social movements such as Pan-Africanism and Ethiopianism to stifle the emergence of a united front among the oppressed. Until well into the 1930s, opposition political groups agitated for no more than a qualified franchise and understood their enterprise to be one of demonstrating to the ruling powers just how far civilization had spread among the native population. Missionary schools must accept responsibility for such actions, even though missionary societies frequently fought to uphold the rights of native peoples within the British Empire.

Finally, the other major knowledge-producing apparatuses to affect early South Africa were European schools and universities, particularly those attended by Afrikaans speakers. The French Revolution, German romanticism, Kuyperian (Dutch) theology, and National-Socialism are all "modern" European intellectual currents that underpinned National party policy after World War II. The notions that capacity for civilization is fixed by race (i.e., genetically determined) and that the object to be civilized is a nation and not an individual flowered in the 1930s as a result of academic contact with Europe and came to fruition in the 1960s with homelands and the policy of separate development. While "backward Boers" beyond the frontier of civilization may have been individually racist, it is not to them that the intellectual justifications for apartheid are to be attributed.

The rest of this chapter discusses the above themes in more detail, beginning at the Cape colony in 1652 and ending after South Africa's emergence from "England's war" in 1945.

SOUTH AFRICA BEFORE STATEHOOD

The Cape as a Dutch Colony

The decision to establish a settlement at Table Bay was taken not by the government of the Dutch United Provinces in Amsterdam but by the Dutch East India Trading Company headquartered in Batavia, although the charter of the company, issued in 1602, granted to its employees many of the political powers which today accrue only to governments. As well as the ability to establish colonies, the company could declare war, negotiate treaties, and recruit military and administrative personnel.[5] The settlement of a band of company employees at the Cape under the leadership of Jan van Riebeeck in 1652 was the direct result of the need for fresh produce and a hospital for the crews of ships on the long voyages to and from the East.

Initial attempts to produce any agricultural crop at all, let alone a surplus, were beset by three fundamental problems. First, with an annual rainfall of between 10 and 25 inches, most of which fell within a few months of the year, the Cape climate was not hospitable to European grains and vegetables, many of which easily succumbed to local pests and diseases. Second, the oft-mentioned labor scarcity at the Cape was due to two factors. Most vexing from the point of view of the whites was that the indigenous peoples could not be induced to work for them—a problem that eventually would become one of the driving forces behind South Africa's labor control policies. Neither the Khoikhoi nor the San were agriculturalists. The San were hunter-gatherers who roamed an area in fairly close proximity to the settlement in search of food, whereas the Khoikhoi were nomadic cattle herders, occupying a vast territory from the Keiskanna River to the Cape point and northward along the Atlantic coast past the Olifants River.[6] Only a few weeks after the van Riebeeck party arrived, the official journal recorded the view that industrious Chinese—who were slaves and servants in other company establishments—might make successful cultivators at the Cape.[7]

The other factor that contributed to a labor shortage was the severe obstacle to immigration posed by the company system of treating all persons who had never been employees of the Dutch East India Company as aliens, forbidden to own immovable property and obliged to leave the colony whenever the government so decreed.[8] Beginning in 1658, the Cape colony joined directly in the East African and Indonesian slave trade in order to secure the required labor, although many imported slaves simply took off into the interior, never to be seen again.

Third, and less frequently cited as a hindrance to agricultural production, was the nature of the settlers themselves. Far from representing a microcosm of Dutch society, employees of the Dutch East India Company usually were drawn from the lower classes. Almost all impoverished, illiterate, and down on their luck, a fair number were sent to the Cape as punishment for some offense. They were not skilled farmers able and willing to adapt their farming methods to a harsh new environment.

Vegetables, wheat, and wine initially were produced by the company. As grain production costs were high, Cape grain was not attractive to passing ships even when available in years of good harvest. Cape wine was expensive and of poor quality. It was only in market vegetables that the Cape's agriculture yielded an advantage to passing ships and to the soldiers occasionally billeted at the Cape to defend the settlement. While the ships and soldiers were there, the farmers enjoyed periods of relative prosperity, but a decline in shipping led to drastic price declines for farm products. For the most part, crop farming during this period was organized around subsistence production; the mining towns that sprang up in the late 1800s as a result of the discovery of diamonds and gold were forced at the outset to import substantial quantities of wheat, maize, meat, and dairy products.[9]

It was the profitability of "stock farming" in the hinterland beyond Cape Town that brought the early settlers very quickly into conflict with the Khoikhoi over grazing lands. Although limited to the market provided by passing ships, the sale of live animals and fresh meat constituted a profitable undertaking for the Cape colonists. But since the Khoikhoi considered cattle a form of wealth and power and so were willing to trade only their old and sick animals to the Dutch, lascivious glances were soon cast in the direction of the "forbidden fruit," as the following entry in Jan van Riebeeck's diary on December 13, 1652, makes clear:

> Today the hottentots came with thousands of cattle and sheep close to our fort, so that their cattle nearly mixed with ours. We feel vexed to see so many fine head of cattle, and not to be able to buy to any considerable extent. If it had been indeed allowed, we had opportunity today to deprive them of 10,000 head, which, however, if we obtain orders to that effect can be done at any time, and even more conveniently because they will have greater confidence in us. With 150 men, 10,000 or 11,000 head of black cattle might be obtained without danger of losing one man; and many savages might be taken without resistance, in order to be sent as slaves to India, as they still always come to us unarmed.[10]

As the company policy of trading with the indigenous peoples for cattle and leaving their lands intact shifted in favor of stealing the former and appropriating the latter, the Khoikhoi vehemently protested. Unable to redress their grievances through negotiation alone, the "Kaapmans" (or Capemen, as the Dutch sometimes called the Khoikhoi) finally issued an ultimatum in 1660; any of their cattle stolen by the company would, in turn, be stolen right back. Van Riebeeck warned of the dire consequences of such a move, and the first Khoikhoi-Dutch war erupted.

Quelled at last by the guns and horses of the whites, the Khoikhoi by 1730 had been completely subjugated. Deprived of their lands and cattle, a few moved farther into the hinterland and merged with the San. Others drifted closer to Cape Town and eked out an existence as best they could. The vast majority, however, survived by serving as menial labor for those who now owned the land and the cattle. In exchange, they received food, lodging, tobacco, and security from attack.[11] Subjugation of the Khoikhoi by the Dutch thus produced the added advantage of supplementing the slave population.

The San were not treated like Khoikhoi stock thieves or criminals; instead, they were hunted down as if they were animals. The white raiders commonly would kill the men and women and take home the children, who were "apprenticed" (along with the Khoikhoi) as farm laborers and usually called "tame Bushmen."[12] Abhorrent and uncivilized as such behavior undoubtedly was, it was not unusual within the context of its time, when European slavers could describe their victims as "almost beasts in human form"; when a Jesuit missionary on the West African coast could write that "the conversion of these barbarians is not to be achieved through love, but only after they have been subdued by force of arms"; and when Europeans increasingly described Africans in general as "bestial" and "brutish" in behavior.[13]

Although many scholars have argued that early European settlers in South Africa did not entertain race-consciousness (that being a nineteenth-century phenomenon),[14] and while the Khoikhoi and the San were treated differently from each other, the dominant group nonetheless constituted the indigenous peoples and their own slaves as "other" in a fourfold sense, according to Hermann Giliomee. First, those who were not European were considered heathen and thus inferior because they were not possessed of what the settlers considered two of the main attributes of civilization, namely Christianity and literacy. Second, the "inferior" peoples were considered intrinsically different and alien, or not fully human. Third, the notion prevailed that the Europeans had a major and legitimate claim to certain privileges and benefits because they were civilized. And fourth, a pervasive fear existed that the inferior peoples had designs on the privileges of the dominant group, a fear that found expression in continual rumors of revolt.[15]

What united the whites as a group was thus a sense of cultural superiority, not race-consciousness. Fear of a less than human other also normalized enslavement and extermination, aligning social practices at the Cape with those of Europeans elsewhere. Yet the dominant group was by no means a united and thoroughly European self even at this early stage. By 1705, those who had left the employ of the Dutch East India Company to farm were calling themselves "Afrikaners," meaning "people of that place," to distinguish themselves from the company employees, whom they referred to as "Europeans." The extent of affinity with Europe appeared so negligible to some travelers that by the end of the eighteenth century Henry Lichtenstein, a German, wrote in reference to the Huguenot clans who had begun arriving after 1688 that "like all other settlers here, they are become entirely Africans."[16]

Company officials in Cape Town meanwhile regarded themselves as "civilized and more enlightened persons" compared to those in the interior of the country, who were described as "lacking in civilization" and as "men without any idea of education, grown up in idleness, and in the unrestrained indulgence of the wild passions of nature."[17] Many officials called themselves "Kaapenaars" as distinct from other whites of the colony, the "Afrikaners." Others in the western Cape, however, preferred the term *Afrikaner* to *Boer* (farmer) or *Hollander*.[18]

In addition to articulating differences based on supposed level of civilization, the whites at the Cape began by the end of the eighteenth century to split along what might be called class lines. Economic frustrations and grievances with company rule were articulated by a small, fairly prosperous bourgeoisie through the forum of the Cape Patriot movement, which started in 1778 in the southwestern Cape. Through contacts with the Patriot movement in Holland, certain Enlightenment ideas were relayed to the Cape and adapted to local circumstances, while the names of Hobbes, Machiavelli, Locke, and other freethinkers were often mentioned.[19]

Even among the bourgeoisie, differences were evident between the Orangists, who supported the aristocratic party in the Netherlands and feared the rising tide of democratic movements in Europe, and the Patriots, who drew inspiration from the struggle of the Dutch Patriots for freedom and popular sovereignty. As the rule of the Dutch East India Company began to crumble by century's end, the Orangists looked to England and the Patriots to France for outside support.[20]

According to J. A. Loubser, the French Revolution unified Dutch colonists at the Cape as "burghers" in opposition to the authorities and provided them with a republican ideal, while the American Revolution also was much debated.[21] These influences were manifested years later in struggles with the British. In 1837, for example, a party of emigrants who left the Cape under the leadership of P. L. Uys resolved "to establish our settlement on the same principles of liberty as those adopted by the United States of America"; in 1849, the Dutch-speaking editor of The Cape of Good Hope Observer wrote, in response to a British plan to settle convicts at the Cape, that "the revolutionary genius of the age has reached even unto the Cape . . . and we are now in a state of war with the government, not a whit less earnest than that which in France transformed Louis Philippe into the Comte de Neuilly."[22]

Obviously the "revolutionary genius of the age" was not applied to relations with the indigenous peoples, but it had, nonetheless, an impact on the Europeans of Dutch origin. As Andre du Toit and Hermann Giliomee have argued, Afrikaner history must be recovered from the nationalist interpretation that later generations have imposed on it—that is, from the notion that Afrikaners always have represented a complete and self-contained nation whose political traditions cannot have any external origins but must arise from within itself. Early Afrikaner political thought, they argue, was associated with the better educated and more experienced members of the Dutch-speaking community, and the intellectual framework and conceptual idiom in which they expressed themselves were usually adapted from the political attitudes and patterns of the wider world around them.[23] That early "habit of fishing in European thought currents," to borrow a phrase from Charles Bloomberg,[24] has remained with Afrikaners to this day and has undergirded a wide range of social practices. The following recent and typical characterization of Afrikaners, therefore, is highly problematic:

> A people who missed the momentous developments of eighteenth century Europe, the age of reason in which liberalism and democracy were born and which had its climax in the great revolution of the French bourgeoisie; a people who spent their time instead in a deep solitude which, if anything took them back to an even more elementary existence than the seventeenth century Europe their forebears had left.[25]

The Cape under British Rule

From 1806 onward, the Cape of Good Hope became a possession of the British Empire, confirmed in 1815 by the Congress of Vienna at the end of the Napoleonic Wars. The peace settlement that succeeded the military defeat of Napoleon was the harbinger of a permanent British settlement at the Cape, of conflict between early settlers and the new administration, and, ultimately, of strong capital and market relations between Britain and South Africa. Its significance in terms of interracial relations must be mentioned briefly as well.

In 1807 the British Parliament passed an act declaring the African slave trade illegal for British citizens. Its effect on the international slave trade was basically minimal, yet the abolition movement—led largely by reformist churches that believed that slave labor was an intolerable obstacle to human progress and an offense against Christian morality—sought to convince the British government to use all means at its disposal to pressure other nations to follow Britain's lead. The Congress of Vienna seven years later provided the first opportunity.

Despite his resentment and over his objections, Viscount Castlereagh, Britain's chief representative at the Congress, was forced by British domestic opinion and political pressure to make the abolition of the slave trade a major issue at the Congress. Moral and religious arguments were supplemented by economic ones, particularly by British West Indian sugar planters recently deprived of their own labor supply, who wanted to see their rivals put on an equal footing.

In the end, Britain, France, Spain, Sweden, Austria, Russia, Prussia, and Portugal joined in an Eight Power Declaration in favor of abolishing the slave trade as soon as possible, a declaration that was attached to the Final Act of the Congress of Vienna. This declaration was considered a major victory for the abolitionists, yet as Paul Lauren has pointed out, states willing to sign general agreements of principle firmly resisted any efforts by others—by appealing to the "larger" principle of sovereignty—to make them practice what they preached. The final texts did not declare the slave trade to be illegal, fix a time limit for its abolition, make a commitment for further action, or even sanction the arrest of slavers.[26] As for the United States, it consistently refused to sign any meaningful international agreement on slavery, even though Congress technically had declared the slave trade to be illegal several years before.

The most notable outcome of the agreement reached at the Congress of Vienna was not, therefore, that slavery declined; in fact, the number of humans exported from Africa to the Western Hemisphere and Arabia actually increased.[27] The major effect of the Congress was that justifications for inhumane treatment of indigenous peoples now recurred consistently to the theme of a civilizing mission.

This theme was soon apparent among settlers at the Cape, as among whites elsewhere. Prior to the Congress, for example, the practice of indenturing the indigenous peoples as "apprentices" was defended simply on the grounds that behavior that was applied to Christians could not be applied without adaptation to "heathens" or "Hottentots." Another defense was to suggest that farmers who lacked "civilization and religion" were the ones responsible for the ill treatment because they were "less capable of restraining their passions."[28] After the Congress the following sorts of claims, made in 1826 and 1832, respectively, became much more commonplace:

Some have gone to great expense, others have engaged in personal activity, in order to do their utmost to make the slaves better members of society, well knowing that their greater degree of civilization would be continued among those people, and that the more they made religious principles their own, the better they would be as servants and the greater the benefits to their owners would be. Once the Government . . . had begun to think of this salutary work, the inhabitants, rather than opposing it, had contributed to the work of civilization, to promote both moral and religious improvement.

Every one must admit that each successive Governor, far from desiring to lower them in the scale of civilization, has had, on the contrary, no other object than to bring them from their wild and savage state to a civilized communion with each other, in order by so doing to afford them an opportunity of becoming capable of social intercourse, and at a proper time to become joint Burghers with us of one society.[29]

Whether for purely self-interested reasons (i.e., the notion that Christian servants were less trouble) or because they came genuinely to believe the truth of their own justifications, Cape Afrikaners under British rule did emerge as the committed champions of a low franchise, or the extension of limited political rights to "free blacks" and former slaves. At the same time, according to du Toit and Giliomee, Cape Afrikaners tended increasingly to adopt British political history, rather than any notions of their own historical rights as Dutch citizens, as their frame of reference.[30] This tendency undoubtedly explains why the British notion of trusteeship articulated by Edmund Burke in 1783 became a euphemism for land dispossession at the Cape under British rule.

The basic premise of trusteeship was that Europeans were not really dispossessing the original inhabitants of their land by force; they were only holding it for them "in trust" until the original inhabitants were civilized enough to know what to do with it. This argument might make sense for colonial administrations that intended someday to leave colonized territories, but for most colonial settlers the notion that they were only "borrowing" land to be one day returned was unsatisfactory. Missionary societies not only in Africa but among Indians in the Americas were educating "heathens" and converting them to Christianity; once "civilized," they theoretically could appeal to the principle of trusteeship and demand their land back.

This potential problem was negated with the help of Swiss jurist Emer de Vattel, who denied any right of sovereignty to "wandering tribes" of hunter-gatherers. Vattel "introduced the human obligation to cultivate the earth as a necessary condition for the natural right of every man or nation to land and property, thus providing a general legitimation for European imperial expansion."[31]

In making this case for the Cape in 1838, the Dutch-educated advocate J. de Wet argued before the Association for the Promotion of Civilization and Literature that his forefathers did no more than "dispose of barren, uninhabited and uncultivated land and make this their property." According to de Wet, the Hottentots were barbarous peoples because they supposedly committed atrocities against each other *and* because they failed to exercise "exclusive and discretionary control over the material things of this world, without anyone else being able to lay claim to them."[32] In the same year, a commissioner for Indian affairs in the United States put the matter even more succinctly and declared that "common property and civilization cannot coexist."[33]

The argument that private property and control of nature were the hallmarks of civilization thus found general expression at a time when the Cape was under British rule. From the outset, important sections of the Dutch-speaking community cooperated willingly with the new British ad-

time up there in spite of the danger. Our sympathies have been appealed to—honorable members have drawn such a dreadful picture of barbarism rushing into the country, and laying everything waste with fire and sword. But in the same breath we are told that the value of farms is increasing at an enormous rate. It is very strange. . . . There is a large army on the frontier, the Kaffirs are completely denuded of their property, they are miserable and starving—then where is [the cause of] the fear? . . . If the colonists occupy the lands of the natives, they cannot expect to sleep upon a bed of roses. . . . It is the Kaffir's uncivilized way of thinking that he has a right to get back the country he has been deprived of, if he can. It is a savage idea, and, no doubt, cannot be found in the breast of any civilized person—although, perhaps, if the French were despoiled of a portion of France, they would very likely try to get it back again. There is a sort of principle in human nature that, if possible, a man will recover that of which he has been dispossessed.[42]

Differences among whites over what are now generally referred to as race relations are thus long-standing and have never broken down neatly along ethnic lines (i.e., with all English speakers on one side and all Afrikaans speakers on the other). These differences and a common affinity with Western civilization among all settlers explain why the term *Afrikaner* has not always meant solely Afrikaans-speaking whites. Many of the struggles within the nationalist movement of the 1930s were not simply differences of opinion over how best to promote Afrikaner interests. They were battles over what an Afrikaner actually was and over whether Afrikaner identity could be freely chosen (the postulate of identity) or was fixed by nature (the postulate of difference). Again, these battles reinforce the notion that subjectivity is socially constituted, not given by nature, and that struggles over identity are central to politics.

There is little evidence to suggest that those who trekked out of the Cape ("Trekkers") to escape British rule saw themselves as a people united by a thirst for independence and inspired by visions of the "promised land." In fact, there were four "promised lands": the Republic of Natal (annexed by the British in 1843); the South African Republic (now Transvaal, annexed by the British in 1877); the Orange River Colony (now the Orange Free State); and the short-lived Republic of Lydenburg. Once the republics were established, according to Giliomee, the particular state in which the Trekkers lived became the focal point of their political identity to such a degree that efforts to create political unity were seriously hampered.[43] Henning Klopper (the first chairman of the Afrikaner Broederbond) felt that moving from the Orange Free State to Transvaal in 1900 was like moving to a different country. According to Klopper, "[W]e were two separate peoples. Although we were all Afrikaners, we had a different system to them, a different way of life almost."[44] Again, the fact that even the supposedly isolated Trekkers were not really a *volk* at the beginning of the twentieth century highlights the role of Afrikaner nationalism in constructing, and not merely defending, a particular subjectivity.

The notion of Afrikaners as a people chosen by God to fulfill a special destiny on a hostile continent is one often traced to the Trekkers themselves. Yet what evidence there is suggests that when the Trekkers spoke of themselves in those terms (which was not often) they described their "calling" in terms acceptable to European audiences. In 1841 the Volksraad of Natal described "Dutch emigrants" as "instruments of God's will . . . for the promotion of Christian civilization among many thousands who, until now, have been left in the deepest darkness."[45] Whether the Trekkers really believed their own justifications for colonial expansion is not the issue. The fact that they felt compelled to defend their actions in what were "normal" European terms was an indication of the strength of their European identity, even while they called themselves "Afrikaners."

Imperialism in the form of foreign investment and warfare undoubtedly was one of the factors that contributed to the eventual constitution of English- and Afrikaans-speaking settlers as separate peoples.

The Anglo-Boer Wars

The discovery of diamonds along the banks of the Vaal River in 1867 soon brought a clash between the British administration at the Cape and the independent republics, for the area of the finds was located right at the point where the borders of the Cape, the Orange River Colony, and the South African Republic (SAR) met. In order to retain control of both the diamond fields at Kimberley and the Cape merchants' trade route to the interior, Great Britain annexed Griqualand West in 1871, justifying the move on the grounds that the whole territory belonged to the Griqua chief Nicholas Waterboer, "who had been prevailed upon to concede his rights to Britain."[46] Major W. O. Lanyon, who took over administration of Griqualand West from Richard Southey in 1875, was commissioned with preparing the new Crown colony for incorporation into the Cape.

The existence of an independent Griqua community is further evidence that not all settlers feared contact with the indigenous peoples. Founded in the early 1800s, the Griquas were a community of whites, Coloreds, Africans, and Khoisan people who had adopted the name Griqua (derived from that of an old Khoikhoi clan) at the suggestion of missionaries. According to Gavin Lewis, the community developed a strong sense of Griqua identity, which lives on among some of its descendants today. For the Griquas, the adoption of a Griqua identity was a voluntary choice on the part of the individual, not a genetic predetermination, and served as a source of self-pride and sense of belonging.[47] The sinking of the Griquas into a generic Colored identity by the National party after 1948, therefore, had little meaning for the people so constituted.

Toward the end of 1876, the Foreign Office in London appointed Sir Theophilus Shepstone special commissioner to the SAR and ordered him to make a full inquiry "into the origin, nature, and circumstances" of the "grievous disturbances in the territories adjacent to our colonies in South Africa" and to annex such territories provided it was "necessary, in order to secure the peace and safety of our said colonies, and of our subjects elsewhere."[48]

When Shepstone led a small British force to Pretoria and annexed the SAR in the name of Great Britain in April 1877, he met with little resistance, for settler morale was very low. The government was practically bankrupt, and its commandos had been unable to conquer the Pedi people to the northeast.[49] But the promises and expectations held out by Shepstone when he took over the government were not fulfilled, and trouble began almost immediately. Paul Kruger and Petrus Joubert set out for London in 1878 to ask for self-government. Their request was refused, and in April 1879 some 1,200 "South African Republicans" started a revolt near Pretoria, demanding independence. On December 16, 1880, a republic was proclaimed at Paardekraal, whereupon British troops arrived to compel the SAR to remain within the empire.

To the surprise and chagrin of Britain, the imperial army was roundly defeated, and from the First Liberation War of 1880–1881 (as later generations refer to it), the Afrikaners emerged victorious. The independence of the republic was recognized at the Convention of Pretoria in 1881 and the London Convention of 1884. Great Britain stipulated in the peace treaties that the republic was to refrain from taxing foreigners more than locals or to attempt to extend its borders (i.e., to lay claim to the diamond fields); it also was not to make treaties with other states, except the Orange River Colony, without Great Britain's approval. "Thus were all difficulties adjusted and the problems of the Transvaal solved"[50]—until gold was discovered within its territory.

The mining capitalists who flooded into the area from Kimberley and elsewhere soon found that conducting business in the SAR was rather different from doing business in the British Cape colony. Well aware of the economic importance of the gold fields, Kruger's government in 1890 encouraged the setting up of the National Bank of Pretoria to conduct its banking business; it also owned a material interest in the railway line that ran from Lourenco Marques (in Mozambique) to the Rand. That the newfound resources were to be exploited was not an issue; the issue was whether locals as well as "Uitlanders" would enjoy a share of the benefits.

Kruger's first move was to ensure that Afrikaners retained all political power in the SAR by laying an increasing number of obstacles in the path toward suffrage of the predominantly British Uitlanders, whose numbers had increased from 48,000 in 1890 to over 100,000 by 1895.[51] In 1882, the period of residence necessary to qualify for citizenship was raised from one to five years, and in July 1887 the same prerequisite, together with the requirement of membership in a Dutch Reformed Church, was laid down for all parliamentary candidates. Finally in 1889, the franchise was limited to those born in the republic.

Even though the Uitlanders possessed 63 percent of the land and 90 percent of the personal property and were paying 95 percent of the taxes, as the leading capitalists, according to Norman Harris, they cared little for citizenship or the vote "and would have given the Transvaal authorities no serious trouble if the proper protection for life, property, personal and corporate interests had been forthcoming."[52] The real grievances of the mineowners centered around the fact that at a time when capital was in short supply, because of the transition to deep-level mining, the Kruger government's economic policies did nothing to alleviate production costs. The mineowners and their technical advisers came to the conclusion that "with efficient government in the Transvaal, the cost of native labor and explosives and coal and imported supplies could be so sliced that the costs of production on the Rand could quickly fall by maybe 15 or 20 percent."[53]

In the 1893 elections, Kruger was reelected president after narrowly defeating Joubert, a candidate more sympathetic to the needs of the mining capitalists. When the pioneer deep-level mine, the Geldenhuis Deep, failed to yield a profit in 1895, despite the spectacular recovery of share prices on the stock market, several of the deep-level mineowners decided that it was "through the unkind economic environment which Kruger's policies had created" that "the high profits which their bold investments would normally have won were being converted to losses."[54] During the closing months of 1895, a plot to overthrow the government was hatched by Cecil Rhodes (then prime minister of the Cape colony) and Alfred Beit.

The exact nature of the plan was never fully revealed, for while Beit and Rhodes were attempting to convince a number of the more skeptical mineowners that seizing Johannesburg by force and placing the SAR under the British flag was the best possible course of action to take, the chief administrator of Rhodes's South African Company in southern Rhodesia unilaterally launched the initiative. At the suggestion of his employer, Dr. Leander Jameson concentrated some 600 of the company's police near the western border of the SAR, to assist the Uitlanders if necessary. On December

29, 1895, he led his troops on the ill-fated "Jameson Raid" to Johannesburg, which ended four days later with his capture at Krugersdorp. Jameson and other leaders of the commandos were sent to London for trial and Rhodes resigned, in disgrace, as prime minister of the Cape.

The Jameson Raid, which rocked the Rand and plunged the mining industry into a full-scale depression, from which it did not recover until the latter part of 1898, did nothing to improve the lot of the average Uitlander. In 1896 laws were passed empowering the state president to expel any alien who was a danger to the public peace and requiring all foreigners entering the SAR to prove that they had either gainful employment or some adequate means of support.[55] Weapons were imported from France and Germany and forts built around Pretoria against future attack.[56]

The annexation of the SAR by Shepstone and the resulting First Liberation War were events that forced Afrikaners, according to Loubser, to become aware of themselves as a nation. At the time, they were not politically united, living as they did in separate states; their views on the concept of Afrikanerdom (i.e., whether it embraced English speakers as well as Afrikaans speakers) differed widely; and they disagreed over whether a united country should be established under British sovereignty or whether a state should be founded on the basis of "Africa for the Afrikaner."[57] What strengthened a nascent nationalist movement, Loubser argues, was the French Revolution, or more specifically the writings of Jean-Jacques Rousseau and his disciples.

In the wake of warfare, Rousseau's notion of the people as a collective personality and as the center of a new social order, which had to be unified to fulfill its calling, exercised a certain appeal. Rousseau's German disciple Johann Gottfried von Herder later developed this idea into the theory of the *Volksgeist* ("people's spirit"), which was seen as the collective, historical personality of each people that gave it its unique character and coherency. God gave such a *Volksgeist* to each nation. Every person was seen by Herder to be first a member of a nation and then an individual; a people thus was regarded as a collective individual with a unique personality—a concept later used by Prime Minister J.B.M. Hertzog.[58]

The influence of Herder's notion that a people's language is an expression of its identity can be seen in the emergence of a movement calling itself the Society of True Afrikaners. It agitated for the public use of Afrikaans in 1875, decades after the British Anglicization policy had gone into effect. Herder's nationalist ideas were developed further by proponents of German romanticism such as Friedrich Schelling, Johann Gottlieb Fichte, and G. W. F. Hegel, who were to emphasize the right of national states to determine their own affairs. Fichte and his disciples were to qualify the people as a biological entity and distinguished between peoples with a higher and lower talent or "giftedness." These nationalist (and racist) ideas found their way to South

Africa in the 1930s and 1940s and were to have a marked impact on the Afrikaner nationalist movement of that era.

In 1897 Sir Alfred Milner was appointed British high commissioner to the SAR; he shared the mineowners' conviction that Britain ought to annex the republic and establish "a self-governing White community, supported by well-treated and justly governed black labor from Cape Town to the Zambezi."[59] On May 4, 1899, he wired London to ask for some "striking proof of the intention of Her Majesty's Government not to be ousted from its position" and insisted that "the case for intervention is overwhelming."[60] In September the Orange River Colony voted to fight with the SAR in the event of a war with Britain; a month later, after the Trekker republics issued an ultimatum demanding the withdrawal of British troops from the SAR frontier, their joint forces invaded Natal and the Cape colony.

Although the Anglo-Boer War (or Second Liberation War) was won by the British—aided by one-fifth of all fighting Afrikaans speakers[61]—at an expense of over 250 million pounds,[62] the Treaty of Vereeniging which ended the war in 1902 was remarkably favorable to the Afrikaners. Despite promises made to blacks, the treaty did not address the issue of franchise rights. It also stipulated that British residents would become eligible to vote after five years' residence in the Orange River Colony and the SAR, but in return the Dutch language could be taught in the schools and used in the courts, and no special taxes were to be levied to pay for the costs of the war. Britain also offered 3 million pounds to the newly appointed civilian administrations to assist with resettlement and provided interest-free loans, for two years, to farmers wishing to resume their occupations. By 1907, both of the defeated states had been granted self-government.

Regardless of how conciliatory the treaty may have been, the "scorched earth" policy used by British troops during the war and the deaths of more than 27,000 Afrikaner women and children in British concentration camps—more than six times the number of commandos who were killed[63]—were not to be easily forgotten. Enthusiasm for Afrikaans-British unification on the strength of a common "Afrikanerness" waned. The Anglo-Boer War thus contributed more than any other single event to the constitution and strengthening of an exclusive, as opposed to inclusive, Afrikaner subjectivity.

Also at this time, academic disciplines such as eugenics, anthropology, and so on were disseminating via "race science" "proof" that different peoples were distinct biological races with special mental and physical characteristics. This literature emerged in the wake of a number of instances of black resistance to white domination globally prior to World War I and presumably was influenced to a certain extent by them. For example, in 1804 a slave rebellion on the French-held island of Saint Dominique, led by an ex-slave calling himself the "black George Washington," ended in independence for the first black nation in the world, to be known thereafter as the Republic of Haiti. Ethiopia repulsed an Italian invasion in 1896 and inspired the ill-fated Boxer rebellion in China four years later. In 1904, the "black" nation of Japan defeated the Russians militarily. The first embryonic Pan-African congress was held in London in 1900; W. E. B. du Bois of the United States formed the Niagara movement in 1905; and the National Association for the Advancement of Colored People (NAACP) appeared in 1909. Zionism and Back-to-Africa movements also began to emerge.

All of these activities frightened European colonizers and led to a flurry of writings in the West about the importance of racial struggle and the inevitable extinction, à la Darwinian theory, of the "inferior" races. When coupled with nationalism, race consciousness produced a proliferation of racial identities among Europeans themselves, who began to speak of an Anglo-Saxon race, a Nordic race, a Celtic race, and so on.[64] Within the context of its time, therefore, the labeling in South Africa of antagonisms between white language groups as a race problem was quite understandable, but the notion that they were separate races with distinct national characteristics worked against the formation of a larger identity.

What tends to be forgotten about the Anglo-Boer War is that it did not involve, as its name suggests, only two peoples; over 13,000 blacks died in the war fighting for the British cause.[65] The South African Native Congress (SANC), therefore, thought it auspicious in 1903 to write to Joseph Chamberlain, the British secretary of state for the colonies, and request the alleviation of certain grievances held by the "Native races." The appeal was largely ignored, but it is nonetheless important because it shows the effect of entanglements with the West on black subjectivity at this time.[66]

The first thing to note about the SANC letter is that it referred throughout to "Native races" and "European races," so the racial discourse becoming prevalent in Europe at the time was clearly apparent. Second, SANC stressed that its interest lay not in the extension of political rights to blacks but in the correction of certain "defects of administration" which worked against "the cultivation of the higher arts of civilization and the moral and religious elevation of the people."[67] In fact, SANC expressed deep gratitude for the "self-sacrificing faith of the Christian nations, foremost among whom are the British Isles," which brought the Gospel of Salvation "to the people that sit in darkness and the shadow of death."[68]

This language may have been nothing more than rhetoric designed to appeal to the particular audience, but SANC's moves to distance itself from less accommodationist elements within the black population suggest otherwise. SANC referred at one point to "church sessessions" which were interpreted as aiming at the eventual overthrow of the established authority of the government and the white clergy. The reference was to those who became known as "Ethiopians." The name reflected the influence of the Ethiopian Church, founded in Pretoria in 1892, and had nothing to do with the Ethiopian defeat of Italy in 1896. Nonetheless, the movement was influenced by "foreign" ideas. As Jean Comaroff has indicated, Ethiopianism was associated with Marcus Garvey, who described blacks as the "dispossessed of Ethiopia." In this way, Ethiopianism linked a South African cultural theme with contemporary developments in North America and with subsequent movements such as Rastafarianism, which *was* influenced by the experiences of the country of Ethiopia.[69] The Ethiopian Church also amalgamated with the American Methodist Episcopal (AME) Church of the United States in 1896. A magistrate in one district complained that the people "appear to be entirely poisoned by American ideas instilled in them by the Ethiopian section."[70]

In reference to these movements, SANC argued that they were purely a church matter and did not pose a threat, for the following reason:

> The black races are too conscious of their dependence upon the white missionaries, and of their obligations towards the British race, and the benefits to be derived by their presence in the general control and guidance of the civil and religious affairs of the country to harbor foolish notions of political ascendancy. The idea is too palpably absurd to carry weight with well-informed minds, and tends to obscure the real issues and to injure the people as a class.[71]

The notion that only the uneducated could possibly want political change was repeated later in the document, when SANC expressed the belief that "the Unity of the Natives for the purpose of attempting to overturn the established authority of the white man is the 'chimera' of ill-informed minds."[72]

What the SANC document demonstrates is that the idea of native unity as a way to counter European control was already circulating, but not among the natives who had been educated by missionaries. Looking for resistance to oppression only among the politically organized, therefore, is a mistake. Missionary societies and their educational institutions during this period were an obstacle to black unity. Mission-educated natives clearly identified with European norms and values; their objective was to assimilate the "civilized" into white society, not to include all blacks. Ethiopianism as a social movement actually was much more subversive than organized political activity because it fostered an identification with oppressed peoples everywhere rather than with the dominant elite, be that black or white.

For all of its modest character, the SANC document demonstrates that natives were well-tuned to race relations in other countries. At different times SANC mentioned "White and Black in the United States of America,"[73] the "opinion of President Roosevelt,"[74] and "the experience of other countries, especially of the Southern States of America."[75] This knowledge reflected the budding ties of native intellectuals to the Pan-Africanist movement and to American "Negroes,"[76] a knowledge that did help to foster both a feeling of Africanness in common with other oppressed peoples and a sense of blackness uniting all peoples of color and of African heritage. The fact that SANC once betrayed itself and spoke of "our race"[77] instead of "the Native races" suggests that a more inclusive identity was already in formation, if fragile.

Evidence for this more inclusive identity also can be found among the so-called Coloreds, whose main political representative, the African Political Organization (the APO, founded in 1902), was defined by reference to Africa, not to skin color. According to Lewis, Coloreds in the early 1900s were strongly influenced by the message of black pride, unity, upliftment, and political assertion promulgated by Francis Peregrino, an Accra-born journalist himself much influenced by the Afro-American leaders Booker T. Washington and W. E. B. du Bois. Peregrino also established links with the AME Church when it began missionary activities in South Africa in the late 1890s. Through these contacts, Peregrino attended the Pan-African Conference held in London in 1900 and thereupon determined to move to Cape Town and spread his message of black pride there. Largely through the pages of his newspaper, the *Spectator*, Peregrino helped mobilize the Colored elites on the basis of their shared blackness and denounced those who felt superior to Africans.[78]

One of SANC's requests was for an imperial commission, to include the question of labor in a larger investigation of the condition of native affairs in South Africa. Such a body, known as the South African Native Affairs Commission (SANAC), was formed in 1903 and deliberated over the problem of labor shortages on the mines for the next two years.

As Adam Ashforth has pointed out, SANAC met at a time when opinion "at home" almost unanimously was opposed to any policy that might be seen as promoting forced labor. (This was one reason why mineowners had to resort to such noncoercive measures as making alcohol freely available at the workplace in order to attract a labor force.) When SANAC convened, it unanimously passed a resolution that affirmed "that forced labor is not countenanced by any South African Government and is repugnant to civilized opinion throughout the country."[79] SANAC continued what already was an established tradition and justified oppressive policies toward indigenous peoples in terms acceptable to a European audience.

SANAC came up with the notion that the practice of reserving portions of land for exclusive native occupation entailed "special obligations" owed by "Natives," which included not only the aboriginal inhabitants of Africa but

also "half-castes" and their descendants. The fact that these people supposedly had come to enjoy the benefits of European civilization provided the basis
for constructing a scheme of special obligations.

Arguing for a reconstructed system of tribalism as a basis for administration
and a central role for the Native Affairs Department, SANAC expressed the view
that communal tenure, a form under which most Reserve or Crown land was
held, was an institution indicative of low levels of civilization and could not be
expected to allow for improvements in productivity. SANAC argued that
individual tenure in concert with measures such as hut taxes would speed the
trek from barbarism to civilization, while alleviating the labor supply problem
by forcing the newly landless to seek a livelihood in the towns.[80] As South Africa
approached statehood, SANAC thus appealed to the concept of private property
and the obligation to cultivate the earth in order to make proletarianization and
landlessness consistent with a civilizing mission.

Toward Statehood

As the two British colonies and the two Afrikaner republics increasingly
became interconnected by railway lines and trading relationships, pressures
to unite increased and "Closer Union Societies" began to spring up. Supported by the Liberal party which had come to power in England in 1905, a
series of pre-union negotiations were held from 1908 to 1909.

The National Convention was assembled on October 12, 1908, to discuss
a draft constitution. The convention was entirely in the hands of colonial
statesmen, who advocated widely different policies in regard to the native
question. While Cape representatives defended a nonracial (if heavily
qualified) franchise, delegates from the north, led by Louis Botha, argued for
a color-bar. Representing Cape farmers, delegate G. H. Maasdorp argued that
his constituents greatly feared the enfranchisement of Africans and wished
to see their voting rights restricted. A number of petitions emanating from or
on behalf of Africans were laid before the convention and advocated "equal
rights for all civilized persons in South Africa."[81]

In a letter setting out Britain's policy on the issue of franchise rights, Lord
Selbourne accepted the principle of enfranchising all white adult males,
"because Europeans could presume to be civilized," and suggested access to
the franchise for blacks who fulfilled such criteria of "civilization" as
education, monogamy, and property ownership.[82]

In the end, the Franchise Committee's final report represented a compromise between the Cape and the northern republics. It recommended that
no registered voters would be disqualified, that existing qualifications in
various colonies would prevail, and that only Europeans would be eligible
to stand as members of Parliament (MPs).

In response to the draft South Africa Act, the black population of the country mobilized on an unprecedented scale to demonstrate opposition to the proposed constitution and sent a delegation to Britain in 1909 to appeal against its provisions when the draft act was submitted to the British Parliament for ratification. Neither the British public nor most parliamentarians were much interested in either the "Colored and Native Delegation" or the draft act. The South Africa bill was ratified without amendment, the franchise was reserved for whites only, and the Union of South Africa went into effect. The "race question," as relations between English and Afrikaner were described, seemed to have found its answer.

That Britain sold out South Africa's blacks for economic reasons is a fairly commonplace assumption. Yet it needs to be remembered that it was *after* the emancipation of slaves, in the second half of the nineteenth century, that racism in the Western world emerged as a fully fledged ideology, supported by the natural and social sciences. As Lauren has argued, those who discriminated on the basis of color did so with a growing awareness of their own race, while those who were discriminated against developed an even more acute race consciousness because constant reinforcement came with every new instance of racial prejudice.[83] What is now South Africa emerged as an independent country at the height of the era of "scientific racism," when the rising biological sciences sought to prove the superiority of whites over all others, and the emerging discipline of anthropology focused its attention primarily upon the physiological differences among races as the chief determinants of their fates. This period was also the epoch when scientific and intellectual opinion transformed Jews from a religious and historical group into a race to be known as Semitic.[84]

The Constitution of the Union of South Africa, therefore, represented not merely the triumph of the "frontier tradition" over "Cape liberalism"[85] but the codification of the scientifically justified Western principle of white supremacy.

SOUTH AFRICA SINCE INDEPENDENCE

When the Union went into effect, the electoral system was biased toward agricultural interests. Almost half of the whites lived in rural areas, the vote was loaded in their favor (rural areas had a smaller number of voters, thus giving a greater value to their votes), and farmers were active in politics—in 1910 over 50 percent of MPs in the governing South African party (SAP) were farmers.[86] This bias is often cited as an example of how the Trekker mentality has prevailed in a South African polity dominated by Afrikaners, but Afrikanerdom still was a highly contested concept among the leading political figures of the day.

Louis Botha (a Transvaaler who became the first postunion prime minister) emphasized a common South African nation (i.e., one that included the English speakers), while nationalists such as Hertzog and D. F. Malan insisted that within the South African polity the English speakers and Afrikaans speakers were different nationalities. They proposed that the streams of English and Afrikaner nationality should flow apart until the Afrikaner stream developed to the level of the English. There was also a white and a black stream. Hertzog, however, regarded Cape Coloreds (whose representatives in the APO decided in 1912 on the term *Cape Afrikaners* as more appropriate than *Coloreds*[87]) as already part of the Afrikaner nation since they met the two criteria for acceptance: they spoke Afrikaans and they were usually members of a Dutch Reformed Church. For Hertzog, Afrikaner identity could be adopted voluntarily and was not fixed by nature. Presumably, for Hertzog, black meant African tribes and was not synonymous with the term native as used by SANAC.

Malan, on the other hand, was a minister of the Dutch Reformed Church, and treated Afrikaner identity as fixed and immutable. He viewed the continued existence of the Afrikaner nation as part of a divine dispensation. Distinguishable by culture, race, history, fatherland, and politics, each *volk* was created by God to fulfill a particular calling and destiny. This notion of the Boers as a "chosen people," willed by God to preserve their distinction from other races (which at this stage still meant the English speakers), was not evident until the second half of the nineteenth century and displayed the influence of Dutch theologian Abraham Kuyper upon teachers and clergy in the interior. Although the world view of the frontiersmen had always borne the imprint of the Bible, their most common reading material, scarcely any of them had claimed to constitute a chosen people in the theological sense. Only in the late 1880s did a number of Transvaal clergy begin to assert such a claim, particularly after one of the chief exponents of the Afrikaans Language movement, the Reverend S. J. du Toit, imported Kuyper's ideas into South Africa.[88] Between 1890 and 1960, according to Bloomberg, most top Afrikaans-speaking theologians did their postgraduate work at Amsterdam's Free University, a school founded by Kuyper.[89]

Conflicting views on questions of political affiliation abounded. When the South African party led by Louis Botha and Jan Smuts formally entered World War I on the side of England in September 1914 by invading the German enclave of South West Africa, it did so in the midst of large-scale opposition from Afrikaans speakers. General de Wet issued a call to arms in the Orange Free State on October 14, and rebellion flickered into open civil war. Botha launched a full-scale campaign and in sporadic encounters 10,000 rebels fought 30,000 government troops. In three months it was all over, but afterwards, as David Harrison has argued, the lines were firmly drawn between the wider nationalism of Botha and Smuts and the narrower nationalism of Hertzog and Malan.[90]

What united the Afrikaans speakers, despite their differences, was also what united all whites, despite their differences: the equation of white with civilization and the belief that the obliteration of white domination would mean the end of civilization in Africa.

The Aftermath of World War I: "Poor Whites" and the League of Nations

With the wartime industrial boom, whites flocked into the factories to escape rural poverty; in 1919 they formed 37.5 percent of the manufacturing work force.[91] At the end of the war came a severe recession, and many proletarianized whites found themselves once again without work. The ranks of the urban unemployed became swelled by three other groups: (1) an increasing number of Afrikaners leaving the land due to a combination of the commercialization of agriculture, a drop in farm prices, and one of the worst droughts in South African history; (2) an estimated 30,000 soldiers returning from voluntary military service overseas; and (3) white mine workers who lost their jobs when the gold price fell and mining capitalists, in order to cut costs, began to substitute cheaper black for expensive white labor. The situation was so bad in rural areas that some whites apparently went to work in the Reserves during ploughing season for the more prosperous natives and were remunerated in kind (i.e., with an animal or crops) rather than in wages. Coupled with the lack of effective segregation in the urban areas, these practices prompted the Dutch Reformed Church to complain that its parishioners were "living with and like Kaffirs."[92]

What made "living with and like Kaffirs" a major problem was not just that it symbolized economic hardship and a breakdown of social injunctions against racial mixing; what was at stake was the maintenance of the boundary between a civilized self and an uncivilized other. European identity was so tied to hierarchy that poverty and the necessity to work for "Kaffirs" symbolized the fall of man; the inability to differentiate the presumed superior self from the inferior other meant that the self had sunk and the whole society had been overcome by barbarism. This fear of "sinking to the level of the Kaffir" prompted an emphasis on standard of living as a necessary if not sufficient condition of civilization.

As an example of this emphasis, an article by philosophy professor Alfred Hoernle, published in the "scientific" journal *Bantu Studies* in the early 1920s, offered three criteria for differentiating the "advanced" or "civilized" person from the "primitive." The first criterion was material standard of life, a concept that entailed differences in housing, clothing, weapons, means of subsistence, and tools. Also entailed was the extent of art—writing as opposed to oral tradition, and history as opposed to myth—to be found in each community.

The second criterion was social organization, and here Hoernle invoked the standard argument that tribal ownership of land and absence of the concept of contract were indicative of primitiveness.

Third, Hoernle claimed that an animistic view of nature was one of the decisive marks of the primitive mind. Animism apparently incorporated two equally important traits: (1) innocence of the scientific concept of impersonal, natural law; and (2) belief that natural objects and events are or may become the instruments of spirits or spiritual forces. Belief in the organic unity of human society with the whole of nature, and in witchcraft, was also mentioned.[93]

On the basis of this sort of "scientific" discourse, the promotion of civilization came to be equated with higher standards of living for the white community, as the following speech by Hertzog indicates:

The Europeans must keep to a standard of living which shall meet the demands of white civilization. Civilization and standards of living always go hand in hand. Thus a white cannot exist on a native wage scale, because this means that he has to give up his own standard of living and take on the standard of living of the native. In short, the white man becomes a white kaffir.[94]

The "poor white" problem after the war was such that no political party could ignore it and hope to stay in office. The South African party was no exception. After Botha's death in 1919, Smuts returned from the imperial war councils in Europe to become premier; his speeches in particular placed support for industry—an issue on which he had once equivocated but was now firmly protectionist—in the context of widening the scope of employment. A coalition government elected in 1924 introduced a "civilized labor policy," effectively reserving certain public sector jobs for whites and Coloreds and giving preferential treatment to those industries employing a high percentage of "civilized labor." This strategy was aimed specifically at ameliorating the economic position of the poor white and resulted in the dismissal of a large number of blacks from semiskilled and unskilled positions.

South Africa's entry into the League of Nations brought its politicians more fully into contact with Europeans who were subjugating colored races on a global scale—not only colonial powers but also white settlers in the United States and Australia. This contact reinforced European identity by bringing South Africa into the club of civilized nations and provided a diplomatic forum within which contested social practices could be justified in standard Western terms. Thus, in a 1929 speech, Prime Minister Jan Smuts felt comfortable claiming that his government's policy of letting rural Africans run their own affairs but under white supervision was in accordance with the trusteeship clauses of the Covenant of the League of Nations.[95]

But the league was not important only because it brought whites together. As a catalyst for demands for racial equality from both within and without its chambers, the League of Nations helped to distance the concept of race from its association with nation and align it more closely with the idea of skin color. In other words, polarization between those peoples who demanded equality and those who refused it turned the struggle for social justice into a fight between two opposing camps—white and black.

To coincide with the convening of the Paris Peace Conference in 1919, the enigmatic American W. E. B. du Bois organized the first Pan-Africanist Congress, which was attended by delegates not only from Africa (including South African blacks) but from all countries in which there had been racial discrimination—including China, Japan, and India—and from racial minorities in North America, South America, and Europe. On the agenda was a discussion of racial discrimination in general and, more immediately, ways to bring "all pressure possible on the delegates at the Peace Table in the interest of the colored peoples of the United States and the world."[96]

In the end, the one officially recognized voice at the peace conference to champion the cause of racial equality was Japan. A so-called colored nation which had militarily defeated a so-called white nation—Russia—in 1904, Japan set out amid great fanfare and cheers from the Pan-Africanists to solicit support for a plan to include an explicit statement on racial equality in the Covenant of the league.[97]

The Japanese determined that Woodrow Wilson held in his hands much of their fate on the issue of race. Yet Wilson was a man who supported immigration restrictions for Asians trying to enter the United States on the grounds that "we cannot make a homogeneous population out of a people who do not blend with the Caucasian race"; who had first introduced segregation into the federal government itself in the belief that "segregation is not humiliating but a benefit"; and who came under tremendous pressure domestically not to give in to the Japanese from people like Senator J. D. Phelan of California, who declared that "equal rights cannot be accorded to Oriental peoples without imperiling our own national existence and destroying western civilization."[98]

The Americans at the peace conference, of course, were not the only "villains." Delegates from Australia and Britain—not to mention South Africa—shared the same attitudes about racial distinction, exclusion, and separation, so that the Japanese quickly realized their "close allies" would not go along with their human rights proposal. A revised amendment, leaving out any mention of race and asking support only for "the principle of equality of nations and just treatment of their nationals,"[99] eventually was passed by a clear majority, although of the Western powers, only France and Italy supported it.[100]

Even the watered-down amendment proved too much for Woodrow Wilson. He declared that it could not be adopted because it had failed to secure unanimous approval, although on at least two other occasions the unanimity "rule" had not been applied. When questioned, Wilson stated that there were simply "too serious objections on the part of some of us" to have it inserted in the Covenant.[101]

With the Japanese proposal defeated, the delegates turned to the important task of carving up among themselves former German territories—mandates, as the delegates chose to call these lands—and promised to govern these territories as a "sacred trust of Civilization" until such time as these "backward" peoples were "able to stand on their own feet in the strenuous conditions of the modern world."[102] South Africa got to keep South West Africa (now Namibia), and Smuts returned home, in triumph, to campaign for the upcoming parliamentary elections.

The racial polarization that the League of Nations helped effect can be seen in a discursive shift among black South Africans after the league's founding. When the South African Native National Congress (later the African National Congress) drew up its constitution in 1919, it spoke interchangeably of colored races, aboriginal races, and Bantu races; in fact, it differentiated among "the whole Bantu people" by equating race with tribe.[103] Less than twenty years later, in 1935, the proceedings of the All African Convention (a meeting attended by so-called Indians and Coloreds as well) spoke of "the White and Black races" and discussed measures to "promote harmony and peace between the two races."[104] Loud applause apparently followed the reading of a telegram to the convention from Moscow, exhorting "the Natives of South Africa to set about their historic task and assist in the struggle of the Negro peoples against exploitation and oppression."[105] A motion to support Abyssinia (Ethiopia) in its "gallant and heroic struggle" against "Fascist Italy" was also carried unopposed.[106]

At the same time, the convention endorsed the imposition of an education or some other qualification as a condition for the acquirement of political privileges;[107] the qualification "was intended to show that the Native was sufficiently developed and educated to be worthy of consultation on matters affecting his own well being and existence."[108] The task of organized political activity, therefore, was to demonstrate how far civilization had spread among the natives. The fact that such a strategy was abandoned within only ten years is intimately tied to the dissemination of a discourse that assumed that black South Africans would never be worthy of inclusion in the political life of white South Africa.

The Upheaval of the 1930s and 1940s

The South African economy suffered a severe setback at the outset of the Great Depression, particularly when Britain abandoned the gold standard in 1931. Widespread public agitation for going off gold and for a government of "national unity" to deal with the economic crisis forced Hertzog into a coalition with Smuts. In the 1933 election, Hertzog and Smuts won a combined total of 135 out of 150 seats, and their two parties (the NP and the SAP) joined together to form the United party (UP).

According to Dan O'Meara, pre- and postfusion ideological definitions among Afrikaners differed first in their delimitations of Afrikanerdom and second in the character of Afrikaner nationalism. The "Hertzogist" conception was voluntarist in that an individual's personal attitude decided whether or not she or he was an Afrikaner. All white South Africans who viewed South Africa as their sole homeland and who accepted absolute language equality and the principle of "South Africa first" were regarded as Afrikaners. Hence, Hertzog made regular reference to Afrikaans-speaking (or sometimes Dutch-speaking) and English-speaking Afrikaners. A broad South Africanism remained the dominant ideology of the United party under Hertzog's leadership.[109]

At the same time, a more ethnically exclusive and fixed delimitation of Afrikanerdom found expression through the Afrikaner Broederbond, founded in 1918, and D. F. Malan's "purified" (Gesuiwerde) National party (G/NP), founded in 1934. These two groups formally embraced the tenets of Christian-Nationalism (C-N), a theological doctrine that came to underpin much of what became known as apartheid.

Rooted in Kuyperian thought and influenced by twentieth-century ultranationalisms (including Nazi Fascism), the doctrine of Christian-Nationalism was formulated as a single, systematic body of ideas only in the 1930s, according to Bloomberg, and was given powerful impetus by the return of intellectuals like Nico Diederichs, Piet Meyer, Geoff Cronje, and H. F. Verwoerd from studies in Germany and Holland.[110]

Christian-Nationalism views God as "Hammadibil," the Great Divider, and insists that differentiation is fully endorsed by the Scriptures. A discourse preoccupied with differences, obvious or hidden, between races, nations, languages, and cultures, C-N draws upon a number of biblical sources to support the claim that God willed national division among the children of Adam and Eve. Genesis 11 is probably the most often quoted:

And the Lord came down to see the city and the tower which the sons of men had built. And the Lord said, "Behold, they are one people and they have all one language; and this is only the beginning of what they will do; and nothing that they propose to do will now be impossible for them. Come let us go down and confuse their language, so that they may not understand one another's speech. So the Lord scattered them abroad from there over the face of all the earth, and they left off building the city.[111]

Any text can be interpreted in a number of ways, and the C-N interpretation of Genesis 11 as an injunction against the sinfulness of "unnatural" racial mixing is one such interpretation. But as a biblical story invoked to justify the practice of apartheid after World War II, the passage from Genesis can be given far less benign meanings.

What the Lord said was that the sons of men were "one people" with "one language"; they were not different "races" or "nations." In unity they threatened God's rule—"nothing that they propose to do will now be impossible for them"—and it was in order to avert that threatened insurrection that the Lord "confused their language" and "scattered them abroad." Genesis 11 thus can be read as an allegory for National party rule after 1948. Playing "God," the government did not simply preserve difference, as it claimed; the NP policy was to maintain the rule of whites by breaking up the unity of black people, by confusing their language via such mechanisms as Bantu education, and by scattering them abroad into impoverished homelands.

To what extent the National party succeeded in its task will be analyzed in later chapters on domestic power relations. Suffice it to say at this point that, although South Africa was considered a "country of nationalities" by some blacks in the 1940s, the conviction of Cronje and others that different nations existed within the European and African communities was not widely shared. According to the manifesto issued by the African National Congress's Youth League (ANCYL) in 1944, for example, the "four chief nationalities" were Africans, Europeans, Indians, and Coloreds, each of which had a "divine destiny" to fulfill. Far from seeing different groups each with its own language and culture within the Bantu race, as Christian-Nationalists did, the ANCYL expressed a belief "in the unity of all Africans from the Mediterranean Sea in the North to the Indian and Atlantic oceans in the South" and argued that "the African people in South Africa . . . suffer national oppression in common with thousands and millions of oppressed Colonial peoples in other parts of the world."[112] From the very beginning then, the doctrine of Christian-Nationalism imported from Europe had to contend against a homegrown ideology of African nationalism, itself the product of struggle between European colonizers and African peoples throughout the continent.

Other important tenets of Christian-Nationalism are that alleged differences are held to be God's will, races do not alter their positions in the superior-inferior hierarchy, and each must simply accept its place in the larger scheme. The notion that a group's characteristics are of an immutable biological or genetic type and are transmitted through blood to succeeding generations was obviously strongly influenced by the Nazi approach to race. In the 1930s, German foreign affairs officers established cultural links with Afrikaners and began to organize cultural-academic exchanges. These links stimulated young Afrikaner postgraduates to take courses in Germany in spite of the language barrier. A sudden emergence of anti-Semitism in Christian-National thought in the 1930s can be attributed to Nazi influence, according to Bloomberg, as there was no indigenous Boer tradition of anti-Semitism before then.[113]

The appeal of arguments invoking race destiny to explain South Africa's problems was so great that they appeared in such places as the "scientific" reports of government-appointed commissions in the 1930s. The Native Economic Commission in 1932 attributed the poor state of the native economy in the Reserves not to overcrowding, but simply to the fact that the "mentality" of the race operating it was "backward," and suggested that the proper role for the "advanced Natives" was to use their own talents in their own areas.[114] Pushing skilled African workers back to the Reserves in the name of development was a practice endorsed by the National party after 1948.

As for Kuyper's doctrine of "sovereignty in own sphere," its influence can be seen in such common Afrikaner phrases as "in every sphere," "in its own area," and, more recently, "own affairs." But if Christian-Nationalism and associated Nazi concepts have lived on to the present, it is not primarily to the National party but to the Broederbond and its affiliated institutions that credit must be given.

It was through the Broederbond's network of extra-parliamentary bodies like the Federation of Afrikaner Cultural Organizations (FAK), the Calvinist Bond, the Voortrekkers, and the Afrikaner National Student-league (ANS), rather than the G/NP itself, Bloomberg has argued, that the Afrikaner nationalism of the 1930s was mobilized. But what is important to remember about the Broederbond is that its chief pressures have been exerted on its own community; that is, on those who share Afrikaans language, religion, and culture but are not aware of themselves as a *volk*.[115] The Bond simply did not appeal to the broad mass of Afrikaans speakers when it was founded, which is one reason it became a secret organization in 1922. Exposing its existence and connection to the G/NP in 1935, Hertzog complained to Malan that his recruitment to the Bond meant that he was now obliged "to discard the policy of national unity with the inclusion of the English-speaking Afrikaner" and "to enter the road of national disunity and disagreement."[116] These ongoing struggles among Afrikaners over questions of identity meant that the nationalist movement of the 1930s had to first create an Afrikaner "nation" before it could defend its interests.

There were two major mechanisms through which the Afrikaner was constituted exclusively as an Afrikaans-speaking white of Dutch origin. First, as O'Meara has pointed out, intellectuals sought to appeal to a mythical and mystified unity of the Boer republican past—its symbols, myths, ideologies, and so on.[117] In this regard, the 1838 Battle of Blood River, when a handful of Trekkers beat back the mighty Zulu nation after praying to God for protection, offered the perfect symbol for the nationalist view of South Africa—a gallant, God-fearing country surrounded by the forces of evil.[118] To recreate the triumph of civilization over barbarism, as the victory at Blood River was remembered, and to link Christian-Nationalism with the heroic Voortrekker ethos, the Broederbond recreated the Great Trek in 1938. In his speech at the erection of the Voortrekker monument that culminated the grand proceedings, Verwoerd spoke of the need for a trek to economic independence for the volk, while the theme of poverty dominated most speeches.[119]

Celebrating as it did the 100th anniversary of the Battle of Blood River, and not the onset of the Great Trek (which began in 1836), the Anniversary Trek helped to downplay historical differences with the British and helped to magnify those with the Africans. But the nationalist movement was as much about constituting a non-English-speaking Afrikaner as it was about separating people of different skin color. A second mechanism for achieving its objective, therefore, was to appeal to the concept of imperialism and to blame all manner of social ills on "foreign British-Jewish capitalism."

Malan blamed the "poor white" problem on "world capitalism which produced the paradox of over-production and poverty and unemployment." Was it not significant, he asked, that Russia, which had "broken with the capitalist system," was the only country free from unemployment during the world's economic depression? Verwoerd, too, admitted that "radical changes such as nationalization of the mining industry or the reorganization of South Africa as a socialist state" were possible solutions. He felt, however, that the tragic sufferings of "poor whites" demanded practical first-aid measures that could be carried out at once.[120]

Throughout the 1930s the Broederbond and its affiliates worked hard to organize Afrikaans-speaking workers into ethnically exclusive trade unions and to establish and promote Afrikaner business interests. Financial groups such as Sanlam and Santam were established at this time, and Christian-

Nationalists fought for control of unions in the mining, building, iron and steel, clothing, and leather industries. Their only real success was in the mines, according to O'Meara, for appeals to nationalism or the mystic unity of the *volk* did little to move workers increasingly organized into nonracial trade unions. Only when Broederbond labor activists began to fight for the material interests of workers against foreign capitalists, "communist" trade union leaders, and cheap African labor did they have much influence.[121]

The fragile unity of the *volk* was sundered again in 1939. Disagreement over South Africa's connection with Britain during World War II tore apart the alliance of Hertzog and Smuts. Hertzog regarded South Africa's entry into "England's war" as a betrayal of South African sovereignty and spoke for those who approved of Hitler's methods of dealing with the Semitic "race." He broke with Smuts and was followed by thirty-seven MPs, representing mainly rural constituencies, into an uneasy alliance with D. F. Malan's "purified" National party.

The war helped concentrate the nationalist movement's thought on the possibilities of achieving a republic, an aim openly espoused by the Ossewebrandwag (OB), founded in 1938 to perpetuate the atmosphere of *volk* solidarity that marked the 1938 Voortrekker celebrations. An openly neo-Nazi movement which at its zenith enjoyed hundreds of thousands of supporters, the OB began to decline with the waning of Germany's star after 1942. But even at the height of its popularity, the OB did not represent the sentiments of anything close to a majority of Afrikaans speakers. There was no conscription, yet when Smuts called for volunteers, roughly one in three eligible Afrikaners joined up to fight with Britain alongside English speakers. In the 1943 election, Smuts increased his majority, receiving 107 seats (to the National party's forty-three) and about one-third of the Afrikaans vote.

As the war came to an end, the Broederbond defined the struggle between the NP and the UP as that between nationalism and liberalism, or the principles of Christian-Nationalism versus those of trusteeship (guardianship, as Smuts called it). It was a struggle that the NP seemed unlikely to win, but one from which it nonetheless emerged triumphant only five years after Smuts's comfortable electoral victory.

It is easy to see apartheid as an attempt to roll back the clock of history by pushing urbanized blacks into tribal Reserves and as a practice totally out of touch with the global march toward racial equality and self-determination for colonial peoples after 1945. Yet apartheid needs to be seen in a larger context, as part of a historical process to defend European civilization on a barbarous continent and to try to justify white domination in terms acceptable to external audiences. To the practice of apartheid and analysis of its place within a web of global relationships binding South Africans to citizens of other countries, the next chapter is devoted.

Summary

This chapter has considered the local effects of struggle involving Dutch and English settlers, colonial administrators, European capitalists, missionary and antislavery societies, and colored races in the League of Nations. It was out of these struggles during the age of colonialism that multiple and overlapping subjectivities were constituted—Afrikaner, native, British, European, African, black, white, Colored, and Griqua. Precisely because these identities are socially constituted and not given by nature, historical contests over their meaning have been an integral aspect of the politics of race relations in South Africa.

Power relations during colonialism also constrained what the struggles between socially constituted subjects would be about. In this regard, the key knowledge-producing apparatuses that shaped understandings of what were normal social practices were the schools and churches affiliated with various European missionary societies. What was normal for whites was whatever European colonizers on the continent were doing, for to abandon European identity meant becoming a native and thus barbaric. Mission influence certainly accounts for the sense of superiority that almost all settlers felt toward the indigenous peoples, although the educated administrative elite often described the "rude" farmers in the interior in the same way that they spoke of the natives.

That same mission influence also explains the "denormalization" of enslavement and extermination as appropriate responses to local resistance and the increasing propensity of settlers to justify white rule by appeal to the necessity for Christian civilization on a barbarous continent. As did settlers in the Americas, settlers in South Africa continually redefined the essence of civilization in order to reinscribe and reconstitute a boundary between the civilized self and barbarous other.

As for the subordinated groups in South Africa, those most closely affiliated with mission schools and churches considered themselves inferior to Europeans yet superior to the largely uneducated mass of their fellow countrymen in the rural areas. While native intellectuals asked for no more than a qualified franchise and the assimilation of the civilized into white society, social movements such as Ethiopianism were disseminating the idea of native unity as a way to counter white domination. Although tribal differences may have been a factor in stifling the emergence of a united front among the oppressed, the fact that an urban/rural split was so prevalent suggests the divisive influence of mission education and religion.

Finally, this chapter has demonstrated the influence on Afrikaner intellectuals of the French Revolution, German romanticism, Kuyperian (Dutch) theology, and National-Socialism. The particular way in which modern European ideas came to underpin National party policy after World War II, and have been used historically to justify white domination, may well be unique to this particular situation. But it needs to be remembered that what the world now knows as apartheid was a product of contact with modern Europe, not of African isolation.

NOTES

1. See Todorov, *The Conquest of America*, especially chapter 3.
2. Quoted in Kammen, *People of Paradox*, p. 34.
3. Scott, *Domination and the Arts of Resistance*, p. 35.
4. See Biko, *I Write What I Like*, p. 88.
5. Magubane, *The Political Economy of Race and Class*, p. 26.
6. Ibid., p. 23.
7. de Villiers, *White Tribe Dreaming*, p. 7.
8. Frankel, *Capital Investment in Africa*, p. 42.
9. Greenberg, *Race and State in Capitalist Development*, p. 74.
10. Quoted in Magubane, *The Political Economy of Race and Class*, p. 27.
11. Greenberg, *Race and State in Capitalist Development*, p. 75.
12. de Villiers, *White Tribe Dreaming*, p. 29.
13. Quoted in Lauren, *Power and Prejudice: The Politics and Diplomacy of Racial Discrimination*, pp. 14, 18.
14. See, for example, Loubser, *The Apartheid Bible: A Critical Review of Racial Theology in South Africa*, p. 5; and du Toit and Giliomee, *Afrikaner Political Thought*. Vol. 1, *1780–1850*, p. 32.
15. Giliomee, "The Development of the Afrikaner's Self-Concept," pp. 7–8.
16. Quoted in de Villiers, *White Tribe Dreaming*, p. 50.
17. See the writings of Truter and Van Ryneveld in du Toit and Giliomee, *Afrikaner Political Thought*, pp. 99, 96.
18. Giliomee, "The Development of the Afrikaner's Self-Concept," p. 10.
19. du Toit and Giliomee, *Afrikaner Political Thought*, p. 4; and Loubser, *The Apartheid Bible*, p. 6.
20. du Toit and Giliomee, *Afrikaner Political Thought*, p. 5.
21. Loubser, *The Apartheid Bible*, p. 6.
22. Quoted in du Toit and Giliomee, *Afrikaner Political Thought*, pp. 283, 291.
23. Ibid., pp. xv–xxv.
24. See Bloomberg, *Christian-Nationalism and the Rise of the Afrikaner Broederbond in South Africa, 1918–1948*, p. 137.
25. Sparks, *The Mind of South Africa*, p. 42.
26. Lauren, *Power and Prejudice*, p. 28.
27. Ibid., p. 29.
28. See the letters by Landdrost R. J. van der Riet to Fiscal J. A. Truter (April 1810) and by J. A. Truter to the colonial secretary, Colonel Bird (February 1811), in du Toit and Giliomee, *Afrikaner Political Thought*, pp. 53–55.

29. The first quote is from the minutes of a meeting of Landdrost Andries Stockenstrom and the heemraden (members of the country court) of Graaff-Reinet; the second is from an editorial in the newspaper *Die Zuid-Afrikaan*. Both are in ibid., pp. 66, 107.

30. Ibid., p. 250.

31. Ibid., p. 199.

32. Ibid., pp. 212–13.

33. Quoted in Kiernan, *America: The New Imperialism, from White Settlement to World Hegemony*, p. 28.

34. Magubane, *The Political Economy of Race and Class*, p. 24.

35. Thompson, *The Political Mythology of Apartheid*, p. 108.

36. Ibid., p. 149.

37. du Toit and Giliomee, *Afrikaner Political Thought*, p. 195.

38. See the letter from Landdrost Anders Stockenstrom to Governor Caledon, dated August 1810, in ibid., p. 158.

39. This language appeared in a letter from Stockenstrom to the colonial secretary, Lieutenant Colonel C. Bird, dated June 1822. See ibid., p. 165.

40. See the letter from the Stellenbosch burghers to the Burgher Senate, dated July 1826, in ibid., p. 104.

41. Letter from Andries Stockenstrom to Lieutenant Governor Young, July 1847, in ibid., p. 180.

42. Speech by J. H. Wicht (a prominent Cape Town property owner and member of the Legislative Assembly) in the Cape Legislative Council, May 1857. Quoted in ibid., p. 187.

43. Giliomee, "The Development of the Afrikaner's Self-Concept," p. 15.

44. Quoted in Harrison, *The White Tribe of Africa*, p. 27.

45. Quoted in du Toit and Giliomee, *Afrikaner Political Thought*, p. 219.

46. Shillington, "The Impact of the Diamond Discoveries on the Kimberley Hinterland," p. 108.

47. See Lewis, *Between the Wire and the Wall: A History of South African "Colored" Politics*, p. 9.

48. Lord Carnarvon, quoted in Harris, *Europe and Africa*, pp. 193–94.

49. Thompson, *The Political Mythology of Apartheid*, p. 169.

50. Harris, *Europe and Africa*, pp. 197–98.

51. Ibid., p. 202.

52. Ibid.

53. Quoted in Van Onselen, *Studies in the Social and Economic History of the Witwatersrand*, p. 12.

54. Ibid.

55. Harris, *Europe and Africa*, pp. 206–7.

56. Sampson, *Black and Gold: Tycoons, Revolutionaries, and Apartheid*, p. 51.

57. On this point, see Giliomee, "The Development of the Afrikaner's Self-Concept," pp. 16–18.

58. See Loubser, *The Apartheid Bible*, pp. 15–18.

59. Quoted in Sampson, *Black and Gold*, p. 52.

60. Quoted in Harris, *Europe and Africa*, p. 207–8.

61. Harrison, *The White Tribe of Africa*, p. 33.

62. Sampson, *Black and Gold*, p. 53.

63. de Villiers, *White Tribe Dreaming*, p. 236.

64. Ibid., p. 51.

65. Harrison, *The White Tribe of Africa*, p. 31.

66. See the document prepared by the executive of the South African Native Congress, 1903, entitled "Questions Affecting the Natives and Colored People Resident in British South Africa," in Karis and Carter, *From Protest to Challenge*, vol. 1, pp. 18–29.

67. Ibid., p. 26.

68. Ibid., p. 18.

69. See Comaroff, *Body of Power, Spirit of Resistance*, p. 272.

70. Quoted in ibid., p. 116.

71. Quoted in Karis and Carter, *From Protest to Challenge*, vol. 1, p. 18.

72. Ibid., p. 28.

73. Ibid., p. 20.

74. Ibid., p. 21.

75. Ibid., p. 28.

76. With regard to ties to Americans, for instance, the 1908 Select Committee on Native Education in the Cape reported that more than 100 Africans from that colony alone had in recent years gone to colleges in the United States and elsewhere. See Odendaal, *Black Protest Politics in South Africa to 1912*, p. 89.

77. Ibid., p. 21.

78. See Lewis, *Between the Wire and the Wall*, pp. 16–18.

79. Ashforth, *The Politics of Official Discourse*, p. 25.

80. Ibid., chapter 1, especially pp. 35–56.

81. Odendaal, *Black Protest Politics in South Africa*, pp. 27–34.

82. See Lewis, *Between the Wire and the Wall*, p. 47.

83. Lauren, *Power and Prejudice*, p. 49.

84. Ibid., pp. 34–35.

85. See Wilson and Thompson, eds., *The Oxford History of South Africa*, vol. 1.

86. Lipton, *Capitalism and Apartheid*, p. 258.

87. The African Political Organization decided on the term *Cape Afrikaners* at its 1912 and 1913 general conferences, a move that Lewis has suggested reflected continued aspirations toward incorporation into the white community, stressing as it did the shared culture of Coloreds with whites. At the same time, the APO continued to call for "race pride" and carried articles on the 1911 Universal Races Congress in London and on the activities of Afro-American leaders such as Booker T. Washington. See Lewis, *Between the Wire and the Wall*, pp. 72–73.

88. On this point, see du Toit, "No Chosen People: The Myth of the Calvinist Origins of Afrikaner Nationalism and Racial Ideology," pp. 920–52.

89. See Bloomberg, *Christian-Nationalism and the Rise of the Afrikaner Broederbond*, p. 10.

90. See Harrison, *The White Tribe of Africa*, pp. 61–64.

91. See Nattrass, *The South African Economy: Its Growth and Change*, p. 173.

92. Harrison, *The White Tribe of Africa*, p. 71.

93. See Hoernle, "The Concept of the 'Primitive,' " pp. 327–32.

94. Harrison, *The White Tribe of Africa*, p. 82.

95. See Giliomee and Schlemmer, *From Apartheid to Nation-Building*, p. 20.

96. Lauren, *Power and Prejudice*, p. 77.

97. The Japanese throughout the conference were described as a "colored race" by delegates from the United States, Britain, and elsewhere. See, for example, ibid., p. 103.

98. All quotes are from ibid., pp. 83, 89.

99. Ibid., p. 90.

100. Ibid., p. 314.

101. Ibid., p. 93.

102. Ibid., pp. 97–98.

103. See Karis and Carter, *From Protest to Challenge*, vol. 1, pp. 76–82.

104. Ibid., vol. 2, p. 31.

105. Ibid., p. 42.

106. Ibid.

107. Ibid., p. 32.

108. Ibid., p. 42.

109. See O'Meara, *Volkskapitalisme: Class, Capital and Ideology in the Development of Afrikaner Nationalism, 1934–1948*, pp. 68–69.

110. Bloomberg's *Christian-Nationalism and the Rise of the Afrikaner Broederbond* remains the seminal work on the theological underpinnings of apartheid. For a Marxist interpretation of Christian-Nationalism and its appropriation by the Broederbond, see O'Meara's *Volkskapitalisme*. For a recent discussion of the Afrikaner nationalism of the 1930s, see Dubow, "Afrikaner Nationalism, Apartheid, and the Conceptualization of 'Race.'"

111. Quoted in Bloomberg, *Christian-Nationalism and the Rise of the Afrikaner Broederbond*, p. 14.

112. Quoted in Mandela, *The Struggle Is My Life*, pp. 19–20.

113. Bloomberg, *Christian-Nationalism and the Rise of the Afrikaner Broederbond*, p. 148.

114. See Ashforth, *The Politics of Official Discourse*, pp. 77–86.

115. Bloomberg, *Christian-Nationalism and the Rise of the Afrikaner Broederbond*, p. 43.

116. Quoted in ibid., p. 109.

117. See O'Meara, *Volkskapitalisme*, p. 54.

118. This point is also made by Harrison in *The White Tribe of Africa*, p. 18.

119. Bloomberg, *Christian-Nationalism and the Rise of the Afrikaner Broederbond*, p. 122.

120. Quoted in ibid., p. 99.

121. See O'Meara, *Volkskapitalisme*, chapter 6.

2

Constituting the Christian and National Self: South Africa in the Postcolonial Era

As chapter 1 demonstrated, the Christian-National idea that South Africa's white and black communities were really composed of distinct cultural (and emergent national) units, cognizance of which should be taken in the constitution of the state, was disseminated in South Africa during the turbulent years of the 1930s and 1940s. Emphasis on the political significance of cultural diversity within African societies emerged in National party thought, according to Ashforth, initially through the work of ethnographers and social anthropologists at Stellenbosch University.[1] Also important were the Institute for Christian-National Education (ICNE) and the South African Bureau for Racial Affairs (SABRA).

The extent to which these institutions succeeded in their allocated tasks will be considered more fully in later chapters on domestic power relations, along with more detailed analyses of government action and resistance to it. This chapter continues the discussion begun in chapter 1, and asks how changing global power relations after World War II have shaped both particular subjectivities and conventional understandings of what are "normal" social practices. In this regard, the most significant factors have been the rise to global economic hegemony of the United States, in tandem with the concerted efforts of antiapartheid activists around the world to isolate South Africa economically and diplomatically; the Cold War between the United States and the Soviet Union; and the decolonization of the African continent.

The economic preeminence of the United States entailed an increasing search by its capitalist classes for investment outlets and trading relationships with the outside world, a search that brought countries such as South Africa ever more fully within the U.S. sphere of influence. The entry of American (and European, and then Japanese) capital into South Africa was by no means automatic, for foreign investment—referred to as "foreign British-Jewish capitalism" in the 1930s—had a long history of negative connotations for many people. In particular, foreign capital conjured up British imperialism and horrors such as the Anglo-Boer War. Once the decision to allow direct foreign investment in South Africa had been taken by the National party, however, it served to strengthen the ties that already bound South Africans to the West and thus kept Western powers to the fore as a point of identification. This reinforcement of Western identity was achieved primarily in two ways.

First, direct foreign investment signaled the abandonment of debates about nationalization and socialism as remedies for imperialism, at least within the white community. This abandonment served to align the South African state more fully with the West not only against the Soviet Union and its East European allies but also against emergent Afro-socialist states on the rest of the continent. In this way capital relations helped polarize South African society between those who identified with the West and its economic systems and those who believed that in Africa's present lay South Africa's future.

Second, the high level of South Africa's dependence on foreign capital and technology for its economic well-being has meant that business confidence in the country cannot be allowed to fall. The South Africa Foundation has been one of the major institutions through which a particular "truth" about South Africa as a stable, peaceful investment outlet has been disseminated. Yet despite such efforts, multinational banks and industries have tended to respond to any form of political situation that affects their investments in South Africa by severing ties to South African entrepreneurs dependent upon their wares, forcing private business and state capital at such times to assume a "progressive" role in demanding meaningful change. Their success has not been automatic; the government, for example, usually has tried to restore business confidence via a mixture of repression and reform, but this type of action results in debates over the utility of Western sanctions that typically have proceeded from the wrong premise. Knowing whether sanctions hurt the South African economy is not as critical as knowing how much political power is actually wielded by those in South Africa most affected by Western sanctions. Politics, and not the economy per se, holds the key to the success of the sanctions movement, although ultimately, the psychological effect on South Africans of symbolically being expelled from the community of Western civilized nations may be the sanctions' most enduring legacy.

There is a difference between sanctions initiated by foreign investors at a time of political upheaval and sanctions put into place by Western governments under pressure from domestic lobbies. The former are typically short-lived and end with a restoration of order, no matter how brutal, while the latter (in theory at least) require some evidence of "meaningful change" in order to be lifted. What exactly constitutes meaningful change is, of course, open to interpretation, but F. W. de Klerk's recent moves to scrap apartheid legislation can be read as prompted in part by a desire to rescind South Africa's pariah status and return it to its historical place within the community of civilized nations. In historical context, antiapartheid movements are the latter-day missionaries and antislavery societies, forcing South Africans either to justify their practices in novel ways or to abandon them altogether.

It is tempting to see South Africa from 1948 until the presidency of F. W. de Klerk as a country that broke from its own previous practices and in so doing moved horrendously out of step with the policies of its Western allies—of the United States in its granting of civil rights to blacks and of Europe in its acknowledgment of the right of colonial peoples to self-determination. If this interpretation is correct, then the post-1948 period in South African history can be remembered as one in which a previously outward-looking people was turned inward by a government recreating a mythical and heroic Voortrekker past—that is, by metaphorically circling the wagons around the *volk* and (armed to the teeth) protecting it from vast numbers of hostile forces. De Klerk, by contrast, would represent that other Afrikaner tradition of collaborating with the British, feeding the Xhosa, appeasing the missionaries, and so on. Tempting as this interpretation is, however, this chapter will suggest that it is not correct, or at least was so for only a brief moment in the early 1980s, for a number of different reasons.

First, in suggesting that there were continuities between pre- and post-1948 practices, I by no means want to suggest that there were not significant differences. As the introductory chapter argued, the policies that the United party (UP) was beginning to effect in 1946 were consistent with the postulate of identity, whereas those of the National party (NP) after 1948 operated from the postulate of difference. Obviously, these conflicting premises entailed vastly different implications for the political practices of the "other." Believing that most Europeans were sincere in their commitment to guardianship, mission-educated blacks organized their political activity prior to World War II around the necessity to demonstrate that the required level of civilization had been reached by the native and Colored populations. The postulate of difference makes such activity futile and requires a different response. But what is important to remember about the two hierarchies of identity and difference is that both have been used to justify dominion over other peoples, differing only in terms of the particular strategies followed. The essential continuity between guardianship and apartheid is that both were designed to perpetuate European civilization—a euphemism for white control and privilege—in Africa; they differed only over how to do it.

Guardianship was long the principle that underpinned the behavior of European colonizers in their relations with colonial peoples; after World War II, European states were forced increasingly to put that principle into effect by granting to their colonies the political right to self-determination. By overturning the UP's plans and insisting that rights for natives be limited and not extended, the NP seemed out of touch with global trends. Yet in some ways the National party was very much in touch; for example, it moved quickly to align itself with the United States in its fight against "Godless communism."

Far from drawing South Africa into the "laager" during the era of the civil rights movement in the United States, the National party went on the offensive and consistently drew attention to its policy of separate development as the solution to race problems elsewhere. The rest of the Western world, so the argument went, was wracked with racial violence and upheaval at a time when South Africa was enjoying unprecedented racial peace and harmony; if the country's major allies desired an end to their difficulties, they had only to look to the example of South Africa to find the answer. At the very least, South Africa as an "important bastion of the free world" should have the right to decide upon its own policies without interference.

As Bloomberg has argued, what the National party has claimed to stand for is not merely white rule based on race; it has also stood for a society modeled on Christian norms. All policies, including segregation, have been justified in terms of a Christian-National Protestant ethic.[2] When it is remembered that President John F. Kennedy defined the U.S.-Soviet conflict as one of "two conflicting ideologies: Freedom under God versus ruthless, godless tyranny,"[3] the emphasis on *Christian* in Christian-National is not incidental. It is a key element in an ongoing effort to retain South Africa's membership within the club of civilized nations by appeal to the Western identity of the country's dominant elite.

In addition, the association of communism with demands for racial equality in South Africa's panoply of security laws was sparked not merely by the alliance of the South African Communist party (SACP) with the African National Congress. It was part of that same effort to retain Western support for the regime by playing up the country's Western character and anticommunist orientation. As Lauren has argued, ever since Lenin became the first white statesman to endorse publicly the cause of racial equality in the 1920s, the question of what relationship, if any, existed between the struggle for racial equality on the one hand and communism on the other was a recurring theme for Western powers.[4] In fact, the practice of labeling any domestic subversive group as "communist" was not invented by the South African state. In the United States, the "red specter of the commune" in the cities in the early 1900s shifted the rhetorical battle between savagery and civilization from Indian conflict to class war. In 1946, the magazine *Nation's Business* stated that "whoever stirs up needless strife in American trade unions advances the cause of Communism," while a struggle by women in New York to retain day-care centers was declared by the *New York World Telegram* to have "all the trappings of a Red drive, including leaflets, letters, telegrams, petitions, protest demonstrations, mass meetings, and hat passing."[5] It is small wonder then that "constructive engagement" has been such a popular policy for the United States in its relations with South Africa and that, as with the movement to end slavery, Western governments have had to be pushed by their own domestic publics to oppose apartheid with anything stronger than loud words.

The shift in global power relationships that the Cold War signaled has been a major factor in keeping South African social practices aligned with those of Western powers, even though the National party has never been able to sell separate development as the solution to everyone's race problems. But a more subtle effect of the Cold War on whites—and an additional reason why blacks fighting apartheid so easily have been labeled communist—is the way it reinforced the historical equation of white with civilization and black with barbarism.

From the discussion in chapter 1, it will be remembered that the major hallmarks of barbarism for Europeans have been lack of Christianity, communal patterns of landownership, and failure to exercise "exclusive and discretionary control over the material things of this world," that is, private property. In theory if not always in practice, a "communist" state espouses all of these traits as virtues and in seeking to spread its message abroad plays on historical fears of "barbarism rushing into the country."[6] This posture can be seen not only in the South African context in phrases such as the "Total Onslaught" but in comments such as those of the American Billy Graham, who at the height of the Cold War talked about "barbarians beating at our gates from without and moral termites from within."[7] The defense of European civilization in South Africa during the Cold War era thus meant resisting any social change that smacked of communism, such as land redistribution, nationalization of industry, or any policy that would lower levels of economic productivity. Preserving civilization, in short, has meant defending capitalism.

With the Cold War officially over only recently, it is too soon to know what the implications will be in terms of Western support for South Africa. The anticommunist rationale presumably has eroded, but given the long history of binding relationships among "Europeans" globally and the willingness of the West to lift sanctions, it seems that Western ties to South Africa can only get stronger in the future. What can be said about the effect of the end of the Cold War, or more specifically of the collapse of communist systems in

Eastern Europe, is that it was one of the contributing factors in the government's decision to unban the African National Congress and the South African Communist party.

No reasonable person, the National party reckoned, could any longer be attracted to the communist ideals of the ANC and the SACP; unbanning them would expose their message as outdated and so weaken support for both organizations, or else it would enable the government to pressure an abandonment of long-held policies such as nationalization on the grounds that they had been demonstrated failures elsewhere. Either way, the National party would be in a much stronger bargaining position vis-à-vis its major rivals once negotiations started. That, at least, was the plan. To what extent it has worked will be considered more fully in later chapters on domestic power relations, but suffice it to say that the elimination of Eastern European funding for the ANC has caused some financial headaches for the organization.

Finally, the argument that South African social practices under apartheid moved the country less out of step with European colonial powers than is commonly assumed can be demonstrated through a brief discussion of the effects of African decolonization. The U.S.-dominated United Nations, which Jan Smuts helped found, kept South Africa tied diplomatically to the West and to the United States in its fight against Godless communism. But it also brought South Africa and colonial powers more fully into confrontation with colonized peoples demanding self-determination. The United States set the ball rolling in 1946 by granting independence to the Philippines. The Europeans followed slowly at first, but by the late 1950s they clearly were ready to throw in the colonial towel and soon began to urge South Africa to "blow with the winds of change." In order not to be seen as out of step with the march of history, the National party began to emphasize the *National* in Christian-National and to activate a policy of separate development.

Whereas guardianship was the principle invoked by South Africa to justify its practices in terms acceptable to Europeans in the colonial era, separate development was the principle in the postcolonial era. Just as "emerging national units" could be found on the African continent, so the argument went, such incipient nations could be found within South Africa itself. African peoples everywhere were demanding independence; by "decolonizing" the "nations" under its protection and granting them self-government, the National party reckoned that it could fend off impending ostracism by pleasing the West (on whom South Africa depended for capital and technology and of which whites felt a part), by pleasing Africa (on which South Africa depended for trade and of which Afrikaners and blacks felt a part), and by placating blacks (on whom capitalists depended for labor and who held the key to political stability). A great deal was at stake in selling the neocolonial project of national separation, so much so that the National party continued trying to sell it to Africa long after it had abandoned hope that the West would buy it.

National separation failed because it was built upon two fundamentally unacceptable premises from the point of view of black South Africans. First, it was built upon the notion of South Africa as a state belonging to only one nation, a white nation. As Giliomee has pointed out, there was a growing tendency after South Africa became a republic in 1961 (and broke from the British Empire) for Afrikaners to see themselves, along with English speakers, as part of a common white South African nation, rather than as a separate nation.[8] African decolonization in this way undermined the Afrikaner nationalist discourse of the 1930s at the same time that it stiffened support for separate development. Afrikaans speakers and English speakers did not consider themselves to be members of different nations whose characteristics were fixed and given by nature; as a result, in the 1960s they were exhorted to choose a common identity based upon racial as opposed to ethnic characteristics.[9] Here then was one of the major contradictions to underpin the National party's project for continuing domination; national identity for whites was to be based upon skin color and could be freely chosen, whereas national identity for blacks was to be hitched to culture and language and was fixed by nature. In other words, the postulate of identity held for whites; the postulate of difference held for blacks. Black South Africans had complained during the colonial era that they were treated as aliens in their own country; any policy that sought to turn the practice of "making foreign" into a political principle could not but be resisted.

The second faulty premise of national separation was not that it appealed to the principle of self-determination but that it privileged the wrong self. Bantu education was the flip side of homelands creation; the latter could not succeed unless the former was able to naturalize tribal identity. In other words, Bantu education was to serve the same purpose as Afrikaner nationalism in the 1930s. Its aim was to tie national identity to the socially constituted group, not to the larger society, and to make the exclusive characteristics of the group the point of identification rather than those common characteristics linking the group to the wider society. This strategy might have worked in earlier eras, but African nationalism for blacks did not mean breaking Africans down into sovereign units for the Xhosa, Shangaans, and so on; such a breakdown was not the lesson of the decolonization occurring on the rest of the continent. It was freedom for the African people as a whole, not for each tribe, that was desired.

One should not conclude, however, that the term *African* has some universal and uncontested meaning. One of the effects of African decolonization was that it brought to the surface struggles over African identity, in the same way that conflict with the British had highlighted contested understandings of Afrikaner identity. These struggles reflect different traditions of African nationalism, themselves based upon voluntarist versus fixed understandings of identity. In one tradition, associated with Marcus Garvey, only two types of people exist in Africa—Africans and colonists. Africa is for the Africans (as the Garveyist slogan goes), so those who think of themselves as Europeans must either leave the continent or assume an African identity. Such slogans as the old "throw the 'whites' into the sea" or, more recently, the Pan Africanist Congress's "one settler, one bullet" are reflective of this particular tradition, which for want of a better term I will call "Pan-Africanist."

What the PAC and others have done is to hoist the National party on the petard of its own neocolonial discourse. If whites want to continue to constitute themselves as Europeans and to treat blacks in the manner of colonial peoples, then they must expect to be treated as foreign settlers, not as fellow citizens. What is important to point out about the Pan-Africanists is that for them *African* is a subjective term, an identity that can be freely chosen and that is not given by birth or heritage. In this sense, Pan-Africanism is closer to the Hertzogist understanding of Afrikanerdom than to that of Malan and the early Christian-Nationalists.

The other tradition of African nationalism is that associated with the current ANC, a tradition that the organization has called "Africanist." This tradition proceeds from the premise that there are different national groups in South Africa that have come to stay; the African group is only one of four. White domination will be eradicated by the building of interracial peace and harmony, not by forcing one group to leave the country or to assume the identity of another.[10] Since this position on groups is not very far from that of the National party, it is easy to see why the ANC is currently a preferred negotiating partner to the PAC.

Whatever the differences between them, neither the ANC nor the PAC has granted legitimacy to the idea of homelands. In fact, the gamble of national separation failed so miserably that it became a catalyst around which antiapartheid forces were able to mobilize sanctions and boycotts against the Pretoria regime. Faced with this situation, the National party in office has responded in two quite different ways to South Africa's pariah status.

One reaction reflects the influence in the National party of P. W. Botha, first as defense minister under Vorster and then as state president. Looking for a way out of trouble in the lessons of a heroic and mythical Voortrekker past, Botha metaphorically circled the wagons around the *volk* and used its accumulated weaponry to attack the enemy. The Western "enemy" was told to "go to hell," the African "enemy" suffered punitive raids into its territory in conjunction with support for antigovernment forces, and the domestic "enemy" was incarcerated without trial, beaten, and murdered. It was Botha's regime that tried symbolically to reenact the 1838 Battle of Blood River. It was Botha who brought Coloreds and Indians into a tricameral Parliament, but when the Trekkers had circled their wagons they always did so around their "loyal servants" as well as around the Boers.

This strategy was bound to fail not only because the enemies refused to be defeated and the servants were not loyal. It failed because the Trekker option could not appeal to the majority of Afrikaners who did not relish isolation and whose sense of national identity was increasingly expanding to incorporate other South African citizens. As a result, when the Boerestaat party (White State party) was launched in 1988 to coincide with the 150th anniversary of the Great Trek, the first South African political party to aim for the establishment of a "white homeland," it attracted only eighty-five people.[11]

Even while the Botha government was "circling the wagons," Afrikaans-speaking whites began casting about for an alternative to neocolonial solutions to domestic problems and to policies built upon a privileging of a mythical heroic subject. The decolonization of Zimbabwe in 1980 suggested to many Afrikaans-speaking whites that intransigence spells disaster. It may have taken ten more years for the seeds of the idea to bear fruit, but the notion that it is better to give a little in order to retain a lot can be traced back to 1980 and the demise of white rule in Rhodesia.

The above introduction has summarized the major themes to be discussed in this chapter. The remainder of the chapter discusses all of these themes in more detail and divides the discussion into three (somewhat overlapping) parts. The first looks at the effects of South Africa's changing economic entanglements with the West, including the impact of sanctions and boycotts; the second looks at the impact of the Cold War between the United States and the Soviet Union, including the U.S. civil rights movement; and the third considers the outcome of African decolonization and independence.

INVESTMENT AND DISINVESTMENT

During its first decade in office, the National party was divided on the issue of what role, if any, foreign capital should play in economic development. On the one hand, debate concerned the nature of foreign investment in the gold mines. Between 1949 and 1955 the new Free State goldfields cost 200 million pounds to develop. The Anglo-American Corporation alone raised more than 23 million pounds in London between 1946 and 1953 and a further 8 million pounds in Europe.[12] The extent of foreign ownership of the mines led some Afrikaners in the National party to advocate nationalization of the industry, but such a move was finally rejected as too radical by most of the party.

On the other hand, more lengthy debates focused on the wisdom of allowing direct foreign investment in the South African economy. Before World War II nearly all overseas investment was in mining shares, but by 1956 the amount of direct investment by British, American, and to a lesser extent Western European corporations, which set up manufacturing subsidiaries behind tariff walls, had overtaken shareholdings and formed nearly 58 percent of total overseas investment.[13] Some Afrikaner economists argued that the country could maintain a fair rate of economic growth without foreign capital and that this would be a preferable way of financing development, since a large foreign sector magnified the economic influence of "outside forces."[14] Others, however, felt that since the amount of capital available from domestic sources was insufficient to meet the need for infrastructure development, for the establishment of industrial undertakings to replace imports, and for the provision of new railway lines and large power and water supply schemes, continued economic growth required foreign capital.

From 1934 until the late 1950s industrial enterprise to replace imports was the major internal generator of growth.[15] As long as the economy maintained a growth rate of over 5 percent a year (which it did from 1946 until 1955), the voices of those who opposed self-capitalization tended to be ignored. But by the end of the 1950s, import substitution began to lose its momentum as the opportunities for replacing foreign with domestic consumption goods, such as food and clothing, were exhausted and the country lacked the degree of technological capacity necessary to replace the more sophisticated intermediate and capital goods required by the manufacturing sector. When the economy was gripped by a fairly serious recession from 1958 to 1961, the National party began to modify its traditionally hostile attitude toward foreign capital, indicated by the following speech of Prime Minister H. F. Verwoerd:

There is a natural desire on the part of every country to retain control over its economic destiny. . . . [T]he encouragement of local capital formation was one of the guiding principles of our financial policies during the last decade. . . . [South Africa] today provides by far the greater proportion of its own capital requirements. But . . . foreign capital can still be of great assistance in the development of our resources. . . . Moreover, in many cases desirable development will not take place without the technical knowledge and business skill which accompany foreign capital. . . . [We] will continue to welcome the participation of foreign investors . . . provided they do not conflict with the general principle of a country retaining control over its economic destiny.[16]

In 1960 the role that the government expected foreign capital to play was spelled out by Dr. Haak, a former minister of economic affairs. He indicated that, although such measures would not be made compulsory, overseas capital was strongly urged to take South African capital as a fully fledged partner and allow South African residents to acquire a louder voice, by share ownership, in determining policy in regard to production and distribution in the private sector.[17]

It was not only the National party during its early years in office that displayed ambivalence toward the idea of direct foreign investment. Blacks as well as Afrikaners had been attracted to the concept of imperialism as an explanation for South Africa's problems in the 1930s; the declaration of the newly founded National Liberation League (a Colored-led organization), for example, called in 1935 for working-class unity between whites and blacks and the destruction of imperialism in collaboration with the struggles of colonial peoples worldwide.[18]

After the war the United States, in particular, was identified as a threat and a danger to the independence of the people of Asia and Africa. In an article written for the magazine *Liberation* in March 1958, for example, Nelson Mandela noted that between 1945 and 1954 the value of private American investments in Africa had leapt from scarcely 150 million pounds to 664 million pounds. Describing imperialism as "a kind of alliance between a foreign ruling power and local reactionary elements for the exploitation by the former of the mineral and agricultural resources of a colonial country," Mandela argued that the American brand was imperialism just the same, in spite of its modern clothing and the sweet language spoken by its advocates and agents. The communist bogey was nothing more than "an American stunt to distract the attention of the people of Africa from the real issue facing them, namely, American imperialism," but the African people were not fooled; they knew who their real friends were. At the United Nations, Mandela pointed out, the Soviet Union, India, and others consistently identified themselves unconditionally with the struggle of the oppressed people for freedom, whereas the United States very often had allied itself with those who stood for the enslavement of others. Judging by events such as "the Little Rock outrage and the activities of the Un-American Witch-hunting Committee," Mandela concluded that, the United States should learn to put its own house in order before trying to teach everyone else.[19]

American capital relations with South Africa, in concert with U.S. anti-communism and behavior at the United Nations, thus alienated blacks even further from the West and strengthened identification with the Third World, although Mandela and others very soon moved to use South Africa's economic dependency to their strategic advantage. In late 1961 members of the ANC and the SACP formed Umkonto We Sizwe (popularly known as

MK) to carry out acts of sabotage, opening a new phase in the liberation struggle by exploding homemade bombs at economic installations and targets of symbolic political significance, such as government buildings. On trial two years later for treason, Mandela explained how South Africa's dependency had influenced the adoption of the new strategy:

> The initial plan was based on a careful analysis of the political and economic situation of our country. We believed that South Africa depended to a large extent on foreign capital and foreign trade. We felt that planned destruction of power plants, and interference with rail and telephone communications, would tend to scare away foreign capital from the country, make it more difficult for goods from the industrial areas to reach the seaports on schedule, and would in the long run be a heavy drain on the economic life of the country, thus compelling the voters of the country to reconsider their position. . . . In addition, if mass action were successfully organized and mass reprisals taken, we felt that sympathy for our cause would be roused in other countries, and that greater pressure would be brought to bear on the South African government.[20]

As for the government and South African capitalists, the sort of alliance between them and multinational corporations that Mandela identified as imperialism was not slow in developing.[21]

Five foreign oil firms—Shell, British Petroleum, Mobil, Caltex (a subsidiary jointly owned by Texaco and Standard Oil of California), and Total—came to dominate all aspects of the oil industry, that is, handling, importing, refining, marketing, and distribution, for some 85 percent of the country's petroleum products. Transnational corporations also helped South Africa build two facilities (known as SASOL I and SASOL II) to manufacture petroleum products from its vast coal reserves.

The diversification of all the major mining houses from gold into other minerals has been assisted heavily with foreign capital, and foreign stockholders continue indirectly to control more than 50 percent of a number of South Africa's largest mines; at the end of 1977, Americans held 25 percent of all the shares issued by South Africa's gold mines. But foreign companies became active directly as well, usually in partnership with South African mining houses, in the exploration and development of a wide range of minerals—titanium, copper, chrome, lead, and uranium. When the indirect and direct investments of the Western European countries and the United States are combined, they represent approximately 20 percent of the value of the estimated total investment in South Africa's mining and mineral industry.

Foreign firms have dominated the South African computer and electronics industry; they have been responsible for most of the imports, sales, installation, and maintenance of high-technology equipment in South Africa. The government's policy of encouraging private firms to design, produce, and assemble various electronic components and equipment in order to lessen the country's reliance on foreign companies has led to the emergence of a small local computer industry; yet the country remains overwhelmingly dependent on foreign companies for the development, supply, and servicing of computers and electronic equipment.

Despite government policies to foster technological self-sufficiency, South African industry in the 1970s was overwhelmingly dependent on imported technology. In a survey of manufacturing firms conducted in 1973, the University of Natal found that 60 percent of those in the sample (169 firms) used foreign technology exclusively, 81 percent (231 firms) stated that more than 75 percent of their technology was foreign, and 90 percent (256 firms) said that more than half their technology was imported.[22] More recently, a report by South Africa's Council for Scientific and Industrial Research (CSIR) blamed balance of payments problems, in part, on high- and medium-technology deficits, which amounted to more than 6 percent of the gross domestic product (GDP) in 1987.[23]

According to recent reports, South Africa's volume of imports continues to rise, with the more important increases recorded under the headings of mineral products (i.e., oil), machinery and electrical equipment, and transport equipment.[24] South Africa's evident lack of self-sufficiency in these areas is causing some concern in economic circles, because in order to meet foreign debt repayments there is a continuing need to run surpluses on the current account of the balance of payments.[25] Trade dependence and financial dependence, in other words, are inextricably linked.

Much of the new business in the long South African boom of the 1960s and 1970s was interlocked directly or indirectly with the military and police machinery and its control of the black population. After the wave of violence and unrest that followed the police shootings of peaceful protesters at Sharpeville in 1960, the defense budget rose sharply, from 22 million pounds in 1960 to 136 million pounds by 1969, a sum that represented 17 percent of the total budget and 2.4 percent of the country's gross national product (GNP). Increasingly, defense and police contracts penetrated into apparently civilian activities. The defense forces took a huge leap under the new minister of defense, P. W. Botha, in 1967, who in one year doubled the numbers in military training in the Citizen Force and Commando Units.

By the time the United Nations voted for a mandatory arms embargo in 1977, after which France discontinued its arms sales, South Africa already was very well equipped with weaponry. But it was by no means self-sufficient, for the more sophisticated weapons required hundreds of components, many of which had to come from abroad, with the help of intricate evasions of the UN sanctions;[26] and the aging British Buccaneer and French Mirages aircrafts—frequently used for cross-border raids—had to be replaced with a South African version of the Mirage which still needed components smuggled in from France, Israel, and Chile.

Transnational banks have constituted the core, as well as the most advanced elements, of transnational involvement in the South African economy. A small handful in the 1970s held about 75 percent of the assets of the twenty largest banks in South Africa, a far higher percentage than foreign firms held in any other sector of the economy. They participated in a full range of financial services for private, parastatal, and governmental activities, providing commercial and merchant banking, discounting and leasing, insurance and pensions, and mutual funds.

South Africa's foreign borrowing soared in the early 1980s as the government embarked on grandiose military strategies of destabilization in neighboring states. The decision of Chase Manhattan Bank to call in its South African loans in September 1985 triggered a foreign loan crisis for the country, which still owes the international banking community an estimated 22,000 million pounds sterling.[27] This crisis was greatly exacerbated by the decision of all other major banks to follow Chase's lead and stop lending to South Africa. However, after P. W. Botha visited Switzerland in October 1988 and urged Swiss bankers to invest massively in the country, two new loans were issued from Swiss banks within the following four months.[28]

Transnational private banks have been the major, but by no means the only, source of overseas funding for South Africa. The International Monetary Fund (IMF)—which, interestingly enough, places South Africa in its European, rather than African, category—sent a team to the country in 1976 to review its economic situation. As the Soweto uprisings rocked the country, the IMF loaned the minority regime $366 million by the end of the year. By the first quarter of 1978, South Africa owed the IMF $485 million. South Africa only gradually reduced this debt, despite soaring gold prices, as it continued to spend heavily to buy oil, military supplies, and machinery and equipment overseas. By January 1979, it still owed the IMF $353 million.

Joint ventures among South African, European, American, and Japanese capital rarely have remained within the boundaries of the Republic of South Africa; in many instances, South Africa has served as a jumping-off point for entry into neighboring states.

Viewed in terms of the corporations that control the shares of companies on the Johannesburg Stock Exchange, the most important in Africa is undoubtedly the Anglo-American Corporation of South Africa,[29] which is also an important investor in the United States. Anglo-American has substantial mining interests in Botswana, Zambia, and Zimbabwe, and through the De Beers Mining Company has a strong interest in diamond mines in Namibia, Botswana, Angola, and Tanzania. It is also important in the metals, engineering, and chemicals industries.

Of the other monopoly groups, Sanlam—the second largest life assurance company behind Old Mutual—is the most important regionally. Its main holdings in the region are the mining company Gencor, the fertilizer and chemicals group Sentrachem, the wholesale and retail group Kirsh, and the construction group Murray and Roberts.

South Africa's parastatal corporations also have been active in the southern African region, particularly in the area of transportation, although the government's privatization initiatives for South African Transport Services (SATS) undoubtedly will change that situation.[30] The third largest company in South Africa after Anglo and Sanlam, SATS is responsible for railways, harbors, air traffic, and some road haulage. An estimated one-third of international cargo for the neighboring states is carried by South African Railways, hence the political importance given by the Southern Africa Development Coordination Conference (SADCC), founded in 1980, to reducing transport dependence on SATS.

The cross-cutting economic relations tying South African government and business to foreign capitalists have had a number of effects in terms of identity and political struggle. First, they have aligned white South Africa more fully with the West through a common affinity with capitalism, after brief flirtations with socialism in the 1930s, but also they have stimulated ties between the National party and the more capitalist-oriented regimes on the African continent.

In 1964, Prime Minister Verwoerd announced that he foresaw the development of a multiracial southern African common market in which none of the member-nations would have political control of any of the others, but in which all would cooperate to their mutual benefit. Although Verwoerd's bid to establish cordial relations with Lesotho, Botswana, and Swaziland brought limited returns, the governments of South Africa and Portugal concluded agreements providing for closer economic relations between South Africa, and Angola and Mozambique; representatives of private business interests set up a South African–Portuguese Economic Institute to promote industrialization and trade ties.[31]

Renewed efforts toward an "outward reach" were made by Prime Minister B. J. Vorster in 1975, at the same time as Portugal's colonies were preparing for independence and the National party was sending the South African Defence Force into Angola, ostensibly to stop the Cubans from gaining access to the country. More recently, President P. W. Botha and Foreign Minister Roelof "Pik" Botha went on what was dubbed "the Bothas' safari" in 1988,[32] which resulted in the opening of trade offices in Mozambique and Lesotho to join the one opened in Swaziland in 1985. In addition to facilitating trade between South Africa and its neighbors, these offices are a form of tacit diplomatic recognition for South Africa as they are often used as unofficial embassies.[33] This recognition may in fact have been the most important objective of the trip for the National party, which saw winning friends and influencing people in Africa as the only way for the country to be let back into the club of European nations.[34]

This theme also has been central to the "new diplomacy" of current President F. W. de Klerk.[35] He and Pik Botha have been insistent in talks with African leaders that the international isolation of South Africa is contrary to the interests of all of Africa; that the establishment of a European common market in 1992 poses serious threats to the future of all states in the southern African region; and that southern African states involved, on the basis of cooperation and good neighborliness, in regional development projects could help offset the isolation and other dangers facing the region as a result of European union.[36] To bolster these arguments, the Foreign Affairs Department in November 1989 published a report in which it insisted that South Africa is part of Africa,[37] and a month later de Klerk let it be known on a visit to the Ivory Coast that South Africa wants to join the Organization of African Unity.[38] More recently, Pretoria has set about expanding ties to other so-called regional (capitalist) powerhouses—Kenya in East Africa, Nigeria in West Africa, and Egypt to the North.[39]

Sanctions and boycotts by most African states have given the Pretoria regime little choice of friends on the continent; only Malawi maintains full diplomatic relations with South Africa. But it is surely no coincidence that South Africa's major ally in Africa has historically been the capitalist-oriented Ivory Coast, and its main self-appointed enemy has been the Marxist-Leninist regime in Angola.

A second major effect of South Africa's global economic relations has been the polarization of struggle within the white community at times of social upheaval—between those wanting to restore international business confidence with concessions to the protesters and those committed to apartheid as a model of race relations the rest of the world should follow. As with other historical conflicts over how to treat the other (e.g., whether the Xhosa should have been exterminated like the San or treated in a friendly manner), these struggles have not broken down neatly along the fault lines of language usage, with all English-speaking whites on one side and Afrikaans speakers on the other.

Struggle was evident after police killed sixty-nine people during a demonstration in the township of Sharpeville in 1960. The shootings and ensuing unrest provoked a massive withdrawal of investors' confidence, giving rise to an immediate business slump. An indicator of this decline in international business confidence was the outflow of foreign capital; capital flows did not move into a positive balance until 1965 (see table 2.1). That the National party would feel pressured by local capitalists to restore this business confidence through granting concessions, rather than resorting to brutality, was what the ANC and others were counting on. In the end, the National party did both, demonstrating the government's difficulty in resolving conflicting demands from within its own ranks and the civil society at large.

In the wake of Sharpeville, large-scale business adopted a two-pronged approach to tackling the problem of the loss of business confidence. First, it sent a series of delegations to the government, culminating on May 12, 1960, with a delegation representing the Afrikaanse Handelsinstitut, the Association of Chambers of Commerce of South Africa, the South African Federated Chamber of Industries, the Steel and Engineering Federation of South Africa, and the Transvaal and Orange Free State Chambers of Mines. These bodies represented the employers of 1.5 million African workers—two-thirds of the country's male African labor force.[40]

The delegation began by observing that in large cities there was a settled urban Bantu population which should in certain respects be treated differently from those in the Reserves; that there was a wide diversity among the Bantu in terms of class, education, and social standards; and that the unrestricted influx of rural Bantu to the towns was undesirable. It then proposed changes in the laws and regulations pertaining to passes, influx control, curfews, and liquor consumption, all of which were recognized as a source of genuine grievances among the African people.[41]

Individual statements made after the state of emergency was declared were another indication of the depth of concern among some domestic capitalists over the loss of foreign investor confidence in South Africa. Dr. M. S. Louw, chairman of Sanlam and other Afrikaans financial concerns, reportedly stated that South Africa must face the fact that its economic future was partly dependent upon "know-how"—that is, technology—and the goodwill and capital of overseas countries. Anglo-American Chairman Harry Oppenheimer reiterated Louw's contention that "we will have to convince overseas countries that we are able to solve our racial problems satisfactorily." After stating in June 1960 that the recent disturbances had affected overseas capital markets in South Africa and had made it more difficult to attract skilled specialist personnel and to obtain essential expert know-how, Oppenheimer insisted that the government must regain the goodwill of Africans and create conditions in which "agitators" would be ineffective.[42]

What business was demanding was hardly a radical solution to the country's problems; it basically was reiterating the old liberal line that urban Africans should be treated differently from rural ones because they were more civilized—

Table 2.1
Total Capital Movements, 1946–1982

Year	Million Rand*
1946	80
1947	352
1948	165
1949	105
1950	182
1951	187
1952	144
1953	113
1954	193
1955	51
1956	35
1957	-47
1958	134
1959	-61
1960	-180
1961	-129
1962	-88
1963	-80
1964	-41
1965	255
1966	141
1967	162
1968	456
1969	180
1970	582
1971	828
1972	448
1973	-45
1974	901
1975	1925
1976	1149
1977	-761
1978	-1294
1979	-2954
1980	-2466
1981	2696
1982	2944

* A minus sign indicates an outflow.

Source: Official Yearbook of the Republic of South Africa, 1984

that is, they had different "standards." The assumption found in much non-Marxist literature that organized business would have overturned apartheid long ago in the name of economic efficiency is thus contestable. Nonetheless, asking the government to recognize that some Africans had genuine grievances which deserved redress meant forcing it to admit that there was something wrong with an apartheid policy supposedly in everyone's best interest. On the wisdom of such an admission, the government was itself divided.

One month after the Sharpeville massacre, the following two speeches delivered the same day—the first by Acting Prime Minister Paul Sauer (the minister of lands) and the second by M. C. de Wet Nel (the minister of Bantu administration and development)—make this clear:

> The old book of South African history was closed a month ago at Sharpeville and, for the immediate future, South Africa will reconsider in earnest and honesty her whole approach to the Native question. We must create a new spirit which must restore overseas faith—both white and non-white—in South Africa. . . . Overseas action could have serious economic repercussions for South Africa. Economic sanctions could be applied. There is only one way to avoid this—a better attitude to the Natives.

> We pay far too much attention to the foreign winds of world opinion and so-called setbacks on the stock market. Unfortunately there are some of our own people and our own newspapers who get into a state of panic about these things. They play into the hands of these elements. I am convinced that the policy of apartheid will serve as a model to the world for the establishment of good race relations.[43]

In the end, the National party tried to appease everyone and ended up pleasing no one. Bantu councils with limited advisory functions were instituted in urban areas, the panoply of liquor laws was amended, and promises were made to make the carrying of passes less onerous; these were the "concessions." At the same time, the NP banned organized political opposition in the name of anticommunism and announced the stepping up of its plans for development of the Reserves so that they could accommodate the "returning Bantu." This last move, a redoubled commitment to apartheid, was taken within the context of African decolonization and was meant to appeal to Africans throughout the continent.

In addition to direct lobbying of government, representatives of both the Afrikaans- and English-speaking business communities established the South Africa Foundation, the main objective of which was to maintain foreign investment, to oppose any threats of trade boycotts, and to "play our part in establishing South African leadership in Africa."[44] As an institution designed to disseminate a particular "truth" about South Africa overseas, the foundation has been extremely effective. Although foreign investment might have flowed back into the country as order was restored, by sponsoring visits to South Africa of influential foreign skeptics and squiring them around under business's tutelage, the foundation managed to turn some doubters into active supporters of the South African system.

Yet even the South Africa Foundation could not prevent the loss of investor confidence that followed the period of upheaval following the Soweto riots of 1976. This loss entailed, first of all, the drying up of foreign loans, which in the 1970s became increasingly important to the South African government and its state-owned corporations. More than fifty U.S. banks were involved in these loans, the majority of which were long-term, but as a result of the events following Soweto, in particular the government moves against Black Consciousness organizations and the death of Steve Biko, pressure on banks to stop lending to South Africa mounted in Europe and the United States. In 1977, South Africa raised only $33.2 million in the international bond and Eurocurrency markets, a mere 3 percent of the 1976 figure.[45] This situation was exacerbated in 1978 when the United States under Jimmy Carter prohibited export-import bank loans to all South African government firms and to private firms with unsatisfactory labor practices.

Second, reflecting concern about the economic and political situation in South Africa, there was little sign of new foreign investment. U.S. companies, which traditionally had retained a majority of their earnings for reinvestment, repatriated nearly two-thirds of their profits in 1978. Third, capital again flowed out of the country in large amounts as a result of internal unrest (see table 2.1). Although part of this outflow was due to the South African government's repayment of loans, a major portion was from the private sector, a sign of waning business confidence in South Africa's long-term economic and political prospects.

What clearly distinguished the foreign corporate response to political instability in South Africa from its response sixteen years earlier was its decision to take some positive action on behalf of blacks. In March 1977 the adoption of six principles espoused by Reverend Leon Sullivan, relating to equality of opportunity in the workplace, was announced by eleven multinationals and several church leaders. Subsequently, more than half of the roughly 350 American corporations in South Africa at the end of the 1970s subscribed to the "Sullivan Principles," as they became known; similar codes were drafted by the European Economic Community, by Canada, and by some private institutions.

Inside South Africa, one of the most important consequences of the unrest in the factories and African townships in the 1970s was the reassertion by "dependent" capital of demands for concessions to the protesters. In immediate response to the Soweto riots, the Transvaal Chamber of Industry (TCI), representing many of the largest manufacturers in the country, submitted in 1976 a memorandum to Prime Minister Vorster that called for a stable urbanized black community, improved wage and job opportunities, better housing with landownership rights, and creation of a middle class of blacks. In a follow-up memorandum written a year later, in August 1977, the TCI made clear that waning business confidence was a major reason for its perception of the necessity for change:

> We have followed with dismay the hardening attitude of overseas investors toward the Republic, and noted the very clear message from the traditional suppliers of foreign loans that they expect to see visible evidence of the move away from discrimination before again recommending long-term investment in South Africa. We have been confused by conflicting ministerial statements, often on matters of important principle. We have realized more and more the indivisibility of political and economic issues in South Africa's circumstances.[46]

Other employers' associations expressed similar concerns. The Associated Chamber of Commerce (ASSOCOM) complained that "a continuation of social instability and the present lack of progress toward a solution which is acceptable to the rest of the world must result in direct and indirect pressures growing stronger. These pressures will be manifested in limited availability of long-term loans to South Africa, a lack of foreign investment and possibly trade boycotts or embargoes."[47]

The "conflicting ministerial statements" of which the TCI spoke were indicative of ongoing conflicts within white society over the appropriate way to respond to mass protest and international criticism. Organized business had not moved very far from its 1960s position in that its solution to race problems still lay in extending rights to only a small portion of the black community, while the National party remained committed to separate development. Nonetheless, the NP did institute a series of educational and economic reforms while recognizing, for the first time since 1948, that some of those classified as African had rights outside the homelands. By doing so, it spawned a host of dissident right-wing movements, the most important of which became the Conservative party (CP).

The CP has long maintained that piecemeal reform can lead only to greater pressures for more meaningful change, and it has been proven correct. The social construction of most blacks as uncivilized began to be rejected by black political organizations in the 1940s. The ANC Youth League argued in 1944 that Western civilization was built upon a destructive view of the universe as a host of individual entities that cannot help being in constant conflict, whereas the African philosophy of life strives toward unity and aggregation; toward greater social responsibility.[48] The questioning of the myth of Western superiority found greater impetus in the writings of Steve Biko, who argued that integration into "white man's society" meant integration into a system based on exploitative values.[49] By the late 1970s, the time had passed when black groups were willing to accept the extension of rights to some but not all of the oppressed; piecemeal reform could only be a stimulus to greater struggle.

When mass unrest and violence erupted again in the South African townships after 1984, the country's relations with the West hit an all-time low. Since then, the United Nations, the European Community, the British Commonwealth, and all of South Africa's major trading partners have taken punitive measures against it and have instituted mandatory employment codes for transnational corporations.[50] During the presidency of P. W. Botha, investment and trade sanctions were in effect, 56 percent of American multinational corporations had disinvested (as well as 19 percent of British and 4 percent of West German companies),[51] international bankers insisted on political reform as a prerequisite to the renegotiation of foreign debt repayments on favorable terms,[52] and both the United Nations and the Commonwealth called for financial sanctions on South Africa.[53] Between 1985 and 1990, $11 billion flowed out of South Africa.[54]

A major factor behind the decision of so many multinational corporations to throw in the towel was not simply a conviction that political instability rendered South Africa's long-term economic prospects woefully bleak; they were under increasing pressure from antiapartheid movements at home to break all ties with Pretoria's white minority regime.

Although antiapartheid sentiment and activities in the United States have been evident since 1912, when the National Association for the Advancement of Colored People (NAACP) helped to organize the African National Congress, it was not until the 1980s that South Africa as a foreign policy issue finally captured the popular imagination. Even in the aftermath of the Soweto riots, a survey conducted by the Public Agenda Foundation in 1979 found that a majority of respondents were only vaguely aware of what was happening in South Africa. Some confused the country with Zimbabwe and even Uganda. And "even those who were well informed said that this was not a subject of great personal interest to them."[55]

As a result of the Free South Africa movement, founded in November 1984, which held daily protests outside the South African embassy in Washington, D.C.; of nightly press coverage of security forces in the townships; and of a five-night broadcast of ABC's "Nightline" from Johannesburg, during which security forces killed nineteen people in Langa on the twenty-fifth anniversary of the Sharpeville massacre, antiapartheid sentiment hardened rapidly. Organized activists called, among other things, for a withdrawal of funds from companies that conducted business with South Africa. By 1986 at least twenty states, sixty-five cities, and more than 100 universities had taken some degree of disinvestment or divestment action.

Multinational corporations were not the only ones that responded quickly to the pressure; American banks withdrew about $400 million from South Africa—roughly one-tenth of their loans—in August 1985,[56] and thirty-seven major banks prohibited lending even to the South African private sector.[57]

In light of what happened after Sharpeville and Soweto, the South African business response to these pressures was predictable in all but two respects. First, in January 1985 a coalition of six employer groups issued a statement calling for government recognition of the right of all groups to ownership of property and employment; free, independent trade unions; equal justice; and an end to the forced removal of people. What was more novel was the call for universal citizenship and meaningful participation for blacks in South Africa's political system,[58] and for amendments to the Group Areas Act.[59] Businessmen severely pounded by consumer boycotts in cities such as Port Elizabeth also pressed the local city councils to open central and suburban business districts to all-race trading and suggested on-site residential rights.[60]

Second, a group of businessmen traveled to Lusaka, Zambia, in 1985 to hold talks with the leaders of the African National Congress, the first time that such a meeting ever had taken place. When asked afterward by a reporter what the future of free enterprise might be under ANC rule, Anglo-American director Zach de Beer responded, "[Q]uite frankly, the ANC frightens me a lot less than a lot of the kids in the townships."[61]

As a result of such activity, Botha's so-called alliance strategy with big business[62] began to exhibit signs of severe strain. In response to a statement by the Federated Chamber of Industries (FCI) in 1986 that it "strongly disapproved" of the new state of emergency and "dissociated itself from the strategy of political repression and economic isolationism,"[63] Botha wrote a letter to John Wilson, the chairman of the FCI:

> Kindly do not trouble me with your points of view if you are not prepared to take the trouble of familiarizing yourself with mine. Unless you, too, come to grips with the security situation in this country and act accordingly, you are bound to pay a heavy price. This is not a threat—it is a considered warning.[64]

Businessmen, not surprisingly, were rather happy to see Botha go and have expressed keen admiration for his successor, de Klerk. So impressed are they with de Klerk's apparent commitment to political reform, negotiation, and change and with his stated appreciation of the need to rebuild foreign business confidence in the country that they gave him a standing ovation at the *Financial Mail*'s 1989 annual investment conference.[65]

Not all whites are as thrilled with F. W. de Klerk as big business is. Apparent death squads, paramilitary civilian units, vigilantism, and other forms of right-wing violence represent the most extreme form of opposition to current National party policy, but what they share in common with more peaceful modes of right-wing resistance is a rejection of policies based upon a postulate of identity, even if those policies are designed ultimately to protect white power and privilege. Questions of whether to negotiate or fight with the other and whether to assimilate or exclude (via extermination if necessary) are once again at the heart of political struggles within the white community (this point will be discussed more fully in later chapters dealing with domestic struggle). The last point to be considered here is the future of Western investment in South Africa, and its implications.

With Botha's replacement by F. W. de Klerk, the situation promised marked improvement. In addition to visiting Africa, the new president set off on a nine-nation tour of Western Europe, where he was warmly received by old friends Great Britain and West Germany as well as by the traditionally more hostile France. Numerous meetings with businessmen, industrialists, and bankers, as well as with heads of state, were held in all the countries de Klerk visited.

The tour promised to be a great success; British Prime Minister Margaret Thatcher pledged to end the ban on new British investments in South Africa, and Spanish and French businessmen planned visits to South Africa to drum up trade.[66] U.S. President George Bush also agreed not to impose new sanctions against South Africa for at least a year.[67] When de Klerk opened Parliament in February 1991 the prospects of sanctions being lifted in the near future looked bright, leading him to predict with confidence that "we shall become part of the international community—finally, fully and with honor and dignity."[68] Yet the prospects for South Africa to regain its former level of economic involvement with the West appear dim at this juncture, even if all sanctions are finally lifted.

First, Japan is now a more important trading partner for South Africa than the United States, Great Britain, and West Germany. In 1988, for example, a year in which South Africa produced about 80 percent of the world's platinum, Japan imported 70 percent of the world supply.[69] Second, the reconstruction of Eastern Europe and the reunification of Germany have increased the likelihood that European businessmen will invest their surplus capital closer to home.[70] The third reason has to do, ironically, with de Klerk's political reforms, which were instituted in part to break South Africa's international isolation.

It is not only that African National Congress Deputy President Nelson Mandela has called repeatedly, since his release from prison, for the strict maintenance of worldwide sanctions against Pretoria.[71] Nor is it just that Mandela frightened investors soon after his release by reconfirming his support for the long-standing ANC policy of sweeping nationalization, particularly in the banking and mining industries where foreign capital is so prominent.[72] As South African economist Howard Preece has argued, investors are generally loathe to put their money into uncertain situations, so that before reinvesting, "private capital will wait not only for the ending of apartheid but also to see how a post-apartheid society develops."[73] The prospects for reinvestment in the short term, therefore, are not bright.

While South Africa's return to the global economy via the West appears unlikely, the eastern route looks much more promising. Western Europeans are not the only ones to see important business opportunities in a rapidly changing Eastern Europe. The South African government angered antiapartheid movements, such as the United Democratic Front (UDF), early in 1990 when it began recruiting East Europeans for skilled and semiskilled jobs in South Africa (although the irony of replacing mostly "liberal" departed whites with the residents of former communist countries was not lost either).[74] Four months later, Trade, Industry, and Tourism Minister Kent Durr announced that South Africa was "breaking new ground" by moving into the Balkans, the Baltic, central and Eastern Europe, Africa and the Far East while also developing the southern Africa regional market. So far, South Africa has established trade missions with Hungary, signed a trade agreement with Poland, and discussed the possibility (during the Namibian independence celebrations) of expanding links with Romania.[75] The government is also trying, eighty-three years after forcibly repatriating Chinese mine workers from Transvaal, to lure wealthy ethnic Chinese from Hong Kong to settle in the country.[76]

Obviously, it is too soon to say with any certainty what will become of all this activity. On the one hand, Western Europe and the United States seem more natural economic partners for Eastern European countries than does the much more distant South Africa. On the other hand, those approached so far have responded with a fairly remarkable degree of enthusiasm to the South African initiatives. What is necessary to point out is that none of these initiatives threaten to undermine an important effect of Western investment in South Africa after World War II, namely, the triumph of capitalism after flirtations with socialism in the 1930s. The commitment of the state to private enterprise is now so strong that struggles over questions of economic justice and redistribution are bound to be at the center of political negotiations for a "new" South Africa for the foreseeable future.

As the following section will demonstrate, it is not only the state that is committed to private enterprise. One of the less obvious effects of the Cold

War between the United States and the Soviet Union has been a reinforcement of the notion of private property as a hallmark of civilization.

THE COLD WAR AND THE U.S. CIVIL RIGHTS MOVEMENT

The League of Nations may have failed to champion the cause of racial equality but it did not put an end to demands for it. Japan promised that proposals for racial equality would "be presented again at every possible opportunity."[77] Pan-African conferences, organized by W. E. B. du Bois and always attended by delegates from South Africa, met in 1921, 1923, and 1927. Marcus Garvey's International Conventions of the Negro Peoples of the World, in which black South Africans also participated, brought delegates from around the world.[78] A League against Imperialism emerged in 1927, one of whose founders—along with such notables as Sun Yat-sen from China, Lamine Senghor from Senegal, Richard Moore and Upton Sinclair from the United States, Jawaharlal Nehru from India, and Ho Chi Minh from Indochina—was J. M. Gumede from South Africa.[79] A League of Colored Peoples formed in 1931.

Since all of these activities were supported, at least verbally, by the Leninist regime in the Soviet Union, they were labeled "red" and dismissed as Bolshevik or communist fronts by many in the West, who sought ever greater control of their colonial populations abroad and tighter immigration restrictions at home. Italy, however, decided to go further and attacked Ethiopia again in October 1935. Haile Selassie appealed to the League of Nations for help against a conquering force which shamelessly bombed Red Cross hospitals, used outlawed mustard gas, and attacked defenseless women and children. In response, league members chose to "note" and "deplore" Italian aggression against Ethiopia but to risk no action that might effectively deter or punish Mussolini's government.[80] Ethiopia, this time, was defeated.

As early as 1943, a special project group of the U.S. Department of State produced draft articles for a United Nations Charter. One of the most important of these prohibited discrimination on the basis of race, nationality, language, public opinion, or religious belief. Absent from the report, however, were any guarantees or measures of enforcement, for the report promised the United States would not "interfere with the laws of some of our states for the segregation of races."[81] No wonder then that South African Prime Minister Jan Smuts worked so enthusiastically for the founding of the United Nations system.

Given this background, along with the conviction of many that South Africa's racial policies were a domestic affair and outside the jurisdiction of the UN Charter, and the fact that the United States through the House

Un-American Activities Committee fought a domestic Cold War as much as it did an external one, it is small wonder that the National party considered the United States an ally after 1948. As Alexander Hepple has argued, former Prime Minister Verwoerd never believed that Britain and the United States genuinely abhorred apartheid. Verwoerd thought the shared anticommunism and common history of colonial practices should make Western states South Africa's allies.[82] And Verwoerd was not far off track. After all, the mounting attacks on South Africa after Sharpeville came largely from the Third World and citizen groups in the West, not from Western governments. The United States, France, and Britain on two occasions vetoed General Assembly resolutions on South Africa—the first time in October 1974, when they blocked an effort to expel South Africa from the United Nations, and again in June 1975 when they opposed a compulsory arms boycott. The notion that the United States always has stood up for freedom and justice around the world says more about the constructed nature of American identity than it does about U.S. policy toward South Africa.

South Africa has been constituted as a Western ally of the United States in three ways. First, at a time when the United States was labeling all manner of social criticism "communist subversion," the National party claimed that it, too, had to fight the Cold War at home as well as abroad. Multiracial trade unions, months of protest in the Transkei in 1960, and organized political resistance to apartheid have all been attributed to white communists who incited the Bantu. The notion that communists were behind the riots in the Transkei apparently prompted laughter in the House of Assembly in 1961; perhaps the National party did not believe even its own justifications. But whether the NP was convinced of its own arguments is irrelevant. The important point is that the Cold War provided a ready-made discourse, a shorthand language through which South Africa could be upheld as Western at a time when pressures for racial equality were mounting. To the charge that its policies were racist, the National party could say, "No, we're anticommunist." As future Prime Minister B. J. Vorster put it succinctly in 1962, "[T]he cold war throughout the world has been stepped up. Why should it therefore not also be stepped up in South Africa?"[83]

The second way that South Africa was constituted as Western was by appeal to the concept of Christianity. Still arguing in 1960 that loss of political control by whites would mean "the end of the Western civilization in South Africa,"[84] the National party nonetheless claimed that "we believe we hold the fort here, not only for the sake of white civilization but also for the propagation of Christianity in Africa. Therefore we do not fight with hate or venom but in faith."[85] Defining the struggle between Eastern and Western nations as that between communism and Christendom, as President Kennedy and others did,[86] the National party claimed repeatedly to represent a society

based upon Christian (i.e., Western) norms and values and justified its
policies consistently in those terms. Maintaining in 1967, for example, that
the policy of separate development could be "tested against the requirements
of Christianity and morality," Prime Minister Vorster insisted that not only
whites but also "the leaders and the masses of the other population groups"
were increasingly persuaded of this fact.[87] He repeated the point at a speech
at Heilbron in August 1968:

> How often did you not hear Dr Malan, Advocate Strijdom, Dr Verwoerd
> and myself say that the policy of separate development does not only
> benefit the Whites, but also benefits the non-Whites, because in terms
> of that policy we created facilities for them which never existed under
> the old policy. We said you may not attend my university, but we did
> not leave it at that. We said we shall give you a university of your own.
> ... That is morality, that is Christianity, that has consistently been the
> policy of the National party and that is how I shall apply that policy.[88]

These justifications for apartheid were intended to appease domestic critics
as much as they were to constitute South Africa as Western. But the outward-
looking nature of these remarks is suggested by the repeated claims of the
National party to have found the answer to everyone else's race problems, as
well as its own. In fact, it defined the country's "calling," using Kuyperian
language, in precisely those terms in 1959:

> The calling of this small nation is to give the world the basis and pattern
> on which different races can live in peace and safety in the future, each
> within its national circle. That is the prescription for the solution of the
> racial problem not only in Africa but throughout the world.[89]

As the civil rights movement in the United States was at its height in the
late 1960s, the National party piously claimed to have taught the world a
lesson about how it was possible to reconcile conflicting groups. As Prime
Minister Vorster argued in 1967, South Africa was not peaceful because of
repression:

> I want to express the hope that our friends in the USA will find a solution
> to their problems. It would be a pity if the leader of the Western world
> could not find a solution to this delicate problem. The peace and the
> quiet and the order we find in South Africa is not due to this or that
> penalty or coercive measure; it is due to the fact that the realization has
> dawned on the masses of every color group in South Africa that separate
> development is not only a policy working in favor of the White, but that

it is equally to the benefit of the non-White. . . . South Africa will serve to show the world how race problems ought to be solved.[90]

No one bought the argument that separate development was a solution to everyone's race problems, and not because the National party had no answer to the charge that its policies were built upon coercion of the majority. The government continues to claim that South Africa is a country of minorities because blacks are not a homogeneous group, so the presumption that there exists a majority to be coerced is fallacious.[91] As for the coercion claim, Vorster argued in 1971 that any realistic policy must entail a measure of compulsion, whether the path chosen was separation or integration. Had not the United States and Great Britain begun to impose sanctions upon those who did not integrate willingly, for example, by busing their children to other neighborhoods?[92]

Apartheid could not be sold because the supposition that it was about respect for diversity was undermined by long-held societal assumptions about white superiority, assumptions that the Cold War served to reinforce. Constituting blacks as innately alien and inferior, D. F. Malan argued in 1954 that differences in skin color were only "the physical manifestation of the contrast between two irreconcilable ways of life, between barbarism and civilization, between heathendom and Christianity, and finally between overwhelming numerical odds on the one hand and insignificant numbers on the other."[93]

If the National party and white society were constituted as Christian, then anyone who opposed them must be non-Christian and by definition communist. But it was not only because blacks were supposedly Godless communists that they were judged inferior. Economic productivity and private property were defined as hallmarks of civilization by Western thinkers in the nineteenth century; it will be remembered from the discussion in chapter 1 that the South African Native Affairs Commission, which met in 1903, described communal land tenure as an institution indicative of low levels of civilization. What made the 1955 Freedom Charter such a threat, therefore, was not simply that it challenged domination by calling for racial equality or threatened sectoral economic interests by demanding nationalization. In asking for land and industry "to be transferred to the ownership of the people as a whole,"[94] the charter was interfering with private property and was seen as advocating the transformation of society from civilized to barbarian. As a result, the charter was considered subversive and blacks, in advocating communal ownership of land and industry, were reconstituted as barbaric. The fact that many enterprises in South Africa at the time were owned by the state did not change the basic conviction that white society was built upon respect for private property and individual landownership.

The assumption that whites are superior because they value private property can be seen explicitly in an interview that Vorster gave to an Afrikaans newspaper in 1980. Arguing that South Africa's mission in southern Africa was tied to the identity of its white people, Vorster claimed that Africa was underdeveloped because it refused private ownership to its people. Vorster concluded that because whites see progress in private ownership and blacks see land as communal property, South Africa could never follow the example of Rhodesia and allow a black majority to govern.[95]

In a variety of ways, South Africa, or more specifically the white community, was constituted and reconstituted as Western during the Cold War between the United States and the Soviet Union. Criticism of its internal policies never stopped the National party from claiming to have "the interests of the free world at heart" and to represent "a very important bastion of the free world."[96] In this regard, the National party has been enormously successful, for it was only in the 1980s that Western states seriously considered symbolically throwing South Africa out of the "club" by imposing sanctions—even then there were those who wanted to argue that apartheid was a "lesser evil" than communism. Duncan Sellars of the Conservative Caucus Foundation in the United States, for example, said in 1986 that Americans must be made to see South Africa as a contest between the United States and the Soviet Union: "We have to stop accepting the Left's agenda, in which the issue is apartheid."[97]

With the Cold War now officially over, South Africa's anticommunist credentials presumably are less important as a mark of its Westernness than other factors, such as respect for minorities and celebration of capitalism and private enterprise. In this regard the National party under de Klerk has wasted no time. Confident that "the events in the Soviet Union and Eastern Europe . . . weaken the capability of organizations which were previously supported strongly from those quarters," de Klerk told Parliament in 1990 that "the collapse, particularly of the Marxist economic system in Eastern Europe, also serves as a warning to those who insist on persisting with it in Africa." Lest anyone should equate state-owned enterprises in South Africa with Marxism, the president went on to say that the government intended to reduce the role of the public sector in the economy and to give the private sector maximum opportunity for optimal performance.[98]

The notion that no reasonable person could be attracted any longer to the tenets of Marxism was reinforced a year later when de Klerk described "the four Ps"—property, prosperity, progress, and participation—as "universal values and ideals" shared by all peoples in South Africa and elsewhere. De Klerk told Parliament that the National party retained its commitment to the protection of private property rights and security of title and tenure and was instituting a Private Sector Initiative to speed the privatization of the economy. Building the "new South African nation" on the basis of "the basic values and ideals of the world's successful democracies and economies" meant that South Africa finally could become part of the international community and "play a full part in the rest of Africa and the world."[99]

South Africa is still trying to sell its policies in terms acceptable to a Western audience. This chapter concludes by arguing that South Africa always tried to sell separate development to Africa as well, even at a time when African states were apartheid's most implacable foes.

AFRICAN DECOLONIZATION AND INDEPENDENCE

Of the fifty-one states admitted to UN membership in 1945, only three—South Africa, Ethiopia, and Liberia—came from Africa; only three were from Asia; and seven came from the Middle East. The vast majority were European or American. With decolonization, that situation was to change. The United States set the ball rolling in 1946 by granting independence to the Philippines. India and Pakistan in 1947, and Burma and Ceylon in 1948, gained independence from the British. The Dutch decolonized Indonesia in 1949. These new nations sponsored an Asian-African Conference at Bandung in Indonesia in 1955 to bring together anticolonial movements in Africa and Asia and forge greater feelings of solidarity. Western opposition to the conference only strengthened the resolve of the Afro-Asian group to push further and support nationalist movements for independence throughout Africa.

Another spurt of independence celebrations occurred in the latter half of the 1950s. In 1956 Sudan achieved independence from Britain, and France relinquished Tunisia and Morocco. Britain gave up Malaya (now Malaysia) and the Gold Coast (Ghana) in 1957. The new Ghanaian leader, Kwame Nkrumah, immediately organized the first Pan-Africanist meeting ever to be held on African soil. Attended, as always, by a delegation of South African blacks, it met in Accra in December 1958.

The year 1960 was the "year of Africa." In that year, when British Prime Minister Harold Macmillan delivered his famous "winds of change" speech to the South African Parliament in Cape Town, fully half of the countries on the continent became independent. By 1961, in fact, the Afro-Asian countries had secured a majority in the General Assembly, thereby altering forever the European and American complexion of the early United Nations.

African independence resuscitated historical fears of the "rape and defloration" of wives and daughters at the hands of the newly liberated,[100] a fear stimulated in no small measure by the alleged rape of nearly 800 white women in the Belgian Congo in 1960. As Pierre Hugo's content analysis of the Afrikaans press at the time has shown, the civil war and any associated political phenomena were side issues to the "big story" of mass rape.

Editorials in *Die Burger, Die Vaderland*, and *Die Transvaler* spelled out that the Congo finally had exposed the folly of liberalism and integration as solutions to race problems, the West did not understand Africa, and communists were poised to take advantage of those who were unqualified to be given independence. Since then, Hugo argues, fears of black violence and of majority rule have been kept alive by the continued prevalence of emotive reporting on African conflicts, especially where whites are involved.[101]

Violence in the Congo in turn revived old differences over whether a united country should be established under British sovereignty or whether a state should be founded on the basis of "Africa for the Afrikaner."[102] Seizing the initiative, Verwoerd proposed to hold a referendum on whether South Africa should become a republic, arguing that "until the Western nations realize more fully what is happening, we should at least combine and protect ourselves."[103] An editorial in the *Rand Daily Mail* remarked wryly that "the whole republican referendum is reduced to the simple question of whether you want your daughter to marry an African, or, more to the point, be ravished by a Congolese soldier,"[104] but Verwoerd knew that fear alone could not swing sufficient support behind the republican ideal. The referendum was cast as a choice about identity. *Not* voting for a republic, Verwoerd argued, meant letting South Africa continue as a state in which the English- and Afrikaans-speaking sections could not unite, while voting for a republic meant cooperating in "developing a united nation."[105] Verwoerd thus undermined all of the Afrikaner nationalist discourse of the Christian-Nationalists and returned to a concept of nation closer to that of Afrikaners such as Louis Botha and General Hertzog. National identity no longer was given by nature or God and it was not distinguishable by such characteristics as culture and language; it could be freely chosen on the basis of political preference through a simple vote of "yes" or "no."

The privileging of race as a hallmark of identity did not sit well with some Afrikaans speakers, who continued to insist that language and not color is the essence of Afrikanerdom;[106] in the end, the republican referendum was carried with only a narrow majority. But the fact that English-speaking Natal voted overwhelmingly against a republic and the Afrikaans-speaking Free State and Transvaal swung the vote suggest that an exclusive Afrikaner identity was still more fragile than an exclusive British identity at this stage.[107]

Republicanism thus strengthened a common white identity and the notion of South Africa as "the only White state in a Black and Colored continent" became more prevalent after the referendum.[108] The founding of a republic also seemed to suggest a "circling of the wagons" against the "African peril." Yet Afrikaner identity historically was tied too closely to Africa to permit isolationism and a "laager" mentality. At the same time as African decolonization was strengthening commitment to separate development, decolonization seemed to provide an opportunity for the National party to portray its policies as based on a respect for, and not a violation of, the principle of self-determination for African peoples.

The notion of South Africa as a country of incipient nations being helped along the path to independence was intended to curry the favor of European decolonizers in the wake of British Prime Minister Harold Macmillan's "winds of change" speech, delivered to the South African Parliament in February 1960:

> We have seen the awakening of national consciousness in peoples who have for centuries lived in dependence upon some other power. Fifteen years ago this movement spread through Asia. . . . Today the same thing is happening in Africa. The most striking of all the impressions I have formed since I left London a month ago is the strength of this national consciousness. The wind of change is blowing through this continent. Whether we like it or not this growth of national consciousness is a political fact. We must all accept it as a fact. Our national policies must take account of it.[109]

The United Nations, of which South Africa was a founder-member, did not object initially to the *idea* of independent South African nations; it complained only later about the way the policy was carried out. In 1961, for example, the secretary general of the United Nations, Dag Hammarskjöld, told Verwoerd that in order to be considered a "competitive alternative" the homelands must meet certain requirements: sufficient and coherent territory, rapid economic growth and industrial development, Africans working outside the homelands should return only on a voluntary basis and had to have their human rights recognized, and the homelands should be allowed to proceed fairly rapidly toward full independence.[110]

But homelands were not aimed only at deflating pressure from the United Nations and from critics in Europe and the United States, as some have suggested.[111] Even before Sharpeville, after Macmillan made his "winds of change" speech, Verwoerd indicated that he viewed his policy as a way to gain friends and influence people on the rest of the continent:

> How can Africa be won? And there we do not see eye to eye very often. . . . If rightly understood, we believe it would seem that what we are attempting to do is not strange to the new direction in Africa but is in the fullest accord with that. . . . The tendency in Africa for nations to become independent and at the same time to do justice to all does not only mean being just to the Black man of Africa, but also just to the White man of Africa.[112]

"Winning" Africa seemed like an uphill battle. Support for African boycotts of South African products already had been raised in 1959 and early 1960,[113] and in June 1960 the Pan-African Federation voted to employ commercial, diplomatic, and political sanctions against South Africa. This boycott was continued by the Organization of African Unity (OAU) upon its formation in 1963; the OAU that same year used its influence in the United Nations to push through a voluntary arms embargo against South Africa. Largely as a result of Kwame Nkrumah of Ghana's vociferous opposition to the Republic of South Africa remaining a member of the British Commonwealth, the country was forced to withdraw in 1961. Yet the National party never ceased to insist that South Africa was in every respect a part of Africa, that it understood "the soul of Africa," and that "Africa understands us."[114] In fact, even after the NP admitted in the 1970s that separate development could not be sold to the West, it insisted that Africa would eventually buy it, as the following speech by Vorster in 1974 makes clear:

> We have tried for years to make ourselves acceptable to Europe and to the U.S.A., to sell ourselves to other countries, especially to countries with a Western viewpoint. We have failed. . . . And that is why I believe that if you want to safeguard South Africa, if you want to make it possible for you to fulfill your vocation, then you must be willing to try to make yourself acceptable to Africa which brought you forth and of which you are a part. . . . Our multi-racial policy of separate development can be sold to Africa and it can be made acceptable to Africa.[115]

Separate development could not be sold to Africa as long as South African blacks rejected it, a basic point about the "soul of Africa" that the National party never quite understood. While Africans in South Africa (other than homeland leaders) remained united in their rejection of a policy that privileged a Zulu or Xhosa identity at the expense of a more inclusive African identity, they were not necessarily united in their understanding of what an African was. Struggles over questions of identity have been at the heart of conflicts between the ANC and the PAC, as later chapters will show in more detail. Suffice it to say here that the PAC follows the precepts of Marcus Garvey and Pan-Africanism in arguing for a conception of African identity as something freely chosen. According to the late PAC leader Zephania Mothopeng, for example, a person is an African "if his only loyalty is to Africa, and he accepts the non-racial, democratic decisions of the African people. He is not going to say he is a minority if he is an African."[116] The ANC, on the other hand, continues to hold to the view that there are four national groups in South Africa, each of which is entitled to basic rights.[117] The voluntarist versus fixed understandings of identity that have split the white community have thus split the black as well, splits which African decolonization helped bring to the fore.

The decolonization of Angola, Mozambique, and then Zimbabwe—all of which espoused Marxism at a time when the Reagan administration in the United States was recommitting the country to fighting the Cold War—raised again the question of what South Africa's relations with the African continent should be. This time the laager mentality, under the initiative of National party leader P. W. Botha, seemed to hold clear sway. Under the banner of a "total strategy" against the "total onslaught" supposedly being waged against the country, Botha set about pumping more money into the domestic arms industry and destabilizing regional states.[118] It was Botha who, symbolically, refought the 1838 Battle of Blood River. Such a strategy was unpopular with businessmen who had investments to protect in the region; it also could not appeal to many of the *volk* whose sense of peoplehood was not based on identification with the mythical heroic Trekkers. According to Adam and Giliomee, Afrikaans speakers by the 1970s were coming increasingly to identify with others on the basis of middle-class values and interests,[119] while Willem de Klerk (the brother of the current state president) maintained in an interview in 1988 that the hallmark of Afrikanerdom remains language; anyone who uses the Afrikaans language and identifies with the Afrikaner culture and way of life is an Afrikaner, blacks included.[120]

Even while the total strategy against neighboring African states was being waged, Afrikaans-speaking whites began asking whether the only lesson to be learned from the Zimbabwean experience was that white South Africans must fight at all costs. A content analysis of articles and editorials published in the Afrikaans press in 1980 shows that Zimbabwean independence was another catalyst to struggles over how to treat the other, and that the idea of negotiation with "meaningful black leaders" was raised before the township unrest of 1984 and the election of F. W. de Klerk as state president.*

In an editorial entitled "Rhodesia and Elsewhere: Lessons for South Africa," *Die Vaderland* suggested in February 1980 that Zimbabwean independence had raised again historical fears for white survival and polarized the citizenry between two competing perspectives: to place power in the hands of "the Black" as soon as possible or to "shoot the whole lot while we're still strong." Between these two extremes was a middle road that needed to be considered, one that would preserve an order "wherein your values and norms have a place and you have the right and power to determine those norms' future." Following this middle road meant accepting three precepts: (1) bring necessary changes while you are still at your strongest; do not wait until circumstances weaken you; (2) negotiate with those who

* The author is indebted to Janis van der Westhuizen for the location and translation of these articles.

will be directly affected by your decisions, and know who their true leaders are—that is, do not talk only to homeland leaders; and (3) remember that social and economic changes necessarily lead to an escalation of political claims, so negotiations need to be conducted on all three levels at the same time.[121]

Support for the notion of a middle way between accommodation and extermination also came from Rowan Cronje, former cabinet minister during the Smith administration in Rhodesia, who told South Africans that if certain sacrifices had been made earlier by whites in his country, such great sacrifices need not have been made later.[122] Cronje's remarks prompted *Beeld* to respond that the sooner changes had been brought about in Rhodesia, the sooner a communist takeover would have occurred,[123] but they also prompted a group of academics to petition the government to talk to "genuine black leaders." The theme that white South Africans should now negotiate with people like Mandela from a position of strength and so retain some control was a recurring one in 1980,[124] despite the persistent claim that power sharing in one political system was not compatible with the self-determination of the Afrikaner *volk*.[125]

That the National party took almost ten years to speak officially to people like Nelson Mandela suggests that other factors—such as township unrest, the end of the Cold War, and the retirement of P. W. Botha—were necessary if not sufficient conditions to begin the process of negotiation. The issues raised in the Afrikaans press at the time of Zimbabwean independence highlight once again how the African experience has shaped understandings of what are appropriate practices in South Africa and brought to the fore conflicting ideals about relations between self and other, identity and difference.

Summary

This chapter continued the discussion begun in chapter 1 of how changing global power relations have shaped both particular subjectivities and conventional understandings in South Africa of what are normal social practices. Investment and disinvestment, the Cold War and the U.S. civil rights movement, and African decolonization and independence have been the key changes examined.

Direct foreign investment in South Africa after World War II was not automatic. Many within the National party during the 1930s and 1940s questioned the norm of both capitalism as a mode of production and imperialism as a system of relations. Once ambivalence toward the idea was overcome and direct foreign investment became—for whites at least—a normal and desirable state of affairs, its effects were twofold. On the one hand, state policy toward both Western and African states reflected the identification of whites with capitalism at a time when blacks warned of the dangers to Africa of American imperialism. However slim the prospects for an "interracial" alliance against imperialism may have once been, they became essentially nonexistent by the end of the 1950s.

On the other hand, direct foreign investment forced private business and state capital during times of social upheaval to demand meaningful change as a way to retain business confidence, thereby engendering struggle with those who wanted to persist with apartheid as a model of race relations for the rest of the world to follow. Government pronouncements and policy shifts after Sharpeville, Soweto, and the 1984 uprisings can be read as attempts by the National party to reconcile conflicting demands from within its own ranks and the civil society at large.

South Africa's major allies came under increasing pressure after World War II to recognize the rights of African and Asian people of color. European states were forced increasingly to grant to their colonies the political right to self-determination, while the United States felt the effects of a concerted and organized civil rights movement. By overturning the United party's wartime plans and insisting that rights for natives in South Africa be limited and not extended, the NP seemed out of touch with global movement in the opposite direction. But whatever may have been the actual situation, the NP moved quickly to avert possible ostracism by reconstituting the country—or at least its white minority—as Western and by casting its racial policies as consistent with changing global norms.

The South African government moved to secure the allegiance of the United States in three ways. First, it portrayed the country as a heterogeneous entity (like the United States itself) that had found the key to racial harmony. Far from condemning or overlooking what the NP was doing, the U.S. government was asked to follow its example. Second, Christian-Nationalism was said to be a Protestant ethic informing state policy; policy that supposedly was quite consistent with the requisites of Christian morality. A society based upon Christian norms and values, by extrapolation, could not possibly be communist. Third, and related to the second point, South Africa was characterized as a bastion of the free world whose efforts to stamp out communist influence domestically (and regionally) made it an integral part of the larger global struggle. For helping the rest of the Western world, South Africa deserved applause, not ostracism.

That the National party has been successful in reconstituting South Africa as Western can be seen, most obviously, in the fact that the only U.S. administration to pressure South Africa without itself being pressured domestically to do so was that of Jimmy Carter. Equally significant, if less obvious, is the fact that the U.S.-dominated International Monetary Fund places South Africa in its European, not African, category.

The NP's task no doubt would have been more difficult had South Africa not appeared to be a capitalist state open to foreign investment. But what needs to be remembered about the defense of capitalism in South Africa is the way it has been articulated historically in terms of the need to preserve European civilization. Communal ownership of land and the absence of the concept of private property have long been considered hallmarks of barbarism by Western thinkers. Because communism is synonymous with barbarism in this way of thinking, anyone or anything advocating ownership of property by the people as a whole is at once culturally inferior and a political threat, regardless of whether formal ties to communist countries or parties exist. The fear, in other words, is not simply of an alien system of thought seizing the country but of a historically contained barbarism finally breaking out and overwhelming civilization. This fear explains why the ANC's Freedom Charter was supposedly a communist document and why blacks themselves—for supporting it—were as yet supposedly uncivilized.

The reinforcement of long-held societal assumptions about white superiority undermined the NP's claims that its policies were based upon a respect for difference and not upon the principle of white supremacy. But the NP used the evidence of decolonization—a trend that revived historical fears of black rape and pillage and thus strengthened a common white (as opposed to separate British and Afrikaner) identity—to justify and instantiate national separation. South Africa was only doing, supposedly, what European colonizers everywhere were doing—that is, respecting the right of African peoples to self-determination.

No single, uncontested understanding among black South Africans exists as to what an African is, but despite differences between the ANC and the PAC over African identity at the height of decolonization, neither organization granted legitimacy to the idea of homelands. The same cannot be said of the United Nations, which complained later about the way the policy was carried out but did not object initially to the breaking down of Africans into sovereign units for the Zulu, Xhosa, and so on. The United Nations thus did not contest, as did black South Africans, the identity of the self to be determined and failed to recognize that what was wanted was freedom for the African people as a whole, not for each tribe.

For a variety of reasons, the National party has faced ongoing and mounting opposition to apartheid. For a brief moment in the early 1980s, the National party under P. W. Botha responded by bringing the "colored servants" inside the laager and symbolically reenacted a heroic Boer past. But the majority of whites were not interested in being latter-day Trekkers; even the Afrikaans-speaking elite looked more to the experiences of decolonizing Rhodesia in 1980 than to those of their own ancestors as a solution to domestic racial problems. It may have taken ten years for the idea of negotiating from a position of strength to take effect, but it was, nonetheless, at the time of independence for Zimbabwe that the idea began to circulate.

NOTES

1. Ashforth, The Politics of Official Discourse, pp. 153–54.
2. Bloomberg, *Christian-Nationalism and the Rise of the Afrikaner Broederbond*, p. xxiii.
3. Quoted in Campbell, "Global Inscription: How Foreign Policy Constitutes the United States," p. 268.
4. Lauren, *Power and Prejudice*, p. 109.
5. See Campbell, "Global Inscription," pp. 276–77.
6. Speech by J. H. Wicht (a prominent Cape Town property owner and member of the Legislative Assembly) in the Cape Legislative Council, May 1857. Quoted in du Toit and Giliomee, *Afrikaner Political Thought*, p. 187.
7. Quoted in Campbell, "Global Inscription," p. 277.
8. Giliomee, "The Development of the Afrikaner's Self-Concept," p. 29.
9. According to Leatt and colleagues, in recent times a shift can be discerned from Afrikaner *volk* nationalism to white nationalism and from ethnic to racial identification. See Leatt, Kneifel, and Nurnberger, eds., *Contending Ideologies in South Africa*.
10. This position was laid out in the manifesto of the ANC Youth League in 1944 and basically has remained that of the ANC to this day. See Mandela, *The Struggle Is My Life*, p. 25.
11. See *Southern Africa Report*, October 7, 1988, p. 6.
12. First, Steele, and Gurney, *The South African Connection*, p. 125.
13. Ibid., p. 126.
14. Lipton, *Capitalism and Apartheid*, p. 269.
15. *South Africa Yearbook*, 1975, p. 340.
16. Quoted in Lipton, *Capitalism and Apartheid*, p. 286.
17. First, Steele, and Gurney, *The South African Connection*, p. 127.
18. See Lewis, *Between the Wire and the Wall*, p. 182.
19. See the article "A New Menace in Africa," in Mandela, *The Struggle Is My Life*, pp. 72–77.
20. Ibid., pp. 167–68.
21. In the Latin American dependency literature, an alliance among the public sector, the multinational corporation, and the domestic capitalist sector has been referred to as "associated-dependent development." See Cardoso, "Associated-Dependent Development: Theoretical and Practical Implications," pp. 142–78; and Evans, *Dependent Development: The Alliance of Multinational, State, and Local Capital in Brazil*.

Information about the role of foreign capital in the South African economy is drawn primarily from three sources: Seidman and Seidman, *South Africa and U.S. Multinational Corporations*; Seidman and Seidman, *Outposts of Monopoly Capitalism*; and Myers, *U.S. Business in South Africa: The Economic, Political and Moral Issues*.

22. See Nattrass, "The Narrowing of Wage Differentials in South Africa," pp. 408–32.

23. *Southern Africa Report*, December 1, 1989, p. 10.

24. Ibid., October 6, 1989, p. 9.

25. Ibid.

26. On this point, see Askin, "The Business of Sanctions Busting," pp. 18–20.

27. See *Southern Africa Report*, December 9, 1988, p. 7.

28. Ibid., February 3, 1989, p. 12.

29. For this discussion of South African investment and trade in Africa, I am indebted to Hanlon's *Beggar Your Neighbors: Apartheid Power in Southern Africa*, particularly chapter 8.

30. In February 1990, SATS announced its decision to go public and break up its diverse operations into five privately run divisions. See *Southern Africa Report*, February 23, 1990, p. 8.

31. South African Institute for Race Relations (hereafter SAIRR), *Annual Survey of Race Relations in South Africa, 1964* (Johannesburg, 1964), p. 127.

32. See *Southern Africa Report*, October 28, 1988, p. 5.

33. Hanlon, *Beggar Your Neighbors*, p. 63.

34. *Southern Africa Report*, October 7, 1988, p. 6.

35. Ibid., November 24, 1989, p. 3.

36. Ibid., September 8, 1989, p. 6.

37. Ibid., November 24, 1989, p. 3.

38. Ibid., December 8, 1989, p. 6.

39. See Wren, "Seeking Respect, Pretoria Bets on Its Strong Economy," p. 4.

40. SAIRR, *Annual Survey of Race Relations in South Africa, 1959–1960*, (Johannesburg, 1960), p. 91.

41. Ibid.

42. Ibid., p. 93.

43. Both quotes are from Sachs, *The Road from Sharpeville*, p. 74.

44. Quoted in First, Steele, and Gurney, *The South African Connection*, p. 222.

45. Myers, *U.S. Business in South Africa*, p. 42.

46. Quoted in ibid., p. 71.

47. Ibid., p. 68.

48. See the ANC Youth League Manifesto, 1944, in Mandela, *The Struggle Is My Life*, p. 12.

49. See Biko, *I Write What I Like*, p. 91.

50. For a comprehensive overview of these measures, see Cooper, *International Business in South Africa, 1988*, pp. 169–86.

51. *Southern Africa Report*, September 15, 1989, p. 8.

52. Ibid., December 9, 1988, p. 7.

53. Ibid., February 10, 1989, p. 12; and September 15, 1989, p. 8.

54. *New York Times*, April 21, 1991, p. E5.

55. Barron and Immerwahr, "The Public Views South Africa: Pathways Through a Gathering Storm," pp. 54–59.

56. Sampson, *Black and Gold*, p. 31.

57. *Africa Report* (September/October 1986), p. 13.

58. *Wall Street Journal*, January 9, 1985, p. 31.

59. *Southern Africa Report*, November 14, 1986, p. 5.

60. Ibid.

61. *Africa Report* (March/April 1986), p. 63.

62. See Libby, "Transnational Corporations and the National Bourgeoisie: Regional Expansion and Party Realignment in South Africa," pp. 291–307.

63. *Southern Africa Report*, October 17, 1986, p. 2.

64. Ibid.

65. Ibid., November 3, 1989, p. 12.

66. Ibid., June 1, 1990, p. 10.

67. Ibid., October 6, 1989, p. 11.

68. At the time of this writing, the European Economic Community had dropped sanctions against South Africa; bans against South African participation in international sporting competition had been lifted; the British Commonwealth had removed bans on tourism and cultural exchanges; and only the question of whether South Africa had released all political prisoners needed to be answered in order for U.S. sanctions to be lifted. Many African nations, in addition, were trading openly with South Africa. The British Commonwealth, however, maintained financial sanctions against the Pretoria regime.

69. Ibid., May 19, 1989, p. 10.

70. This fact was confirmed in a recent speech to the South Africa Foundation by British Foreign Secretary Douglas Hurd. See *Southern Africa Report*, March 23, 1990, p. 11.

71. See ibid., March 16, 1990, p. 5; and April 20, 1990, p. 12.

72. More recently, Mandela has expressed support for the notion of a "mixed economy," but the overall ANC position on this issue remains somewhat unclear. See *New York Times*, June 22, 1990, p. 1.

73. *Southern Africa Report*, February 16, 1990, pp. 11–12.

74. Ibid., January 12, 1990, p. 6.

75. Ibid., May 4, 1990, p. 12.

76. Ibid., March 16, 1990, p. 12.

77. Lauren, *Power and Prejudice*, p. 104.

78. Ibid., p. 109.

79. Ibid., p. 118.

80. Ibid., p. 120.

81. Quoted in ibid., p. 147.

82. See Hepple, *Verwoerd*, p. 193.

83. See the speech made by Vorster at the time of the second reading of the General Law Amendment Bill, designed to make sabotage a treasonable offense punishable by death. Reprinted in O. Geyser, ed., *B. J. Vorster: Select Speeches*, pp. 53–55.

84. M. C. de Wet Nel, quoted in Giliomee and Schlemmer, *From Apartheid to Nation-Building*, p. 42.

85. Hendrik Verwoerd in January 1960, quoted in Hepple, *Verwoerd*, p. 176.

86. See the letter from Verwoerd to voters written September 1960 in ibid., p. 177.

87. See Geyser, *B. J. Vorster*, p. 78.

88. Ibid., p. 97.

89. Minister of Bantu Administration and Development M. C. de Wet Nel, quoted in Harrison, *The White Tribe of Africa*, p. 169.

90. Quoted in Geyser, *B. J. Vorster*, p. 84.

91. As information officer for the National party, for example, Stoffel van der Merwe argued in 1986 that in South Africa "all groups are minorities, and the protection of minority groups against domination by another group or combination of groups will have to be an important feature of any future political dispensation." See *Africa Report* (March/April 1986), pp. 69–71.

92. See a speech given by Vorster at Stellenbosch University in February 1971, reprinted in Geyser, *B. J. Vorster*, p. 126.

93. Quoted in Sparks, *The Mind of South Africa*; see also Malan, "Apartheid: A Divine Calling."

94. The Freedom Charter has been reprinted many times; see the transcript in Mandela, *The Struggle Is My Life*, pp. 46–54.

95. See the interview with Vorster in *Die Burger*, March 14, 1980.

96. See the speeches by Vorster in 1970 and 1971, reprinted in Geyser, *B. J. Vorster*, pp. 111, 136.

97. Quoted in Finnegan, "Coming Apart over Apartheid: The Story behind the Republicans' Split on South Africa," pp. 19-23, 40–46.

98. See the transcript of the speech in *Southern Africa Report*, February 9, 1990, pp. 7–16.

99. Address by State President F. W. de Klerk at the opening of the Parliament of the Republic of South Africa on February 1, 1991, pp. 2–3. Transcript available from the South African Consulate, Beverly Hills, Calif.

100. See the letter from the Stellenbosch burghers to the Burgher Senate, dated July 1826, in du Toit and Giliomee, *Afrikaner Political Thought*, p. 104.

101. See Hugo, "Towards Darkness and Death: Racial Demonology in South Africa," pp. 567–90.

102. See Giliomee, "The Development of the Afrikaner's Self-Concept," pp. 16–18.

103. Quoted in Hepple, *Verwoerd*, p. 178.

104. Quoted in Harrison, *The White Tribe of Africa*, p. 165.

105. Hepple, *Verwoerd*, p. 177.

106. See, for example, the editorial in *Beeld* entitled "Afrikaner with 'New Eyes' toward the Future," May 3, 1980.

107. Of the 1,800,748 whites entitled to vote, 1,663,872 did so. Those in favor of a republic totaled 850,458, and those against 775,878. In Natal, 42,299 voted in favor and 135,598 against. See Hepple, *Verwoerd*, p. 178.

108. See, for example, the speech given by Vorster at the University of the Orange Free State in 1967, in Geyser, *B. J. Vorster*, p. 73.

109. Quoted in Lauren, *Power and Prejudice*, p. 217.

110. See Giliomee and Schlemmer, *From Apartheid to Nation-Building*, p. 101.

111. See, for example, Gerhart, *Black Power in South Africa*, p. 254.

112. Quoted in Botha, *Verwoerd Is Dead*, pp. 55–56.

113. This support came from the All-Africa Trade Union Federation and the All-Africa People's Conference. See SAIRR, *Annual Survey of Race Relations in South Africa, 1959–1960*, p. 276.

114. See the speech by Verwoerd given in 1967. Reprinted in Hepple, *Verwoerd*, p. 75.

115. Ibid., p. 246.

116. See the interview by Ameen Akhalwaya, "Zephania Mothopeng: Free at Last," in *Africa Report* (January/February 1989), pp. 31–33.

117. See, for example, Nelson Mandela's interview with the *Washington Post*, June 27, 1990.

118. For a good overview of the "total strategy," see Hanlon, *Beggar Your Neighbors*, chapters 1 and 2.

119. See Adam and Giliomee, *Ethnic Power Mobilized*, pp. 123–24.

120. Interview with the author, Rand Afrikaans University, Johannesburg, June 1988.

121. See "Rhodesia and Elsewhere: Lessons for South Africa," *Die Vaderland*, February 21, 1980.

122. See "Do It Now—Message to South Africa," *Beeld*, March 22, 1980.

123. See "Change Does Not Prevent Communism," *Beeld*, April 1, 1980.

124. See, for example, "Rhodesia's Lessons for South Africa Written in Cillie Report," *Die Burger*, March 5, 1980; "South Africa Must Learn from Rhodesia," *Die Transvaler*, March 7, 1980; "Accept Results in Rhodesia—MP," *Die Burger*, March 7, 1980; "The Halter Pulls Tighter," *Rapport*, March 9, 1980; "Mugabe Looks at S.A. Press," *Beeld*, March 10, 1980; and "Talk Can Prevent Bloodbath in South Africa," *Die Transvaler*, May 12, 1980.

125. See, for example, "Powersharing on This Level Will Never Work," *Die Transvaler*, September 6, 1980.

II

The Uneven Effects of Normalization: Resistance, Struggle, and Social Change

3

Domination and Resistance in the Pre-Apartheid Era

Chapters 1 and 2 looked at how global relations of power have constituted particular subjectivities and shaped understandings in South Africa of what are normal social practices. Attempts by the dominant groups continually to repackage and resell domination in terms acceptable to Western and African audiences were a recurring theme in part I; how those normalizing practices both affected and were influenced by the behavior of the oppressed themselves was not the object of analysis. The purpose of chapters 3, 4, and 5 is to tell the other side of the story and to analyze the relation between modes of domination and practices of resistance at various sites within the territorial space known as South Africa.

Power, from a Foucaultian perspective, is always analyzed in terms of struggle, conflict, and war; as part I demonstrated, the struggles and conflicts that global power relations have engendered frequently have involved struggles over questions of identity and over appropriate relations between self and other. This is equally the case when relations of power are more localized, that is, when what is involved is the dominant in its immediate relations with the oppressed. Splits and fissures over the identity of Coloreds, for example—over whether they were Afrikaner because they shared the language of Afrikaans or black in common with other oppressed peoples—began even before the Union of South Africa went into effect.

James Scott has argued that relations of domination are always, at the same time, relations of resistance; once established, domination does not persist of its own momentum. A good deal of the maintenance work consists of the symbolization of domination by demonstrations and enactments of power, the purpose of which is to naturalize domination among the subordinate groups. Ritual enactments that seem to suggest the unquestioned acceptance of power relations—such as a black South African bowing and saying "Ja, baas" when questioned by a white person—are what Scott calls the public transcript of power. Yet if the elite-dominated public transcript tends to naturalize domination, some countervailing influence manages to denaturalize it as well, for behind the official story is always a hidden transcript of resistance, specific to a given social site and to a particular set of actors. This hidden transcript contains not only speech acts but a whole range of practices, which in peasant societies often take the form of poaching, pilfering, clandestine tax evasion, and intentionally shoddy work for landlords.

What are the countervailing influences that manage to denaturalize domination? As mentioned in the introductory chapter, Scott argues that the inability of the dominant to destroy entirely the autonomous social life of subordinate groups—their churches, social clubs, coffee houses, and so on—is the indispensable basis for a hidden transcript; that is, it provides the social space within which a dissident subculture can flourish.[1] Such a transcript has certainly been evident in South Africa, where those most removed from white society and the discourse of the civilizing mission— such as peasant members of independent African churches—have been least acceptant of particular practices of domination. At the same time, the importance of these autonomous social spaces explains why struggles to retain autonomy often have been as central to political resistance as demands for representation in the state.

Resistance, then, need not be organized, or even overt, and often will be localized and focused on the conditions of everyday life—precisely where normalization seeks its greatest effect. As John Brewer has argued in regard to South Africa, this is not politics in a narrow sense, if politics is taken to be the organized pursuit of goals within a constitutional framework, but politics in the wider sense of struggle against oppression. The very reason why opposition has been directed through ordinary life, Brewer argues, is precisely because narrow forms of political expression have been denied.[2]

Lack of organization and cohesion does not mean that localized resistance has no effect on the practice of domination. First, consider the effect of resistance on the behavior of what might be called the dominant economic elite. Mineowners, for example, were among the first to demand hut taxes (the nonpayment of which was common) and to pass regulations to generate an adequate supply of low-cost labor. This chapter will show, however, that they did not do so until a wide variety of noncoercive measures—such as making cheap alcohol freely available at the workplace and recruiting heavily in rural areas—had failed to attract a significant number of blacks away from their other occupations in peasant farming, domestic service, railroad construction, diamond digging, and so on. Since the "dignity of labor" was supposed to "civilize the natives," rejection of proletarianization was implicitly a rejection of the whole discourse of the civilizing mission.

Even after measures had been taken to restrict the economic autonomy of blacks and force them down the mines, breach of contract, smuggling, drunkenness, and even strike action—all of which were illegal—were widespread forms of resistance to poor pay and work conditions, forcing greater attempts at control over working-class lives.[3] The compound system for mine workers, a panoply of laws prohibiting the sale of alcohol to blacks, increased police surveillance in urban areas, and prohibitions on the right to strike are all practices originating out of resistance to domination rather than from class struggle among competing white groups.

Second, consider the effect of resistance on the state. It is tempting to see the promulgation of ever more onerous legislation as indicative of enormous state power and the odd "progressive" law before 1948 as prompted by some shift in the material interests of the white community. Yet both types of state action are more a symptom of insufficient state capacity to exercise power over black lives than they are of effective state control. Power from a Foucaultian perspective is neither given, nor exchanged, nor recovered, but rather exercised, and it exists only in action. When black South Africans have resisted domination by ignoring the edicts of the state, they have exercised power and have not been its victims.

Finally, localized forms of resistance to domination hold the key to understanding the particular form that modes of mass resistance have typically taken. Black resistance often is portrayed in the literature as following an evolutionary trail from peaceful appeals and deputations to mass civil disobedience to violence to economic boycotts, and so on.[4] Such a view might be consistent with the history of various political organizations, such as the African National Congress, but organized activity does not tell the whole story of black resistance to domination. As this chapter will show, the people in rural areas were boycotting white traders and puppet political institutions long before urban-based political groups advocated the widespread adoption of such tactics. If these practices eventually were to become widespread in urban areas, it was not due to some evolutionary progression from one stage of resistance to another or to the diffusion of behavior from town to countryside. Migratory labor policies facilitated the circulation of ideas about strategies of resistance by enforcing the physical mobility of the black population. But the origins of the most prevalent forms of resistance to domination now employed in South Africa are to be found in the rural and not urban areas.

The argument here is not that all practices of domination are necessarily resisted by all oppressed people. The point here is that neither domination nor resistance is ever either uniform or universal. The dissemination and acceptance of a certain practice as normal are bound to be uneven, like the spread of capitalism, so that some groups but not others accept certain practices as normal, while the same groups accept some norms and reject others. This explains the relative rarity of (and difficulty in sustaining) mass unity movements as well as the historical existence of political conflicts among the subjugated.

The rest of this chapter elaborates on these themes in more detail, beginning before South Africa became a state and culminating with the National party victory in 1948.

THE PRE-UNION ERA

The British Colonies: The Cape and Natal

As mentioned in chapter 1, before the British Empire took control of the Cape colony from Holland in 1806, labor for the Dutch settlers was provided mainly by the subjugated Khoikhoi and by slaves brought from Mozambique, Madagascar, and the East. The European farmers sometimes drew distinctions between slaves, baptized slaves, and *swart vry burghers* ("free black citizens"). By the end of the eighteenth century, slaves had taken over domestic service, the skilled trades, small-scale retailing, and the heavy farm work in the western Cape. The 26,000 slaves in the colony outnumbered the European freemen, so that slavery had clearly become an integral part of Cape society.[5]

After the British abolished the importation of slaves from the East in 1807, the need for indigenous labor to supplement the forced labor supply became more pressing, and white farmers demanded greater control over the 1,500 free blacks and 14,000 Khoikhoi at the Cape colony. The result was a proclamation issued by the governor of the Cape, Earl Caledon, on November 1, 1809; the proclamation called for the "Hottentots" (Khoikhoi) to be provided with "an encouragement for preferring entering the service of the inhabitants to leading an indolent life."[6] They thereafter were required to have a fixed "place of abode," but they could not own land and could not move from district to district without a certificate known as a "pass" issued by the *landdrost*. As H. R. Hahlo and Ellison Kahn have argued, "this 'class legislation' . . . fixed the status of the colored people—as a group—at the level of labor, and no higher,"[7] even though Cape society never formally enslaved the Khoikhoi as it did other peoples.

By Ordinance Number 50 of 1828, the 1809 enactment and all other proclamations affecting the status of the Khoikhoi were swept away, and Khoikhoi competence to own and purchase land was proclaimed. By 1841, legislation at the Cape brought all servants, black and white, under one law.

Yet class legislation affecting the indigenous peoples, Bantu-speaking as well as Khoikhoi, was a key aspect of the European conquest of the interior. The very ordinance that preceded the egalitarian Ordinance Number 50 authorized field-cornets to issue passes to Africans entering the colony across the frontier in search of work. And both the Khoikhoi and Bantu speakers were brought under the laws regulating relations between masters and servants. The 1856 Masters and Servants Act in the Cape imposed compulsory registration for contracts and penal sanctions for the servant's breach of contract. Desertion, failure to begin work at the stipulated time, drunkenness, negligence, insolence, and similar misdemeanors on the part of the servant also entailed criminal consequences.[8] Amendments to the law in 1873 added special penalties for farm servants, including hard labor, spare diet, and solitary confinement.

When Britain gave representative government to the Cape in 1853, it granted the franchise to all male subjects of the Crown who were twenty-one years old, could read and write, and earned a minimum annual salary of fifty pounds or possessed landed property worth at least twenty-five pounds.[9] The Cape franchise was, in theory at least, "nonracial," and black voters were a significant political force. Political associations concerned with voter registration, township grievances, and education were also in some evidence, although, as André Odendaal has argued, they tended to be under the leadership of mission-educated, "detribalized" Africans who had been encouraged to denounce uncivilized local customs and believed themselves to be inferior to Europeans.[10]

Although the bulk of agricultural labor at the Cape was provided by either the Khoikhoi or slaves, Bantu speakers were beginning to enter the service of white farmers by the mid-nineteenth century. In part, these were people displaced as a result of upheavals in the interior stemming from the formation of the Zulu state, people who frequently intended to return home when the situation became more stable. Under prevailing conditions, when the cash economy was so little developed, African squatting on white farms was the only way to insure an adequate supply of labor, which explains why many settlers apparently "kept and fed" the Xhosa "with a view to induce them, by kind treatment, to stay with them as servants."[11] Few European farmers could afford wage inducements, while most could afford to offer grazing rights to a few African families. Some settlers even let out their land to rent-paying African tenants, although most attempted to control production themselves.[12]

The system of African squatting did not necessarily bring, as it did for the Khoikhoi, the destruction of African peasant society. Indeed, around the peripheries of white settlement there remained a number of Bantu-speaking states that had retained ownership of their land and formal political autonomy: the peoples of the Transkei, of Ciskei, of Zululand; of what are now Botswana and Lesotho; and to some extent the Swazi, the Lobedu, and the Pedi.[13] But increasing agricultural production in the middle and later nineteenth century, without substantial changes in agricultural methods, brought greater concern over labor supplies, a rise in land values, and hence the pressure for expropriation on the indigenous inhabitants. White farmers, previously content with two or three families on or near their land, began to complain constantly about the shortage of labor.

Labor shortages on white farms at the Cape were exacerbated by the discovery of diamonds at Kimberley in 1867, which suddenly accelerated the demand for both skilled and unskilled labor. For the three years following the first find—the era of "river diggings" or reclamation of alluvial deposits—most of the diggers were either white farmers from the neighboring districts who did the digging in their spare time or southern Tswana from Griqualand West, wherein the diamond fields of Kimberley and the lower Vaal were located. The Tswana soon became extensively engaged in selling diamonds to white traders, prospectors, and dealers, the proceeds from which were reinvested in the rural economy via purchase of cattle, sheep, goats, wagons, and horses.[14] Along with the Xhosa of the eastern Cape, the Mfengu of Ciskei, and the Sotho of Basutoland (now Lesotho), the Tswana of Griqualand West responded to the opportunities provided by the rapidly expanding consumer market of Kimberley and engaged in a "virtual explosion of peasant economic activity" in the 1870s.[15]

After most of the readily available surface diamonds had been picked up and white adventurers set out for the more valuable "dry diggings" in 1871, direct African involvement in the diamond trade declined. Africans continued to prospect on the river diggings but were prevented from entering the Kimberley fields by the white diggers who, perhaps because they feared that the dry diggings soon would be exhausted, were determined to prevent African participation in the spoils. Complaining that the natives stole the stones, the whites burned their tents, beat them if they tried to dig, and introduced a system of passes to keep them from the fields. Kimberley quickly became essentially a white city, with blacks allowed to enter only as laborers or servants.[16]

The colonial government at the Cape soon began to extend its control over the diamond fields and thus over independent African communities. In 1874 it annexed Griqualand West, a move that sparked a local rebellion in 1878. Cape officials thereafter instituted a policy of reserving land confiscated from the rebels for "loyal" Africans, rather than white settlers, so that by the 1890s, very few of the original land titles remained in Griqua hands. For a number of years thereafter, Europeans feared that the African and Griqua people among whom they lived would "combine" in a "rising."[17]

Labor legislation at Griqualand was based on the Cape Masters and Servants Act of 1856 and on Proclamation 14 of August 1872. Under these provisions, a servants' registry was established to contract all servants, but the registry came to apply only to natives, who were required to carry a pass at all times.

Despite being deprived of much of their economic autonomy as a result of land dispossession and restrictions on access to the diamond fields, local blacks had a "hidden transcript" of resistance and found a way to profit from the diamond industry. Soon after Griqualand West was annexed to the Cape, the Kimberley representatives in Parliament (Josiah Matthews, Joseph Robinson, and Cecil Rhodes) demanded an inquiry of the diamond mining industry. The parliamentary inquiry concluded that illicit diamond buying (IDB) threatened to jeopardize the entire future of diamond mining and argued that "exceptional circumstances" required "exceptional and stringent legislation for the protection of this industry."[18] The protective measures demanded were a barrage of labor legislation and enforcement of existing statutes, which promised to tighten employer control over the material and social lives of workers.

The canteens, which were the central institutions of African working-class lives, were believed to be the crucibles of the IDB trade. Although a bill was introduced for the total prohibition of liquor to Africans, only the limited objective of a prohibition on consumption and sale in the locations and mining areas was achieved. The system of searching workers on entry to and exit from the mines was recommended and finally promulgated and implemented. An expanded police force increased its vigilance in relation to African migrants, and the number of pass arrests soared throughout the 1890s.

Another piece of important legislation was the Diamond Trade Act, which established a maximum penalty for IDB of fifteen years, or five years and banishment from Griqualand West. The act also gave police officers wide powers of search in public and private places.

The final salvo in this barrage of legislative activity was the demand for the enforcement of the compulsory feeding and lodging of Africans on their employers' compounds. The political strength of merchants and their rhetoric of free trade managed, however, to keep compounds off the statute book; only at the end of the decade, when the De Beers Mining Company monopolized diamond production, did the mineowners control parliamentary representation. In 1884, unable to solicit parliamentary support for closed compounds, the most powerful companies began to build barracks to isolate African workers from the towns.

With the shift from open to underground mining, the vastly increased amounts of capital required for development work and machinery necessitated an uninterrupted supply of labor in crucial departments of mining. Parliamentary debate again centered on the pros and cons of the closed compound system, presented by its adherents as of infinite benefit to Africans themselves. This time, the mineowners effected a compromise with the opposition—comprised of white miners who refused to be compounded and storekeepers and liquor traders who feared the loss of African business—by making two important concessions. First, they undertook to buy all merchandise required for the compound stores from dealers in Griqualand West. Second, they disclaimed any intention of compounding white workers. The Compagnie Française began the system in January 1885 with 110 recruited Africans engaged in Natal. The Kimberley Central followed suit in April 1885 with 400 Africans, who promptly struck, but once the strike leaders had been dismissed, the others began work. In July 1886 De Beers closed the compound on 1,500 Africans, who immediately struck but failed to hold out for long. Prior to this time, the company built a compound for 300 African convicts.[19]

With the annexation by the Cape government of the Transkei and the Ciskei, the African population of the Cape increased by over a million, and African voters who had formed only 14 percent of the electorate in 1882 accounted for 47 percent in 1887. The Cape Parliament thereupon passed a Voters' Registration Act, which disqualified all those who had become voters by virtue of their occupation of tribal land. Thirty thousand people found themselves disenfranchised, demonstrating again how communal land-ownership was linked to barbarism and thus used to justify political exclusion.

A newspaper editor named John Jabavu led African protests against the act, but to no avail. The 1892 Franchise and Ballot Act raised property qualifications even further because the black vote continued to affect results in a number of constituencies. Africans again opposed the act unsuccessfully. The "nonracial" franchise at the Cape was therefore more illusion than reality in that "civilized standards" were raised whenever blacks threatened the dominant position of Europeans. Nonetheless, the black mission-educated elites continued to believe in the slogan of "equal rights for all civilized men." They supported the British side in the Anglo-Boer War when imperial officials, such as Milner and Chamberlain, promised "equal laws, equal liberty" for all races in South Africa in the event of a British victory.[20]

Legislation pertaining to relations between masters and servants, to passes, to liquor, and to closed compounds came at the behest of mineowners who could not induce a labor supply via wages alone. Farmers, on the other hand, were to be the main beneficiaries of the establishment of a system of permanent "native locations" in the rural areas. First promulgated in the eastern Cape by Governor Glen Grey, who mandated sufficient space between the locations to allow the spread of European settlements in order that "each European emigrant would thus have it in his power to draw supplies of labor from the location in his more immediate proximity,"[21] "locations" were delineated by Lieutenant Governor W. O. Lanyon in Griqualand West in 1877.

Coupled with the promulgation of hut-tax obligations, the new patterns of landownership were intended to draw Africans forcibly more fully into the cash economy, as well as to facilitate the access of white settlers to nearby sources of labor. Yet in 1886, the magistrate of the Umzimkulu district reported that hut taxes and rents were being withheld, so that landowners and traders had to go to court to secure writs against those who defaulted on their debts.[22] The rent and rate boycotts so prevalent in African townships 100 years later thus had their roots in much earlier resistance to proletarianization in rural areas.

In the face of boycotts, the effective imposition of native locations and hut-tax collection required stronger measures. Aimed primarily at increasing the flow of wage labor from the Transkei to the mines, the Glen Grey Act of 1894 promulgated a labor tax, deprived Africans who held land under individual tenure of the right to count their holdings as a franchise qualification, and instituted a council system to provide for partial local self-government.[23] Within only a few months, however, popular hostility to the act had become so threatening that local officials sought urgent changes in legislation.

The initial approach of the magistrates wanting to publicize and implement the Glen Grey measures was simply to seek the approval of headmen, but this tactic was to backfire. The capitulation of the headmen was a signal for more overt defiance by the common people, who organized large meetings, refused to pay the labor tax, and sent petitions and protests to the colonial administration.[24]

The Transkei Native Vigilance Association (TNVA), led by Enoch Mamba, emerged in reaction to the council system. Consisting of educated, Christian Africans who were dissatisfied with the powers exercised by traditional leaders—calling them "red heathens" who were averse to all civilization[25]— the TNVA aimed to articulate popular grievances which could then be properly submitted to the General Council for consideration.[26]

Although the TNVA met with official hostility from the start, a Select Committee recommended abandonment of the labor tax in 1903. Enthusiasm for the individual tenure clause also cooled. These were obvious political concessions to the protesters, whose most effective weapon—the withholding of taxes—was to be used so frequently over the coming years. The Cape administration, however, sought as rapidly as possible to extend the district council system, for segregated local councils were a means to increase political openings for Africans without accepting them as full and equal participants in colonial politics.[27] Councils also would assume responsibility for spending on local services, thereby freeing the colonial administration of these costs. The council system, therefore, was an important forerunner of the system of Bantu Authorities instituted in the 1950s and subsequently expanded as Bantustans, again in the wake of widespread popular protest.

Even the eventual implementation of district councils represented a victory of sorts for the protesters, who after 1903 instituted an effective boycott of the councils until they were administered by popularly elected Africans, rather than by white functionaries or chiefs and headmen. As William Beinart and Colin Bundy have pointed out, the hostility to whites and insistence that Africans must administer their own affairs were indicative of the influence of Ethiopian separatist churches and their message of black self-help and assertiveness.[28]

Given all of the opposition to the councils after 1894, constant rumors of native unrest among white settlers were not without foundation, although the colonial administration often thought the settlers overreacted to what were rarely violent protests. Worried by the emergence within local communities of leaders who seemed to be articulating widespread grievances and troubled by agitators ("agitators" usually referred to educated blacks), settlers demanded tougher action to control the natives. A 1908 Locations Act was designed to establish tighter control over the renting of private farmland to Africans, but when rumors of rebellion began circulating in 1909, the magistrate in Griqualand East advised against its implementation.

As Gail Gerhart has pointed out, the strongest white disapproval was reserved for educated blacks who imitated European ways and aspired to some form of work above manual labor.[29] Enoch Mamba's TNVA would seem to be an obvious point of reference, yet even those elite-led groups out of direct touch with the masses, such as the South African Native Congress (SANC), were considered by the early 1900s to represent a threat to order and stability. It is tempting to put white fears of SANC down to emotional hysteria, particularly when SANC demanded only "equal rights for all civilized men" and devoted as much energy to the "upliftment" of "the native races" as to harassing the government. But there is a sense that even SANC threatened to undermine white domination by challenging the status quo.

SANC's 1903 letter to Joseph Chamberlain (discussed in chapter 1) is a document that was highly critical of labor practices in the mines at the same time as it resisted the idea of native unity as a way to counter European control. SANC rejected completely the "normal" argument that the native preferred living in absolute idleness to advancing the progress of the country and so had to be forced to work for his own good. Also totally false, according to SANC, was the notion that natives were demoralized by high wages paid during the Anglo-Boer War and that they lived by stock stolen from farmers. The scarcity of labor was due not to innate defects in the indigenous people but to "scandalous irregularities under the old regime at the Rand," to "the sudden depression of wages before the effects of the war," and to "the impressions formed of . . . evil conditions." Capitalist demands for a cheap labor supply, and not worker sloth, were said to be the root cause of the labor problem.

SANC politely requested an imperial commission to investigate the labor question in a larger investigation of the condition of native affairs in South Africa. But its prediction of what would happen in the absence of economic justice contained an only thinly veiled threat:

> For South Africa, labor troubles are just commencing. . . . It is not a race question, although radical differences in life and language, and such questions as general treatment, rates of wages, accommodation, food, etc., give rise to more bad feeling on this, and the Master and Servant question, than any other subject . . . and the attempts to reconcile low wages with high living, we may readily believe from the example of other countries will continue to agitate the country long after the present generation has departed.[30]

Concern about agitators like SANC, which did not require "communists" in order to protest capitalist practices and economic inequality, also may have been behind passage of the School Board Act of 1905. In the same year that the South African Native Affairs Commission (SANAC) argued that the "educated Natives" should be distinguished from the "more solid and experienced men who are in closer touch with the masses,"[31] the School Board Act made education compulsory for white children but not for those not of European parentage or extraction. De facto segregation in education actually already existed, as low-fee or free mission schools attended primarily by poor blacks existed alongside a better-funded, nondenominational school system for those who could afford to pay fees—mainly whites. Still, the School Board Act was opposed bitterly by educated blacks such as those in the newly formed African Political Organization (APO). The APO believed that education brought with it the civilized status that supposedly was the prerequisite for political rights,[32] and it fought hard to mobilize public opposition to the act. But the act's defeat seemed preordained, as the more "liberal" Progressive party supposedly had sponsored the act in the first place.

Nonetheless, the struggle was not entirely wasted, according to Gavin Lewis, for it helped arouse the political awareness of the Colored elites as never before.[33] As for the act itself, it paradoxically may have had at least one positive impact: it helped turn the steady stream of black South Africans attending educational institutions abroad into more of a flood. In 1908 the

Select Committee on Native Education in the Cape reported that more than 100 Africans from that colony alone had in recent years gone to colleges in the United States and elsewhere.[34]

In general, the idea of international cooperation with blacks overseas, and thus the formation of an inclusive black identity that would challenge the later notion of Coloreds and natives as different peoples, were furthered by an increasingly active African press. For example, the Accra-born journalist Francis Peregrino (a so-called Colored) began producing a newspaper for blacks called the *South African Spectator* in 1900. Peregrino, who in the 1890s had run his own newspaper in the United States, was heavily influenced by Booker T. Washington's message of self-help and W. E. B. du Bois's insistence on the need for black unity and political assertion. This influence was evident in the pages of the *Spectator*, which rejected all theories of racial inferiority, stressed black pride, and urged blacks to adopt habits of sobriety and respectability.[35]

Despite attempts to foster black identity, Peregrino was unable to prevent a branch in Kimberley of the Colored People's Vigilance Society (CPVS), which he founded in 1901, from segregating "colored Afrikander" and "native" members on the grounds that otherwise "the color question was always broached."[36] Splits and fissures over the identity of Coloreds—over whether they were Afrikaner because they shared the language of Afrikaans[37] or black in common with other oppressed peoples—thus began even before the Union of South Africa took effect.

In colonial Natal, the underlying principle adopted by the *Volksraad* (parliament) was racial segregation, with the simultaneous enforcement of contracts of service between African squatters and European farmers by way of stringent pass laws and the "apprenticeship" of African children. With the discovery after annexation by the British in 1843 that the coastal lands of Natal were suitable for sugar plantations, white farmers raised a continual clamor for the breakup of the African locations set up earlier by Sir Theophilus Shepstone and the abrogation of tribal practices that recreated an autonomous space for Africans within traditional peasant economies. They did not object to the existence of locations per se; rather, a committee of inquiry appointed in 1852 to investigate the problem of labor shortages attacked the amount of land available to the African because it allowed him "to follow idle, wandering, and pastoral lives or habits, instead of settling down to fixed industrial pursuits."[38]

The farmers failed to "disperse the Reserves," but they created hut taxes and restrictions on landholding that Africans could escape only by living on white farms, the number and size of which continued to expand. In 1875 whites farmed 2 million acres, by 1893 this figure had risen to almost 6 million acres, and by 1904 whites were farming over 7 million acres.[39] Law

Number 11 of 1865 disenfranchised native voters other than those specially given the vote by the lieutenant governor.

The response of mission-educated Christian Africans was to become more assertive politically, developing European-type political organizations alongside the establishment of independent African churches and newspapers. The Natal Native Congress (NNC), for example, was founded during the Anglo-Boer War of 1899–1902, with the aim of cultivating Africans' awareness of their rights and acting as a forum for airing grievances. Although it asked only that Africans be represented in Parliament by sympathetic whites, the movement was symptomatic of ever-increasing African interest in political affairs and organization at the grassroots level. This interest was fostered by the dissemination of newspapers to even the most remote farms and locations.

None of the programs of the Ethiopian (separatist) church movement expressed explicit political aims, but in practice African nationalist sentiments frequently were expressed openly. As Odendaal has argued, religious movements were an extension of formal political organizations—or perhaps the other way around—because churches spread out more than political associations at the grassroots level.[40]

In 1905 SANAC published its report on the barbarous nature of communal land tenure in the Reserves and proposed that individual land tenure and hut taxes would speed the civilizing of natives into wage laborers (see also chapter 1). One of the most outspoken critics of the SANAC report was the South African Native Congress (SANC), which rejected the proposals at the same time as it accepted the premise that rural Africans needed to be "civilized." In Natal, however, the report was followed by disturbances that culminated in the outbreak of a full-scale rebellion in 1906.

It was only in 1897 that the Zulu kingdom had been incorporated into the colony of Natal and only in the early twentieth century (i.e., much later than elsewhere) that white occupation of land within Zululand had taken place. The effect of this longer history of autonomy, according to Gerhard Mare and Georgina Hamilton, was to leave a legacy of unconsolidated land occupied by Africans, and the symbols of continuity, resistance, and apparent Zulu political and cultural coherence that could be used by subsequent regional leaders to mobilize support by appeal to the "Zulu Nation."[41] The question of Zulu identity is important in terms of contemporary politics and will be raised again in subsequent chapters, when struggles between the ANC and the Zulu-based Inkatha Freedom party are discussed in more depth.

Unrest in Natal was present ever since the end of the Anglo-Boer War; it was an unrest exacerbated by the imposition of a poll tax on all adult males in the colony at the end of 1905. This tax was part of SANAC's proposal to raise revenue and force Africans into wage employment. When the rebellion of Chief Bambatha broke out in the Greytown district, martial law was proclaimed and the militia was sent to quell unrest in disaffected areas. The rebellion continued throughout 1907 and resulted in the massacre by British troops of between 3,000 and 4,000 of Bambatha's followers. Bambatha's head was cut off and displayed to prove that he was dead and the rebellion over.

According to Odendaal, the rebellion was a cogent factor in promoting the idea of broad-based political cooperation among Africans throughout South Africa,[42] in much the same way that the Anglo-Boer War fostered a sense of Afrikaner nationhood. Bambatha also helped shift the site of struggle from the land to the workplace, not only because proletarianization was increasing rapidly but because the brutal force used by the colonial authorities was attributed to mineowners. Newspaper editor A. K. Soga, for example, blamed mineowners for the repression—aimed, he said, at impoverishing Africans and forcing them to the mines—and encouraged vigilance associations to think about strikes and labor disputes as "a phase of the coming struggle between capital and labor."[43] Again, the adoption of class analysis to explain relations of domination was beginning to take shape among Africans well before communists came along to incite the Bantu.

In 1885, the Natal colony addressed a petition to the queen of England for the introduction of convict labor, but it was unsuccessful. Seasonal labor was recruited from Mozambique and other surrounding areas. Eventually, the British settlers in Natal convinced the British government to import indentured Indians, some 6,500 of whom arrived between 1860 and 1866.[44] After their period of indenture was over, most remained as laborers, servants, traders, and professionals as well as in many other occupations.

Even the racial construction of South Africa as a country comprised of officially classified whites, Coloreds (the offspring mainly of marriages between slaves and white settlers), Indians, and Africans would not have been possible without African resistance to proletarianization, for without it there would have been no Colored or Indian population of which to speak.

The Afrikaner Republics: The Orange River Colony and Transvaal

In the Orange River Colony (ORC; now the Orange Free State) and Transvaal (or South African Republic, as it was then called), as in the British colonies, the need of white farmers for land and labor found expression in a number of statutes, proclamations, and ordinances designed to push unwilling Africans out of the subsistence economy. Both parliaments claimed that all natives within the limits of the respective republics were their subjects, liable to taxation and to service with European farmers but denied citizenship and legal equality.[45] An 1855 proclamation in Transvaal, for example, prohibited the holding of landed property outside of the native locations by noncitizens, which effectively prevented landownership by Africans since only Europeans were eligible for citizenship. A Masters and Servants Act was enacted in Transvaal in 1880. The 1893 Towns and Villages Act in the Orange Free State gave town councils the right to establish locations for coloreds (by which was meant both Africans and people of mixed blood) in urban areas. Fifteen years later the Rights of Colored Persons in Respect of Fixed Property Act aimed at weakening the position of African squatter-peasants on white farms.

The question of who or what a "colored" was came up again in 1905 when Sir Alfred Lyttleton, the British colonial secretary, proposed a draft constitution for self-government of the two republics that limited the franchise to whites only. Seeing hopes dashed for the extension of the Cape's nonracial franchise to the other colonies, the Coloreds in the APO sent a deputation to the Transvaal and ORC governments to convey their grievances and approved a petition to the king of England asking for intervention to secure franchise rights. By asking for the franchise for Coloreds only and not for all blacks, the petition aroused concern among some Colored leaders over the movement away from a commitment to black unity.[46]

The APO's Abdullah Abdurahman rejected criticism on the grounds that the Treaty of Vereeniging, which ended the Anglo-Boer War, denied the franchise to natives only, not to Coloreds, and claimed that the protection of existing rights for Coloreds was a first step toward a broader enfranchisement for all blacks. Abdurahman wrote to the West Ridgeway Committee, pleading for the extension of franchise rights and repeating the arguments used in the petition to the king. The committee's response, apparently, was to suggest that most whites in Transvaal and ORC interpreted the term *native* as including both Africans and Coloreds, not the former only. It thereby rejected Abdurahman's claim that the Boer delegates to the Treaty of Vereeniging had not meant to exclude all nonwhites from the franchise because the distinction between aborigines and Coloreds was well understood.[47]

No doubt there were those for whom the term *native* meant "aborigine" only. But the SANAC report also defined *native* as meaning both an aboriginal inhabitant of Africa and "the so-called colored people,"[48] suggesting that the notion of the Coloreds as a distinct people separate from Africans was not prevalent among whites at this time.

The APO may have been acting purely out of tactical expediency and may not have been reneging on its commitment to equal rights for *all* civilized men. Still, its decision to organize political action around a specifically Colored identity helped strengthen the sense of a separate identity among rank-and-file APO members, according to Lewis.[49] The APO was ambivalent over how best to achieve the objective of integration into white-dominated society. Should it emphasize unity with other oppressed peoples (which the very name, *African* Political Organization, implied), or should it focus on the shared culture of Coloreds and Afrikaans-speaking whites? This ambivalence was to surface again and again in coming years, with conflicting understandings of identity often at the heart of political struggles and fractures within the so-called Colored community itself, as elsewhere.

With its battle to secure franchise rights defeated, the APO turned to other issues, particularly to education and to what for Abdurahman was a personal obsession, namely, alcoholism among the Colored people. The practice of paying farm workers in alcohol, to which Abdurahman attributed the problem of widespread drunkenness, soon spread to the gold mines as well, where mineowners struggled to find noncoercive means to overcome black resistance to proletarianization.

In the early years of gold mining, the industry complained constantly of labor shortages and almost from its inception turned to the state for assistance in generating an adequate supply of low-cost labor. As SANC pointed out in its 1903 letter to Chamberlain, the problem was caused less by physical scarcity, or idleness, than it was by the reluctance of Africans to seek employment in the mines for both economic and social reasons. Economically, the wages paid for unskilled work fell below the subsistence level necessary for a man to support his family. In fact, mineowners on three occasions—in 1890, 1896–1897, and 1902—actually lowered wages, the first time by 14.2 percent.[50] The social unattractiveness of mining stemmed from the fact that African workers on the Rand, as at Kimberley, were confined to all-male compounds, even though the smuggling factor was not as important for low-grade gold as it was for diamonds.

Had their range of employment options been more limited, Africans might have been compelled by personal imperative, rather than state action, to accept the low wages, dangerous work, and compound living offered by the mining capitalists. Yet as a result of the gold discoveries, their range of employment opportunities in both town and countryside increased rather than diminished. The growth of mining areas in the countryside offered profitable openings in the locations and on white farms to African farmers, who apparently adapted to the improved market opportunities more quickly than the majority of whites.[51]

Employment opportunities in towns also were good; for example, Johannesburg evinced a notable demand from the moment of its establishment for domestic servants of all colors and both sexes. Much of the early demand for black male servants, in particular, came from middle- and upper-class families who considered a team of houseboys a prestigious asset. During the 1896–1898 depression, boardinghouse keepers and other householders began substituting cheap unskilled black labor for more expensive semi-skilled white servants from Europe. The demand for houseboys, therefore, increased and, for a variety of reasons, most of these positions came to be filled by Zulu speakers drawn from neighboring Natal. By 1899 there were several hundred houseboys at work on the Rand whose average monthly wage was eighty shillings—thirty shillings higher than the average wage paid to black miners. Although the mineowners remained silent about this condition on the eve of war, in time they expressed their strong disapproval of the wage disparity.[52]

From 1890 onward, groups of Zulu-speaking washermen—often drawn from the same rural areas in Natal that supplied the Rand with many of its houseboys—established themselves along the banks of the Braamfontein River and soon dominated Johannesburg's hand-laundry business. Bound together in an ethnically based organization, which in some respects resembled a medieval European craft guild, they named their association *AmaWasha*, which had a membership of over 1,200 by 1895.[53]

Migration of workers to German South West Africa to work for the railway companies and the military presented another opportunity to Africans, particularly those from the Cape. In 1910 the chairman of Rand Mines went so far as to demand that the Transvaal government approach the Cape with a view to stopping such recruitment. The Cape government took the position that it would discourage recruiting and would grant no further licenses to recruit but that legislation would have to await a new Union Parliament, soon to come into being. By November 1910, 3,000 Cape workers had left and others followed.[54]

As already mentioned, mineowners first devised a number of noncoercive strategies to solve the labor supply problem, particularly as opinion "at home" almost unanimously was opposed to any policy that might be seen as promoting forced labor. In 1889 the gold-mining companies came together to form the Chamber of Mines, the objectives of which were to prevent ruinous wage competition among them by fixing wage rates and to centralize control over recruitment of the labor force. In 1897 the chamber organized its own labor-recruiting organization, known as the Rand Native Labor Association, out of which two other associations were to grow. The Native Recruiting Corporation (NRC) was responsible for the centralized recruiting of mine labor from within South Africa itself and from Botswana, Lesotho, and Swaziland, while the Witwatersrand Native Labor Association (WNLA) recruited from areas further afield. These two institutions were to control the recruitment of labor for the gold mines throughout the following eighty-year period, combining once again in the late 1970s into one organization known as the Employment Bureau of South Africa Limited, or TEBA.[55]

Mine workers drawn from outside of South Africa's boundaries lowered the competition for labor between the Rand and white farmers, so the Transvaal government was willing to assist the Chamber of Mines to enlarge the geographic area from which it recruited African labor through the negotiation of labor contracts with other countries. As early as 1898, some 60 percent of the gold mines' work force was provided by Mozambique. Although the relative importance of that country as a source of labor declined somewhat over the course of the twentieth century, the proportion of foreign workers as a whole—from Lesotho, Botswana, Mozambique, Swaziland, and Malawi—in South Africa's gold mines had climbed by 1973 to 80 percent of the total.[56]

In lieu of wage inducements, mineowners used alcohol as a primary means of attracting and stabilizing their labor force. But reliance on alcohol was not merely insufficient to assure a continuous labor supply; it very soon contributed to an exacerbation of the problem it was meant to correct. By 1895 it was estimated that between 15 percent and 25 percent of the black labor force was permanently unfit for work because of drunkenness, and the Chamber of Mines realized that, as a result, "the scarcity of labor was intensified, as companies able to get them had to keep far more boys in their compounds than were required on any one day to make up for the number periodically disabled by drink."[57] Shortly after the onset of the depression in 1896, mineowners advocated the legislation of a total prohibition of the sale of alcohol to black mine workers. Members of the *Volksraad* were divided over the issue, but when Act 17 of 1896 was passed, it contained a "total prohibition" clause to be put into effect on January 1, 1897.

An inadequate supply of workers and inefficiency due to drunkenness were only two of the unskilled labor problems with which mining capitalists had to contend. Another was the fact that desertion and breach of contract by African miners was a major cause of labor turnover, either as a response to wage-rate adjustments or to poor living or working conditions. By the early 1890s, mineowners came to the conclusion that their labor needs would not be satisfied without a measure of state coercion because Africans, in a variety of ways, actively resisted mine work if at all possible.

One of the first actions of the Mine Managers' Association (MMA) after its formation in 1892 was to set up a Committee on the Native Labor Question which acted as a pressure group from below on the Chamber of Mines. According to the committee's first report issued in 1893, there were three crucial areas that the chamber should insist the Transvaal government attend to. First, it was argued, the government should carry out the proletarianization of labor through an increase in the hut tax:

It is suggested to raise the Hut Tax to such an amount that more natives will be induced to seek work, and especially by making this hut tax payable in coin only; each native who can clearly show that he has worked for six months in the year shall be allowed a rebate on the Hut Tax equivalent to the increase that may be determined by the state.[58]

Second, the state was expected to carry out the mobilization and acquisition of the labor force once it had been compelled to seek cash earnings. And third, the state was expected to see to the question of the regulation and retention of labor, once it had arrived at the mines, through the pass laws. In 1896, after discussions between the mining industry and the Kruger government, which dated back to March 1894, the government promulgated a hut tax law and pass regulations to facilitate the control of black workers on the Witwatersrand.

In the early years, the social composition of the mine labor force was noteworthy because local-born whites were by and large not directly involved in the mining industry. The technical difficulties of deep-level mining, the scale of investment that it required, and the absence of an indigenous skilled work force meant that in the initial stages the industry was forced to resort to the introduction of skilled immigrant workers to perform certain tasks and to oversee the production process in general. The mining companies substituted whenever possible cheaper black for more expensive white labor in a range of occupations and insisted that white gold miners supervise increasing numbers of black workers.

Amid rising concerns about the future of white labor in the mines, the white Mine Workers' Union (MWU) in 1893 successfully lobbied the *Volksraad* for legislation that would bar black workers from blasting operations in the mines. The Chamber of Mines opposed the first statutory color bar established in Transvaal on the grounds that a test for miners should be based on competence, not color,[59] but it was unable to prevent either the initial act or subsequent amendments which set aside a wide range of mining occupations for whites.[60]

After the defeat of the Afrikaners in the Second Boer War of 1899–1902, the British administration of Lord Milner brought a new mood to the pass laws and the mining industry in general, even though blacks had participated in the war on the side of Britain as both combatants and noncombatants. Armed blacks raised the specter, yet again, of a native uprising, so that after the Treaty of Vereeniging the pass laws were applied more vigorously, tax defaulters were dealt with more speedily, land was appropriated more systematically, and wages were reduced less hesitantly. The year 1908, for example, saw passage of the Gold Law, which prohibited blacks from hiring or owning property in municipal areas and proclaimed residential segregation. The Native Tax Act of the same year differentiated between squatter-peasants and labor tenants on farms, taxing the former more heavily so as to force them into the labor market.

The outcome of all of this was that Africans deliberately withheld their labor, giving rise to an acute shortage in the mines. As Odendaal has argued, the "African labor supply was not, as might have been supposed, an inert mass there to be manipulated and exploited at will."[61] It was, in fact, quite politically sophisticated, thanks again to the influence of separatist churches and their educational institutions.

It was on the Rand that the foundation for the first African mass movement along truly national lines was established—namely, the Ethiopian church— by Mangena Mokone and a number of others. They called themselves Ethiopians in reference to a number of biblical texts, which they interpreted as a promise of the evangelization of Africa. The church was to be open to all Africans and it was to be run by African leaders.

By the end of the nineteenth century, the Ethiopian movement had gained thousands of adherents and spread throughout South Africa. It also had amalgamated with the African Methodist Episcopal (AME) Church in the United States, founded by a former slave to encourage black assertiveness.[62] As already mentioned, the church was not explicitly political in nature. But it was more subversive than formal political organizations in the way that it articulated dissatisfaction with white rule, propagating autonomy and native unity—rather than integration into existing society—as the way to counter European domination and fostering a sense of common black identity with oppressed peoples everywhere. Associated with Marcus Garvey, Ethiopianism was in essence the first major Pan-African social movement in South Africa and thus an important forerunner of more overtly political Pan-Africanist movements such as the PAC and Black Consciousness.

Another American religious "import" to the Rand was the Christian Catholic Apostolic Church in Zion, founded in Chicago in 1896 and intro- duced to the black populations around Johannesburg and Natal in 1904. Repeated government commissions in the early years of the twentieth century expressed suspicion that Zionism might be "mischievously" crossing the boundaries between religion and politics. Abstinence from smoking among the first Zulu Zionists, for example, was perceived by white farmers as an act of resistance against a labor system that used tobacco as a mode of payment.[63]

To deal with labor shortages in the mines, consistent attempts were made to increase the efficiency of unskilled labor after 1903 by controlling the illicit drink traffic that persisted despite prohibition and regulating health condi- tions in the compounds. Furthermore, Milner agreed to the importation of Chinese contract laborers, even though white workers increasingly were available due to the war, rinderpest (a crop disease), and the discharge of British soldiers from the army. The Labor Importation Ordinance of 1904 legalized the first importation of Chinese laborers, some 21,000 of whom arrived by the end of the year.[64] In 1902, 1906, and 1907 white miners struck to protect their skilled positions and their rights to organize against management and have some control over their working conditions.

The practice of importing foreign workers was discontinued after 1907. But the state continued to intervene directly in securing a labor supply through the establishment in 1907 of the Government Native Labor Bureau and through the regulation of recruiting conditions and agreements.[65] Native recruitment was often accompanied by the retrenchment of whites, a process that brought recurring and accelerating violence to the mines.

In the course of the 1907 strike, troops were used to control serious outbreaks of conflict between mining capital and labor. Production was maintained by the large numbers of unemployed local whites who entered the industry for the first time as scabs and then as permanent laborers, but, after the strike was broken, the Botha/Smuts government insisted on a "definitive ratio in mining of 'civilized labor' to indentured natives."[66] It also sought more forceful means to restrict the level of white labor militance through passage of the Industrial Disputes Prevention Act of 1909. The act established a Department of Labor for Transvaal and made provision for the prevention of strikes and lockouts by whites and for the settlement of disputes by conciliation after investigation.[67]

Whereas overt confrontations between management and labor tended to be the rule with white workers influenced by their industrial experiences in Europe, African resistance to conditions in the mines assumed more the form of a "hidden transcript," perhaps explaining why African resistance so often has been overlooked. The most common forms of resistance were breach of contract and desertion, drunkenness, illicit alcohol trafficking, diamond smuggling, and failure to perform a minimum amount of work, but wage reductions frequently prompted more ambitious strategies. In the wake of the wage reductions of 1890, for example, African workers at the Anglo-Tharsis Mine blew up the mine manager's house with dynamite. During the wage reductions of 1896–1897, mineowner Julius Wernher complained that the theft of gold amalgam was being carried out on a tremendous scale. Even strike action by Africans, a weapon they resorted to increasingly as the twentieth century wore on, was not unheard of prior to the Act of Union. In 1902, following the wage reductions that accompanied the formation of the Witwatersrand Native Labor Association, African miners at the Consolidated Main Reef Mine went on strike in protest against the higher wages being paid to African workers by contractors working outside WNLA agreements.[68]

The Act of Union in 1909 did nothing to threaten the labor control system in any of the four territories shortly to amalgamate into the Union of South Africa. Indeed, legislation promulgated after 1910 reflected ongoing resistance to various practices of domination and the efforts of white society to gain greater control over the material and social lives of blacks.

Toward the Union of South Africa

The formation of "closer union" societies created feelings of apprehension among many Africans about federation. Louis Botha of the South African party (SAP), for example, stated before the Transvaal Labor Commission that, if he had his way, he would break up "native Reserves" and force Africans onto the labor market.[69] Yet Africans had faith in Britain and in the Cape delegates to the National Convention. The release of the draft South Africa Act in February 1909, which reserved the franchise for whites only, thus came as a rude shock and galvanized organized political activity on an unprecedented scale.

In addition to numerous regional meetings, SANC convened a South African Native Convention in March 1909, the first occasion on which African political leaders and associations in various colonies had cooperated formally. According to one of the delegates, the draft act represented the interests of the capitalists and the landed elite. Yet despite the class analysis, the whole tone of the convention reflected the influence of missionary and other Western agencies. Protests were respectful and temperate and went to great lengths to prove the loyalty of Africans and their suitability to participate in formal politics.[70]

The African Political Organization held its annual conference in Cape Town a month later. To resounding cheers from the delegates, Abdurahman opened his presidential address on a theme of black unity, declaring that by the term *colored* he meant "everyone who was a British subject in South Africa, and who was not a European."[71] Yet in reaffirming commitment to the Cape liberal franchise as the appropriate basis for a united government, the APO was rallying together the black elite and leaving unquestioned the exclusion of the mass of the "uncivilized" from formal politics.

Once the four colonies had drawn up a ratified draft South Africa Act, the focus of the unification issue shifted from South Africa to Britain, where the draft constitution was to be submitted for assent to the imperial Parliament. SANC and the APO each sent three delegates, Indians in Transvaal sent two, one of whom was Mahatma Gandhi, and the Transkeian Territories General Council submitted a petition. The Indians were treated with some suspicion by the others because their basic grievance with white law and custom at this time was that they classified and treated them as natives. It is clear that neither Indians nor Coloreds were considered a distinct race at this time. But despite suspicion, the recognition of a common lot did bring about a degree of solidarity among the various black groups.[72]

The South Africa Act was passed without amendment in 1909, and the new country acquired a constitution which, as chapter 1 argued, was a codification of the scientifically justified Western principle of white supremacy. It also acquired a new prime minister, Louis Botha, whose South African party had a constitution that bound it to "maintain white standards." This maintenance was to be done by protecting white workers from undercutting by black workers, whose "resisting power to capitalist exploitation" was supposedly inferior to that of Europeans.[73]

FROM UNION TO THE NATIONAL PARTY VICTORY, 1910–1948

Domination and Resistance from Union to World War I

In terms of organized political activity, the most significant developments after the return of black groups from London were the attempts to consolidate SANC into a permanent national organization. After its second annual congress in March 1910, SANC decided to concentrate on issues that affected the everyday welfare of Africans (rather than on moral appeals for the franchise) and to accommodate not only the educated elite but also traditional leaders with mass followings. Resolutions concerning railway facilities, pass laws, land purchase for Africans, labor legislation, and so on, were sent to the government when the first session of the South African Parliament met in October 1910.

Africans were not happy with the premiership of Louis Botha, even though he appointed some "liberals" to his cabinet and released Zulu Chief Dinizulu from jail in Natal. Walter Rubusana decided to run for election to the Cape Provincial Council as an independent, arguing that the natives recognized the superiority of the white man and only wanted equal opportunity and an open door. His election to the Tembuland seat was a powerful psychological boost for other Africans, for this was the first time that an African had stood for and won a legislative position in South Africa.[74]

Meanwhile, Abdurahman told delegates to the 1910 APO conference that the organization must concentrate on the "rights and duties of the Colored people of South Africa, as distinguished from the native races." At the same time, he exhorted members to cooperate with Africans to "fight together for the welfare of all the colored people."[75] This distinction between Coloreds as people of mixed race and coloreds as all blacks reflected ongoing ambivalence over questions of identity, over where to draw the boundaries between self and other. On occasion the boundaries were drawn more narrowly than around all people of mixed race. For example, in 1910 some Cape Muslims sought to establish an organization catering exclusively to Cape Muslim interests, an idea attacked by leading Muslim clerics on the grounds that a separate organization for "Malays" would "weaken the political organization of the colored peoples as a whole—the African Political Organization."[76]

As long as white society scarcely differentiated blacks from each other—lumping everyone together under the umbrella term *native* or *colored*—the more inclusive black identity tended to hold sway. But when Afrikaans-speaking whites like Hertzog defined people of mixed race as part of the Afrikaner nation and thus entitled to certain privileges denied to Africans, the attractiveness of black unity as an organizing strategy began to be contested more and more.

While formal political organizations were grappling over which identity to organize their activities around, African mine workers in 1911 went on strike at the Dutoitspan, Voorspoed, and Village Deep mines, as if to prove that their "resisting power to capitalist exploitation" was not inferior to that of white miners. Management readily responded with police and mob violence, imprisoning African strikers under the masters and servants laws.[77] The two pieces of legislation that almost immediately succeeded the end of the strike were prompted by recognition of the power of African resistance to capitalist exploitation, so soon after its presumed weakness.

The Native Labor Regulation Act of 1911 was the more far-reaching of the two acts. By subjecting African workers to criminal sanctions for striking and for breach of labor contracts, the act severely circumscribed the bargaining rights of African mine workers. In addition, all Africans were required to obtain a pass before they could leave their place of residence to seek employment elsewhere, travel from one labor district to another, seek employment in an urban area, take up employment, or leave the area of a mine.[78]

Opposed by the Chamber of Mines but supported by the MWU and the Labor party, the 1911 Mines and Works Act was promulgated to prevent Africans from performing skilled work in the mines. Such work could be performed only by those holding "certificates of competency," and under the terms of the act such certificates were granted to whites only in Transvaal and Orange Free State. Certificates granted to blacks in the Cape and Natal were not valid in the northern provinces.

In farming, persistent demands for legislative and other restrictions in order to make cheap labor available continued after Union. In 1911 the Native Settlement and Squatters Registration Bill was introduced. It aimed to increase the availability of labor on white farms by placing onerous taxes on semi-independent African squatters, while entirely exempting farm laborers in fixed employment from taxation. A clause of the bill also debarred African syndicates from buying land.

The South African Native National Congress—the African National Congress, as it was renamed in 1925—met in January 1912. For the first time, mass-based leaders cooperated enthusiastically with the educated elite on an interregional basis. Although the conference stressed African loyalty to the government, it expressed particular concern about the growing restrictions on access to land for the indigenous population. It also talked about the lot of women, deprecating, in particular, proposed legislation which allowed for the medical examination of prospective female domestic servants on the grounds that it was "not only degrading to the native women, but also a piece of pernicious class legislation."[79]

Delegate John Dube declared that the American leader Booker T. Washington should be the guiding star of ANC policy, a policy of "deep and dutiful respect for rulers whom God has placed over us" and hope that British democratic ideals ultimately would triumph over color prejudice and class tyranny.[80]

"Deep and dutiful respect" did not prevent the squatters' bill from becoming law as the infamous Land Act of 1913. Supported by mineowners, this act restricted the renting of land to Africans in European areas, the system of farming-on-the-half (whereby Africans cultivated and lived on a white landowner's property in exchange for giving up half the harvest), and African landownership. The president of the Chamber of Mines, for example, argued that the act would ensure that "the surplus of young men, instead of squatting on the land in idleness . . . earn their living by working for a wage."[81] Chiefs also were rewarded for persuading their subjects to earn the money for taxes in the mines, and traders encouraged blacks to buy on credit and then pay off their debts by mine work.

Needless to say, the Land Act sparked widespread resistance in the rural areas, where "deep and dutiful respect for rulers" was less common than struggles for autonomy, particularly in Transkei where it fed on long-held grievances about the forced dipping of cattle. Supposedly intended to prevent disease, the dip often killed the animals; peasants saw compulsory dipping as part of a larger scheme to deprive them of their livelihood.

Administered as it was through the council system, cattle dipping became one of the grievances around which popular resentment of the councils crystalized. The government in its broader reaches thus came under attack while the antidipping movements lasted.[82]

Rural people sought by force of argument to defeat the new regulations. A number of protests centered upon the fact that people had not been consulted and the popular will had been ignored. Plans were made to oust councillors from their positions; the plans included petitions, insolence, disrespect, and in some cases threats of violence and death.

Once the initial protests at public meetings had been overruled, a wide range of delaying tactics and passive resistance were practiced. Attempts also were made to outflank the local representatives of state power and appeal for help elsewhere. When they failed to achieve the desired result, new political forums and organizations were formed to represent the popular will.[83]

By November 1914 the main impetus for heightened opposition to dipping came from secret committees seeking more radical solutions. Direct action took the form of threats against, or actual attacks on, loyalists and state employees; it spilled over into raids on vacated trading stores; and in extreme cases it involved preparation for armed attacks on magistracies and the police, whose functions often were performed by local headmen. Opponents of dipping, in effect, turned against those chiefs who had "sold them to the government without consent."[84] Attacks on and opposition to "stooges" clearly are not only "modern" South African phenomena but practices originating with traditional peoples in rural areas.

Violent opposition to dipping was thought to be a form of behavior "learned" from labor disturbances on the Rand in 1913–1914;[85] officials in Pretoria proposed in 1914 to suspend dipping in restive districts. The chief magistrate, however, feared that the native uprising in the Transkei would spread to other areas of South Africa. The Smuts government authorized the mobilization of troops, and the people were eventually quelled. But the threat to the state posed by unrest in the Transkei was to persist for a number of years. Meanwhile, the country prepared for war.

World War I and Its Aftermath

Were it not for the onset of World War I, the South African party probably would have been ousted by the Labor party in the 1915 general election. The SAP's unpopularity was due in part to its forceable suppression of a strike in 1913 on the New Kleinfontein Mine—during the course of which black and white workers cooperated with one another and struck together. The unpopularity also was due to the passage (in response to a general strike called by the South African Federation of Trades in 1914) of the Riotous Assemblies Act, which imposed penalties for picketing and "similar acts designed to interfere with the right of persons to remain in employment when a strike was in progress."[86] As a result of these actions, the Labor party succeeded in securing a majority in the Transvaal Provincial Council with the aid of the votes of white mine workers.

The swing away from the Botha-Smuts government continued in the form of armed rebellion and then open civil war, and the SAP's chances in the 1915 election looked rather slim. But the advent of global war enabled it to stage an election campaign based upon an appeal to English-Afrikaner national unity and thereby soundly to defeat the Labor party. The newly reelected government's insistence in 1915 that the Chamber of Mines recognize white trade unions constituted an attempt to mitigate the hostility of white miners who were traditional Labor party supporters.

Although no recognition of the right to organize extended to blacks, struggles against capitalist exploitation flourished among black workers during the war, particularly those employed in manufacturing. Between 1915 and 1922 the number of industrial establishments on the Rand increased from 862 to 1,763, while the black working class engaged in nonmining activities swelled from 67,111 in 1918 to 92,597 in May 1920.[87] Particularly after the formation of Clements Kadalie's Industrial and Commercial Workers' Union (ICU) in 1918—which by 1927 reached a peak membership of 100,000 members[88]—the incidence of strikes by blacks on the Rand and in the port cities rose dramatically (from twelve in 1914 to forty-seven in 1919 to sixty-six in 1920)[89] for a number of reasons.

First, the decline of subsistence agriculture was so rapid that by 1920 manufacturing and commerce did not employ migrant males; they employed whole families of workers who had little or no ties with the land and no means of subsistence other than the selling of their labor power.[90] This situation affected both whites and blacks, although as a result of the 1913 Land Act blacks were affected more. When inflation began to bite in the middle of 1917, prices spiraled and hardship was widespread, but blacks were affected more deeply because their wages, unlike those of whites who received war bonuses and cost-of-living allowances, remained relatively unchanged. The political atmosphere on the Rand—and, indeed, in most other urban areas in South Africa—became highly charged as blacks began to realize that they could not live on their meager wages:

> The [Natives] have had some unpleasant riots in Johannesburg, which were suppressed by police, into whose methods an enquiry is now being held. There is a sullen feeling of discontent among the Natives all through the Union. They have broken away from their old friends and advisers, and we are within a measurable distance of some very serious trouble.[91]

In 1918 a boycott of mine stores was organized by Shangaan miners on the East Rand, and in June 1918 Johannesburg's sanitary workers struck in support of higher pay. In December 1919 the ICU launched a strike of its mostly Colored members on the Cape Town docks, demanding an end to food exports—which were blamed for food price inflation—and higher wages. In cooperation with the Cape Federation of Labor and the white railway workers' union, the ICU brought 2,000 workers out on strike for fourteen days and succeeded in gaining a minimal increase in wages in 1920.[92] This event helped galvanize all sections of the black working class into militant agitation, including the massive 1920 strike of 71,000 African mine workers.

Two other factors appeared to contribute to the increase in black labor militancy during and immediately after World War I. One was the "demonstration effect" of white worker action. The speed with which the Johannesburg municipality caved in to a municipal engineers' strike in May

1918, which plunged the city into darkness for five successive nights and resulted in a 23 percent pay increase to *all* municipal workers as a result of the action, was an object lesson to black workers on the Rand and precipitated the action taken by black sanitary workers. Major strike movements on the Rand in 1919 and 1920 coincided with a white building workers' strike together with a ballot for a general strike and in February 1920 with a ballot for another white mine workers' strike. The relationship between white and black militance was not lost on employers, particularly mineowners:

> It is possible that if the leaders of White Labor had realised the effect of their actions, South Africa might have had less unrest in the past, and would probably have been saved the spectacle of an organized Native proletariat. How serious this movement may be in the future will appeal to all who give a few moments' consideration to the question, and it is the duty of all—employers and employees alike—to see that they so order their affairs that the country is spared Native uprisings and perhaps years of upheaval.[93]

As Philip Bonner has pointed out, equally as important as the demonstration effect "was a sense of weakening in the power bloc, which black workers felt they would be able to exploit. Certainly the repressive capacities of the state were stretched to the limit at these times."[94]

Against this background of labor militance and industrial unrest, the APO decided in 1919 to launch its own attempt to organize Colored workers, but the Federation of Labor founded by the APO soon collapsed from lack of support. Established craft unions refused to abandon the nonracial Cape Federation of Labor and accused the APO Federation of attempting to divide "the whole working class into separate camps," while unskilled Colored workers flocked to the ICU. Lewis argues that the APO simply was unable to convince workers of its ability to obtain better working conditions and wages for its supporters,[95] but the lack of appeal of an organization built upon an exclusively Colored identity was undoubtedly a factor as well.

Evidence of working-class solidarity with whites, and the fact that the best-organized and most militant group active among black South Africans during the 1920s was the newly founded South African Communist party (SACP), suggest that "class" was a more powerful mobilizing tool than a narrowly constituted ethnicity at this time. Communists initially joined the ICU and tried to reorganize the scattered and diffuse movement into industrial branches.

Yet the sharp resentment of the SACP by ICU leaders, who tended to see the struggle in South Africa in nationalist and anticolonial, rather than class, terms, implies that the idea of black unity had as much appeal as class unity for the black South African working class. Eventually, the SACP was expelled from the ICU and began to establish its own industrial unions and strive by various means to attract Africans to the party. In this regard, the most significant move probably came in 1928, when the SACP announced that its aim was a "black republic" in South Africa as a first stage toward the eventual founding of a workers' republic. That year, three members of the central committee were black, as were many of the SACP's rank-and-file membership. More conciliatory moves also were made toward the ANC, hitherto regarded as a reactionary movement.

Whatever the reasons for it, labor militance, in concert with white economic hardship and the activities of the SACP, contributed to fears about the decline of European civilization and the determination to preserve it by maintaining higher standards of living for the white community. These fears were compounded by an intensification of political struggles in many parts of rural South Africa in the 1920s and by changing forms of rural popular protest. Largely urban-based national and regional political movements, such as the ANC (whose 1919 constitution provided for an Upper House of Chiefs within Congress), the ICU, the SACP, and the Wellington movement, began to organize workers in rural districts and solidify urban/rural bridges. Independent African churches also grew rapidly in some areas.

As an example of this rural resistance, early in 1922 the people of the Herschel district in the eastern Cape realized that, while commodity prices were dropping in the urban areas, they remained static in Herschel. A boycott of shops in the area was organized by 3,000 women "strikers" who manned picket lines, some armed with sticks. In calling themselves strikers, the women were associating themselves with the postwar wave of strike action in the urban areas, particularly on the Rand, where the participation of women in mass movements was a regular occurrence. In 1925, women started a boycott of schools, complaining that teachers were agents of the state and attacking the ideological hold of the "progressives"—that is, of those who wanted to bring civilization to the natives.[96]

As Beinart and Bundy have shown, the targets of mass action increasingly became those who collaborated with the state. Emphasis shifted more and more to attempts to secure local autonomy rather than to protect remaining African rights in a common society.[97] In this regard, the founder of the Wellington movement, Wellington Buthelezi, reflected the thinking of rural people in his message of liberation, which stressed religious and political separatism, black political unity, and rejection of white people and the state. Buthelezi himself was strongly influenced by Garveyism and exhorted the people to have faith in help from American blacks, while urging them not to pay their taxes.[98]

Many rural people were not particularly troubled by the growing emphasis on segregationist policies that all of this protest activity helped inspire, seeing the policies as a step in the direction of greater self-government and local control. The African National Congress and the progressives, however, reacted negatively to the growing political influence of General J. B. M. Hertzog's National party. The 1919 constitution of the ANC, for example, indicated that the aim of the movement was to air African grievances in the present and to work "when the time is right" for the eventual representation of Africans in the government of the country. The support of sympathetic whites in the quest for change also was considered desirable.[99]

Questions of identity and of relations between self and other were, therefore, at the heart of political differences between rural people attracted to Garvey's Pan-Africanism and the urban-based organizations run by the mission-educated elite. The PAC's later split from the ANC was but one more instance of this type of conflict.

Described by Marc de Villiers as "a ferocious effort to preserve what collective security was left"[100] among Europeans, the principles that were to guide government policy toward natives in the 1920s were political control of "radical" chiefs, restriction of black access to skilled employment, rigid separation of black and white workers both socially and economically, and strict control over black movement both to and within the urban areas. These principles were endorsed by the government-appointed Stallard Commission, whose 1921 report concluded that "the Native should only be allowed to enter urban areas which are essentially the white man's creation when he is willing to enter and minister to the needs of the white man, and should depart therefrom when he ceases so to minister."[101]

Numerous pieces of legislation codified these various principles. The Native Affairs Act of 1920 gave to the central government the power to appoint or depose tribal chiefs, the Apprenticeship Act of 1922 allowed unions and management to regulate jointly the training and supply of apprentices and to exclude Africans from the skilled trades in the urban areas, and the 1922 Native Taxation and Development Act forced all adult African males to pay a poll tax of one pound a year and every male occupant of a hut in the Reserves a local tax of ten shillings. The Natives (Urban Areas) Act of 1923 contained a number of clauses: it provided for the accommodation and management of Africans in segregated sections of urban areas and for legal limits on the number of Africans who could remain in the towns, it enabled the prohibition of public gatherings of Africans outside a native residential area, it provided for the forceable removal of "idle and undesirable" Africans to a work or farm colony for up to two years, and it prohibited the transfer of land in urban areas from European to native without official consent.[102]

The SAP's defeat at the polls in 1924 signaled public dissatisfaction not with the postwar legislation designed to preserve European civilization but with Smuts's handling of the Rand Rebellion of 1922. After a sharp fall in the gold price in 1921, the Chamber of Mines announced plans to withdraw the Status Quo Agreement, signed with white unions in 1918, which held constant the ratio of African to white miners. In response to the chamber's plans to retrench an estimated 2,000 white jobs, the MWU called a strike. The walkout that began in the coal mines and spread to the gold fields eventually led to a general strike encompassing 30,000 white workers, under the famous slogan "workers of the world unite for a white South Africa." The government responded with military forces brought from all over South Africa; over 250 people were killed and hundreds more were wounded or imprisoned.[103]

The Rand Rebellion was to be the last major confrontation between capital and white labor in South Africa. As its price for joining hands with the National party of General Hertzog—who claimed in 1919 that Coloreds should be given political and economic, but not social, equality with white Afrikaners, with whom they shared a language, history, and undivided loyalty to South Africa—the Labor party demanded entrenchment of the advantageous position of white workers. In addition to the creation and reservation of employment for whites in industry and the state sector, a series of legislative measures designed to circumscribe the economic advancement of Africans resulted.

The Interwar Years

Once in office, the Pact government (as the alliance of the National and Labor parties was known) introduced three acts which formed the basis of its "civilized labor policy": the Industrial Conciliation Act of 1924, the Wage Act of 1925, and the 1926 Amendment to the Mines and Works Act of 1911. A government circular issued in 1924 defined *civilized labor* as "the labor performed by persons whose standard of living conforms to the standard generally regarded as tolerable from the European standpoint." *Uncivilized labor*, by contrast, was that "rendered by persons whose aim is restricted to the requirements of the necessities of life as understood among barbarous and undeveloped peoples."[104] This circular set an important precedent for a range of practices designed to equate high standards of living for the white community with the defense of European civilization on a barbarous continent.

The Industrial Conciliation Act provided for the registration and regulation of trade unions and for the prevention and settlement of disputes between employers and employees by conciliation. It made no reference to color, but the term *employee* was defined in such a way as to exclude workers whose contract of service or labor was regulated by any native pass laws and regulations. The effect was to deny to pass-bearing Africans the right to belong to registered trade unions and, therefore, from participating in collective bargaining procedures on the same terms as other employees.

The Wage Act of 1925 established a wage board designed to investigate and to recommend the conditions of labor and of wages and other payments for labor. The act applied to all workers and to unorganized industries or to those in which an industrial council (a necessary preliminary to collective bargaining under the terms of the Industrial Conciliation Act) had not been established. Its purpose was to guarantee civilized rates of pay and employment in areas not protected by collective bargaining agreements.[105] Africans could resort to the Wage Act only to determine their wages and other conditions of employment and not for anything else.

The 1926 Amendment to the Mines and Works Act entrenched the job color bar on the mines against challenges to its legality. The Chamber of Mines financed an unsuccessful campaign against the 1926 amendment—the first well-financed campaign against segregation and discrimination measures since Union.[106]

In addition to the above acts, the government reserved certain public sector jobs for whites only and gave preferential treatment to those industries employing a high percentage of "civilized labor." This strategy was specifically aimed at ameliorating the economic position of the poor white and resulted in the dismissal of a large number of blacks from semiskilled and unskilled positions.

A series of measures also were enacted to wipe out forms of resistance to domination already widely practiced and to control movement. The Native Labor Consolidated Taxation Act of 1925 tried to stamp out tax boycotts by making failure to pay native taxes a criminal offense, as did the Native Taxation and Development Act of 1926 which required a taxable African to produce on demand his tax receipt or face criminal charges. The 1932 Native Service Contract Act imposed penalties, including whipping, for breaches of contract, thereby trying to prevent such breaches where masters and servants laws had failed. Restrictions on movement were tightened by the 1927 Native Administration Act, which in addition to creating a separate administration for Africans in the country enabled the government to prevent African entry into any area designated as a pass area. The Natives (Urban Areas) Amendment Act of 1930 imposed curfew regulations on urban townships.

According to the South African Institute for Race Relations (SAIRR), in 1930 there were 42,262 convictions under the pass laws, of which about 39,000 were in Transvaal alone.[107] Yet despite the pass and influx control restrictions and harsh measures pertaining to farm labor, Africans did not accept their lot passively and did not remain in the rural areas. They continued to move to the cities during the interwar years, due to a combination of the continued decomposition of peasant communities and the slightly higher wage rates paid by urban employers. Between 1921 and 1936 the urban African population doubled, demonstrating the lack of state power to restrict access to the towns of those determined to move.[108]

Other noteworthy legislation enacted by the Pact government was the Immorality Act of 1927, which imposed a Unionwide ban on sexual intercourse outside marriage between Europeans and Africans; the Liquor Act of 1928 (an updated version of pre-union prohibition measures), which restricted the serving of liquor to blacks in hotels and licensed restaurants; and the Franchise Laws Amendment Act of 1931, which removed all voting qualifications for whites while retaining the income or property test for black males in the Cape and Natal.

As Hertzog had promised, Coloreds were to be included with whites in the government's civilized labor policy, so that one of the most immediate effects of the Pact victory was that it brought to the fore apparent differences among Coloreds over questions of their identity. The African National Bond (ANB) was formed in 1925 as a self-professed "Colored wing or branch of the Nationalist Party." It aimed to "cultivate a spirit of national pride" in cooperation with whites and rejected the APO's policy of amalgamating the colored races on the grounds of the Coloreds' supposed separate identity. The ANB also urged Coloreds not to despise their Afrikaans heritage and backed the establishment of a separatist Colored church under the Reverend J. H. Forbes.

By the end of 1925, the ANB claimed 6,000 members, in contrast to the APO's 10,000. But when in practice, if not in theory, it became apparent that the civilized labor policy benefited whites almost exclusively, support for the ANB soon evaporated. Combined with the absence of any coherent and reasoned argument by ANB leaders as to what exactly constituted the basis of a separate national or racial identity for Coloreds, Lewis argues that the organization's rapid decline indicated how its existence depended on material rewards rather than on any genuine conviction of the existence of a separate Colored identity.[109]

The APO rejected the civilized labor policy from the start as "nothing but white or European labor" and made black unity the pivot of its efforts to fight the government's legislation. Between 1927 and 1934 the APO launched four conferences of black organizations, attended not only by organized groups such as the ANC, the ICU, the Garveyites, the South African Indian Council, and the Griqua Union but by delegates chosen by a host of black church, welfare, vigilance, and voters' associations throughout the Union and South West Africa.[110] Despite the formation of groups such as the ANB, the Pact government's legislative enactments strengthened a common black identity among all the oppressed peoples. This explains the strong hostility of both the Nationalists and the ANB to the APO's "Non-European Conferences," even though the leading figures rejected proposals to adopt such confrontationist tactics as pass burning and reaffirmed commitment to their established policies of moderate protest and appeal.[111]

In 1934 the South African party of Smuts and the National party of Hertzog fused to form the new United party. This union prompted the followers of D. F. Malan to break with Hertzog and set up a new "purified" National party demanding the total segregation of Coloreds, along with Africans, from whites. This split within Afrikanerdom was not really so surprising, given the differing conceptions of identity held by Hertzog and Malan (discussed in chapter 1). Hertzog and Smuts seemed to make strange bedfellows, as the former's aim of providing separate political representation for white and black clearly went against the prevailing liberal principle of "equal rights for all civilized men" that the latter always espoused. Yet Smuts acquiesced in the passage of several "Native Bills" that Hertzog insisted were necessary in order to fend off a combined black onslaught against white rule.

Appealing increasingly to the principle of trusteeship and to the defense of European civilization, slogans calculated to find sympathetic ears in the League of Nations at the time, Smuts tried to appease Africans to some extent. He stressed the importance of preserving African cultures and traditions (projecting the Glen Grey Act, for example, as a major progressive step since it granted a form of local government to the Transkei) and promised to make more land available for African settlement in return for placing Cape voters on a separate roll.

Appeasement of the League of Nations and Europeans was easier than appeasement of local blacks. Much of the land to be released for Africans "was already well occupied by Natives,"[112] so that the Hertzog-Smuts bills were met with united black opposition throughout the country via the forum of the All-African Convention (AAC) which met in 1935. The AAC rejected the principle of trusteeship as inapplicable to a situation in which whites formed part of the permanent population of a country. It described as "erroneous and misleading" the "common assumption that the South African conception of trusteeship is identical with that evolved and pursued in her colonies by Great Britain."[113] Hertzog's "Native Bills" would "relegate the African people permanently to the position of a child race," would create two nations in South Africa with inevitably clashing interests, and would lead inevitably to unnecessary bitterness and racial strife. In light of this, the AAC argued that "the only way in which the interests of the various races which constitute the South African nation can be safeguarded is by the adoption of a policy of political identity."[114]

The AAC's call for a qualified franchise to achieve its stated objective obviously reflected, as did the appeal for a common identity embracing both white and black, the influence of moderate elites and their ongoing commitment to equal rights for all civilized men. Treating the African people as a "child race" was not the problem; relegating them to that status permanently, instead of letting them develop, was. Within the context of the time, when the public commitment of the dominant to the normal discourse of liberalism was weakening, it was precisely that same liberal discourse that constituted the moderate demands of the oppressed as a threat. The oppressed, in other words, were challenging the discourse of the dominant, not merely echoing it. By appealing to the existing norm of a civilization criterion for the exercise of political rights in a common society, a position consistent with the postulate of identity, the AAC was challenging the emerging norm of separate racial representation that was consistent with a postulate of difference. Within only ten years, all major political organizations in South Africa—both white and black—were to abandon liberal precepts, but for a brief moment in the 1930s when there was the paradoxical situation in which a discourse long used by the dominant to normalize inequality became a major weapon of resistance to change in the hands of the oppressed. As a result, groups such as the AAC were considered an immediate threat, and not because of the strength of "ancestral memories of the black sea pressing against the meagre Afrikaner breastworks."[115]

In 1936 the Representation of Natives Act and the Native Trust and Land Act were promulgated. The former act removed African voters in the Cape from the common roll and instead provided them with three white representatives in Parliament and a Natives' Representatives Council (whose members were partially elected but whose functions were purely advisory) to which to take their grievances. The latter act claimed to settle finally the division of South Africa's land between white and black by defining a number of "released areas" to be acquired for the occupation of Africans. Plots were to be available on a leasehold basis only; Africans were prohibited under any circumstances from buying land outside the Reserves. As previously stated, much of the land to be released was already occupied by Africans anyway.

The Pact government tried to stem African migration to the towns (which persisted despite pass and influx control restrictions) with the Native Laws Amendment Act of 1937. A "foretaste of the apartheid legislation to come,"[116] the act intended to make segregation in the urban areas more effective, to institute greater control over entry of Africans into urban areas, and to provide for the removal from the towns of "surplus" Africans. It also created rural exchanges to assist in the distribution of farm labor and discontinued prohibition of "Kaffir beer" in urban townships (or locations).

The act was defended by Smuts on the grounds that "the proper way to deal with this influx [of Africans into towns] is to shut it off at its source and to say that our towns are full, the requirements are met, we cannot accommodate more natives, and we are not going to accept any more except in limited numbers."[117] With this statement, Smuts indicated his support for Hertzog's labor policies. Yet only five years later he defended a relaxation of the pass laws on the grounds that African urbanization could not be stopped: "You might as well try to sweep the ocean back with a broom."[118] This remarkable about-face cannot be explained without reference to the rapid socioeconomic changes South Africa underwent as a result of the outbreak of World War II, to the activities of urban-based resistance movements, and to the general anticipation of independence for colonized peoples that the war helped engender among the local African leadership as elsewhere.

World War II and Its Aftermath

During the 1930s the ANC had all but collapsed due to internal dissension, disillusionment with liberal politicians who did little to defend African voters in 1935–1936, and a dwindling of popular support. Not until the tumultuous decade of the 1940s did the ANC rise from its lethargy and begin to try to organize a mass movement.

The disruption of the global capitalist economy as a result of World War II led to a rapid expansion of manufacturing and of the size of the urban African population. Moreover, the movement to the towns was becoming an increasingly permanent process, particularly since African women began to join the labor force. The 1939–1940 report of the Native Affairs Commission estimated the number of permanently urbanized Africans to be 750,000. The Broome Commission found that in 1946 nearly one-quarter of Durban's African population could be regarded as permanently urbanized.[119]

The influx of Africans to the cities was accompanied by a resurgence of militancy and an epidemic of strikes, sparked mainly by poverty among urban blacks but also in part by strikes in the copper belt of northern Rhodesia (Zambia) by European and African workers in May 1940. These strikes apparently "aroused the keenest interest and concern among African workers in the Union."[120]

Economic militancy manifested itself in two different types of activity. One type was what Tom Lodge has called "popular subsistence movements," which attempted either to resist increased subsistence costs or to reduce the price of survival.[121] Although not affiliated with any of the organized political groups, these movements were to have a lasting impact on the politics of opposition. The Alexandra bus boycotts of 1940 and 1945, for example, which came in response to attempts to raise bus fares, demonstrated the effectiveness of the economic boycott, a tactic that was to be used again and again in later years.

The Johannesburg squatter movements of 1944 to 1952, which were motivated and sustained by housing shortages on the Rand, not only provided their own housing but also established courts, rudimentary policing, food cooperatives, social services, employment opportunities, and legal advice.[122] So prevalent during the mass protests of the 1980s, what has been called "people's government" or "alternative structures" already enjoyed a long heritage by then.

The second major type of activity was provided by organized African labor. In the period from 1941 to 1949, 1,685,915 African work hours were lost due to strike activity, nearly ten times those lost in the comparable period from 1930 to 1939. During the course of World War II, more than 300 strikes involving over 50,000 blacks took place, as a result of which Africans won wage increases in private industry averaging over 50 percent.[123] Finally spreading to the mines, worker militance culminated in the 1946 strike of 40,000 African mine workers, the first large-scale work stoppage organized by an African labor organization, the African Mine Workers' Union. In addition to the conventional insistence on regular wage increments and cost-of-living allowances, demands centered around abolition of the compound system, the pass laws, and formal tribal divisions in the mines.

For the ANC leadership in Johannesburg, the workers' struggle that was to have the greatest impact on its outlook was that of the African mine workers. Although defeated after one week by the Smuts government, the 1946 strike nevertheless impressed upon the newly founded ANC Youth League (ANCYL), in particular, the potential for collective action and mass support which the movement had systematically failed to exploit.

By 1944, when the ANCYL was founded, a new mood of defiance and self-assertion was clearly evident among Africans in all walks of life. Gerhart has suggested that many blacks experienced a sharpening of race-consciousness during the Italian invasion of Ethiopia in 1935–1936, when the white world stood aside as one of Africa's two independent black states fell to conquest.[124]

The effects in South Africa of nationalist movements on the African continent were readily apparent in the ANCYL's founding manifesto, which opened with a rejection of the long-held assumption that the white race was on a higher plane of achievement in the civilization of the West than the African. Dismissing the long-disseminated view that a belief in the organic unity of human society with nature is "barbaric,"[125] the Youth League described Western individualism as highly destructive. The notion that Europeans were letting the African "develop along his own lines" by acting as trustee was said to be a bluff, designed to mislead the world into thinking that Africans were being helped, when in reality the intent of trusteeship was to make white domination "secure and unassailable."[126]

Rejecting the principle of trusteeship for the principle of self-determination (a move that placed it closer to rural movements than to the existing leadership of the ANC), the ANCYL defined the self as all Africans in the Union of South Africa and its objective as national freedom for the African people. In this regard, it emphasized nation-building via education as an urgent political prerequisite to fighting oppression and reaction. Only by attacking as a united force could Africans escape the kind of defeat that befell their forefathers, who fought European settlers as isolated tribes instead of pooling their resources.

The ANCYL manifesto was a revolutionary document in the sense that it marked the first clear rejection by an organized political movement of the normal claim that Europeans were on a higher plane of civilization than blacks. It ushered in a new phase in the liberation struggle because the rejection of liberal principles implied the futility of demonstrating to Europeans just how far civilization had spread among the natives.

At the same time, the manifesto rejected the Pan-Africanism of Marcus Garvey, which wanted Europeans to "Quit Africa," and embraced instead the African nationalism of Anton Lembede (who died in 1947), a nationalism that displayed clear traces of the Christian-Nationalism espoused by certain Afrikaners. The ANCYL creed, for example, opened with a belief in the "divine destiny of nations," and the four "national groups" in South Africa —Africans, Europeans, Indians, and Coloreds—were said to differ from each other both historically and culturally. The mother country of Indians was supposedly India; the Indians' main contribution to the liberation struggle of the Africans simply was not to impede it. The Coloreds had no motherland— presumably, they were South Africans—and their objective was to organize "a Colored People's National Organization to lead in the struggle of the National Freedom of the Coloreds."[127] This discourse of "divine destiny" and the understanding of national identity as given by culture and history rather than as something freely chosen placed the ANCYL's nationalism closer to that of the Christian-Nationalists than to that of the Pan-Africanists, even though assumptions about genetic inferiority and differentiation within the Bantu race were never accepted as normal by the ANC.

While the ANCYL's African nationalism and rejection of liberalism constituted a break with the traditional ANC leadership, they also marked a certain retreat from the black unity theme of the 1930s. But not all black groups followed the ANCYL in this regard. Reminiscent of the Black Consciousness leader Steve Biko, a young Colored teacher named Ben Kies argued in 1943 that the only way white rulers in South Africa had maintained their dominance for so long was through a highly successful policy of "divide and rule," giving preferential treatment to one black group while oppressing another, in a process of "piecemeal enslavement." "Vicious racial myths" percolated throughout society so that each group felt superior to the other and formed sectional organizations confined to their own group. The solution, Kies argued, was to break down the racial myths, forge national black unity with a mass base, and launch a united struggle against segregation and for full democratic rights.[128] In contrast to the ANCYL's goal of African unity by appeal to an exclusively African history and culture, Kies advocated the building of a broader black nationalism among all those oppressed by the existing system.

Kies and others urged the All-African Convention, which drew most of its support from African teachers in the Ciskei and Transkei (i.e., from the traditional bases of support for black unity), to take the lead in forming a united front against aggression, a call which led to the formation of the Non-European Unity Movement (NEUM) in 1944. The ANC, however, refused to attend the first Unity Conference and never reached any form of agreement with the NEUM despite the efforts of Kies and others. The South African Indian Congress also turned down an invitation to affiliate with the NEUM. By the time World War II ended in 1945, divisions over which national identity to organize resistance around were at the heart of political differences among the oppressed groups and were to shape the nature of struggle throughout the postwar period.

The government's response to these unfolding developments was at first somewhat predictable. In 1941 it took steps to prevent interracial worker organization by passing the Factories, Machinery and Building Work Act, which mandated separate places of work where employees of different races worked in the same room. A year later, it promulgated the War Measures Act, which totally prohibited strikes by African workers and provided for a system of compulsory arbitration. In 1943 a Colored Advisory Council was inaugurated to advise the government on matters pertaining to Colored welfare, a move consistent with the UP's increasing commitment to racial segregation. But after Hertzog's breakaway from Smuts and the latter's increased parliamentary majority following the 1943 election, South Africa's labor control system began to unravel.

Much consideration was given by the newly reelected government to the issue of African trade unions, which, although officially prohibited by the Industrial Conciliation Act, numbered about 120 by the end of the war and represented 158,000 workers.[129] Over opposition from the minister of mines, the minister of labor in 1943 called a conference of representatives of European and African trade union bodies, of African representatives in Parliament, of employers, and of various other interested parties to consider the question of the recognition of African unions. Smuts stated in 1945 that the government had agreed in principle to the registration of trade unions for African workers, but the minister of railways had already (a year earlier) offered facilities to African railway and harbor workers for the organization and recognition of unions similar to those for European workers. In 1947 an amendment to the Industrial Conciliation Act which provided for the recognition of African unions was tabled. It was not clear whether they were to be under the same machinery as for white and Colored unions.[130]

The argument for a policy of facilitating the orderly development of a stable African work force was most fully expressed in the final report of the Native Laws (Fagan) Commission, appointed in 1946 to consider the operation of laws relating to Africans who lived in or near urban areas for industrial purposes other than mining. After much investigation, the Fagan Commission took the view that the African was not to be regarded as a foreigner or a visitor in urban areas and that with industrialization should come the provision of homes and security for African industrial workers. The use of migrant labor also was to be reduced within as narrow limits as possible. The report concluded that, while some measures of separation and of differential, but not discriminatory, legislation might have to be recognized as desirable, the African must be integrated into the industrial development of the country and in local affairs must be accorded some measure of executive authority in his own urban areas.[131]

That the Smuts government accepted the Fagan recommendations is not really surprising since in 1945 it had passed two pieces of legislation consistent with them. One was the National Education Finance Act, which freed African education from its constricting dependence on African taxes. The other was the Workmen's Compensation Act, which brought African farm workers and domestic servants under the provisions of the existing law. The year 1946 saw passage of the Disability Grants Act, which extended to all black disabled workers the same benefits enjoyed by whites; the Unemployment Insurance Act, which encompassed the majority of African industrial workers within its ambit; and the Native (Urban Areas) Amendment Act, which increased the amount of revenue available to municipalities for expenditure on social services for Africans. Provision for recognition of African trade unions, as already mentioned, was tabled in 1947.

Here then was South Africa in the 1940s; almost a carbon copy of itself during the "reform decade" of the 1970s. The Smuts reforms were not indicative of the sudden abandonment of a commitment to white domination—Smuts's insistence that compromise was the best way to "save the position of European civilization in South Africa" demonstrated that clearly.[132] "Give a little in order to keep a lot" was Smuts's implicit motto, as it is now the motto of the National party under de Klerk. Also like de Klerk and like his own liberal predecessors, Smuts was recommitting the government to the postulate of identity, to the notion that some blacks were part of the national self even though the vast majority were inferior and must remain excluded. It would be tempting to see this shift as the effect of Smuts's shedding of Hertzog in 1943 and of his return to his own liberal heritage. But Smuts had moved much closer to Hertzog's position on segregation by 1937. What the Smuts reforms represented was a codification of existing practices—trade unions that already operated were to be recognized, Africans already in the urban areas were to be granted some measure of authority, and so on. In this sense, the reforms were testimony to the power of black resistance and to the ineffectiveness of state control, just as later reforms were; to an implicit acceptance that "the ocean" could not be "swept back with a broom" because decades of legislation designed to prevent unionization and urbanization had clearly failed in their task.

But the Fagan recommendations were not what many of the white electorate wanted to hear. Rejection of the Fagan recommendations was a major plank in the electoral platform of the Christian-Nationalist-inspired National party, which defeated the United party in the 1948 election and achieved a narrow parliamentary majority based upon a minority of votes. As its leaders saw the situation, if African workers were allowed to become completely integrated into the urban economy, nothing would stop them from struggling to gain political power in a common society.

How exactly the National party intended to prevent either integration or political struggle was not always clear at the time. Metaphorically speaking, it was not obvious whether the NP proposed to sweep back the ocean more vigorously, buy a bigger broom, replace the broom with a sea wall, or divert the ocean into rivers and streams. In other words, it was not clear what the word *apartheid* during election campaigns actually meant. But when it became evident that the National party had far more in mind than simply a stricter enforcement of existing legislation, black resistance in a multiplicity of sites was an almost immediate response, as chapter 4 will attempt to demonstrate.

Summary

This chapter began an analysis of the relation between modes of domination and practices of resistance at various social sites within the territorial space known as South Africa. It is indisputable that normal practices of domination in South Africa—such as land dispossession—have been bound up historically with the necessity for mineowners and farmers to acquire and control labor. But only by uncovering a range of black practices of resistance to proletarianization is it possible to understand the particular forms that labor control has taken. In other words, the treatment of black laborers cannot be explained only by reference to the structural constraints imposed by deep-level mining or to the greater militance of whites, for blacks were never an inert and easily manipulable mass. It was their ability to recreate work opportunities outside of the mines and white farms—in traditional agricultural pursuits, in more novel, urban-based occupations such as the hand-laundry business, or in neighboring states—that made labor shortages such a problem in need of solution.

Only when various "benign" enticements, such as widespread alcohol distribution, failed to attract a sufficient labor force did mineowners turn to the state for assistance. Restrictions on landownership and hut taxes were meant to benefit both mineowners and white farmers, and undoubtedly they sped up the disintegration of African peasant communities and the proletarianization of African labor. Yet the more that the state attempted to exert control over black lives, the more resistance it provoked, necessitating greater attempts at control which prompted, in turn, increased and more spectacular acts of defiance. In their striving to retain as much political autonomy as possible, the people in rural areas have resorted to such strategies as tax evasion, boycotts of puppet political structures, demonstrations, and armed rebellion. Those forced off the land often have accepted mine work but then resisted poor pay and working conditions by resorting to smuggling, breach of contract, drunkenness, and strike action. Others have moved to the urban areas in defiance of a panoply of laws intended to restrict their entry and keep them available as labor for white farmers.

Increasingly onerous legislation in South Africa is an effect of black resistance, representing attempts by the state to tighten control over black lives in the face of an evident failure to do so. For a brief moment in the 1940s, a different type of response seemed possible when the Smuts government moved to recognize African urbanization and workers' rights (as well as limited political autonomy) instead of struggling to stamp them out. In the context of a postwar depression, such moves became politically unpopular and were reversed by the National party. But the UP's policies (which were consistent with the postulate of identity) and those of the NP (consistent with the postulate of difference) were in essence two sides of the same coin. Both came in response to black resistance, although they clearly reflected very different understandings of what constitutes appropriate strategy in dealing with the political practices of the "other."

Black resistance to normal modes of domination prior to 1948 thus explains the particular practices of the economic elite as well as the legislative outpourings of the state. Rural-based opposition to the loss of land and local autonomy also embodied and enabled many of the strategies that later became mass-based, such as consumer boycotts and rejection of imposed political institutions. As Scott pointed out in his postulate of the "hidden transcript," localized acts of resistance may have important economic and political effects while sustaining a "culture of resistance" until the time is more conducive to mass action.

While this chapter has argued for the importance of black resistance, it also has sought to explain the historical absence of mass struggle, as well as political struggles among the subjugated, in terms of the uneven effects of normalization. Organized political protest did not challenge the norm of white superiority until the 1940s or the norm of treating non-Western-educated African peoples as barbaric and in need of upliftment. Formal organizations were striving for the assimilation of the civilized into white society, while rural-based social movements, such as Ethiopianism, were struggling for autonomy under the influence of doctrines of black unity and self-help. At the same time, the urban-based movements never treated as normal the idea that Africans would be better off working for whites than they would cultivating their own land.

In resisting domination, the subordinate groups in South Africa, as elsewhere, often have disagreed over the question of what specific demands to make on the dominant. They also have disagreed over the question of what particular identity they should organize their activities around. In South Africa the question of identity perhaps has been more salient for the Coloreds than for any other group, for they have differed over whether to constitute themselves as Afrikaners, as blacks, or as a distinct Colored people. The acceptance by some of an identity imposed from above inevitably has generated conflict with those who argue for embracing a common identity and for the consolidation of a united front among the oppressed.

Finally, this chapter has demonstrated how changing social norms may be reflected within the particular practices of specific resistance movements. The ANCYL took the unprecedented step in 1944 of rejecting the norm of white supremacy at the same time as it embraced the emerging norm of treating South Africa as a country of national groups. This step may have been politically expedient, but it nonetheless undermined the idea of black unity as a way to fight oppression.

NOTES

1. See Scott, *Domination and the Arts of Resistance*, especially chapters 1, 3, 4, and 5.

2. Brewer, *After Soweto: An Unfinished Journey*, p. 5.

3. Whether or not such practices as drunkenness are acts of political resistance or merely social problems is open to interpretation; I would not want to deny that widespread drunkenness can cause problems such as enhanced poverty (when wages are drunk away), domestic violence, and so on. But within the context of a situation, as in South Africa, where alcohol has been bound up with practices of domination (both farmers and mineowners have paid their workers in alcohol; prohibition has been instituted at various times; police have used the excuse of "beer raids" to harass "subversives," to name but a few of these practices), the case can be made that breaking laws related to drinking is a political act.

4. See, for example, Gerhart, *Black Power in South Africa*.

5. Greenberg, *Race and State in Capitalist Development*, pp. 74–75.

6. Quoted in Hahlo and Kahn, *South Africa: The Development of Its Laws and Constitution*, p. 794.

7. Ibid.

8. Ibid., p. 774.

9. See generally, Mbeki, *South Africa: The Peasants' Revolt.*

10. Odendaal, *Black Protest Politics in South Africa*, pp. 5–16.

11. This language appeared in a letter from Stockenstrom to the colonial secretary, Lieutenant Colonel C. Bird, dated June 1822. See du Toit and Giliomee, *Afrikaner Political Thought*, p. 195.

12. Beinart and Bundy, *Hidden Struggles in Rural South Africa*, p. 49.

13. Legassick, "South Africa: Forced Labor, Industrialization, and Racial Differentiation."

14. Shillington, "The Impact of the Diamond Discoveries," p. 103.

15. Bundy, "The Emergence and Decline of a South African Peasantry," pp. 373–76.

16. Sampson, *Black and Gold*, p. 47.

17. Beinart and Bundy, *Hidden Struggles in Rural South Africa*, p. 46.

18. Quoted in Turrell, "Kimberley: Labor and Compounds, 1871–1888," p. 61.

19. Ibid., p. 65.

20. See Lewis, *Between the Wire and the Wall*, pp. 14–15.

21. Quoted in Magubane, *The Political Economy of Race and Class*, p. 93.

22. Beinart and Bundy, *Hidden Struggles in Rural South Africa,* p. 54.

23. See Davenport, "Civil Rights in South Africa, 1910–1960," pp. 11–28.

24. For a discussion of the entire episode, see Beinart and Bundy, *Hidden Struggles in Rural South Africa*, pp. 138–66.

25. Odendaal, *Black Protest Politics in South Africa*, p. 45.

26. Ibid.

27. Beinart and Bundy, *Hidden Struggles in Rural South Africa*, p. 149.

28. Ibid., p. 160.

29. Gerhart, *Black Power in South Africa*, p. 32.

30. See SANC, "Questions Affecting the Natives and Colored People Resident in British South Africa," especially pp. 23–25.

31. Quoted in Ashforth, *The Politics of Official Discourse*, p. 34.

32. See Lewis, *Between the Wire and the Wall*, p. 30.

33. Ibid., p. 34.

34. Odendaal, *Black Protest Politics in South Africa*, p. 89.

35. See Lewis, *Between the Wire and the Wall*, pp. 16–18.

36. Ibid., p. 18.

37. According to Allister Sparks, it was the slaves who invented Afrikaans and taught it to whites, while political prisoners from the Dutch East Indian colonies were the first to write in Afrikaans. See Sparks, *The Mind of South Africa*, pp. 79–80.

38. Quoted in Greenberg, *Race and State in Capitalist Development*, p. 77.

39. Nattrass, *The South African Economy: Its Growth and Change*, p. 70.

40. Odendaal, *Black Protest Politics in South Africa*, pp. 82–86.

41. See Mare and Hamilton, *An Appetite for Power: Buthelezi's Inkatha and South Africa*, pp. 15–18.

42. Odendaal, *Black Protest Politics in South Africa*, p. 68.

43. Quoted in ibid., p. 69.

44. Magubane, *The Political Economy of Race and Class*, p. 77.

45. Hahlo and Kahn, *South Africa: The Development of Its Laws*, p. 795.

46. See Lewis, *Between the Wire and the Wall*, p. 36.

47. Ibid., pp. 36–38.

48. See Ashforth, *The Politics of Official Discourse*, p. 33.

49. See Lewis, *Between the Wire and the Wall*, p. 37.

50. Richardson and van Helten, "Labor in the South African Gold Mining Industry, 1886–1914," pp. 77–98.

51. See Van der Horst, *Native Labor in South Africa*; and Bundy, "The Emergence and Decline of a South African Peasantry."

52. Van Onselen, *Studies in the Social and Economic History of the Witwatersrand*.

53. Ibid.

54. Beinart and Bundy, *Hidden Struggles in Rural South Africa*, pp. 166–90.

55. Nattrass, *The South African Economy: Its Growth and Change*, p. 137.

56. *Southern Africa Report*, August 28, 1987, p. 6.

57. Quoted in Van Onselen, *Studies in the Social and Economic History of the Witwatersrand*, p. 15.

58. Quoted in Bozzoli, *The Political Nature of a Ruling Class: Capital and Ideology in South Africa, 1890–1933*, p. 41.

59. Lipton, *Capitalism and Apartheid*, p. 112.

60. Greenberg, *Race and State in Capitalist Development*, p. 313.

61. Odendaal, *Black Protest Politics in South Africa*, p. 39.

62. Ibid., pp. 25–26.

63. Comaroff, *Body of Power, Spirit of Resistance*, p. 218.

64. Greenberg, *Race and State in Capitalist Development*, p. 164.

65. Richardson and van Helten, "Labor in the South African Gold Mining Industry," p. 88.

66. See Wilson, *Labor in the South African Gold Mines, 1911–1969*.

67. See Schaeffer, "The History of Industrial Legislation as Applied in South Africa with Special Reference to Black Workers," pp. 49–55.

68. See Richardson and van Helten, "Labor in the South African Gold Mining Industry," p. 92.

69. Odendaal, *Black Protest Politics in South Africa*, p. 114.

70. Ibid., pp. 168–80.

71. Quoted in Lewis, *Between the Wire and the Wall*, p. 50.

72. Odendaal, *Black Protest Politics in South Africa*, pp. 197–216.

73. Quoted in Lewis, *Between the Wire and the Wall*, p. 66.

74. Odendaal, *Black Protest Politics in South Africa*, p. 246.

75. Quoted in Lewis, *Between the Wire and the Wall*, pp. 57, 59.

76. Quoted in ibid., p. 58.

77. Greenberg, *Race and State in Capitalist Development*, p. 156.

78. Ehrensaft, "Phases in the Development of South African Capitalism: From Settlement to Crises," p. 74.

79. Quoted in Odendaal, *Black Protest Politics in South Africa*, p. 277.

80. Ibid.

81. Quoted in Lipton, *Capitalism and Apartheid*, pp. 119–20.

82. Beinart and Bundy, *Hidden Struggles in Rural South Africa*, pp. 191–221.

83. Ibid.

84. Quoted in ibid., p. 217.

85. Ibid.

86. Schaeffer, "The History of Industrial Legislation," pp. 49–50.

87. Bonner, "The Transvaal Native Congress, 1917–1920," p. 272.

88. On the ICU, see Sachs, *The Road from Sharpeville*.

89. Magubane, *The Political Economy of Race and Class*, p. 125.

90. Bozzoli, *The Political Nature of a Ruling Class*, p. 181.

91. J. X. Merriman, quoted in Magubane, *The Political Economy of Race and Class*, p. 124.

92. See Lewis, *Between the Wire and the Wall*, p. 101.

93. Quoted in Bozzoli, *The Political Nature of a Ruling Class*, p. 184.

94. Bonner, "The Transvaal Native Congress," p. 290.

95. See Lewis, *Between the Wire and the Wall*, p. 100.

96. On these women's movements, see Beinart and Bundy, *Hidden Struggles in Rural South Africa*, pp. 222–69.

97. Ibid.

98. Ibid.

99. See Karis and Carter, *From Protest to Challenge*, vol. 1, pp. 76–82.

100. de Villiers, *White Tribe Dreaming*, p. 265.

101. Quoted in Magubane, *The Political Economy of Race and Class*, p. 125.

102. Hahlo and Kahn, *South Africa: The Development of Its Laws*.

103. Greenberg, *Race and State in Capitalist Development*, p. 315; and Lipton, *Capitalism and Apartheid*, p. 113.

104. Quoted in Lewis, *Between the Wire and the Wall*, p. 132.

105. Greenberg, *Race and State in Capitalist Development*, p. 316.

106. Lipton, *Capitalism and Apartheid*, p. 113.

107. SAIRR, *Annual Report, 1933* (Johannesburg, 1933), p. 38.

108. Magubane, *The Political Economy of Race and Class*, p. 126.

109. See Lewis, *Between the Wire and the Wall*, pp. 128–47.

110. Ibid., p. 141.

111. Ibid., p. 142.

112. SAIRR, *Annual Report, 1937* (Johannesburg, 1937), p. 15.

113. See Karis and Carter, *From Protest to Challenge*, vol. 2, pp. 31–32.

114. Ibid., p. 32.

115. de Villiers, *White Tribe Dreaming*, p. 276.

116. Ibid., p. 277.

117. Quoted in Magubane, *The Political Economy of Race and Class*, p. 126.

118. Quoted in Lipton, *Capitalism and Apartheid*, p. 21.

119. Magubane, *The Political Economy of Race and Class*, p. 127.

120. SAIRR, *Annual Report, 1940* (Johannesburg, 1940), p. 29.

121. Lodge, *Black Politics in South Africa since 1945*.

122. See Bonner, "The Politics of Black Squatter Movements on the Rand, 1944–1952," pp. 89–115.

123. Burawoy, "The Capitalist State in South Africa: Marxist and Sociological Perspectives on Race and Class," p. 316.

124. See Gerhart, *Black Power in South Africa*, chapter 3.

125. See, for example, Hoernle, "The Concept of the 'Primitive.' "

126. See the transcript of the manifesto in Mandela, *The Struggle Is My Life*, pp. 11–13.

127. Ibid., pp. 19, 26.

128. See Lewis, *Between the Wire and the Wall*, p. 215.

129. SAIRR, *Annual Report, 1945* (Johannesburg, 1945), p. 9.

130. Ibid., 1944–1947.
131. Ibid., 1947, p. 2.
132. See Lewsen, *Voices of Protest,* pp. 210–12.

4

The National Party and the Postulate of Difference: Multiracialism and National Separation

An Afrikaner sociologist, Geoff Cronje, first introduced the term *apartheid* into the lexicon in the 1940s, and an Afrikaner Nationalist government elected in 1948 then adopted it as its governing principle. These two factors have led a number of scholars to attribute the "problem" of South Africa to the National party as representative of Afrikaners; scholars then explain the problem in terms of some characteristic peculiar to Afrikaners themselves. This type of analysis presupposes that South Africa after 1948 differed markedly from South Africa before 1948 and that the essential characteristics of the difference can be identified and explained. Such identification and definition, however, have proved more difficult than expected.

The word *apartheid* means "separation" or "apartness." It is often distinguished from "segregation" in being more systematic and far-reaching, even though *separation* and *segregation* mean virtually the same thing when translated. Sam Nolutshungu has argued, for example, that although the National party did not invent apartheid, since much of the racial legislation it promulgated merely extended and consolidated pre-1948 laws and practices, "it can be credited with insisting more than any of its predecessors on the maintenance of this system and of a more comprehensive, authoritarian, and doctrinaire policy in all these matters, and especially in regard to labor."[1] In this view, apartheid represented less a new system than a redoubled commitment to the existing one; less an example of change than a preservation of stasis. Such a view actually was shared by many South Africans in 1948, who alternatively took the position that the National party was simply more honest about its discriminatory commitments than the UP, or that the NP was dishonest in leading voters to believe that it planned something new when it did not.

This notion of apartheid as a renewed commitment to the status quo before Smuts's wartime reforms is understandable, if ultimately incorrect. It is understandable because much of the postwar legislation issued by the National party had a certain repetitive ring, being no more than a reissuing or restating of laws already on the statute books. As with all previous influx control laws and other measures designed to regulate labor (such as increased police surveillance over all aspects of black lives), postwar legislation can be interpreted as an ongoing attempt by the state to exercise power over blacks in the face of an evident failure to do so. Put simply, new measures of control would not have been necessary had the existing ones been working effectively.

Apartheid has been described as "an imposition of a minority on a majority" and as "legislated segregation,"[2] but these definitions also imply that apartheid is not a post-1948 phenomenon attributable only to Afrikaners. Legislation forcing blacks to carry passes, for example, was instituted during the 1800s in the British-administered provinces of Natal and the Cape at the behest of English mineowners and farmers, not at the behest of Dutch settlers. What then was different about the post-1948 era, other than a refusal to accept that "the ocean" could not be "swept back with a broom"? This chapter argues that apartheid was fundamentally the production of racial and national identities in South Africa, as well as the "foreignization" of a large proportion of the South African population. It differed markedly from its predecessors because it was based on the postulate of difference, not on the postulate of identity.

As stated previously, the postulate of identity does not presuppose equality between self and other; the other is deemed an inferior version of the self. It does, however, hold out the possibility that through "development" or "upliftment" the other can come to resemble the self and thus be considered worthy of integration and eventually assimilation. Both the nonracial Cape franchise and Smuts's reforms, exclusionary as they were in protecting European civilization, were nonetheless consistent with the postulate of identity as they extended limited rights to those blacks who had acquired the necessary traits—such as Christianity and private property—constitutive of the civilized self.

The NP rejected "a policy of integration which must lead eventually to assimilation"[3] because it would supposedly mean "the end of the Western civilization in South Africa, the political eclipse of whites and everything they have built up over a period of more than 300 years."[4] It proposed instead a policy of separation. Its project was not to legislate segregation—dismissed as mere "fencing off" by Malan in 1944[5]—but to legislate difference in a manner consistent with the tenets of Christian-Nationalism. God-given, and thus fixed, cultural/national diversity among different races was supposedly the hallmark of South Africa, a diversity of which cognizance should be taken in the constitution of the state. This discourse was of course racist in that it attributed the so-called inferiority of the non-European nations to biogenetic qualities and in so doing doomed them to permanent exclusion from white society. Consistent with the postulate of difference, blacks were considered inherently alien and so any attempt to assimilate them could lead only to trouble and strife.

Yet the National party, within the global context of the times, could never admit openly to being racist or resort to strategies, such as physical extermination, that in earlier eras, as well as Nazi Germany, the postulate of difference had entailed. What the NP claimed instead was that it was merely allowing blacks to administer their own affairs under white guardianship, a practice consistent with that of colonizers elsewhere. Smuts had long made the same argument to justify earlier practices, an argument rejected by the All-African Convention in 1935 on the grounds that trusteeship could not be applicable to a situation in which whites formed part of the permanent population of a country along with blacks. But in insisting that its policies formally recognized innate cultural differences among the black people themselves, as well as their incipient nationhood, the NP claimed to be much more closely in tune with Western colonial practices than other governments had been.

The NP also sought to fend off challenges to white rule by refiguring the conventional way in which the problem of South Africa was understood. If the issue of a recalcitrant group of white settlers oppressing a single black group is reframed as the difficulty of a plural society holding together hostile or dissociated groups within a common territory,[6] then the political problem shifts from the question of how to empower a majority to how the rights and freedoms of each minority can be guaranteed and protected.[7]

As this chapter will demonstrate, the NP's project required acceptance by the oppressed of a variety of identities imposed upon them from above. First, they were to accept the definition of themselves as Colored, Indian, white, or African although such classifications had little meaning for many. The so-called Coloreds, in particular, were self-defined as Afrikaners, coloreds, blacks, Griqua, Malay, and so on but only rarely as Coloreds. Even the short-lived African National Bond, which in the 1920s had organized political action around the idea of a distinctively Colored nationality, emphasized above all Afrikaans heritage, while its very name suggested an African self-understanding.

Second, black nations were to forget the prevalent association of race with skin color and return to an older understanding of race as synonymous with nation or tribe. This required them to overlook the fact that different national identities for Afrikaners and English-speaking South Africans did not preclude their collapse into a single racial category called "white."

The arbitrary drawing of boundaries between subjects and the racialization (as well as nationalization) of their identities were bound to be contested by some and accepted by others, thus generating both resistance to the NP's practices and struggles among the oppressed over how to overcome domination. Neither type of struggle particularly troubled the government throughout the 1950s. But when the crushing of armed rebellions in 1960 sparked unprecedented global pressure for change, the NP responded with minor concessions and the "gift" of "national" independence for the African races.

All of this is not to suggest that the National party took office with a fully drawn blueprint of future plans from which it methodically worked, or that all of its various strategies were even internally consistent. The NP methodically insisted throughout the 1950s, for example, that guardianship and not independence was what it had in mind for the people under its control. What needs to be considered is the question of why the arbitrary classification of people as different races, tribes, and nations was never accompanied by any systematic set of criteria on which such differentiation was supposedly based. The South African Bureau for Racial Affairs (SABRA), for example, claimed to know that Coloreds formed a distinct group that differed from other communities in that it possessed certain characteristics of a spiritual and traditional nature. Such characteristics, however, were never defined.[8]

One could argue in this regard that the Nationalists were simply lax or that divide-and-rule strategies ultimately rely on brute force, not on reasoned argument, to succeed. Nonetheless, the National party frequently has claimed that its policies are based on knowledge of the other, or "experience,"[9] and that in recognizing cultural difference and granting autonomy on that basis, it is doing for others what the Afrikaner (or European) has demanded for the self. It is these sorts of arguments that suggest why ambiguity and incoherence have been an inescapable element in the National party's classification schemes and not simply an accidental oversight.

The criteria by which the National party might define peoplehood among blacks could not help but be vague and incoherent after 1948 because no universally accepted measure by which white society defined itself was available at the time. As discussed in previous chapters, the hallmarks of civilization shifted continually over time, the meaning of the term *Afrikaner* was often highly contested among so-called Afrikaners themselves, and the notion that English- and Afrikaans-speaking whites formed a single nation was what Afrikaner nationalism had fought in the 1930s. In an important sense, then, the National party could not provide systematic criteria by which to differentiate blacks from each other and from whites because whatever measure was chosen—Christianity, private property, religion, culture, language, even skin color—would result in an inability to differentiate many of the black others from the white self. In other words, the lack of a clearly defined self and the lack of an easily recognizable boundary between self and other were precisely what made ambiguity a political imperative and not a mere oversight.

At the same time, the NP tried to constitute a clearly defined self and demarcated boundary by proceeding from the premise that blacks were innately inferior and alien. Yet such a premise did not allow for the sort of openness to cultural contact that deep knowledge of the other actually would require, that is, that would enable the NP to classify difference in any meaningful way. Struggles against cultural contact (other than in a highly mediated way through the writings of ethnographers and others) were after all what Afrikaner nationalism had involved since the 1920s. It is inherent in the postulate of difference that the supposedly alien other can never really be known; he can only be feared or despised. The frequent claim by white South Africans to "know blacks" usually is based on such dubious evidence as conversations with gardeners, that is, on knowledge drawn from within the context of a highly inegalitarian power relationship. The NP's supposed recognition of cultural and national differences actually is based on ignorance derived from fear, which is again the reason its classification of the unknown other has been arbitrary and inconsistent.

Despite these difficulties (or perhaps because of them), the NP turned to what Foucault calls knowledge-producing apparatuses to normalize its new practices of domination. This chapter shows how struggles over Bantu education have been central to black resistance to domination since 1948, particularly during the era of so-called reform analyzed in chapter 5.

The multiplicity of other forms that resistance took between 1948 and 1973 also is documented here. An ongoing "hidden transcript" of resistance to attempted social and economic control involved such practices as nonpayment of taxes, illegal entry to the towns, illicit beer brewing and sale, and so on. Numerous pieces of legislation issued by the state, such as the Prevention of Illegal Squatting Act of 1951, can be understood only as attempts to stamp out such practices. The sabotage and bombing campaigns of the early 1960s were within the genre of a hidden transcript as the identities of those involved were meant to be kept secret. And in an important sense, the dissemination of Black Consciousness philosophy throughout schools, universities, and other community groups was a hidden transcript of resistance to domination that enabled the mass protests that shook South Africa within a very few years.

After 1948 there was a greater tendency of the oppressed to engage in practices that involved open confrontation and defiance. These included boycotts of buses, whole towns, and puppet structures; the defiance campaign of 1952; the antipass campaign of 1960; and the armed rebellion in Pondoland in 1960. All of these activities were indicative of the failure of the National party's divide-and-rule strategy, but in a sense they were enabled by the postulate of difference on which that very strategy was based. By closing off every avenue of incorporation for civilized blacks into a common society, the NP forced elite blacks to throw in their lot with the oppressed masses in a way scarcely done before, thus inviting mass organization in a way that the old liberal system never had. The NP also brought home the futility of organizing political action around the demonstration to whites of just how far civilization had spread among the natives, for if natives never were to be deemed worthy of inclusion in a common society, then the only answer was to force whites through mass action to relinquish power against their will. Forms of resistance prevalent in rural areas in an earlier era thus came to be the dominant modes of struggle everywhere after 1948.

Apartheid paradoxically provided the social conditions for the mass struggle it was designed to prevent. Black Consciousness and Steve Biko were able to succeed in the 1970s where the Non-European Unity Movement and Ben Kies had failed earlier because common oppression strengthened the production of a common black identity. But this does not mean that struggles among the dominated were not evident and fierce or that the effects of normalization were nonexistent. Mass struggle is not necessarily synonymous with a united front or total uniformity of vision and purpose. Reflective of the uneven effects of normalization, struggles within the ANC over whether to accept the idea of South Africa as a country of nationalities and demand equal rights for all national groups spawned a dissident rival movement, the Pan Africanist Congress (PAC).

The rest of this chapter will consider the various themes discussed above in more detail, beginning with the National party victory in 1948 and concluding just before the era of "reform" that began in 1973.

IMPLEMENTING MULTIRACIALISM: APARTHEID FROM 1948 TO 1959

Although now used widely as a synonym for domination, the term *apartheid* in 1948 was by no means universally understood by South Africans outside of National party circles. For example, the *Torch,* a Colored newspaper, declared that the National party victory in the 1948 election meant only that "segregation will now be called apartheid." The United party, it explained, "prefers the hypocritical method of covering up the knuckle-duster in a silken glove, while the Nationalists approach their victim with an open weapon."[10] The *Torch* therefore represented the view that the "Nats" were basically the same as the UP, only more honest. In contrast, the editor of an annual survey published by the "liberal" South African Institute for

Race Relations (SAIRR) basically accused the NP of pretending to stand for novel policies when in fact it had nothing new in mind:

> The word which has come into general use as a convenient description for this [National party] policy, the word "apartheid," is one which has proved as ambiguous as its predecessor "segregation." It has been interpreted by various speakers who have supported it, and particularly by speakers anxious to commend it to the Non-European public, as being the creation of a new and large Bantu state. Some speakers have referred to it as "Bantustan"—but it is to be compared not with Pakistan, but with Utopia or with Plato's Republic "laid up in the Heavens."
>
> On the territorial side the new policy does not aim at anything more, at most, than implementing the provisions of General Hertzog's Native Trust and Land Act of 1936. What is true in Apartheid is not new and what is new is not true.[11]

At a time when first India and then Pakistan were decolonizing, the word *apartheid* connoted independence, not segregation, although creating a large state called Bantustan was not the National party's intention, in 1948 or thereafter. The editor of the SAIRR's annual, in that regard, was correct. The popular misperception was so great, however, that a Congress on Native Policy held by the Dutch Reformed Churches in Bloemfontein in early 1950 passed a resolution supporting the idea of total territorial segregation. This led D. F. Malan to reiterate quite categorically that such was not his government's intention:

> It is not the policy of our party and it is nowhere to be found in our official declaration of policy. On the contrary, when I was asked in this House on previous occasions whether that was what we were aiming at, when we were accused of aiming at total territorial segregation, I clearly stated . . . that total territorial segregation was impracticable under present conditions in South Africa, where our whole economic structure is, to a large extent, based on Native Labor. It is not practicable and it does not pay any party to endeavor to achieve the impossible.[12]

The dismissal by the SAIRR of NP policy as "nothing new" was less accurate, although understandable in light of party speeches both before and after the election. National party campaigners rejected the Fagan Report and promised instead a return to the 1921 Stallard principles. These principles declared that Africans should be in the white areas only on a temporary basis and for a limited purpose, that they should retain their links with the Reserves to which they must eventually return, and that stricter influx control and the extension of migrant labor to industry would enforce these principles.[13] The minister of mines in August 1948, for example, argued that "there should be a migratory labor policy, not only as it is on the mines but in the country generally."[14]

Yet aside from the extension, rather than reduction, of migrant labor, the National party accepted three of the key principles of Fagan. These were that the South African economy was fully dependent upon black labor; that the natives were in the urban areas to stay, if only for short periods of time; and that at the level of local government they should be given some authority to run their own affairs. Evidence of acceptance of the first premise can be found in the above-quoted speech by Malan; evidence of acceptance of the other two can be found in another NP speech given the same year:

> The biggest problem in connection with Native administration today is the situation in the urban areas. . . . It is admitted that Natives should remain in the urban areas, but it is explicitly stated that they should have no equal political or social or other rights with Europeans. They may live in urban areas, where they cannot have such rights and cannot be regarded as permanent inhabitants. In their own separate residential areas, however, the intention is that they should gradually be given the opportunity of serving their own people. Ultimately it is intended that for every location or Native township there should be a council or councils of Natives, under the guidance of the local authorities or the Department of Native Affairs, who can manage the affairs of the location or of such Native township.[15]

Once the confusion about "Bantustan" had been cleared up, therefore, those who took pronouncements such as the above as evidence of "nothing new" in NP policy were to be forgiven. What seemed in the offing was a synthesis of the policies of the United party circa 1937 and 1945. In the former period, the UP still was trying to control African urbanization; the National party's extension of migrant labor to industry was intended to serve the same purpose. By 1945 the UP recognized the inevitability of the African presence in the towns and began to consider granting some political authority at the local urban as well as rural level, in accordance with the principle of trusteeship; the National party's plans for township councils "under the guidance of the local authorities" was motivated by the same recognition and in accordance with the same principle.

Yet had the NP really proposed "nothing new," it probably would not have stayed long in office. Its innovative plans were revealed, in fact, in the very same speech cited above, which continued as follows:

As far as possible members of the same race or tribe should be housed together so that the tribal relationship can be restored and maintained. On the farms, there is no question of equality. The relationship of master and servant is maintained on the farms and there is no danger that conditions on the farms will develop in the same way as in the cities, where they are working with the Europeans on an equal footing—which gives rise to all kinds of undesirable conditions.[16]

If Africans were working with Europeans on an equal footing, one wonders what had become of the civilized labor policy, designed to prevent precisely that. The major significance of the above quote, however, is that it demonstrates how the National party strategy for white domination involved "retribalizing" Africans—whose tribal identities, if they ever existed, obviously had broken down or they would not have needed to be "restored"—by appealing to the notion of ethnic difference and separating them residentially on that basis.[17] As an indication of government thinking, the quote is also noteworthy for the way in which the speaker treats the terms *race* and *tribe* synonymously. It reflects the Afrikaner nationalist view of racial identity as constituted more by ethnicity (culture, language, religion, and so on) than by skin color, a view that enabled the NP to treat not only African tribes as races but Coloreds and Indians as races as well.

The first prime minister of the ruling National party, D. F. Malan, was the first to separate white from black, a move that affected mainly whites and Coloreds who in urban areas often lived in mixed residential neighborhoods. But he also undertook to separate the black population (who until then had lived together and identified with each other, even though Africans were supposed to live in segregated townships),[18] on the basis of what Afrikaner nationalists claimed were distinctive cultural differences. In this regard the key legislative enactment of the National party was not the Group Areas Act but the Population Registration Act, which purported to offer so-called objective or scientific criteria for differentiating whites from Coloreds, from natives, from Indians.

Prior to 1948 all of South Africa's inhabitants were deemed by whites to belong to one of four groups: natives (or Africans, or Bantu; at times this also meant Colored); Coloreds (a category that included not only those of mixed blood but also Cape Malays, the Khoikhoi, and the San; at times this term simply meant all blacks); Asiatics (which included Chinese and Indians); and Europeans (namely, all those who traced their descent from the European continent and from Great Britain). Since there was no formal system of racial classification, however, the dividing lines between these various groups were always blurred and often shifting. This problem was reflected in the fact that "Colored" in the old Orange River Colony meant simply "black"; that

"Native" as used by SANAC in 1903 meant indigenous peoples as well as those of mixed blood; and that Indians in 1907 complained that they were treated and classified as Africans.

Under the terms of the Population Registration Act of 1950, the South African population was to be classified as white, Colored, native, or Asian (almost always referred to as "Indian"). The shift from "European" to "white" perhaps suggests an increasing association of racial identity with skin color, but, as mentioned before, Afrikaner nationalism tended to think of race as primarily a cultural phenomenon (hence the distinction in the late eighteenth century between the English race and the Afrikaner race). It probably reflected growing Afrikaner attachment to the land (the name, after all, means "people of Africa") and unease with the "colonial" or "alien" connotations of the term *European*.

How was the racial identity of each person to be determined? The act defined a white person as one "who in appearance obviously is, or who is generally accepted as a white person, but does not include a person who, although in appearance obviously a white person, is generally accepted as a colored person." How could someone who was physically "obviously a white person" be "generally accepted as a colored person"? Again, culture or ethnicity—"way of life"—was to be the determining factor, not skin color. But since Coloreds historically have spoken Afrikaans and belonged to Dutch Reformed Churches, classification of numerous "borderline" cases depended upon such nebulous phenomena as the color of a person's cuticles, the identity of the individual's friends, or how much curl was in the hair, all supposedly indicative of highly fixed cultural identities derived from "blood" and "heritage."[19]

A Colored person was simply one "who is not a white person or a Native," a totally negative definition implying that Coloreds were neither self nor other but a nongroup in between. A native was a person "who in fact is or is generally accepted as a member of any aboriginal race or tribe of Africa." Here again, the terms *race* and *tribe* are used synonymously, indicating that their interchangeability in the above speech was no mere coincidence. To decide whether a person was a member of "a race or tribe of Africa," the test of descent or "preponderance of blood" was to be adopted. This meant that a person could be classified as a native even though, for example, she had spent her entire life among Coloreds, had never spoken a native language, and had a husband classified as Colored.[20] But these mitigating factors were irrelevant within the tenets of Christian-National thinking, which treated identity as an inherited trait as opposed to a freely chosen characteristic.

Continual appeals for reclassification and the resort of the Race Classification Board to such "infallible" measures as the "pencil test" in the hair and the "cuticle test" only serve to illustrate the lack of clearly identifiable differences between supposedly distinct cultural groups. The continual resort to appearance criteria was necessitated, in other words, by the similarities in "way of life" across the various groups. Race classification legally inscribed social difference; it did not merely recognize it. As a result, the Population Registration Act was one of the most far-reaching of the National party's legislative innovations.

Yet for all of the attempts at massive social engineering that it entailed, the Population Registration Act was in many ways a confused and internally inconsistent document, reflecting the lack of a clearly defined self in white society. First, the "races" were defined in different ways: white and Colored were defined by skin color, native was defined by country of origin, and Asian was defined by continent of origin. This lack of uniformity reflected the multiple constructions of the self as variously European (defined by continent of origin), English and Afrikaans of Dutch heritage (defined by country of origin), white (defined by skin color), and Afrikaner (defined by both continent and skin color). Any one of these criteria—country, continent, color—could have been applied in a consistent manner to differentiate the population, but consistency was not conducive to the requirements of white domination at the time. Country of origin as a defining hallmark of race would have split the required common identity among whites, continent of origin would have made classification of Coloreds impossible (were they European or African?), and color would have created a single black majority in contradistinction to a white minority. The politics of social diversity as a way to maintain domination thus made inconsistency an imperative, not an oversight.

Second, if the Afrikaners were a distinct nation separate from English speakers, why were they lumped together as white by the very people who insisted on Afrikaner essentialism? Prime Minister Vorster claimed in the late 1960s in reference to these differences that "one could hardly imagine" a country in which there were "sharper clashes in the past between language groups than right here in South Africa."[21] Yet these clashes did not preclude the sinking of difference into a common identity. Identity for whites and difference for blacks were thus encoded within the very wording of the Population Registration Act, even though they were not elevated to the level of political principles until the 1960 republican debate.

Third, there were no less than eight subcategories for the race defined as Colored. In terms of the NP's insistence that natives were a heterogeneous group of nations, it made sense to subclassify them as Sotho, Xhosa, Zulu, Shangaan, and so on—this subclassification scheme was then used later to justify homelands. But if Coloreds were a distinct and homogeneous group, why break them down into Griqua, Cape Malay, and such noncategories as "other Colored"? Were "other Coloreds" supposed to be a distinct nation within the larger racial group, in the same way as Afrikaners or Zulus supposedly were? Presumably not, as there has never been a homeland called Cape Malaysia or a territory designated as Other Coloredland.

What these contradictions and ambiguities highlight is the essentially arbitrary way in which the postulate of identity for whites and difference for blacks was put into actual practice. The National party was not working from a fully drawn blueprint for the future but was muddling along in a context of black resistance to domination and conflicting understandings of identity within white society. These conflicts were particularly evident in the case of Coloreds, who variously had been classified as Afrikaners and natives and who were now a racial nongroup subclassified into other nongroups that were supposed to have a distinct national identity. Socially constructing identity and difference, not merely recognizing them, was the NP's ambitious, if ill-implemented, strategy for maintaining white domination.

The 1950 Group Areas Act generally is considered one of the cornerstones of apartheid for two reasons: (1) because it mandated separate residential areas for the different races, and (2) because it created a legal precedent for forcibly moving people not only from town to country, as before, but from one urban area to the next. Whereas previous Urban Areas Acts had sought to segregate white from African, Group Areas was to segregate all race groups from each other. For the first time, entire urban townships were moved to make way for white settlement, such as the Johannesburg mini-city of Sophiatown which became the Afrikaner suburb of Triomf. Group Areas was one side of the coin, and the 1936 Land Act was the other; together they enshrined in law the forced removal of black people from their land and property.

Group Areas was also significant in a couple of other respects. On the one hand, it recognized that Africans were a permanent feature of urban life, thus implicitly conceding the failure of previous influx control measures. On the other hand, it recognized that racial identities had to be legally constructed and reproduced, for they were either nonexistent or too fragile to survive in mixed residential neighborhoods. The most innovative feature of the Group Areas Act, therefore, was not that it legislated segregation but that it legislated difference.

Apart from repealing the 1946 Unemployment Insurance Act in 1949, the NP, during its first three years in office, was preoccupied with the issue of political representation and social separation, not with labor policy. This preoccupation contrasted with the emphasis during the election campaign on extending migrant labor. In 1948 the Asiatic Land Tenure and Indian Representation Act of 1946 (which gave Indians in Natal and Transvaal representation by three members of Parliament) was repealed. The 1949 Prohibition of Mixed Marriages Act proscribed marriage between whites and

Africans; it did not, however, preclude marriage between Africans and Coloreds. Perhaps to correct the oversight, the Immorality Amendment Act of 1950 extended the existing prohibition on sexual contact between blacks and whites to contact between whites and all others, including Coloreds. Finally in 1950, the National party promulgated the Suppression of Communism Act, which banned the SACP and defined communism as any act likely to promote racial hostility.

At this point, the ANC decided to implement its Programme of Action, adopted at its 1949 annual conference after considerable pressure from the Youth League. Reflecting the ANCYL's conviction that the time was ripe for mass action and noncooperation with the government (as opposed to the old method of deputations and petitions), the Programme of Action indicated that the ANC's ultimate goals were national freedom, political independence, and self-determination. The immediate objective was the abolition of all "differential political institutions." Boycotting these "dummy institutions" and educating people on the question, as well as using tactics such as strikes, civil disobedience, noncooperation, and work stoppages, would provide the means to these ends.[22]

Three major demonstrations were held in urban areas in 1950. The first was a Freedom of Speech Convention, the second was a May Day or Freedom Day demonstration against discrimination, and the last was a National Day of Protest against the new Group Areas Act. The May Day demonstrations involved a one-day work stoppage and were very successful, particularly around Johannesburg, where more than half the African work force stayed at home. This success occurred in spite of a government ban on demonstrations and meetings and of the arrival of thousands of police who opened fire on protesters, killing eighteen people. The National Day of Protest, supported by the South African Indian Congress (SAIC), was also a major success in terms of attracting mass support.[23]

At the same time, a dispute over land and stock going back three or four years erupted in an outbreak of violence in Witzieshoek, on the border of Basutoland (now Lesotho). African peasants had been ordered to cull their stock and cease using watersheds as grazing lands because of the adverse effect on white farming areas nearby. They refused to do so, instead petitioning the minister to appoint a commission of inquiry into their grievances. The government eventually did appoint a commission in November 1950, but it was too late to avoid bloodshed. The "disturbances" in Witzieshoek that month left fourteen Africans shot dead by police and two policemen killed. Many Africans were arrested or imprisoned, and their leaders were deported.[24]

These urban and rural protests did nothing to shake NP commitment to differential political institutions; they may only have strengthened it. In 1951 the Separate Representation of Voters Act removed Colored voters in the Cape from the common roll, in breach of the entrenched clauses in the Act of Union requiring a two-thirds majority to do so. Until a 1968 amendment to the principal act abolished all Colored representation, Coloreds were allotted four (white) representatives in Parliament and two in the Cape Provincial Council. As Lewis has argued, this disenfranchisement, along with the totally arbitrary and offensive definition of certain people as Colored in terms of the Population Registration Act, made organizations catering solely to peculiarly Colored concerns an increasingly anachronistic affair. Apartheid thus forced a sense of common purpose among groups meant to be kept apart, so that the post-1948 period was marked by a growing convergence of interests with African and Indian organizations.[25] At the same time, the major Colored organizations—such as the Colored People's National Union—did not refer to themselves as African (as the old APO had done), did not extend membership to non-Coloreds (as the NEUM continued to do), and organized around the presumption of a particular national identity. Their actions suggest a shift away from the 1930s emphasis on a common black identity and at least a willingness on tactically expedient grounds to work within the dominant terms of social reference.

The NP soon turned to the problem that had plagued previous governments and defied legislative solution, namely, how to control the rate of urbanization when impoverished people were determined to move to the towns. The NP's own policies in a sense exacerbated the unworkability of influx control because the extension of migrant labor to industry meant the breaking up of settled urban families; keeping such families together, in addition to the quest for work, was now a powerful incentive for people to remain in town illegally. In an effort to exert greater control, the government passed the Prevention of Illegal Squatting Act in 1951. This forbade anyone from entering upon any land or building, or any native location or village, without permission.

The effectiveness (or rather lack thereof) of this measure is reflected in a number of subsequent pieces of legislation. The 1956 Natives (Urban Areas) Amendment Act entitled a local authority to order out of an urban area any native whose presence was deemed "detrimental to the maintenance of law and order." The 1957 Native Laws Amendment Act tried to prevent migrant workers in the mines from bringing their wives or other women to stay with them by prohibiting unauthorized entry into a native village or hostel. The 1963 Bantu Laws Amendment Act tried to prevent domestic servants from bringing their husbands or other males to stay with them by prohibiting more than one servant per white household. The 1970 Bantu Laws Amendment Act made the same provision applicable to white farms. And the 1983 Laws on Cooperation and Development Amendment Act tightened controls on the entry to urban areas of the families of qualifying migrants. Not until the scrapping of influx control in the late 1980s did the NP admit the futility of trying to "sweep back the ocean with a broom," although people from independent homelands continue to be subject to passport checks and immigration control.

The government was also forced to turn its attention more systematically to the whole issue of "native administration" when the Natives' Representatives Council (established in 1936) went on strike and open defiance loomed among rural people. As Mbeki has pointed out, the whole council system and its participants had given up hope of sharing in government and were talking loudly of independence. In the beginning, whites had trusted these institutions to turn discontent and aspirations inward, but the annual council sessions had served merely to bring peoples' representatives from all over the country together and enable them to hammer out common demands. Pressure for self-rule, therefore, was coming from inside the Reserves, from African urban ranks, and even more strongly from outside the country, for colonialism everywhere was seen to be on the decline.[26]

The National party had to find a new way to administer natives and devise a system under which Africans appeared to be managing their own affairs. An important sector of African people in the country therefore had to be won over to the government. The NP decided to woo rural chiefs, working on the theory that, if it could keep a firm grip on them, they in turn would swing a threatening club over the heads of the middle-class elements. Together, the chiefs and the middle class would keep the peasantry underfoot. These schemes coincided with swelling popular opposition to the council system and turned most of the peasantry against the government's "hirelings," but the NP did get most of the chiefs to accept its declarations about self-rule and development.[27]

The 1951 Bantu Authorities Act established Bantu Tribal Authorities in place of the Natives' Representatives Council, which was abolished. Instead of an elected umbrella organization representing all Africans, the act instituted subcouncils—based on tribal and ethnic groups—whose members would be largely selected by the government. How this was to promote self-rule was unclear; in response to protests from whites, Malan insisted that even in their own areas natives would remain under European guardianship.[28] What is clear in retrospect is that the act, prompted by rural protest, became part of the larger project of retribalization. Tribal affinities were obviously (and paradoxically) breaking down in rural areas, because of the council system, as well as in urban areas under the impact of industrialization.

What is important to remember about the act, however, is that according to one of its provisions the establishment of Bantu Authorities was not compulsory; they could not be imposed on any rural area without consultation with the people concerned. In practice this simply meant consulting the local chief, whose position was dependent upon an uncritical attitude toward the government. But, as the ANC's Mzala recently suggested, "it is interesting to speculate what the apartheid government would have done had the Bantu Authorities Act been consistently rejected by all the chiefs, as the ANC had suggested."[29]

Rejecting the NP's claim that Bantu Authorities meant self-government and democracy, the ANC, in concert with the South African Indian Congress, decided to respond to all of these various National party initiatives with a more sustained display of popular opposition to the NP's intentions.

The Defiance Campaign of 1952 and Its Effects

At a meeting held at Bloemfontein in December 1951, the ANC and the SAIC decided that unless the government revoked six of its discriminatory laws before February 29, 1952, protest demonstrations to herald further resistance to the government's policies would be held on April 6, 1952. Prime Minister Malan was informed of this decision in a letter in January which referred to "a rising tide of bitterness and tension" among Africans and protested against "legislation that continues to insult and degrade the African people."[30] Malan rejected the demands for repeal of the pass laws, the laws restricting African ownership of cattle, the Bantu Authorities Act, the Group Areas Act, the Separate Representation of Voters Act, and the Suppression of Communism Act. He also warned of severe consequences should the demonstrations take place.

On April 6—the 300th anniversary of van Riebeeck's landing in South Africa—thousands of people all over the country held demonstrations in the form of mass meetings and prayer meetings. As these failed to impress or bother the government, the commencement date for the Defiance Campaign proper was confirmed.

On June 26, 1952, a nationwide civil disobedience campaign against the apartheid system was launched. It was the largest nonviolent resistance movement ever seen in South Africa and the first mass campaign pursued jointly by Africans and Indians. In the months that followed, more than 8,000 blacks, mainly in the urban areas, went to jail for infringing apartheid laws by ignoring pass regulations, entering railway coaches and waiting rooms for "Whites Only," and ignoring curfews.

Despite the newly adopted ANC emphasis on noncooperation, the resisters tried to cooperate as fully as possible with the authorities. Letters were written to the magistrates, warning them of what was going to be done as well as when and where it was going to take place. The names of relevant leaders also were given in advance. Plans often were disrupted by the police as a consequence, and rearrangements were made necessary. Members of the

ANC also adopted a policy of addressing the courts when arrested in the hope of reaching both the government and the white community.[31]

The government appeared beyond the reach of the campaign leaders, twenty of whom were arrested and convicted under the Suppression of Communism Act. The ANC's Chief Albert Luthuli was deposed from his chieftainship in September 1952 for refusing to withdraw from the Defiance Campaign, whereupon the Amakholwa tribe, of which he was the head, refused to elect a new chief on the grounds that the whole tribe were members and supporters of the ANC.[32]

Despite repressive measures, the number of volunteers for the campaign increased progressively from the last days of June until the end of October. News at the beginning of October that India had moved successfully at the United Nations to have South Africa's racial policies debated in the General Assembly gave the leaders a shot in the arm; they called for an intensification of the campaign in response.

Suddenly, in November and December, the number of volunteers for the campaign dropped because of an outbreak of rioting in Port Elizabeth, Johannesburg, Kimberley, and East London. Fears that the police would provoke riots in order to find an excuse to suppress the campaign violently had been voiced even before the campaign started.[33] The ANC reaction to the rioting was therefore to condemn the police as responsible for the violence and to demand an immediate and impartial commission of inquiry. Instead, the government imposed a curfew.

The ANC reacted with the organization of a one-day strike in Port Elizabeth on November 10. The strike was 96 percent successful, but after sporadic violence the Defiance Campaign, harassed by government intimidation and propaganda, expired.

With hindsight it is easy to say that a civil disobedience campaign, by challenging the moral authority of the law in a manner that minimized violence and did not seriously inconvenience the white population, would not represent a strong enough challenge to change government policy. By informing the authorities beforehand of their plans and appealing for white support via courtroom appearances, the ANC and the SAIC can appear both naive and pathetically out of touch with the times, as well as hopelessly wedded to the old methods of deputations and petitions. But such an assessment would be too harsh, for within the global context of the time, the Defiance Campaign seemed likely to be an effective method of achieving meaningful change.

The extent to which the Defiance Campaign actually replicated Gandhi's nonviolent methods in India has generated some debate.[34] The campaign was, nonetheless, clearly influenced by Gandhian tactics, not only in terms of their providing the SAIC with an example to follow, but in terms of their proven success; India (and Pakistan) had become independent in 1947. In an era when the demise of colonialism appeared imminent *without* massive violence, emulating the tactics employed by one of the very first states to be granted its independence made some sense, particularly when that state was using its position within the United Nations to challenge South Africa's discriminatory laws.

At the same time, decolonization was an uneven process and in 1952 had not spread to Africa at all. The European powers were displaying varying degrees of willingness to fight to retain their empires and evidenced not the slightest intention of criticizing racial policies in South Africa that were not much different from those in colonial territories everywhere.

The General Assembly debate on South Africa resulted in the appointment, over South African protest, of a three-member fact-finding commission to study the extent to which racial legislation might affect the maintenance of peace and security in the country. Submitted by Chile, Haiti, and France in October 1953, the commission's report stated that serious discrimination against non-Europeans was contributing to interracial tensions and recommended that the United Nations give all possible moral, intellectual, and material help to South Africa in an endeavor to alleviate its problems.[35] It did not, however, suggest anything stronger should South Africa refuse the help offered to it.

As an original member of the United Nations, South Africa undertook, as a result of these actions, a general obligation under articles 55 and 56 of the UN Charter to promote the human rights of its citizens without regard to race, sex, language, or religion. But sovereignty as then interpreted prevented discussion of internal policies unless a dispute between states or a situation "likely to threaten international peace and sovereignty" was involved.[36] South Africa, as a consequence, was under no external pressure to act on its obligation.

The National party thus was not seriously challenged either internally or externally; nevertheless, the Defiance Campaign did have some political effect. Sustained mass protest, orchestrated and coordinated by an Indian/African alliance, clearly demonstrated the failure of the government's efforts to prevent mass protest by legally constituting distinct racial affinities. In addition, the ANC's paid membership was estimated to rise from 7,000 to 100,000 members—"with many times that number of politically conscious supporters"[37]—*despite* government repression and police strong-arm tactics. Stronger measures, not an admission of defeat, were to be the National party response.

Most obviously motivated by the Defiance Campaign were the 1953 Public Safety and Criminal Law Amendment acts. These were formal successors to Proclamation 276 of 1952, which banned meetings of more than ten Africans without permission and fined anyone who caused Africans to resist or contravene any law. Exceptions to the meetings rule were religious services, sports gatherings, entertainment, weddings, and funerals, hence the highly politicized nature of these events in later years. The Public Safety Act enabled the government to declare a state of emergency in the event that public safety or order was seriously threatened; the Criminal Law Amendment Act totally proscribed opposition to "supposedly" discriminatory laws and raised penalties for acts of defiance.

More subtle responses came in a variety of guises. The 1952 Abolition of Passes and Coordination of Documents Act had significance as more than an example of doublespeak (i.e., abolishing a pass by renaming it a "reference book"). Whereas the old pass was nothing more than a travel permit—an internal visa—the new document contained an identity card prescribed by the Population Registration Act, in which was recorded all information relating to the holder. In form as well as in content, the South African pass became like the American "green card" (which also must be carried by "resident aliens" at all times), revealing how it has functioned to inscribe foreignness in a large proportion of the domestic South African population.

Passed in 1953, the Bantu Education Act transferred education for Africans from the Department of Education to the Bantu Affairs Department and placed the financial burden for schooling on the parents. Whereas education for whites was both free and compulsory up to the age of sixteen, no laws mandated African attendance at school.

After introduction of the act, all African schools, including those run by churches and missions and all private schools had to adopt a common syllabus (quite different from the one for whites) or be deregistered. One objective of the act clearly was to foist on schools, whether they wanted it or not, an inferior type of education designed "to fit the Bantu more effectively for their future occupations,"[38] namely, as unskilled laborers. Economically, the act was intended to ensure that blacks would not be able to compete with whites for better-paying jobs. But since state subsidies to mission schools were also to be progressively eliminated over a four-year period, the act clearly had a political purpose as well.

In introducing the Bantu Education Bill to Parliament, the minister of education defended it by saying:

Native education should be controlled in such a way that it should be in accord with the policy of the State. . . . Good racial relations cannot exist when the education is given under the control of people who create wrong expectations on the part of the Native himself.[39]

"Wrong expectations," presumably, were those that held out the possibility of eventual equality between white and black. Since mission schools historically had fostered feelings of racial inferiority in their black pupils, they hardly seem in retrospect to have been politically subversive institutions. That they were considered so by the NP can perhaps be explained by two factors. First, mission schools traditionally despised heathen and barbaric customs, so driving a wedge mainly between urban and rural Africans, but they also emphasized Christian brotherhood and solidarity. Christianity thus was a detribalizing force because it nurtured nontribal affinities and was feared accordingly.

Second, mission education was conducted in English, not in any of the Bantu languages, so that those exposed to it had a tool for sharing ideas with members of other tribes. Again, the result was to drive a wedge between English and non-English speakers and at the same time to germinate cross-tribal affinities among those equipped with the same language and experiences.

The Bantu Education Act thus was significant in terms of the National party's political strategy of multiracialism because it instituted a system of "mother tongue" as opposed to English-taught education in primary school. It also reorganized syllabi to shift emphasis from common to tribal histories and customs, disseminating in the process a particular truth about black people in South Africa—the supposedly historical basis of their socially constituted identities. As a result, education in South Africa has been an enormously political issue and the focus of much protest activity—not only because it has prevented black economic advancement but because of its role in the larger practice of retribalization.

The year 1953 also saw passage of the Native Labor (Settlement of Disputes) Act. This act explicitly barred Africans from the registered trade unions and provided for them a separate system of native labor committees to be chaired by white labor officers appointed by the minister of labor. Strikes and lockouts by Africans also were prohibited under the terms of the act, presumably to prevent a recurrence of politically motivated strike action such as that at Port Elizabeth in 1952.

The ANC's immediate response to this legislation was to organize a boycott of primary schools in protest against differential education, but this response presented the problem of what to do with children roaming the streets. Since independent schools were illegal, the ANC organized "cultural" clubs, which conducted education under cover of cultural activities. This action was patently illegal too; the government eventually forced these institutions to close down,[40] but some of them managed to last for up to three years.[41]

As a corollary of the Bantu Education Act, the NP introduced the Native Trust and Land Amendment Act of 1954. This introduced a system of ethnic segregation within African townships; that is, Zulus were supposed to live in one area, Xhosas in another, and so on. Consistent with the larger aim of breaking down the common Africanness that existed in urban areas, the act was massively opposed and ultimately never enforced.

Commissioned by the National party in 1950, the report of the Tomlinson Commission was issued in 1954. This report supplemented the underlying premise of Bantu education by providing "scientific" proof for the claim that Africans were not a single homogeneous national group. Finding subgroups that differed by language and "general cultural characteristics," the commission claimed that the role of the state was no longer one of assisting in the transition from barbarism to civilization but of facilitating the development of each separate culture in its own sphere to the highest degree possible. The capacities for each culture to develop, in this view, were racially determined. The task of the educated Bantu was to aid materially in the development of their culture as a whole, rather than to try to assimilate into superior white society.[42]

The Kuyperian language, the presumption of cultural development as something genetically determined, and the rejection of the premise that the barbarous other could ever come to resemble the civilized self were all consistent with the postulate of difference and made the Tomlinson Report an important document in the dissemination of a particular truth about South Africa in coming years. As Tomlinson himself said later, "[T]here hasn't been a single Parliamentary Session since 1956 that this report hasn't been referred to,"[43] although substantive recommendations, such as for the expansion and consolidation of Reserve lands, were never implemented.

Despite its system-supporting thrust, the Tomlinson Report serves to demonstrate the socially constructed and ultimately arbitrary nature of the NP's approach to difference. According to the report, the all-embracing traditional unit in the social organization of Bantu society was the tribe, hence its claim that "culturally, there are points of similarity as well as difference between the various groups and their subgroups." Cultural difference was defined principally in terms of linguistic divisions, of which the commission found four—Nguni, Sotho, Venda, and Shangaan-Tsonga.[44] This understanding of culture was consistent with a particular Afrikaner view that makes language the hallmark of a nation and was in essence a summary of the findings of such disseminators of "truth" as the journal *Bantu Studies*. Containing numerous articles on such "exotica" as rainmaking, initiation rites, folk tales, herbal medicines, witchcraft, and so on, all of which were cultural practices supposedly universal among the Bantu, the journal in the 1920s and 1930s devoted most of its coverage to linguistic differences among the various tribes.[45]

The consistent application to the Bantu of language as a hallmark of nationhood should have resulted in only four homelands, not ten. Why was there a Venda but not a Nguniland? Again, the simple answer is that NP policy operated from the premise that blacks were inherently alien and unassimilable; beyond that, there was no fully drawn blueprint for social engineering that informed particular practices after 1948. The frequent claim to "know" the other is no more than an attempt to justify socially constructed, arbitrary, and highly contested classifications of national difference.

As already mentioned, an immediate effect of the Defiance Campaign and subsequent legislation was a massive growth in ANC membership after 1952. But this growth presented the organization with two different kinds of problems: police informers among the new recruits and the difficulty of maintaining a nationwide network when the top leaders were arrested and banned. To overcome these problems, it devised what became known as the "M-Plan" (after its formulator Nelson Mandela), which was designed to shield the ANC from collapse in the face of government repression. The plan involved the establishment of a cellular network at the grassroots level, which through a hierarchy of middle-level leaders would maintain constant communication with the national executive. Although enjoying only sporadic success at first, the M-Plan nonetheless facilitated the transition to underground politics, as will become apparent later.[46]

The larger outcome of the new legislation was the founding of the Congress Alliance, made up of the executive committees of the ANC, the SAIC, the South African Congress of Democrats (COD), and the South African Colored People's Organization (SACPO). The alliance convened a conference representative of all South African population groups on June 26, 1955, known as the Congress of the People. It was here that the now-famous Freedom Charter was adopted unanimously by the member organizations. Government legislation, therefore, only instilled in various political organizations greater determination to work together.

But toward what end did these organizations work? The famous Freedom Charter, to which the ANC continues to subscribe, identified the people of South Africa as African, European, Indian, and Colored, and under the heading of "All National Groups Shall Have Equal Rights!" declared their aim to be "equal status in the bodies of state, in the courts, and in the schools for all national groups and races." Discussing the significance of the congress beforehand, Chief Luthuli noted how this was "the first time in the history of our multi-racial nation that its people from all walks of life will meet as equals."[47] The state chose, of course, to focus on those aspects of the Freedom Charter considered threatening to the status quo, such as demands for nationalization, but the framing of demands for rights in the dominant terms of multiracialism and multinationalism was indicative of the normality of speaking in such ways. This discourse was important in shaping the nature of the political demands that could emanate from the ranks of the oppressed.

Majority rule, for instance, implies an aggregation of individual wants or preferences within a single entity and is not a demand that can be accommodated within a system built upon group rights.

The same year as the Congress of the People met, the ANC's National Executive Committee held its annual conference. The committee rejected the latest UN report on South Africa; while condemning the country's racial policies, the report declared that their implementation was "slowing down" and was characterized by "gradualism" and "flexibility." This was not to be the last time that the outside world misunderstood what was happening in South Africa, but it provoked the ANC to respond that "by the time the world comes to learn about some aspects of apartheid, its implementation is well ahead in the country."[48]

A year later, in 1956, trouble began in northwest Transvaal when a tribal meeting, pressed by the government to accept Bantu Authorities and education, rejected both in May. Chief Moroamche, who led the meeting, was then deposed by the government and deported to the Transkei in March 1958. Local people refused to pay taxes until Moroamche was restored, and rioting broke out in several villages. More than 200 people were arrested in one incident alone. In the end, the small and scattered nature of the Reserves in Transvaal made it easy for the government to crush and isolate open resistance.[49]

From 1955 to 1958 African women in both urban and rural areas were leading the struggle against passes, extended to them by the euphemistically named Abolition of Passes Act of 1952. Twice they presented themselves in large numbers at the Union Buildings in Pretoria, unsuccessfully demanding a hearing with the prime minister. In early 1957, in the Zeerust area of Transvaal, crowds of women forced the minority that had taken out passbooks to surrender them, and the books were burned. In most cases, these demonstrations were led by ANC members and supporters—hence government officials attributed the Zeerust disturbances to ANC "agitators." The Federation of South African Women (FSAW), however, also organized a major (unsuccessful) protest against the carrying of passes in 1958.

The ANC planned an antipass campaign of its own but was forestalled for ten days by the newly formed Pan Africanist Congress. How that campaign came to be implemented, and what its wide-ranging political effects were, are the topics for discussion of the following section.

IMPLEMENTING NATIONAL SEPARATION: APARTHEID FROM 1959 TO 1973

As a political organization separate from the ANC and its Youth League, the PAC was established in April 1959. Cabled greetings from Kwame

Nkrumah of Ghana and Sekou Toure of Guinea were read out, underscoring the determination of the new group to identify its cause with that of continentwide anticolonial struggles.[50] Much has been made of the fact that PAC founders had tried unsuccessfully a year earlier to seize control of the ANC leadership and to oust communists from the movement.[51] But these actions by the Africanist wing of the ANC (so-called because of its association with the popular Pan-Africanism of Nkrumah and other African leaders) were more than a mere power play. Dissociation from the ANC was triggered by the conviction that the ANC was no longer true to its tradition of African nationalism. The PAC constituted itself as the real representative and embodiment of that tradition, although what was at stake was actually conflicting understandings of the meaning of that tradition for contemporary political struggle.

The basic gripe of those who seceded from the ANC was with the Freedom Charter—the product, they felt, of the ANC's alliances with other congresses—because it was in "irreconcilable conflict" with the movement's 1949 Programme of Action. The clause in the charter that asserted that in South Africa "the land belongs to all who live in it," for example, was said to be a betrayal of African nationalism because it suggested that the land no longer belonged to the indigenous people but was to be shared with Europeans. Just as offensive was the emphasis in the charter on "group rights"; parts of the charter stated that "all national groups shall have equal rights" and that "all national groups shall be protected by law against insults to their race and national pride."[52] The African nationalism of the PAC did not distinguish Africans from Coloreds and sought to consider Indians outside of the "arrogant and opportunist" merchant class as candidates for inclusion as well. The ideal South Africa, the secessionists argued, would guarantee individual rather than minority rights because "we are fighting precisely that group exclusiveness which those who plead for minority rights would like to perpetuate."[53]

The Freedom Charter also was criticized for being a political bluff, promising a utopia around the corner but not indicating how to reach it. It was "utterly useless," argued Potlako Leballo, "to go around shouting empty slogans such as 'the people shall govern,' 'the people shall share,' without identifying the political steps necessary to effect such a government."[54] Leballo suggested that the ANC was being made a tool and a stooge by "interested parties" that were anxious to maintain the status quo. Cited as evidence were the ANC's use of class analysis (which supposedly saw all workers as equally oppressed, whether black or white), its endorsement of group rights, and its acceptance of the normality of multiracialism. PAC President Robert Sobukwe argued that "multiracialism" implied some kind of "democratic apartheid," or "racialism multiplied," and was to be resisted:

Against multi-racialism, we have this objection that the history of South Africa has fostered group prejudices and antagonism, and if we have to maintain the same group exclusiveness, parading under the term of multi-racialism, we shall be transporting to the new Africa those very antagonisms and conflicts. Further, multi-racialism is in fact a pandering to European bigotry and arrogance. It is a method of safe-guarding white interests irrespective of population figures. In that sense it is a complete negation of democracy.[55]

The NP and, to a certain extent, the ANC are still wedded to "democratic apartheid," and the PAC continues to struggle against multiracialism and group rights, as chapter 5 will show. What is historically significant about the PAC is not that it began a tradition of noncollaboration with whites, although this fact is easy to focus on. Its significance lies in the fact that it refused to accept the supposedly fixed yet arbitrary constructions of identity imposed by the National party and proposed instead the adoption of an African identity by all those whose full and only loyalty was to the continent of Africa. It rejected prevailing understandings of identity as given by such fixed traits as place of origin or skin color (as encoded in the Population Registration Act) and substituted the much more voluntarist criterion of loyalty to the land of one's birth and acceptance of the idea of majority rule. Anyone, by this formulation, could be an African if they chose, even white people.

In terms of actual strategy, the PAC criticized the ANC for having no political program of its own and simply reacting to the political program of the government of the day. To break from the action-reaction syndrome, the PAC proposed that Africans should fashion a new society through "positive action," that is, through relentless execution of the 1949 program.

In this regard the PAC devised what it called the "status campaign." The campaign would not have as its main target government legislation but was to consist of boycotting stores and other facilities until black people were treated as customers or with respect as persons. The basic objective was to convince the masses that they must win their own liberation through collective action and determined struggle and must not rely on court cases and negotiations on their behalf by sympathetic whites. In numbers, Africans had bargaining power; once they realized this, they would have greater self-respect and could negotiate with other members of society as equals. The status campaign, therefore, saw the exorcism of feelings of racial inferiority, inculcated over generations, as a necessary first step toward liberation—hence its similarity to the later programs of Black Consciousness.[56]

Had it been carried out, the status campaign would have put onto a nationwide and more systematic footing a form of political protest that

Africans had been using locally for generations; namely, the economic boycott. In this sense, the status campaign was less a new strategy than it was a building upon the historical practices of those outside of the formal, mission-influenced organizations. But no sooner had the status campaign been announced in August 1959 than it was abandoned in favor of a "positive action campaign," the forerunner of the antipass campaign that led to the Sharpeville massacre.

Designed as a mass protest against the pass laws, the positive action campaign seemed to have the government as its main target and thus was not in keeping with stated PAC policy. Its aim, according to PAC activist Philip Kosana, was to put pressure on industrialists who would then appeal to the government to lift the pass laws so that the work force would be able to return to work.[57] The campaign also was not simply a reaction to legislation introduced in 1959—namely, the Promotion of Self-Government Act (which provided for the abolition of African representation in Parliament and the creation of offices of commissioners general to provide the emergent "Bantu national units" with "guidance and control")[58] and the so-called Extension of University Education Act (which segregated tertiary education and restricted entry to the white universities).

To be launched on March 21, 1960, the campaign may have been a cynical move to preempt support for a similar campaign by the ANC (planned for ten days later), but there seems to have been more to it than that. Ngubane has suggested that the idea for the status campaign was abandoned due to the discouragement of Ghanaian leaders to whom the PAC looked for inspiration.[59] This explanation appears plausible in light of the history of connections between black South Africans and liberation movements elsewhere on the continent.

Other developments occurring at the time also seem to have convinced the PAC to shoot for something more spectacular than consumer boycotts. Ghana and Guinea were becoming independent, and Kenyans were forcibly driving Europeans out of East Africa. Anthony Sampson, an editor of the black magazine *Drum* in Johannesburg in the 1950s, has described how the Mau Mau rebellion in Kenya and the transformation of the colonial Gold Coast into independent Ghana reverberated throughout the townships, with small boys calling themselves Jomo (after Kenya's Kenyatta) or Kwame (after Nkrumah, Ghana's first leader).[60] The militant spirit of the youth seemed proof enough that "the masses" were ready for action.[61]

International pressure on South Africa to change its racial policies also seemed to be on the upswing. At a conference held in November 1959, the newly formed All-Africa Trade Union Federation appealed to all African peoples, the international free labor movement, and democratic governments everywhere to use their influence and power to refuse markets for South

African goods. Unions representing seamen and dockworkers were urged to withdraw their services from firms importing or exporting goods to South Africa. Further support for a boycott was given at the second All-Africa People's Conference held in Tunis in January 1960.[62]

The UN General Assembly adopted a resolution on South Africa in November 1959. It expressed deep regret and concern that the Verwoerd government had not yet responded to previous appeals to reconsider policies that impaired the right of all racial groups to enjoy the same fundamental rights and freedoms. The assembly stated its deep conviction that policies that accentuated or sought to preserve racial discrimination were prejudicial to international harmony. The assembly was convinced that the South African government's policies were not simply a matter of domestic jurisdiction but were an international subject of the utmost importance.

The countries that opposed the resolution, not surprisingly, were Britain, France, and Portugal. The United States supported it, the head of its delegation stating that "apartheid is a violation of human rights buttressed and sanctified by law."[63]

Harold Macmillan delivered his famous "winds of change" speech to the South African Parliament in Cape Town on February 3, 1960:

We have seen the awakening of national consciousness in peoples who have for centuries lived in dependence upon some other power. Fifteen years ago this movement spread through Asia. . . . Today the same thing is happening in Africa. The most striking of all the impressions I have formed since I left London a month ago is the strength of this national consciousness. The wind of change is blowing through this continent. Whether we like it or not this growth of national consciousness is a political fact. We must all accept it as a fact. Our national policies must take account of it.[64]

In the same way that the global political climate appeared conducive to the Defiance Campaign in 1952 it also may have seemed hospitable to a positive action campaign in 1960, or at least not hostile to it. Plans for the campaign clearly had been made before Macmillan's speech, but the desire to demonstrate "the strength of this national consciousness" and force national policy to "take account of it" may have boosted the commitment of its organizers. After March 21, 1960, African men were urged to turn themselves in at police stations and court arrest for being without passes.

The "year of African decolonization"—1960—will go down in South African history as the "year of the Sharpeville massacre." It was, more generally, a time when the National party found itself confronted with nationwide, full-scale rebellion, not only throughout the urban townships but in the rural areas as well.

Sharpeville, Pondoland, and After: 1960–1963

In Johannesburg and Pretoria, events were undramatic. Robert Sobukwe, leader of the PAC, was arrested along with a small group of men at the Orlando police station for being without a pass. In Pretoria, six men presented themselves for arrest at the Hercules police station, had their names taken, and were sent away. In other parts of the country, however, events took an ugly turn.

At Sharpeville, an African township near the industrial center of Vereeniging, fifty miles south of Johannesburg, a crowd of 5,000 gathered. A much larger crowd of 20,000 which had gathered at nearby Evaton was dispersed by low-flying Sabre jets, but at Sharpeville the aircraft failed to intimidate people. Police reinforcements were brought in, and by early afternoon 300 police faced the crowd. When a scuffle broke out, which breached the wire fence around the police station, the less experienced officers (perhaps influenced by the memory of the recent deaths of nine policemen attacked and killed while on a liquor raid at nearby Cato Manor) began shooting indiscriminately, killing sixty-nine people and wounding 180 others.[65] The majority of the killed or wounded were shot in the back.

In the days that followed the shootings, Vereeniging was held in the grip of a general strike by the workers of the townships. In the tense atmosphere of the weeks that followed, violence erupted as mass protest hardened into determined resistance; eighty-three black civilians were killed and 365 injured in riots that occurred between March 21 and April 9.[66] After three weeks of mass gatherings, pass burnings, stay-at-home strikes, and arrests and clashes with the police, the government, after a brief suspension of the pass laws, declared a state of emergency and banned the ANC and the PAC.

In the Pondoland area of the Transkei, meanwhile, peasant resistance erupted into a full-scale revolt, resulting in the arrest in 1960 of 4,769 men and women, of whom 2,067 were eventually brought to trial.[67] The government finally suppressed the revolt by bringing in the military to assist the police, by using guns, armored cars, and jets against the unarmed peasants. But it took much longer than three weeks to suppress the revolt. By the time the rebellion was put down, the Pondos had completely smashed the Bantu Authorities system. Members of the Tribal and District Authorities had fled. "People's courts" were dealing with collaborators, and chiefs were in the protective custody of the government.

Although meetings were declared illegal in March 1960, they were held anyway and were attended by thousands of peasants. Because of the location of the meetings, the movement became known as "Intaba" ("the mountain"). At one meeting, the police emerged from the bushes and fired on the crowd, killing eleven people. Afterward, the government announced the appointment of a commission of inquiry, composed of Bantu administration officials, to hear popular grievances.

What the people demanded was withdrawal of the Bantu Authorities and Education acts, representation in Parliament, relief from increased taxes, the abolition of passes, and the removal of Paramount Chief Botha Sigcau. Once again the so-called tribal peasantry, in rejecting all "differential political institutions," demonstrated that government policy was about creating tribal affinities, not recognizing them. These people were no more tribal than those in the towns.

When the commission's response to these demands was deemed unsatisfactory, the Pondos at a meeting on October 25 announced rejection of its report and the continuation of the struggle. They decided not only to stop paying taxes—a historically popular form of protest—but to do something that is often considered a 1980s phenomenon. In protest at the uncooperative attitude adopted by most whites from the nearby town of Bizana, who had been asked to support the struggle, to be civil to Africans, to not report meetings to the police, and to not replace striking workers with scabs, the Pondos determined to boycott the town.[68] For weeks on end, all shops in Bizana were boycotted, bringing the commercial activities of traders to an almost complete standstill.

In urban areas, where the army and police concentration was higher, the struggles engendered by the Sharpeville massacre were short and sharp. In Pondoland, by contrast, resistance lasted several months and assumed a truly mass character that was lacking elsewhere. In addition, the aim of resistance shifted from the alleviation of local grievances to the attainment of basic political ends. The Intaba adopted the full program of the ANC and its allies as embodied in the Freedom Charter (although the demand for civility from whites seemed PAC-inspired), bringing home to the ANC the fact that it needed to link the struggles of peasants with those of workers in the towns.[69]

Within a year of being banned, both the ANC and the PAC moved from strategies of nonviolence to the selective use of force; caught between police repression aimed at destroying the organizations and grassroots pressure in favor of violence, most leaders saw no other choice. A vocal minority, however, opposed the new plan, especially after Chief Albert Luthuli won the Nobel Peace Prize in 1961.[70]

In late 1961 members of the ANC and the SACP, including whites, Coloreds and Indians, formed Umkonto We Sizwe ("spear of the nation" in English) to carry out acts of sabotage. They opened a new phase in the liberation struggle by exploding homemade bombs at economic installations and targets of symbolic political significance, such as government buildings. Umkonto turned to the still-legal South African Congress of Trade Unions (SACTU) to recruit volunteers.

By 1962 at least three distinct underground organizations were active: Umkonto We Sizwe; Poqo ("we stand alone"), which was connected with the PAC; and the National Liberation Committee, another ANC offshoot. Between October and mid-December of 1962, forty-five sabotage attempts were reported, of which thirty-three were successful.[71] By mid-1963 Umkonto alone claimed more than seventy acts of sabotage.[72]

The National party government devoted substantial energy to wiping out these challenges to its authority. The crushing of Poqo proved relatively simple. It took the police nineteen months, however, to crack Umkonto—a testament to the success of the ANC's M-Plan. Finally, after a tip-off thought later to have come from a CIA operative at the American Embassy, the security police in July 1963 captured Umkonto's leaders in Rivonia, a white suburb of Johannesburg.

With the decapitation of the major underground movement, the regime put to an end, at least temporarily, any form of organized resistance within the country, armed or otherwise. As Stephen Davis has pointed out, the next phase of the ANC's liberation struggle, which involved rebuilding the party's shattered underground from external bases, had to await fundamental geopolitical changes in the region.[73] To conclude from all of the government repression, however, that the events of 1960 and thereafter had no or only a fleeting impact on South African politics would be entirely mistaken, for the National party tried in myriad ways to deflect criticism of its policies both at home and abroad.

As discussed in chapter 2, the Sharpeville shootings and ensuing unrest provoked a massive withdrawal of investors' confidence, giving rise to an immediate business slump. That the National party would feel pressured by local capitalists to restore business confidence through granting concessions, rather than resorting to brutality, was what the ANC and others were counting on. In the end the NP did both—granting concessions while banning protest and rounding up political leaders—but it could not resort to brutal repression only because of the way that the international community responded to the domestic upheaval.

The decolonization of Africa, set in motion by the independence of the Sudan in 1956 and Ghana in 1957, provided more than an important stimulus to the 1960 antipass campaign by instilling in South African blacks a renewed sense of efficacy and purpose. It also turned apartheid from a purely domestic concern into an international issue of some magnitude.

At the Pan-African Federation conference that took place at Addis Ababa in June 1960, the decision was made to employ commercial, diplomatic, and political sanctions against South Africa. This boycott was continued by the Organization of African Unity (OAU) upon its formation in 1963, which the same year reiterated a call made by individual African states in 1961 for trade sanctions against South Africa. At least two non-African countries—Indonesia and Kuwait—then severed trade relations and closed their ports and airports to South Africa, bringing to eleven the number of non-African countries to do so.[74] The OAU also called on the United States—then trying to extend its diplomatic influence in Africa at the expense of the Soviet Union—to choose between independent Africa and the colonial powers.

In 1961 the Union of South Africa became a republic and, largely as a result of Nkrumah of Ghana's vociferous opposition to South Africa remaining a member of the British Commonwealth, the country was forced to withdraw.

In April 1960 the UN Security Council passed Resolution 4300 (with Britain and France abstaining), which called for an end to apartheid. In November 1962, UN General Assembly Resolution 1761 called upon members, "separately or collectively, in conformity with the charter" to break diplomatic relations with South Africa, to close ports to South African vessels, to forbid their flag vessels to enter South African ports, to boycott South African trade, and to suspend landing rights for South African aircraft.[75]

With the influx into the United Nations of seventeen new African nations in 1960 as a result of decolonization, Resolution 1761 clearly reflected the growing willingness of Africa to use the United Nations as a weapon to isolate South Africa internationally. Finally, in December 1963, the UN Security Council (with U.S., British, and French support) adopted Resolution 182, which proscribed shipment to South Africa of arms and materials for arms manufacture. Britain and France stated that they would cut off supplies of weapons that could be used for internal suppression but would continue selling equipment that might be needed for defense against external aggression.

In the immediate aftermath of Sharpeville, an anti-South African rally at Trafalgar Square in London drew 12,000 people, and the British Anti-Apartheid Committee organized a boycott of South African goods for the month of March. In the United States, meanwhile, a conference of concerned groups and individuals sponsored by the American Committee on Africa passed a resolution on South Africa. It urged Washington to cease buying gold and strategic raw materials from South Africa if other sources were available, to advocate a consumer boycott of South African goods, to urge dockworkers to refuse to unload these goods, to try to persuade the organizers of the World Trade Fair not to grant South Africa a pavilion, and to attempt to persuade businessmen not to invest in South Africa.

Other than actions taken at the United Nations and a carefully worded statement from Washington that the U.S. State Department hoped that "the African people will be able to obtain redress for legitimate grievances by peaceful means,"[76] South Africa's major trading partners and sources of capital displayed open distaste for punitive measures against the Pretoria regime. Time and again calls for economic sanctions within the United Nations or from the OAU were opposed; if external pressures for change had any influence on the future course of South Africa's policies, it was not from this quarter that they emanated.

In terms of internal responses, the degree of social upheaval that followed Sharpeville brought to the fore differences within white society between those wanting to restore international business confidence via concessions to the protesters and those committed to apartheid, as chapter 2 discussed. The government's initial posture was one of intransigence. When the opposition in Parliament demanded to know what the official response to the State Department's message would be, Prime Minister Verwoerd insisted that once concessions were started in order to retain the friendship of Western countries, reform would not stop until the eventual one-man, one-vote system and the handing over of the country to black domination had been reached. The National party did not, however, hold out against concessions for long.

The path that the National party chose to follow was one that would please business; that is, it tried to appease the protesters, while driving a deeper wedge between urban and rural Africans, and clearly intended to fend off world pressures and domestic protests. After miraculously surviving an assassination attempt against him in May 1960 by David Pratt, a wealthy middle-aged farmer and businessman, Verwoerd announced the packet of concessions that the government had decided to offer. Read on his behalf in Parliament by the minister of finance on May 20, the prime minister's statement contained the following provisions:

- The government had decided to take steps to prevent the incitement from continuing;

- The Department of Bantu Administration would be equipped to enable it, in every city with a large urban Bantu residential area, to supervise the administration of the Bantu through the municipal authorities concerned. While the disturbances had not affected the policy of separate development, they had affected public opinion in such a way that the government would now be able to apply certain aspects of policy that had been under consideration for some time but that previously did not have the necessary support;

- "Practically useless Native Advisory Boards" would be replaced by urban Bantu authorities with limited, though real, authority over

Bantu residential areas, under supervision of the municipalities concerned. They also would have a measure of judicial authority;

- A greatly increased police force within the residential areas had become essential;

- The government intended bringing about certain changes to remove the necessity for liquor raids. At the same time, it would guard against crime, including the illegal liquor trade and the manufacture of dangerous concoctions;

- The government was unable to abandon the reference book or influx control systems—nor could exemptions be considered. The size of the reference book, however, would be reduced, and the Department of Bantu Administration was trying to introduce methods to make this document what it was originally intended to be—a means to facilitate Bantu administration. It aimed to make the system such that the Bantu would experience all the advantages and privileges, instead of the disadvantages, which were never intended;

- The government fixed minimum wages, and any employer was free to increase these. While it was undesirable for the government to exercise compulsion, it wanted to encourage employers to pay more by rationalization of their trades and by improving the productivity of their workers. The government would ensure that the machinery that existed for Bantu workers to negotiate with their employers was implemented to a greater extent;

- In that part of the country where the Colored community was a natural source of labor, it was wrong to allow the Bantu to enter in great numbers. The government's policy for industries in these areas to make the best use of Colored labor would be implemented more strictly;

- The Bantu homelands must be enabled to provide for both their increase in population and the returning flow of Bantu. The government had decided to concentrate immediately on the development of industries on the borders of the Reserves.[77]

Other than the 1961 Urban Bantu Councils Act, which authorized the establishment of elected African councils to advise the government and white authorities on minor local matters, the main legislative enactment of the above proposals in regard to urban Africans was a flurry of amendments to South Africa's panoply of liquor laws. The Liquor Amendment Act of 1961 removed all restrictions on the sale of alcohol to blacks over eighteen years of age and established a National Liquor Board. Amendments to the principal act in 1962 and again in 1963 made it possible for Coloreds and Indians to hold licenses for the sale of liquor in their own group areas, permitted Africans to supply each other (gratis) with alcohol, and declared it no longer illegal for employers to supply free liquor to black employees. The 1962 Bantu Beer Act rendered it no longer an offense for Africans to be in possession of beer, thus removing the necessity for what had become almost daily liquor raids in African townships such as Sharpeville.

Such measures rather effectively managed to kill two birds with one stone. They removed, in a climate of urban unrest, a major source of tension between township residents and the police; and they catered to the interests of commercial farmers by opening up a large domestic market for their processed products. Mineowners, historically the major advocates of prohibition but now anxious for a restoration of order, voiced no opposition to the changes.

Other noteworthy legislation promulgated in the aftermath of Sharpeville was the Native Laws Amendment Act of 1962, which empowered the Bantu Investment Corporation to assist Africans in urban areas or rural townships adjacent to the Reserves (the so-called border areas); the 1963 Rural Colored Areas Act, enabling occupiers of land in Colored areas to elect advisory boards with powers of local self-government; and, in particular, the 1963 Transkei Constitution Act, which granted limited self-government to the 3 million Xhosas in the Transkei territory whether they wanted it or not.

The creation of independent African homelands in South Africa was not motivated simply by a determination to divide and rule, to rid South Africa of the source of its political problems, or to cater to the changing economic interests of particular whites, although these considerations undoubtedly played a part. As Mbeki has argued, the government hoped that, by advertising its "gift" of self-government to Africans, it would silence world censure of its policies and slow down the surge of an inclusive African nationalism in the rural areas.[78]

Nor was separate development aimed only at deflating pressure from the United Nations and critics in Europe and the United States, as Gerhart has suggested.[79] Even before Sharpeville, after Harold Macmillan made his "winds of change" speech to the South African Parliament, the grand architect of separate development clearly indicated that he viewed his policy as a way to gain friends and influence people on the rest of the continent. At the launching of the Transkei on its path to "independence" in 1963, Verwoerd stated again that "in the light of the pressures being exerted on SA [South Africa], there is no doubt that eventually this will have to be done, thereby buying for the white man his freedom and right to govern himself."[80] In the same year, Verwoerd proposed the idea of a multiracial common market in southern Africa in which all member-nations would cooperate to their mutual benefit. The fact that these moves were branded later as deliberate attempts at domination of all Africans—politically at home and economically in the rest of the region—was a clear indication that separate development could not be sold. But the attempt to sell it was nonetheless induced by widespread political unrest in South Africa in 1960.

Had the homelands been granted a genuine form of local autonomy, they might not have generated the ire that they obviously did. The PAC, for example, reacted to the activities of homeland leaders by drawing a distinction between the geographic tribalism of Kaiser Matanzima of the Transkei and the political tribalism of KwaZulu Chief Gatsha Buthelezi. The first, according to PAC President Robert Sobukwe, consolidated the rural population—and nothing more—whereas the latter tried to win support in urban areas, thus weakening unity of purpose among urban blacks. In other words, Sobukwe drew a distinction between those claiming to speak only for rural people in their demands for autonomy and those trying to break up a sense of common African identity by appeal to such concepts as "Zuluness." Hence, harsher criticism was meted out to Buthelezi than to his other Bantustan colleagues.[81]

In reality, the homelands were never even self-governing, let alone independent. The Transkei Constitution Act of 1963, for example, made the sixty-four chiefs in the Legislative Assembly responsible to the government of South Africa, not to the Transkeian voters, because their appointments had to be approved by the state president. Only forty-five members of the assembly were elected. It had no power over defense, police, foreign affairs, immigration, communications, currency, or customs. Any piece of legislation passed by the Legislative Assembly could be vetoed by the republic's government. Mbeki described Transkeian self-government as "sleight of hand," "fraud," and "toy telephones."[82]

Absence of real power, therefore, contributed to the lack of legitimacy of homeland institutions, but even if they had had any real power, it is doubtful whether rural people would have accepted them. Built as they were upon the sands of a tribal affinity which did not reflect people's self-understanding, the homelands could not appeal to a people who had fought for eleven months to destroy Bantu Authorities and education and who did not see themselves as citizens of "foreign states."

Between Concession and Reform: 1963–1973

Having smashed organized political opposition, the government attempted yet again to freeze and even curb the growth of the number of Africans who qualified to be in the urban areas. Two Bantu Laws Amendment Acts were passed in 1963 and 1964. The former tightened the provisions of the Natives (Urban Areas) Act (amended in 1945) by prohibiting Africans living in servants' quarters from sharing their quarters with any other African. It also disallowed occupation by more than five Africans of land or premises in the white parts of town without government permission, and it stated that any "undesirable" African could be summarily ejected from an urban location. The latter proscribed all trading by Africans outside the Reserves and townships, forced unemployed Africans to pay the costs of their own removal from urban areas, mandated registration of all new service contracts, and rendered it an offense for anyone other than a local authority to sell Bantu beer.

Manufacturing capital vociferously opposed both of the above measures. In 1963 a combined memorandum was submitted to the Department of Labor by some of the largest employers' organizations in the country—the Association of Chambers of Commerce, the Federated Chamber of Industries, the Steel and Engineering Industries' Federation, the National Federation of Building Trade Employers, and the Motor Industry Employers' Association. The memorandum severely criticized legislation seen as designed to give government sweeping powers of control over the movement of labor and the presence of Africans in the urban areas. The lack of provision for consultation with employers was also deplored, as was the undermining of the security of residence of urbanized Africans.[83]

A year later, these same organizations were joined by the Trades Union Congress of South Africa (TUCSA), the African Chamber of Commerce, and others in a collective appeal that "restrictions on the mobility of labor should be progressively relaxed in the interests of economic growth."[84] The government, however, remained intransigent; the deputy minister of labor in 1964 reiterated that:

> The entire basis of the presence of the Bantu in the White areas rests on the labor he performs. . . . We say very clearly to the Bantu in the whole of South Africa, "You may be in the White areas in order to come and work there, but not to vote for Parliament there. . . . If you misbehave as laborers, if you are unworthy laborers, you cannot remain here."[85]

The 1967 Physical Planning Act designated certain controlled areas within which no new industrial development involving the use of African labor might in the future be undertaken without the approval of the minister, and it placed limitations on the number of Africans who could be employed in a trade in the metropolitan areas. A year later, the Community Development Amendment Act gave the minister blanket power to prohibit the issuing of trading licenses in a group area where development had been frozen. These measures had very little impact on the pace of African urbanization, but they did reflect the government's determination to channel industrial development away from white areas and toward the homelands.

To prevent political organization across racial lines, the National party in 1968 issued the Prohibition of Political Interference Act, which made it illegal to (1) belong to a racially mixed political party, (2) assist a political party of another racial group, (3) address any meeting to further the interests of a political party or candidate from another racial group, and (4) receive money from outside South Africa to further the interests of such a candidate or party.[86] The act clearly was aimed at the Progressive Federal party (PFP), as the only South African political party then in existence with a nonracial membership.

The NP in 1968 established separate Colored and Indian councils with purely advisory functions. These were to prove unworkable. Rather than being abolished, however, they were in effect converted into elected chambers in the new three-chamber Parliament established in 1983. Bophutha-Tswana and Venda were granted "self-government" in 1971.

Although no organized opposition in the country existed to protest this legislation, all resistance had not ceased. With regard to the ANC, for example, Oliver Tambo's executive committee decided in 1967 to initiate joint military operations with Joshua Nkomo's Zimbabwe African People's Union (ZAPU) in Rhodesia. In 1968 Portuguese troops ambushed twelve PAC men on their way through Mozambique to South Africa. In 1969 the ANC party conference mandated reconstruction of the party's shattered underground, with new attention paid to South Africa's black youth. Over the next few years, the ANC began the slow process of quietly reconstructing an internal network while waiting for more states in the region to achieve independence from colonial rule.[87]

The emergence of the South African Students' Organization (SASO) in 1969 was also, according to Mzala, a manifestation of the desire among university students to fill the political gap that the banning of all major opposition groups had opened up. By the beginning of the 1970s, SASO had increased rapidly its membership and had been accepted as a relevant liberation group, although its *modus operandi* and stated objectives were very different from those at least of the ANC, then trying to appeal for youthful support. Rejecting all value systems that sought to make the black person a foreigner in the land of his birth and negate his basic human dignity, SASO insisted that black people should build up their own value systems and see themselves as self-defined and not as defined by others. Through a reclaiming of black history and achievements, SASO sought to build up a pride among black people in themselves, their achievements, their community, and their history.[88]

The Black Consciousness philosophy espoused by SASO easily can be dismissed as "nonpolitical" if one takes a narrow view of politics as merely the organized defense and promotion of certain rights. But within the context of South Africa in the late 1960s, the doctrine of Black Consciousness was the most radically subversive political discourse that the National party had yet encountered. Black Consciousness rejected all of the various elements on which the defense of white domination stood: the postulate of difference and the policy of separate development (which made blacks aliens and inferior and thus denied their basic humanness), socially constructed and arbitrary classifications of black people (which made them defined by others rather than by themselves), and the production of certain truths about people's identities and histories through such mechanisms as Bantu education (which did not enable black people to develop a sense of pride in themselves or their achievements). It was the dissemination of Black Consciousness thinking throughout schools, universities, and other community groups that in an important sense was a hidden transcript of resistance to domination that enabled the mass protests which shook South Africa within a very few years.

Here then was South Africa at the beginning of the 1970s: run by a government committed to separate development and troubled little by either organized political opposition outside of educational institutions or by external pressure. By the end of the decade, however, that same government had instituted all manner of socioeconomic reforms, as rapidly and as surprisingly as the United party had changed its policies between 1943 and 1947. It did not take a war to push South Africa along the path of reform a second time, but it did, as before, require a combination of global political changes and localized resistance to get the government moving. Chapter 5 is devoted to explaining the National party "reforms" of the past few years.

Summary

This chapter has looked at how the post-1948 South African system of domination (up to the era of "reform" that began in 1973) differed from the previous one and what sorts of struggles that new system engendered. It began by suggesting that those who thought apartheid represented less a new system than a redoubled commitment to the existing one were to be forgiven, because much of the postwar legislation issued by the National party was no more than a reissuing or restating of laws already on the statute books. As with all previous influx control laws and other measures designed to regulate labor, postwar legislation can be interpreted as an ongoing attempt by the state to exercise power over blacks in the face of an evident failure to do so; new measures of control would not have been necessary had the existing ones been working effectively.

At the same time, it is doubtful whether the National party would have remained long in office had it really offered nothing new. Not synonymous with white domination, which is an enduring and structural characteristic of the South African situation, apartheid refers to a historically contingent set of political practices by which that same domination has been effected and preserved. It differed markedly from its predecessors in the sense that it was based on the postulate of difference and not on the postulate of identity.

Rejecting a policy of integration in favor of separation, the National party's project was not to legislate segregation but to legislate difference in a manner supposedly consistent with the tenets of Christian-Nationalism. God-given, and thus fixed, cultural/national diversity among different races was supposedly a hallmark of South Africa, a diversity of which cognizance should be taken in the constitution of the state. Consistent with the postulate of difference, blacks were considered inherently alien and so any attempt to assimilate them could lead only to trouble and strife.

Had multiracialism been simply the recognition by the state of existing social differences, it might have escaped complicity in the perpetuation of white domination. The problem was the arbitrary and inconsistent construction of social difference as racial in order to separate the population on that basis. Working against the historical production of a common black identity as well as against more localized affinities such as those of the Griqua (who became a Colored subgroup), the Tshidi (who became Tswana), and the Mfengu (who became Xhosa), the NP relied on Bantu education for the success of its project. Black schools were to write the past and present of South Africa in multiracial terms so as to strengthen the identification of blacks with the group to which they had been arbitrarily assigned. This policy explains the highly politicized and contested nature of black education since the Bantu Education Act of 1953.

Resistance to the National party during the period covered in this chapter was most widespread and national in scope in 1960; it was then that urban- and rural-based movements simultaneously engaged in armed rebellion. Occurring within the context of African decolonization and independence, this resistance provoked an unprecedented amount of global pressure on South Africa in the form of capital flight, UN resolutions, and economic boycotts. As a response to demands for autonomy and self-determination, the homelands policy was totally inadequate, but territorial separate development was nonetheless an attempt by the National party to appease Africans everywhere.

Organized political resistance to apartheid all but ceased after 1964—testimony indeed to the repressive capacities of the state at this time. But rather than considering this period as one in which all resistance vanished, this chapter has argued for recognition of the continued workings of a hidden transcript. As a movement that contributed to the mass protests of later years, the philosophy of Black Consciousness was radically subversive for a number of reasons. First, it called into question the norm of considering South Africa as a country of nationalities as opposed to a single country made up of peoples of different origins. As had the Pan Africanist Congress, Black Consciousness tried to reestablish the once prevalent norm of black unity (as opposed to an interracial alliance) as the way to fight oppression. Second, Black Consciousness rejected all approaches to difference that treated blacks as foreign and inferior to whites. Most obviously, it refused the idea of homelands, but it also delegitimized the particular truths about people's identities and histories disseminated throughout South African schools and universities. Only by the voluntary adoption of a common black identity and reclamation of a doctrine of self-affirmation could the victims of oppression hope to improve their lot.

As in earlier eras, the policies of the state after 1948 cannot be understood without reference to a range of practices of resistance to domination. But the subordinated continued to struggle among themselves over what to demand, how to demand it, and in whose name (i.e., by appeal to which identity) the demands should be made. Differences among the ANC, the PAC, and Black Consciousness may have made the emergence of a mass unity front impossible. But they are rooted, nonetheless, in fundamentally political considerations about the nature of the self and appropriate relations between the self and others.

NOTES

1. Nolutshungu, *South Africa in Africa: A Study of Ideology and Foreign Policy*, pp. 375–76.

2. Motlhabi, *The Theory and Practice of Black Resistance*, pp. 3–5.

3. See the speech by Paul Sauer in Lewsen, *Voices of Protest*, p. 284.

4. M. C. de Wet Nel, 1960, quoted in Giliomee and Schlemmer, *From Apartheid to Nation-Building*, p. 42.

5. Ibid., chapter 2.

6. A large academic literature is devoted to consideration of plural societies; for a good overview, see Greenberg, *Race and State in Capitalist Development*, pp. 16–18.

7. See *Africa Report* (March/April 1986), pp. 69–71.

8. See Lewis, *Between the Wire and the Wall*, p. 265.

9. In a recent article on Afrikaner nationalism, Saul Dubow discusses the three major concepts invoked historically to justify apartheid: scripture, science, and experience. See Dubow, "Afrikaner Nationalism, Apartheid, and the Conceptualization of 'Race.' "

10. Quoted in Lewis, *Between the Wire and the Wall*, p. 258.

11. SAIRR, *Annual Report, 1947–1948* (Johannesburg, 1948), p. 2.

12. Quoted in SAIRR, *Annual Report, 1949–1950* (Johannesburg, 1950), p. 2.

13. Lipton, *Capitalism and Apartheid*, p. 22.

14. Quoted in SAIRR, *Annual Report, 1947–1948*, p. 49.

15. D. Jansen, quoted in SAIRR, *Annual Report, 1949–1950*, p. 2.

16. Ibid., p. 3.

17. Although the implementation of such a policy may have been new, the idea for it was not; the Afrikaner Broederbond as early as 1933 apparently envisaged settling different

African tribes in separate areas. See Giliomee and Schlemmer, *From Apartheid to Nation-Building*, p. 45.

18. Motlhabi, *The Theory and Practice of Black Resistance*, p. 9.

19. For a discussion of the "pencil test," the "blue bum test," the "eyelid test," and other equally ludicrous means for differentiating whites from Coloreds, see Beresford, "Tragicomedies of Apartheid Bigotry," p. 11.

20. On the Population Registration Act, see Hahlo and Kahn, *South Africa: The Development of Its Laws*, pp. 795–97.

21. Quoted in Geyser, *B. J. Vorster*, p. 75.

22. Motlhabi, *The Theory and Practice of Black Resistance*, p. 44.

23. Ibid.

24. See Mbeki, *South Africa: The Peasants' Revolt*, chapter 9.

25. See Lewis, *Between the Wire and the Wall*, p. 262.

26. See Mbeki, *South Africa: The Peasants' Revolt*, chapter 3.

27. Ibid., chapters 3 and 8.

28. SAIRR, *Annual Survey of Race Relations in South Africa, 1951* (Johannesburg, 1951), p. 24.

29. Mzala, *Gatsha Buthelezi: Chief with a Double Agenda*, p. 53.

30. Quoted in Muller, *Five Hundred Years: A History of South Africa*, p. 433.

31. Motlhabi, *The Theory and Practice of Black Resistance*, p. 57.

32. See Mzala, *Gatsha Buthelezi*, pp. 55–56.

33. Motlhabi, *The Theory and Practice of Black Resistance*, p. 62.

34. Fatima Meer, for example, sees the Defiance Campaign as simply passive resistance and therefore similar to Gandhi's method and the method adopted by South African Indians. Oliver Tambo, on the other hand, has differentiated the "aggressive pressure" of the Defiance Campaign from the "passive reaction to oppressive policies" of Gandhi's strategy. See Meer, "African Nationalism: Some Inhibiting Facts"; and Tambo, "Passive Resistance in South Africa."

35. SAIRR, *Annual Survey of Race Relations in South Africa, 1952–1953* (Johannesburg, 1953).

36. See McHenry, "The United Nations and Decolonization," pp. 4–10.

37. Walshe, *The Rise of African Nationalism in South Africa*, p. 420.

38. D. F. Malan, quoted in Weinberg, *Portrait of a People: A Personal Photographic Record of the South African Liberation Struggle*, p. 79.

39. Quoted in SAIRR, *Annual Survey of Race Relations in South Africa, 1952–1953*, p. 67.

40. Weinberg, *Portrait of a People*, p. 81.

41. Motlhabi, *The Theory and Practice of Black Resistance*, p. 55.

42. See Ashforth, *The Politics of Official Discourse*, pp. 155–72.

43. Quoted in ibid., p. 153.

44. Ibid., p. 159.

45. Quoted in SAIRR, *Annual Report, 1949–1950*, p. 2.

46. See Davis, *Apartheid's Rebels*, chapter 1.

47. All quotes are from Mandela, *The Struggle Is My Life*, pp. 47, 51, 54.

48. Quoted in Motlhabi, *The Theory and Practice of Black Resistance*, p. 49.

49. Mbeki, *South Africa: The Peasants' Revolt*, chapter 9.

50. See Gerhart, *Black Power in South Africa*, chapter 6.

51. See, for example, Ngubane, *An African Explains Apartheid*, pp. 100–101.

52. The Freedom Charter has been widely reprinted; the quotes here are from Mbeki, *South Africa: The Peasants' Revolt*, pp. 153–57.

53. Quoted in Motlhabi, *The Theory and Practice of Black Resistance*, p. 81.
54. Quoted in ibid., p. 76.
55. Quoted in ibid., p. 82.
56. Ibid., pp. 80, 92–93.
57. See Lodge, *Black Politics in South Africa*, p. 218.
58. See Hahlo and Kahn, *South Africa: The Development of Its Laws.*
59. Quoted in Motlhabi, *The Theory and Practice of Black Resistance*, p. 93.
60. See Sampson, *Black and Gold*, p. 78.
61. Gerhart, *Black Power in South Africa*, chapter 5.
62. SAIRR, *Annual Survey of Race Relations in South Africa, 1959–1960*, (Johannesburg, 1960), p. 276.
63. Quoted in ibid., p. 277.
64. Quoted in Lauren, *Power and Prejudice*, p. 217.
65. *New York Times*, March 22, 1960, p. 1.
66. SAIRR, *Annual Survey of Race Relations in South Africa, 1959–1960*, p. 68.
67. On the entire revolt, see Mbeki, *South Africa: The Peasants' Revolt*, chapter 9.
68. Ibid., p. 123.
69. Ibid.
70. Davis, *Apartheid's Rebels*, chapter 1.
71. *Africa Today* (April 1963), p. 3.
72. Commission on U.S. Policy toward Southern Africa, *South Africa: Time Running Out*, p. 170.
73. Davis, *Apartheid's Rebels*, chapter 1.
74. The other nine were the Soviet Union, the People's Republic of China, India, Malaysia, Antigua, Barbados, Jamaica, British Guiana, and Surinam.
75. Doxey, *Economic Sanctions and International Enforcement*, p. 537.
76. Quoted in Botha, *Verwoerd Is Dead*, p. 59.
77. SAIRR, *Annual Survey of Race Relations in South Africa, 1959–1960*, p. 104.
78. Mbeki, *South Africa: The Peasants' Revolt*, chapter 1.
79. See Gerhart, *Black Power in South Africa*, p. 254.
80. Quoted in Ballinger, *From Union to Apartheid: A Trek to Isolation*, pp. 469–70.
81. See Motlhabi, *The Theory and Practice of Black Resistance*, p. 83.
82. See Mbeki, *South Africa: The Peasants' Revolt.*
83. SAIRR, *Annual Survey of Race Relations in South Africa, 1963* (Johannesburg, 1963).
84. Quoted in SAIRR, *Annual Survey of Race Relations in South Africa, 1964*, p. 187.
85. Ibid., p. 186.
86. SAIRR, *Annual Survey of Race Relations in South Africa, 1968* (Johannesburg, 1968).
87. Davis, *Apartheid's Rebels*, chapter 1.
88. See Mzala, *Gatsha Buthelezi*, p. 86.

5

From Difference to Identity: The Era of "Reform," 1973 to the Present

T he assassination of Hendrik Verwoerd was a turning point, the beginning of the end of the apartheid era, the start of the modern period. After 1966 the tribe began—but slowly!—to lose faith in the vision; some of them began to see what they had done.[1]

The above quote is indicative of what John Brewer has described as a fairly widespread belief about South Africa since 1971; namely, that the collapse of Afrikanerdom's confidence in apartheid, because of the changing social and economic position of Afrikaners, has been responsible for its relaxation.[2] Embedded within this belief are the assumptions that Afrikaner confidence in, and commitment to, apartheid have steadily eroded over the last two decades or so and that changed material interests have been primarily responsible for the shift.

Another prevalent view of the role of Afrikaans-speaking whites in contributing to social change begins not from the premise that confidence in apartheid has diminished, but that confidence in the Afrikaner self has increased. From this perspective, apartheid was the product of the "group inferiority complex among Afrikaners"[3] and could be removed like a scaffolding once the edifice it was designed to protect was strong enough to stand without it:

By the end of the 1970s the Afrikaner had grown in self-confidence as his role in the running of South Africa's affairs had expanded. . . . The Afrikaner "identity" nurtured by the Broederbond, was no longer under the threat that it had been before 1948. The Republic had been won and had endured. The country was prosperous and the Afrikaners' place in it secure.[4]

Although this chapter argues that black resistance has been a more important catalyst to social transformation over the past few years than the changed material interests of particular whites, there is no disputing the claim that some alteration within the Afrikaans-speaking white community has contributed to that transformation. But the question of exactly what the Afrikaners—or whites, more generally—have lost confidence in, and why, needs to be addressed in order to consider how the post-1948 South Africa has been reconstituted.

The crisis of confidence in white society that many commentators emphasize may be considered a crisis of confidence in the power of the state to fulfill two of the promises made since 1948: the promise to control African physical and economic mobility and the commitment to territorial separate development. In both cases, black resistance to the NP's machinations is a more convincing explanation for the crisis than greater confidence in the self among Afrikaners.

With regard to the issue of control, more blacks than whites lived in the white areas by the time Verwoerd departed, despite legislation passed in the 1960s designed to slow down or even reverse urbanization. That trend only continued under Prime Minister B. J. Vorster. The urban African population increased by 1.5 million between 1970 and 1980;[5] huge illegal squatter camps, such as Crossroads outside Cape Town (which despite police harassment has become as large and permanent as the legal Cape townships of Mitchell's Plain and Khyelitsha) are stark testimony to that fact. In the same way that Smuts's United party lost confidence by 1945 in the ability of whites to "sweep back the ocean with a broom," it became evident by the mid-1970s that African urbanization was beyond the control of the ruling National party and its supporters. Hence, pass laws were relaxed, and legislation pertaining to home ownership in urban areas was promulgated.

The National party, despite its encouragement of "border industries" and the prohibition of strikes and trade unions, has not been able to channel economic activity back to the homelands. A spate of labor legislation since 1973 has attempted to reverse this situation. The problem is not just a function of the reluctance of white businesses to move and their tolerance of worker organization, although these have certainly been factors.[6] Even when the white economy has been unable to provide jobs for those from rural areas, their inhabitants have migrated anyway, often being absorbed into a rising informal sector estimated to account for between 25 percent and 35 percent of overall economic activity.[7] Mostly hawkers, small convenience store owners, liquor and soft drink retailers, and builders, the "informals" are, according to one recent report, "changing the face of retailing in black areas." They even have their own association—the African Council for Hawkers and Informal Businesses (ACHIB)—to represent their interests.[8]

The ten-year period from 1973 to 1983 might be termed the first phase in the National party's reform process. It was an era in which the NP both broke and implemented the different commitments it had made since 1948. What was broken was the promise made in the late 1940s that natives would never have any rights in urban areas or be regarded as permanent inhabitants—they were accorded some rights as workers and allowed to own their own homes (if not the ground on which they rested). What was implemented was the notion of urban councils run by Africans but under the guidance of the local authorities (as predicted by the NP in 1949) and independence for four of the so-called homelands. Driven by the immediate need to find a way to appease mass demands for change while leaving apartheid intact, the first phase of the reform process was in essence a study in logical inconsistency. The granting of limited rights and local political autonomy implicitly was a recognition that blacks shared with whites a common South Africanness and was consistent with the postulate of identity. The ongoing commitment to separate development, in contrast, was evidence that the postulate of difference had not been abandoned. Blacks were both citizens and foreigners, self and other.

Another inconsistency lay in the ongoing claim that Indians and Coloreds were different nations; yet no homelands had been allocated for them as for Africans. The people in these groups were both self and other as well. The way this particular problem was resolved, by P. W. Botha, was through the writing of a new constitution in 1983 which created a tricameral Parliament— one chamber each for whites, Indians, and Coloreds. This second phase of the reform process—from 1983 to 1990—merely added new inconsistencies to the old ones. Whereas the rights accorded to the African nations were essentially dependent upon the ability of the individual to secure work— otherwise they would be removed to a homeland—those granted to Indians and Coloreds were accorded on the basis of race. In other words, Africans had rights as workers; other blacks had rights as racial groups.

Not only was the second phase inconsistent, but it invited further struggle by undermining the usual argument for exclusion of Africans on the basis of radical difference. At various times, Coloreds as well as English-speaking whites have been constituted as Afrikaners, so a redrawing of the boundaries of the national self to include "brown Afrikaans speakers" made some sense. But at no time in history have the Indians ever been constituted as such. The lack of any sound historical or contemporary basis for such incorporation was of enormous political significance, for if an alien people like the Indians—that is, a people never acknowledged to share any racial or cultural characteristics with whites—could be incorporated into a common (if structurally separated) central government, there was no longer any logical reason for excluding the alien Africans.

Only since 1990 and the capitulation of the de Klerk regime to the idea that all blacks will have certain rights on the same basis, that of their common South Africanness, did the move away from the inconsistencies of the first two phases of reform and the end of the commitment to separate development really become manifest. In a 1988 interview, former newspaper editor Willem de Klerk (the brother of the current state president) offered a succinct explanation for this change. "Apartheid," de Klerk said, "failed because blacks rejected it."[9] In this regard, it is important to emphasize not only such indicators of rejection as mass riots and demonstrations but also the struggles against Bantu education that have wracked South Africa since 1976 in particular. As argued in previous chapters, the ability of the government to sell the idea of separate development required the breaking down of an inclusive black identity and the normalization of socially constituted differences within the black population. The key to such an ambitious project was the dissemination through knowledge-producing apparatuses of a particular truth about South Africa, its history, and its peoples.

The open challenges to Bantu education that began in 1974 and culminated in the Soweto riots, the boycotts of official school syllabi that began in Colored schools in 1980 and spread throughout the country, and more recently the people's education movement in black townships throughout South Africa are all indicative of far more than dissatisfaction with inferior facilities and poorly trained teachers. The determination of students to recover what Foucault calls "subjugated knowledges"—that is, lost or deliberately silenced histories that challenge normal constructions of social reality—is indicative of the widespread failure of Bantu education to normalize multiracialism and national separation. It is also indicative of the success of Black Consciousness as a counter-discourse or hidden transcript of resistance that spread rapidly throughout South Africa after the founding of the South African Students' Organization in 1969.

One way to justify homelands is to deploy an argument long used in regard to political action in rural areas; that is, to suggest that those who live there are quite content and that only agitators out of touch with the aspirations of the rural masses actually disapprove of separate development. But the demands in recent months by most homeland leaders for reincorporation of their territories into South Africa, as well as the massive display of support for the ANC and other nontribal organizations within the homelands themselves, render such justifications increasingly obsolete.

It needs to be stressed, however, that processes of normalization are always uneven and are often the source of conflict among the oppressed themselves. In this regard, the most severe conflict in recent years has pitted the Inkatha movement (now renamed the Inkatha Freedom party, or IFP) of Gatsha Buthelezi against the various affiliates of the African National Congress and of Black Consciousness. There certainly are fundamental and ongoing differences between the ANC and Black Consciousness philosophies; they are reflected in their contrasting uses of the term *black* to refer to Africans only or to all oppressed people. That the former usage of the ANC accords with the understanding of most whites suggests its greater willingness to consider South Africa a multiracial society. But Buthelezi's organization of political action around appeal to an exclusive Zulu nationality is what unites the others against Inkatha. Buthelezi buys into the philosophical rationale (the tribe equals nation equation) of separate development even while he resists the idea of a separate Zulu homeland. He would become less dangerous but would nonetheless remain a political threat even without the active support that he has enjoyed from the South African state.

As this chapter will demonstrate, the demise of apartheid is indicative of the abandonment of the postulate of difference on which National party policy since 1948 has rested. The NP project is not to eliminate white domination but to perpetuate it in different ways. The extent to which the shift to a postulate of identity is due to a secure Afrikaner self, supposedly able to survive without the aid of racial legislation, however, is somewhat complicated.

As argued in earlier chapters, Afrikanerdom has never been united over where to draw the boundaries between the Afrikaner self and the non-Afrikaner other; at various times, Coloreds and English-speaking whites have been constituted as Afrikaners. What the decolonization of Africa and domestic resistance to domination have brought home to many whites—English-as well as Afrikaans-speaking—is that security is not consistent with the idea of South Africa as a state belonging to only one nation, a white nation. The boundary between the national self and alien others has shifted due to the failure of attempts to normalize multiple national identities among black South Africans. Acceptance of the necessity for universal franchise by the National party means that blacks are now citizens, not resident aliens. They no longer, therefore, need to carry a passbook.

At the same time, it needs to be remembered that the defense of civilization has been a far more prevalent justification for white domination in South Africa than Afrikaner self-determination, even from the National party. As argued in earlier chapters, the maintenance of higher living standards for the white community, the protection of private property, and the commitment to capitalism more generally have all been invoked at various times to constitute a boundary between a civilized self and a barbarous other. If whites have greater confidence that their domination can persist without racial legislation, then such confidence is warranted in these areas. The privatization of the economy and the National party's refusal to redistribute land guarantee that South Africa's most important economic assets, and thus the country's wealth, will remain in white hands. The legislative cover of a civilized labor policy is no longer required. The various opposition movements of course know this, which explains why the battleground already has begun to shift from demands for representation to economic justice.[10]

Another issue concerns the confidence of the white community that the boundaries between arbitrarily constituted races can be maintained in the absence of the Population Registration Act; in other words, whether multi-racialism has been so normalized that it can reproduce itself after the legislative scaffolding has been removed. Without some fixing of the notion that group identity exists and that regardless of the size of their memberships each group has a right to equal political representation in the state, the whites have no discursive weapon with which to fend off the idea of majority rule.

In this regard, there has been some confusion as to what exactly the National party is up to, in the same way that there was confusion in 1948 over what the term *apartheid* meant. Writing in 1982, Willem de Klerk described the new policies of F. W. Botha as "in essence a politics of compromise which looks to close cooperation [with other racial groups] but with full retention of self-determination, group rights and the full main-tenance of an own sphere of life." The borderline, de Klerk went on, "will be drawn at self-determination—in the church, in politics, education, living space, and group facilities. These are the non-negotiable aspects which the Afrikaner will defend with force of arms."[11]

When President de Klerk told Ted Koppel during an interview for ABC's "Nightline" in February 1990 that there are not only whites and blacks in South Africa but different races and nations, he seemed to be reaffirming, and not repudiating, decades of National party commitment to multi-racialism. The Afrikaner novelist Andre Brink recently insisted that, although South Africa might be one nation soon, "every small group, ethnic or otherwise, would still be forced to have its own identity: that terrible password of South African society."[12]

On the other hand, United Democratic Front (UDF) cofounder Alan Boesak has pointed out that F. W. de Klerk does not talk about "group rights" and mentions instead "protection for minorities." "Has there really been a shift in thinking from group rights to minority rights?" asked Boesak in 1990, or "is minority rights simply a new phrase for group rights?"[13] Unfortunately, the answer to the latter question seems to be "yes," for National party spokesmen occasionally use the terms *groups* or *minorities* interchangeably, in the same way that they interchanged *race* and *tribe*.[14] The concept of community rights increasingly is bandied by government spokesmen, raising the question of whether this is simply a euphemism for group or minority rights. The difference, supposedly, is that minorities and groups previously were defined by race whereas communities may be defined by where they live, their common interests, or culture.[15] But the National party's recent proposals to reserve one-half of town council seats in an expanded local authority system for people elected by property owners and renters suggest that community rights are not race-blind. Since millions of blacks have no real homes, this type of move would give whites a major advantage in many areas, as they own most property.[16]

What seems to have changed is not the normality of talking in terms of group identity but the way in which that identity is supposedly constituted. In terms of the Population Registration Act, identity was fixed by the state and supposedly given by such inherited traits as blood or heritage; the ability freely to choose an identity was simply not an option. Now, however, de Klerk has made it clear that although a new constitution must protect the group rights of the four existing races, he envisages the political incorporation of a fifth group comprised of those South Africans who do not wish to identify themselves by race. This is still "groupness" as the number of groups has expanded to five and has not disappeared, but the option for self-definition is consistent with de Klerk's emphasis on national identity as something freely chosen and not fixed by nature. It remains to be seen what would happen if the majority of the population simply defined themselves as South African.

Willem de Klerk suggested in 1988 that the National party would have to abandon plans for a race federation because such a federation would not be acceptable to blacks. He predicted a move toward more of a territorial dispensation. South Africa would be divided into provinces (some of which would be the so-called independent homelands) with all voters on a common roll and protection for minority rights. This is essentially what the National party's recent program for universal suffrage—discussed in more detail later—amounts to. Many aspects of the program have been rejected by the major opposition groups, but the accuracy of de Klerk's prediction demonstrates once again the way in which particular National party policies are the effect of black resistance.

The final point to consider about the new South Africa is the extent to which physical barriers among the various races will be maintained in the absence of the Group Areas Act. There apparently has been no rush so far by blacks to buy in white neighborhoods,[17] but the National party has nonetheless moved to restrict black access to white schools and neighbor-hoods—two of the nonnegotiables that Willem de Klerk mentioned in 1982—in two ways. First, in announcing in September 1990 the opening of state schools to students of all races, Education Minister Piet Clase made it clear that "autogenous" or own-group education must remain an option, an insistence repeated by President de Klerk a few months later.[18] The practical way in which this option is to be kept alive, apparently, is by requiring a poll of at least 80 percent of parents in which 72 percent must approve before a school can become nonracial. Perhaps this is what community rights actually refers to—the right of white civil society, with the backing of the state, to continue to control the lives of the country's black majority.

Second, the government has tabled the Residential Environment Bill, which would maintain norms and standards of existing neighborhoods and would prevent their physical deterioration. Although neighborhoods would not be allowed to exclude residents on the basis of race or religion, they would be free to set their own standards for what was acceptable.[19] In other words, they could appeal to standards as a euphemism for racial exclusion.

ANC Deputy President Nelson Mandela already has stated that the organized resistance movements must be "vigilant against statements which are said to be calculated to protect standards. We regard these as a euphemism to protect white privilege."[20] If the appeal to standards is fundamentally a way for the government to maintain white privilege without itself being the focus of struggle—that is, if the intention is to localize the defense of white domination and make it the responsibility of each community and the private (largely white) business sector—there are bound to be implications for future political struggle against domination. Already, the Congress of South African Trade Unions (Cosatu) and the popular United Democratic Front have begun to loosen their ties to the ANC in order to give themselves greater freedom to challenge policy at the local level. The two have joined forces with several housing rights organizations to form a new civic association. According to Cosatu's general secretary, Jay Naidoo, the organization is redefining its role and becoming more, not less, political. "Unless a political transition is accompanied by a meeting of the needs of the people," Naidoo has argued, "that transition will be a mere illusion."[21] Localized struggles always have been prevalent, as previous chapters demonstrated. But such actions as boycotts of white towns, consumer boycotts, and various worker-initiated forms of protest such as stay-aways and strikes will remain as vital an element in the struggle against white domination as the actions of such formal political organizations as the ANC.

As far as the organized opposition to the National party is concerned, it may be useful to place the various groups along a spectrum, not in terms of left or right (always ambiguous and contested terms) but according to how inclusive or exclusive, fixed or voluntary, are their understandings of identity. In this regard, the most unambiguously open and voluntarist is the PAC, which advocates national liberation and self-determination for Africans, defined as anyone who is loyal to Africa, considers himself or herself as African (rather than as European or Indian), and opposes white privilege.[22] The most closed and fixed is the Conservative party (CP) and its assorted right-wing affiliates, which define the self to be determined as an Afrikaans-speaking white of Dutch heritage.[23]

In between are the preferred negotiating partners of the government, the ANC and the IFP, which share with the National party a fair amount of inconsistency or ambiguity on the issue of identity. The NP takes an open and voluntarist approach to identity in its appeal for nation-building on the basis of a common South Africanness, but it seems wedded to some notion of group, or minority, or community, identity as fixed by culture and heritage.[24] The ANC continues to express a commitment to nonracialism—that is, to a common South African identity—but nonetheless remains wedded to the clauses in the Freedom Charter giving each national group the right to establish its own schools, to give instruction in its own language, and to retain its own culture and religion.[25] As for the IFP, Buthelezi speaks often of the "warrior blood" coursing through the veins of the Zulu nation,[26] yet his opening of the movement to non-Zulus and refusal to accept independence for KwaZulu reflect some commitment to a more broadly and voluntarily constituted identity.

All of these differences and ambiguities reflect an ongoing lack of consensus in both white and black society and suggest that, along with more localized struggles, conflicts over identity and over appropriate relations between the self and other will continue to undergird the politics of the new South Africa as they did the old.

The rest of this chapter discusses the above themes in more detail. The discussion is divided into the three phases of reform mentioned earlier: 1973–1983, 1983–1990, and 1990 to the present.

THE FIRST PHASE: LIMITED RIGHTS FOR AFRICANS, 1973–1983

As the global economic recession of the early 1970s began to make itself felt in South Africa and news of the surrender of colonial administrations in Angola and Mozambique filtered into the country, an unprecedented number of strikes and work stoppages involving Africans erupted, initially in Natal (see table 5.1). Not only was economic activity disrupted, but instances of violence and social unrest were common. On September 11, 1973, for example, police were called to Anglo-American's Western Deep Level Mine at Carletonville to force striking miners back to work. What actually transpired was unclear, but the following day, twelve African miners had been shot dead and a number of others wounded. When this news was released, Anglo-American's headquarters were besieged by (mostly white) students demanding an inquiry into the shootings.

The response of mineowners to the strikes was to call upon the government to make concessions to black workers. Harry Oppenheimer, the

Table 5.1
Strikes and Work Stoppages in South Africa, 1970–1984

Year	Number of Strikes and Stoppages	Number of African Employees Involved
1970	76	3,210
1971	69	4,067
1972	71	8,711
1973	370	90,083
1974	384	57,656
1975	274	22,546
1976	245	26,291
1977	90	14,950
1978	106	13,578
1979	101	15,494
1980	267	56,286
1981	342	84,706
1982	394	---
1983	336	---
1984	469	---

Source: South Africa Yearbook (various years).

chairman of Anglo-American, asked in 1973 for government recognition of African trade unions on the grounds that blacks would never accept "that the organization of labor which is regarded as right and necessary for white workers, not only in South Africa but throughout the Western world, is not suitable for them."[27]

As for the government, its immediate response was one of suspicion that the strikes were not motivated purely by economic frustration. In 1973 the minister of labor, D. J. Geyser, stated:

The strikes in Natal are following a pattern which indicates that they are not purely connected with higher wages. . . . The conduct of these particular workers and their reluctance to negotiate indisputably show that the agitation for trade union rights offers no solution and is only a smoke screen behind which there are other motives. . . . The government cannot permit wage claims to be converted into disturbances which can prejudice the good order of the state. The situation is being closely watched and there will be no hesitation in taking action against those responsible for any incitement in this regard.[28]

Despite this initial suspicion, the government in 1973 passed the Bantu Labor Relations Amendment Act, which legalized strikes and lockouts for Africans not employed in certain essential industries. It also established a separate, alternative committee system for Africans in lieu of the extension to them of full trade union rights. The National party in 1973 came to the same realization that the United party had in 1947 when it recognized that legislation designed to prevent worker organization and strikes had failed.

The labor unrest of the early 1970s was to have a large impact on the nascent Black Consciousness movement (BCM), which along with prying black politics away from white liberals sought to unite and bring solidarity among black workers. A loose affiliation of community action, education, and labor groups working mostly at the grassroots level, the BCM was bound more by a common philosophy than by a particular political program. Originating with the founding of SASO in 1969 and with the inauguration of the Black People's Convention (BPC) in 1972, BCM aimed to promote self-reliance, critical awareness, understanding of the community and its problems, and a sense of positive self-identity. Described in the following passage by SASO's first president, Steve Biko, the similarities between the philosophy of the BCM and the PAC, which preceded it, are most evident in the way that Biko talks about identity:

The call for Black Consciousness is the most positive call to come from any group in the black world for a long time. It is more than just a reactionary rejection of whites by blacks. The quintessence of it is the realization by the blacks that, in order to feature well in this game of power politics, they have to use the concept of group power and to build a strong foundation for this. . . . The philosophy of Black Consciousness, therefore, expresses group pride and the determination by the blacks to rise and attain the envisaged self. At the heart of this kind of thinking is the realization by the blacks that the most potent weapon in the hands of the oppressor is the mind of the oppressed. Once the latter has been so effectively manipulated and controlled by the oppressor as to make the oppressed believe that he is a liability to the white man, then there will be nothing the oppressed can do that will really scare the powerful masters. Hence thinking along lines of Black Consciousness makes the black man see himself as a being, entire in himself, and not as an extension of a broom or additional leverage to some machine.[29]

For Black Consciousness as for the PAC, identity was not something given by nature and fixed over time but was to be chosen freely and realized in action. Blacks were invoked to "rise and attain the envisaged self." Had he lived, Biko might have had some interesting reflections on the similarities and differences between his approach to identity and that of F. W. de Klerk; the current state president in his emphasis on the task of building a South African nation also treats the nation as an envisaged self to be attained through some form of collective action, although he undoubtedly would not want that self to be defined as black.

Frequent references in the work of Steve Biko to the writings of Franz Fanon, and his insistence that liberation means freeing the mind of the oppressed from settled beliefs that normalize existing power relations, suggest a similarity between the thinking of the BCM and that of other African intellectuals. Biko, in fact, resisted the widely held notion in the 1970s that Black Consciousness was influenced by the "American 'Negro' Movement" and argued that "it seems to me that this is a sequel to the attainment of independence by so many African states within so short a time."[30] He also pointed to an influence on the movement of more localized practices of resistance to white domination, in addition to the continentwide forces just mentioned:

> Through the work of missionaries and the style of education adopted, the blacks were made to feel that the white man was some kind of god whose word could not be doubted. . . . The attitude of some rural African folk who are against education is often misunderstood, not least by the African intellectual. Yet the reasons put forward by these people carry with them the realization of their inherent dignity and worth. They see education as the quickest way of destroying the substance of the African culture. . . . How can an African avoid losing respect for his tradition when in school his whole cultural background is summed up in one word: barbarism?[31]

Whatever its official connections (or lack thereof) to the PAC, Black Consciousness was a modern movement in the tradition of Pan-Africanism, which had informed both rural struggles for autonomy through the influence of the Ethiopian churches and anticolonial struggles on the African continent through the formal Pan-African congresses. This tradition can be seen in the Black Consciousness message of self-help, black pride, and lack of faith in the doctrine of liberalism. With its emphasis on reclaiming African culture and history, on withdrawal from direct confrontation with the government, on working within the confines of the law, and on avoiding violence, the BCM seemed like a very tame successor to the ANC and the PAC. The government, in fact, rejoiced at the founding of SASO, seeing it as representing some form of "tribal consciousness."[32] Yet a successful BCM, the National party finally realized, would represent one of the greatest threats it had ever had to face, and not only because SASO and the BPC were advocating foreign disinvestment, organizing student strikes, and planning "Viva Frelimo" rallies to celebrate Mozambiquan independence.

By rejecting differentiation between urban and rural Africans, and among Africans, Coloreds, Indians, and whites, the BCM threatened to denaturalize the whole system of multiracialism. Since "black" meant all victims of white oppression, even white people could in theory join the BCM, as evidenced by Biko's close collaboration with the white newspaper editor Donald Woods. This perspective is what made Black Consciousness such a radical and subversive discourse, threatening enough to the state that Steve Biko was murdered in a police prison cell in 1977.

Black Consciousness and Steve Biko were able to succeed in the 1970s where the Non-European Unity movement and Ben Kies had failed earlier because common oppression strengthened the production of a common black identity. Given its origins in the universities, the BCM was to have a major impact on the youth of South Africa and thus, directly and indirectly, on the Soweto protests and their aftermath. But it was not only against Bantu education that the BCM directed its struggle. According to the ANC's Mzala, one of the most discussed topics within the leadership and ranks of SASO in the beginning of the 1970s concerned the position of Chief Buthelezi. SASO was not impressed with the chief's portrayal of himself as an opponent of apartheid and a reluctant participant in the Bantustan scheme. The organization felt that the creation of an "I am a Zulu" attitude that Buthelezi stood for threatened to undermine the unity forged through struggle in the decades since the foundation of the ANC in 1912.[33] Whether or not one accepted so-called independence for one's homeland was not the key issue for SASO; the question was whether political action was to be organized around a common black identity or by appeal to a more exclusive identity, such as Zuluness.

The Inkatha movement which Buthelezi revived in 1975 was in essence the complete opposite of what the BCM stood for. Intended as an organizational power base outside of the legal framework of the Bantustans, Inkatha was to enable Buthelezi to confront the critics of his political positions. Yet as Mzala has pointed out, this exposed the essential paradox in Buthelezi's political stance. While trying to project a role for himself in the larger South Africa, he was forced to turn to the only political constituency readily available to him—that is, the Zulu people trapped within the framework of the Bantustans.[34] Inkatha's stated aim was that of "fostering this spirit of unity among the people of KwaZulu throughout Southern Africa, and between them and all their African brothers in Southern Africa." It was also agreed that the organization would help to "promote and encourage the development of the people of KwaZulu, spiritually, economically, educationally and politically."[35]

The difference from other organized resistance movements can be seen in the fact that terms such as *nation* or *nationally* in the constitution of Inkatha did not mean the African people as a whole as understood by the ANC, or the more inclusive definition of *African* as understood by the PAC, or all black oppressed people as understood by the BCM. *Nation* referred to "KwaZulu citizens" in terms of the Bantu Homelands Citizenship Act of 1970;[36] that is, it meant all Zulus throughout South Africa whether they resided in KwaZulu or not. Certainly, it would be possible to argue that the Zulus were once a nation—Buthelezi's frequent references to Kings Shaka and Cetshwayo are part of the project of recreating that national identity.[37] But even if one accepts the extraordinarily high membership figures (over 1 million in 1985) that Buthelezi claims for Inkatha,[38] it remains the case that no other black leader has claimed to oppose apartheid while accepting the notion of national diversity among the African people.

The Struggle Intensifies: Soweto and Its Aftermath, 1976–1983

The violence and social unrest that erupted in South Africa on June 16, 1976, and continued more or less unabated for more than a year were the worst that the country had ever seen. By February 1977 the death toll stood at 575; of the total, 451 were said to have died "as a result of police action," and 134 of these were under the age of eighteen.[39]

The immediate cause of the disturbances was the inferior system of education for Africans, instituted by the Bantu Education Act of 1953. This system had long been resented by both students and parents; the government's announcement in 1974 that by the following year all African schools must conform to its policy of equal use of Afrikaans and English in the classroom was the straw that broke the camel's back.

Pleas to the government to reconsider from teachers, parents, and community leaders were ignored. School strikes and boycotts took place in the first months of 1976, but still the government would not reconsider. SASO therefore decided to organize a rally at Orlando stadium in Soweto, a township of Johannesburg, to be followed by a protest march through the city streets. On June 16 several thousand high school students arrived at the stadium. Their entry was blocked by South African police, who opened fire on the protesters. The planned rally and march never took place.

The violence that erupted in Soweto immediately after the shootings spread within days to townships in Pretoria, Cape Town, and the western Cape, then to Port Elizabeth and the eastern Cape. It also flared sporadically in Durban and the homelands. What followed was more than a year of upheaval and violence, including school boycotts and strikes, student marches, demonstrations, the burning of schools, labor unrest, and clashes with the police. Steve Biko was found dead in a police cell, fueling the disturbances in Port Elizabeth. Yet in spite of the fact that townships were practically under martial law, the campaign against Bantu education was intensified. By the time the mass protests petered out at the end of 1977, the government had dropped the school language issue, although it had become clear by then that far more than poor schools was at stake.

The less direct impetus to the challenge was both the BCM and the successful conclusions of the struggles for independence in Mozambique and Angola. Late in 1974 university students had defied a government ban and held a "Viva Frelimo" rally in Durban to celebrate the victory of the Mozambiquan liberation movement. A similar rally took place at the University of the North. The police showed up in force and arrested many black students. But the renewed sense of defiance and militance that the collapse of Portugal's colonies had stimulated was clearly evident at the subsequent trials, and not only among the students. The accused Africans regularly entered the courtroom singing freedom songs. They raised their fists in a Black Power-type salute and shouted "Amandla!" ("Power!"), to which spectators in the courtroom would respond "Ngawethu!" ("Is ours!").[40] The press kept readers throughout the country informed of this continuing demonstration of defiance.

The newly independent Portuguese territories of Angola and Mozambique soon began providing material and military support to resistance movements from South Africa (the ANC and PAC), from Namibia (the South West African People's Organization, or SWAPO), and from war-torn Rhodesia (ZAPU and the Zimbabwe African National Union, or ZANU). The Pretoria government used various methods to clear these movements out of the neighboring states, but the ANC adapted quickly to the circumstances. In an outer arc of "sanctuary states" (Angola, Zambia, Tanzania) it housed military camps, administrative offices, and educational institutions. An inner tier of "transit states" (Botswana, Swaziland, Mozambique) served as only temporary bases and as clandestine infiltration routes to funnel guerillas into and recruits out of South Africa rapidly.[41] Thousands of young blacks who fled South Africa after Soweto received military training in Africa, as well as in the Soviet Union and other communist countries.

Within a short time, these guerillas began to reenter the country, link up with the domestic underground, and commit some spectacular acts of sabotage against key government targets. Largely dormant during the 1960s, the ANC's M-Plan cells formed the basis for the rapid revival of an internal underground after 1977, in rural as well as urban areas.

The change of strategy to bombings and sabotage that the smashing of organized opposition prompted was much more successful in the 1970s than it had been after Sharpeville, thanks in part to the geopolitical changes in the region. Official figures put the number of terrorist incidents in South Africa over the fourteen years that followed the banning of the ANC at only fifty-five; between October 1976 and May 1981, 112 attacks on government buildings and explosions in the country were reported.[42]

The South African government was beset by a host of other problems as well. One was the outflow of capital (discussed in chapter 2) that the Soweto riots prompted. Another was the adoption by the UN Security Council of Resolution 418, which declared that the global arms trade with South Africa (but not apartheid per se) constituted a threat to world peace and was therefore illegal. This measure strengthened the voluntary arms embargo imposed against South Africa in 1963 by making it mandatory.

In December 1977 the UN General Assembly approved a recommendation to the Security Council for a mandatory oil embargo against South Africa, but this measure was effectively vetoed by the abstention on the vote in the Security Council of Great Britain, the United States, and France.

As for the Western world, Great Britain displayed once again its unwillingness to rock the boat of its mutually beneficial economic relationship with South Africa. By the late 1970s, however, Britain was no longer South Africa's major trading partner; that role had been taken over by the United States.

Under the administration of Jimmy Carter, the United States moved quickly to signal its displeasure to Pretoria. In 1976 it adopted a policy limiting sales of computers to South African government departments and public agencies. A year later, it prohibited the export or reexport of any item to South Africa or Namibia that the exporter "knows or has reason to know" will be "sold to or used for" the South African military or police.[43] In 1978 the United States reduced the staff of its military attaché in Pretoria and also prohibited export-import bank loans to all South African government firms and to private firms with unsatisfactory labor practices.

Other Western states also moved against South Africa. Even before the UN mandatory arms embargo was imposed, France announced its intention to discontinue arms sales to the Pretoria regime. Canada in 1977 withdrew its commercial consuls from South Africa and ended the availability of its Export Development Corporation facilities for sales to the government in South Africa. Then in 1979 Sweden passed the South Africa Act which prohibited any new investment in South Africa, including reinvestment of earnings.

Inside South Africa one of the most important consequences of the unrest in the factories and African townships in the 1970s was the reassertion by "dependent" capital of demands for concessions to the protesters (again see chapter 2). An important means through which major industrialists sought to lobby government was the Urban Foundation, established in late 1976 after a conference of leaders of business and industry was held in Johannesburg. The foundation intended to improve the lot of urban Africans in four areas: education and training, housing, employment, and the physical environment. Conspicuously absent from the program was any mention of political rights for urban Africans or the lot of those Africans forced to live in the homelands. Nevertheless, in response to local (and some multinational) business pressures from major employers, as well as to the recommendations of the

Wiehahn and Riekert commissions published in 1979 (enacted from the Wiehahn Commission was the recommendation for trade union recognition for Africans; from the Riekert Commission, the granting of permanent urban residence to Africans with Section 10 rights), the government implemented a series of reform measures. Legislation pertaining to education, housing, and the physical environment is summarized in table 5.2; that pertaining to economic opportunities for Africans is summarized in table 5.3.

Also implemented after Soweto (in 1977) was the vision expressed by the National party in 1949 that urban Africans would one day be allowed to manage their own local affairs. According to the government, the setting up of community councils was an attempt to accommodate the political aspirations of Africans in urban areas since they were denied participation in the central organs of state power and yet had no affinity with the homeland structures created for them. Formalized in the Black Local Authorities Act of 1982, which gave the government the power to both establish and abolish them, community councils were massively rejected almost from the beginning and essentially collapsed after the wave of unrest that engulfed South Africa again after 1984.

The government adopted only piecemeal the recommendations of the Wiehahn and Riekert commissions and made no moves to remove the pass laws from the statute books or to consider the possibility of the political incorporation of blacks within a common system. This position reflected both an ongoing determination of whites to retain political and economic control and their fear of black empowerment. Even while the reforms were being implemented, the National party was trying to sell homelands to Africa and proceeded to grant independence to the Transkei in 1976, to Ciskei in 1977, to Venda in 1979, and to BophuthaTswana in 1981. This combination of reform and ongoing commitment to national separation resulted in the logical inconsistencies in policy mentioned earlier. Africans were granted some of the economic and social rights that whites had long enjoyed and were accorded some limited political authority at the local urban as well as rural level. These steps were essentially those taken or proposed by Smuts after the end of World War II and were in accordance with the principle of trusteeship and the postulate of identity. At the same time, blacks continued to be denied any possibility of incorporation into a common political system and were supposed to channel their aspirations for national self-determination into the politics of Pretoria-created Bantustans. Such inconsistencies reflected ongoing conflicts within white society about relations between the self and other, but even if the white community had been willing to live with them (and many were not), the black community rejected them out of hand.

Even the measures most obviously designed to fend off youthful protest against Bantu education, such as the commitment to build more schools and

Table 5.2
Improvements for Africans in Education, Housing, and Physical Environment,
1976–1981

Year	Legislation	Summary
1976	Medical University of South Africa Act	Provided for the establishment of a medical university for Africans near Ga Rankuwa.
1977	Bantu Education Amendment Act	Provided for the building of more schools in Soweto and other townships. Choice of language for instruction to be left to the schools, committees, and boards concerned.
	Bantu Universities Amendment Act	Conferred greater autonomy on the three universities for Africans (their curricula having formerly been strictly controlled by the Department of Bantu Education).
	University of Durban-Westville Amendment Act	Provided for the admission of other races to the university for Indians.
	University of the Western Cape Amendment Act	Provided for the admission of other races to the university for Coloreds.
1978	Bantu (Urban Areas) Amendment Act	Provided for urban Africans to own their own homes, on a 99-year leasehold basis.
1979	Education and Training Act	Made African education free and compulsory.
	Universities for Blacks Amendment Act	Provided for the opening of Fort Hare, Zululand, and Turfloop to all Africans.
	Housing Amendment Act	Provided for housing loans for Africans on the same terms as for other races.
1981	Technikons (Education and Training) Act	Provided for Technikons (trade schools) to be established for Africans.
	Vista University Act	Provided for the first all-African university in the white areas. Campuses planned for Soweto, Cape Town, Port Elizabeth, Bloemfontein, and Vereeniging.
	Laws on Cooperation and Development Amendment Act	Provided that a site acquired by a non-African might be used by one African only for residential purposes.

Table 5.3
Improvements in Economic Opportunities for Africans, 1973–1982

Year	Legislation	Summary
1973	Bantu Labor Relations Amendment Act	Legalized the right of some African employees to strike.
1974	Second General Law Amendment Act	Repealed the Masters and Servants laws and the penal section of the Bantu Labor Act of 1964.
1976	Bantu Employees In-Service Training Act	Provided for the in-service training of African employees at both public and private centers.
	Second Railways and Harbor Acts Amendment Act	Provided for African employees from the homelands, previously not eligible for these industries' pension funds, to qualify.
1977	Bantu Labor Relations Regulation Amendment Act	Extended provisions of the 1973 act. Also provided for Africans to become members of the Central Bantu Labor Board.
	Workmen's Compensation Act	Brought African compensation in line with that of other racial groups.
1979	Black Taxation Amendment Act	Abolished the poll tax for Africans.
	Housing Amendment Act	Provided for housing loans for Africans to be brought into line with those of other racial groups.
	Industrial Conciliation Amendment Act	Africans outside of the homelands allowed to join trade unions, although racially mixed trade unions are specifically forbidden.
	Laws on Plural Relations and Development Second Amendment Act	Revised the tax scale for Africans. The threshold at which they would be liable for payment of taxes raised from R360 to R1200 per annum.
	Unemployment Insurance Amendment Act	The scope of the principal act was widened to include Africans earning less than R546 per annum.
1981	Labor Relations Amendment Act	*Employee* redefined to include all African workers. Provision also made for the establishment of racially mixed trade unions.
	Police Amendment Act	Extended the principles of the 1958 act, in order to provide for the payment of allowances to retired black police officers and their dependents.
	Unemployment Insurance Amendment Act	Broadened the scope of the 1966 act to include certain African miners under its terms.
1982	Second Unemployment Insurance Amendment Act	Extended the provisions of the main act to include Africans from the homelands.
	Manpower Training Amendment Act	Made provision for the payment to employers of training allowances for African workers.

grant greater autonomy to black universities, did not really go to the heart of student dissatisfaction with the nature of the education they were being given. Reflecting the influence of SASO and Black Consciousness philosophy, Colored students initiated an educational boycott in 1980 which took as its objective the "conscientization" of the black masses through the dissemination of new versions of South African history that challenged accepted truths.[44] Police action failed to end the boycott, and Prime Minister P. W. Botha finally suggested that an inquiry into the desirability of a single educational system for all races be instituted.[45] The National party's first phase of reform, from 1973 to 1983, was therefore a dismal failure as a strategy to fend off black resistance and create loyalty to the system among those outside of the African homelands.

THE SECOND PHASE: INCORPORATION OF INDIANS AND COLOREDS, 1983–1990

In order to understand the second phase of the NP's reform process, it is necessary to return briefly to 1980; as chapter 2 argued, it was during the decolonization of Zimbabwe that the debate over power sharing began in earnest. A content analysis of articles and editorials published in Afrikaans newspapers at this time reveals an emerging consensus that the way to avoid losing everything, as Zimbabwe's whites apparently had done, was to negotiate a political settlement to South Africa's problems with the genuine but not too radical leaders of the country's black majority. Substantially less consensus within the Afrikaans-speaking white community was apparent from the evidence in the press on the issue of with whom exactly the National party should negotiate to share power.

Despite a fairly widespread conviction in 1980 that the ANC and Namibia's still-outlawed SWAPO were no more than agents of the Soviet Union to bring communism to southern Africa, editorials did mention the need to talk to the leaders of these two groups. *Die Transvaler* in May, for example, argued that "it does not help to say that Mandela is a communist and we do not want to talk to Sam Nujoma. . . . South Africa has to bring the black leaders to the conference room and talk to them."[46] Nujoma also was described in *Beeld* as a "legitimate" interlocutor by Piet Cillie, chairman of the publishing conglomerate Nasionale Pers. Regarding Mandela, Cillie expressed less certainty, saying that he did not know whether "Mandela has to be fetched" because it was not clear how much support he still enjoyed.[47] Another black leader with less international but substantial national stature mentioned at the time was the Soweto civic leader Ntatho Motlana. He was described by *Die Vaderland* in February as "a formidable leader among his own people."[48] No one mentioned Chief Gatsha Buthelezi.

With hindsight it is easy to see that the most significant articles in terms of subsequent developments were those that advocated political incorporation of the Coloreds. *Die Burger* in March, for example, claimed that Zimbabwe's "lesson for South Africa" was that "he who wants to retain everything runs the risk of losing everything," and that, in order to avoid this, "urgent work must be done to assign the Coloreds of South Africa with effective political authority."[49] It is also easy to see that the ongoing exclusion of the majority of blacks implicit in such a stance could only contribute to greater, and not less, political struggle in the future. But what needs to be pointed out is how the eventual political incorporation of the Coloreds reflected ongoing differences within Afrikanerdom over the identity of the self and appropriate relations between the self and others.

Two articles published in the Afrikaans press in 1980 serve to illustrate the nature of these differences. An anthropology professor from Potchefstroom University, M. van Wateren, wrote in *Die Transvaler* in September that power sharing between "*radically* different race groups" (emphasis in the original) was an unrealistic dream that could not be made to work in South Africa; the greatest lesson to be learned from Zimbabwe, according to van Wateren, was that "what does not belong together cannot merely be amalgamated in the belief that moderation will be upheld."[50] Left unspoken was the question of whether all, or only some, race groups were radically different, thus leaving open the possibility for selective incorporation. But the article was nonetheless a clear example of the presumption that blacks are inherently alien and unassimilable, that is, of the postulate of difference upheld by many anthropologists since the 1930s and by the NP since 1948.

In reflecting on Ian Smith's Rhodesia, an editorial by Piet Muller in *Beeld* in March could have been referring to contemporary South Africa when it said that the talk about a bastion of Western civilization and civilized standards is to be translated as "high living standards." More important, the editorial used the occasion of Zimbabwean independence and the fear and uncertainty for the future that it was engendering among South Africa's whites to rethink the identity of the Afrikaner self.

What made the future seem dangerous for many Afrikaners, according to Muller, was that for too long attempts had been made to build the future upon erroneous suppositions. For many years the *volk* had been told that the essence of their peoplehood lay in color, not in the language, culture, and history within which the real substance of Afrikaner *volkwees* ("nationhood") was located. If the Afrikaner wanted to participate in a meaningful way in the ongoing conversation about South Africa's constitutional future, he would have to reexamine the fundamentals of his *volkwees* and decide in what way he was different from other nations.

Muller went on to suggest that the protection of group rights would necessarily have to be the cornerstone of any new constitutional dispensation and that groups were by nature culture groups and not merely color groups. For the sake of his future, the Afrikaner would need to learn to look with new eyes at South Africa and not merely think of himself as the heir of the British Empire in southern Africa. He would have to make it clear in his own mind that what was at stake was the continued existence of the *volk* and not merely the retention of a privileged position, as was so often the case in the old colonies. It had become essential that "all Afrikaans-speakers—white and brown—accept each other as members of the same cultural group."[51]

The new constitution promulgated in 1983 by Prime Minister P. W. Botha (who became state president in 1984) can be interpreted as a political compromise between the opposed positions within Afrikanerdom that the articles by van Wateren and Muller represented. Coloreds were incorporated into a central government, then under the exclusive control of whites, as a separate race group rather than as a cultural group to be amalgamated with Afrikaans-speaking whites. Had Muller's suggestions been taken seriously, the concept of white would have ceased to have had any political meaning, opening up the question of the basis for political inclusion in Parliament of English-speaking whites. But the fact that the concept of white did not cease to have political meaning demonstrates Muller's point that for many Afrikaners the essence of their peoplehood lay in color rather than in language, culture, and history.

Nowhere in 1980 was the possibility of the political incorporation of Indians mentioned, yet the 1983 constitution created a tricameral Parliament with one chamber each for Indians, Coloreds, and whites. At various times, Coloreds as well as English-speaking whites have been constituted as Afrikaners, so a redrawing of the boundaries of the national self to include "brown Afrikaans-speakers" made some sense. But at no time in history have the Indians ever been constituted as such. The question of why Indians were incorporated probably has a very simple answer—no homeland existed for them and the National party did not know what else to do with them. But the lack of any sound historical or contemporary basis for such incorporation was nonetheless of enormous political significance. If an alien people like the Indians—that is, a people never acknowledged to share any racial or cultural characteristics with whites—could be incorporated into a common (if structurally separated) central government, why could not others? In other words, the second phase of reform invited only greater struggle because the usual argument for exclusion of Africans on the basis of radical difference (as exemplified by van Wateren) was undermined by the mere existence of a tricameral Parliament.

The policies of P. W. Botha in the early 1980s were a symbolic reenactment of the 1838 Battle of Blood River. Botha did not exactly rescind the rights granted to Africans by B. J. Vorster after Soweto, but one piece of legislation in particular made it clear that the idea of a permanent African population in urban areas (let alone political rights) was not accepted by all whites. The 1983 Laws on Cooperation and Development Amendment Act introduced controls on the entry to urban areas of the families of qualifying migrants, making it more difficult for men who qualified for urban rights to have their families live with them. The act required the acquisition of "approved accommodation," in addition to a regular source of income, before the families of permanent residents could legally reside with them. Many simply came anyway, but by mandating jobs and housing as prerequisites for urban residence at a time when both were in short supply, the act sent a clear message to Africans that hope of further reform on their part was simply wishful thinking.

Formerly South Africa's minister of defense, Botha pumped money into the domestic arms industry and went on the attack against neighboring African states that harbored ANC and PAC "terrorists." Brought into the tricameral Parliament as junior partners to whites, the Coloreds and Indians were symbolically the servants who fought with the Boers inside the wagons at the Battle of Blood River. Africans were the enemy—"communists"—who must be excluded by force rather than integrated by negotiation. Botha did not waste time trying to justify the ongoing exclusion of Africans by appeal to the usual argument about radical difference. As Joseph Lelyveld has put it, Botha "fobbed off black political aspirations by changing the subject, changing the time scale, waxing philosophic, or promising 'practical policy away from politics.' "[52] Botha did this because there was no longer any basis for the usual argument, because the support of Western powers such as the United States under Ronald Reagan and Great Britain under Margaret Thatcher did not require it (only anticommunism), and because blacks demonstrated more massively than ever before that they simply would not buy it.

The Politics of Refusal: 1984 to the Present

It was during the referendum campaign for the new constitution in 1983 that the United Democratic Front (UDF), a loose coalition of about 700 organizations (including the ANC and various Black Consciousness groups), was founded. Somewhat reminiscent of the Congress Alliance of the 1950s, the UDF tried unsuccessfully to defeat the constitutional proposals by a massive display of nonracial solidarity in the form of peaceful protests and demonstrations.

The activities of the UDF soon were supplemented by a variety of other forms of resistance to the new constitution and to urban local authorities for

Africans, as well as to apartheid more generally. Widespread unrest began in early 1984 in Atteridgeville, a township near Pretoria, where African students boycotting schools stubbornly resisted government attempts to force them to return to class. Their example spread to other townships, and school boycotts—first under the slogan of "liberation before education!" and then the more BCM-type slogan of "education for liberation!"—came to be a permanent feature of township life. When the new African town councils in the Vaal triangle, southeast of Johannesburg, sought to raise rents, residents attacked and burned the rent and administration board offices in Sebokeng. Public buildings, shops, and banks were destroyed in other townships of the Vaal triangle, including Sharpeville.

By the beginning of 1985, strikes by African trade union federations, year-long "stay-aways" from school, protests, police and military action, and massive funerals forced the government to declare a state of emergency. With the townships out of police control, Law and Order Minister Adriaan Vlok declared that the army intended to quell the unrest and "to show that the state can be in authority of the situation, that it has the machinery to be in command of a particular situation."[53] Tribal battalions were introduced into the army, and homeland military services were beefed up.

The magnitude of violence after Soweto pales in comparison to that occurring since September 1984. During the first five months of 1986 alone, 504 people died in more than 10,000 unrest-related incidents; 1,599 were injured,[54] forcing the government to reimpose on June 12 of that year (four days before the tenth anniversary of the Soweto uprising) the state of emergency that had been lifted three months earlier. The University of Natal has estimated that between September 1984 and December 1988 over 4,000 persons lost their lives, including nearly 190 white and black soldiers and police.[55] Adriaan Vlok was forced to admit in 1988 that "in some areas it is not going well."[56]

Although easily overlooked because of media and academic preoccupation with urban townships, a large share of the violence and political unrest sweeping South Africa in the mid-1980s took place in so-called ethnic Reserves, largely in the form of attacks on government institutions there. Many people in rural areas, as earlier chapters demonstrated, historically have supported the ANC or other nationally based organizations and have rejected tribal politics, so much so that the state of emergency imposed on the Transkei in 1960 was not lifted until November 1989.[57] With Botha-inspired South African aggression against neighboring states harboring ANC fighters, the ANC hoped that allied homelands headed by ministers "looking the other way" could become neutralized sanctuaries for its military wing Umkonto.[58]

The success of this ANC strategy has been somewhat uneven, due more to the nature of homeland leaders than to lack of popular support for the ANC.

But ANC fighters have often infiltrated the republic through parts of BophuthaTswana; a base of ANC support has existed within kaNgwane; and the ANC has been suspected of piloting ongoing espionage activity in black homelands—in the Transkei, in particular.

Since the unrest supposedly peaked in 1987, the South African Bureau for Information has claimed regularly that the security forces have the situation under control and that the number of disturbances is abating. Yet violence in Natal has invited comparisons to Beirut; violence flares every day in other parts of the country in scores of incidents. In only the first twelve days of March 1990, 104 people were killed in violent incidents; thirty-one died in only forty-eight hours.[59] The latest figures for 1991 published by the South African Institute for Race Relations put the number of deaths in political violence during the first quarter of the year at almost 600.[60]

It is not only the amount of violence that distinguishes the current uprisings from those of previous challenges. Many more people, using a multiplicity of tactics, are now involved. As antiapartheid activist David Webster pointed out before his murder by unknown gunmen, the state of emergency was responsible for a rethinking of the kind of politics that could be engaged in but by no means for the end of politics altogether. What happened was a move away from "microphone politics," mass meetings, and so forth to grassroots-level organization (a reflection of the influence of Black Consciousness as well as an effect of repression). Street committees, area committees, block committees, and so on are much more seriously organized than before. "People in the townships are bruised," Webster argued, "but they're determined."[61]

What Alan Boesak has called the "politics of refusal" entails a united front of labor unions, consumers, civic organizations, schools, and "guerilla" groups involved in active noncollaboration with the government. Motivated in part by a drive to push government administration out of the townships and replace it with "people's power"—the ANC strategy of "making the country ungovernable"—and by a shift in focus toward more grassroots issues involving the daily lives of township residents, this form of resistance is rooted in the historical experiences of protest of both urban and rural people. "Stay-aways" from work and school, strikes and acts of civil disobedience, protest marches, and prison hunger strikes have been joined by three kinds of community-based mass action. First, "people's courts" and militia units have been established to administer justice in local areas.[62] Second, consumer boycotts of white businesses (sometimes of entire towns, such as Boksburg, Carletonville, and Welkom) have been instituted to bring black suffering to the attention of whites in a nonviolent manner or to punish right-wing voters.[63] Third, there have been boycotts by at least 4 million people in fifty-four townships of rent and service payments to the South

African government.[64] In addition, while indiscriminate violence against whites remains infrequent, determined resistance to the police and security forces and attacks against the property of reactionary businessmen have been coupled with political assassinations—"necklace" murders—of alleged black collaborators and government stooges such as African town councillors and policemen.

The current uprisings are also distinguishable from those of previous challenges in that there are no longer only two sides to the conflict, that is, government and opposition. Now there is Inkatha as well. During the school boycotts of 1980, Buthelezi went on record saying that he wanted to train an army to keep order, to prevent the destruction of schools, and to control riots. A year later, the first Inkatha paramilitary training camp near Ulundi in Natal, known as Emandleni Matleng camp, was established.[65] It was established to employ violence against the opponents of Inkatha. Although there is no definitive link to the camp, the camp was implicated in the 1983 attack on the University of Zululand. After a rampage by an estimated 500 Inkatha warriors left five students dead, Buthelezi justified the violence in terms that were to become increasingly familiar over the next few years.

Blaming non-Zulus for campaigns of denigration and vilification against himself personally (rather than against the Inkatha "syllabus" that he had introduced into KwaZulu's schools), Buthelezi claimed that the proud sons and daughters of a "warrior nation" must inevitably respond with counter-violence.[66] In a sense, then, it was not only Botha who was symbolically reenacting scenes from a heroic and glorious past. Invoking the tradition of resistance to colonial conquest associated in African history with Zulu Kings Shaka and Cetshwayo, Buthelezi sought to reconstitute a lost Zulu nation by appeal to heritage and warrior blood. In the process, he constituted all political opponents as Xhosas or non-Zulus.[67]

After the founding of the UDF, the focus of Inkatha attacks against its enemies shifted from universities and students to urban townships and a host of UDF affiliates. At various times in 1986, these attacks were attributed to the "warrior blood coursing through [Zulu] veins,"[68] to the "anger of ordinary men and women in the street,"[69] and to "human frailty."[70] Buthelezi blamed "the External Mission of the ANC and its internal surrogate, the UDF," for creating "a climate in which violence has been so vigorously stimulated."[71] He was no doubt correct in insisting that the violence was not all one-way (from Inkatha to the UDF), but it was not only its supposed status as a violent organization that made the UDF seem threatening to the leader of Inkatha.

As Mare and Hamilton point out, there must have been a fair amount of confusion in 1975 about the relationship between the ANC and Inkatha because Inkatha was "formed by a man who refers frequently to his ANC membership, and even more frequently to the fact that he had been asked to participate in bantustan politics by ANC leaders, who places Inkatha within both a Zulu history and an ANC history, and whose movement uses the ANC colors and uniforms similar to those of ANC members."[72] Not surprisingly, an attitude survey of Inkatha supporters conducted in 1977 found that 50 percent also supported the ANC.[73] According to Mzala, Buthelezi's selective appropriation of ANC history was deliberate, for his assumption of the mantle of the internal wing of the ANC (which is perhaps why he always referred to "the ANC mission-in-exile") would legitimize his position and give him strategic leverage in his battles against his critics.[74] But then along came the UDF, a movement whose nonracial emphasis on alliance-building placed it far closer to the traditions of the ANC than to an organization catering to the Zulu nation. The UDF, in other words, tore the ANC mantle from Inkatha's shoulders and revealed it for what it was—a purely "ethnic" organization.

Despite government repression and Inkatha violence, community-based, grassroots-level resistance was not stamped out by the Botha regime. Neither was the United Democratic Front. As Steve Mufson has put it, "when the government chops off the head of the UDF by detaining its executive committee members, the UDF body politic grows another head."[75] Brought on by consumer boycotts, the collapse of the administration of the townships, the continuing unrest, the imposition of sanctions from abroad, and the accelerating disinvestment, the crisis of confidence in apartheid mentioned by many commentators was manifest in a number of ways by the late 1980s. These manifestations were the decision of the Nederduitse Gereformeerde Kerk (NGK, the Calvinist Dutch Reformed Church) to declare apartheid a serious sin and to open its membership to all races; the numerous trips of prominent Afrikaner businessmen and intellectuals to various locations in Africa to meet with the ANC; the major splits, for the first time, to the left of the National party (that is, the formation of the Democratic party and of a "progressive" Afrikaner newspaper, *Vrye Weekblad*); the electoral support received by the Conservative party (which split from the NP in 1983); and the appearance of death squads, bombings, and other forms of right-wing violence.

Buffeted by all of these pressures, the National party instituted a number of changes to apartheid legislation. Under Botha, passbooks for blacks, influx control, job reservation for whites, and prohibitions against racially mixed sexual relations, marriage, trade unions, and political parties were all scrapped. According to Willem de Klerk, these changes were prompted by "an impatience and despair in the country. There is a realization among whites that the current policy is unacceptable to the majority of South Africans and to the international community, that the current policy is part of the problem, not the solution."[76] But with the three "pillars of apartheid"—Group Areas, Population Registration, and Land Acts—remaining on the statute books, no meaningful solution to the country's problems appeared forthcoming. As David Harrison has argued, "by the time Botha had become Prime Minister Apartheid was far more than a policy which could be repealed, an ugly aspect of an otherwise normal society. It was a total way of life, written into the constitution and enshrined in law. Apartheid had developed an unstoppable momentum of its own."[77]

Initial hopes that a solution acceptable to all might lie with Botha's successor, F. W. de Klerk, were soon dashed. In the same way that the SAIRR in 1948 doubted there was much of a difference between Smuts and Malan in terms of policy, the liberal weekly *Southern Africa Report* suspected that the only difference between Botha and de Klerk was one of manner. According to editor Raymond Louw, de Klerk "talks amiably and fluently in both languages without passion . . . while Botha's style is aggressive and hectoring, punctuated by 'you-listen-to-me' finger-waving." De Klerk's air of reasonableness left an impression on the country, reeling from "a decade of bullying" by President Botha, that a new era of reform was about to dawn. But through his speeches and those of his party followers, the newly installed NP leader had shown that reform had reached a dead end, "that he will pursue sterile apartheid policies and that he has no fresh ideas to offer."

Most of the evidence for this conclusion was drawn from an interview on the Afrikaans Sunday-night television program, "Netwerk," during which de Klerk stuck rigidly to the National party's apartheid policies of "own affairs" and "general affairs," the preservation of group rights, and "protection for minorities." He also opposed a one-man, one-vote system in a unitary state as the "death knell" for South Africa. He announced instead his intention to pursue Botha's thinking by instituting a National Forum which would give blacks the role of advisers in lawmaking. "Diversity of population," de Klerk said, "demanded the recognition of distinctive interests for which power bases should be created under which control over these interests could be exercised." The wording may have varied slightly from Botha's, according to Louw, "but the language was the same and it upheld the principle of the apartheid tricameral parliament with the 'fair referee' being the (white) state president elected by the majority vote of the ruling (National) party."[78]

Along with de Klerk's speeches, the ongoing commitment of the National party to white schools and neighborhoods led many people to subscribe to the "no fresh ideas" thesis. To demonstrate dissatisfaction with the pace of government reform and the hollowness of its claims that "apartheid is dead," a coalition of antiapartheid groups called the Mass Democratic movement (MDM) launched a second Defiance Campaign, thirty-seven years after the ANC and the SAIC launched the first one. By courting arrest at white hospitals and beaches, the campaigners aimed to show that even "petty apartheid" had not disappeared. In contrast to the first Defiance Campaign, the latest one was planned to be short-lived (peaking with the

September 1990 parliamentary elections) and had the outside world as its focus perhaps more than the National party.[79]

No sooner was the NP returned to office than Transkeian leader Major General Bantu Holomisa told the BBC world service radio that he wanted his territory reincorporated into South Africa and was prepared to hold a referendum to find out if Transkeians would agree with him.[80] Apparently they might, because two months later, in November 1989, a crowd of between 65,000 and 80,000 people packed a soccer stadium in Umtata, Transkei, to attend a rally for Walter Sisulu and six other ANC members recently released from jail. Amid shouts of "viva, viva ANC" the guests of honor urged Transkeians to send delegates to the Conference for a Democratic Future, planned for December 9, and said the ANC army, Umkonto, was alive and well in the Transkei alongside Holomisa's army.[81]

Since then, almost all of the independent black homelands and nonindependent self-governing states have been engulfed in what one commentator described as "popular eastern Europe-style revolts against the dictatorships and corruption of their rulers."[82] In Gazankulu in February 1990, government services were paralyzed as workers went on strike. Organizers demanded the resignation of Chief Minister Hudson Ntsanwisi and the abolition of government-sponsored youth and cultural organizations. Similar bouts of unrest, with huts burned down and people killed, occurred in Lebowa and Venda. Military factions seized power in Ciskei in February and in Venda in March. After the coup in Ciskei, the new leaders demanded reincorporation into South Africa; this coup was followed almost immediately by mass marches in BophuthaTswana against high rentals and service charges and in support of reincorporation.[83]

And still the National party had nothing new to offer. When the government spoke of power sharing it envisaged the participating entities to be groups (four racially defined groups and perhaps one other), not individuals. As de Klerk's vaunted five-year plan released in October 1989 made clear, each group would have autonomy over its own affairs but would agree on general affairs affecting the state as a whole on the basis of consensus. At the general affairs level, the size of the participating entity would not be the decisive factor; as de Klerk put it, all groups, irrespective of size, would have equal voting power and power of the veto.[84] What this plan represented was presentation by a minority of guidelines for a constitution that would enable it to maintain the status quo of white domination and exercise control over the majority through use of the veto. It was multiracialism by any other name and had nothing to do with majority rule or nonracialism.

The opposition forces, of course, knew this. As political prisoner Walter Sisulu emphasized at a press conference after his release from jail, the government was still talking in "group" philosophies, while the ANC was seeking a nonracial democracy, and those concepts were worlds apart.[85] ANC representative Thabo Mbeki told Ted Koppel in an interview for ABC's "Nightline" in February 1990 that the most pressing matter then facing opposition forces was the issue of group versus individual representation.

And then, within the space of only a year, everything seemingly changed. Mandela was out of prison, all opposition groups were unbanned, the National party wanted to negotiate with "genuine black leaders," the discourse had shifted from groups and minorities to "community rights," the "pillars of apartheid" were slated for removal, universal franchise was promised, and a new, mutually acceptable constitution for the country was to emerge from the government's four-phase reform process: a climate for talks, talks about talks, negotiations about a new constitution, and implementation of the constitution.[86] Almost overnight, it seemed, the National party's own politics of refusal to end apartheid had shifted to a politics of negotiation for a new South Africa.

All of this led many in the West to speak of change in Eastern Europe and South Africa in the same breath; the notion that apartheid was dying along with communism. Since apartheid generally connotes white domination, it was the whole system of white control in South Africa that was now, apparently, on the way out. F. W. de Klerk was the Mikhail Gorbachev of southern Africa—a visionary leader committed to fundamental change and progress toward a new South Africa. The willingness of Western states to lift sanctions demonstrates the unproblematic way in which this particular interpretation of events in South Africa over the past few months has been accepted.

As stated earlier, there has been a certain studied ambiguity in much of the National party's policy initiatives, leading at least some commentators to wonder whether it is all "just an exercise in co-option and manipulation."[87] The ambiguities over such terms as *community rights*, *standards*, and *generally acceptable alternative measures* need to be considered in evaluating the meaningfulness of the recent changes in South Africa's racial order.

Two other points also require emphasis. First, as mentioned earlier, white domination and apartheid are not synonymous. White domination describes an enduring, structural characteristic of the South African situation, while apartheid refers to a historically contingent set of political practices by which that same domination has been effected and preserved. The de Klerk regime may be in the business of finding new political practices that will leave the basic situation intact and that will not transform it. Second, if Harrison is correct that apartheid has become a "total way of life," then it may not necessarily disappear once the legislative scaffolding has been removed, particularly if "acceptable alternatives" are those intended to keep that same way of life intact. With these caveats in mind, the question of how exactly the new South Africa is to differ from the old one will be addressed in the final part of the chapter.

THE THIRD PHASE: WHITE DOMINATION AND THE POSTULATE OF IDENTITY, 1990 TO THE PRESENT

From the Politics of Refusal to the Politics of Negotiation

Although concrete policy proposals are conspicuous by their absence, it is in President de Klerk's February 1990 speech to the opening of Parliament—during the course of which he unbanned all major opposition groups—that a discursive shift away from the postulate of difference is first detectable. Less an indicator of something totally new in the offing, the speech is notable for the way in which it reinvigorates "civilization" as the entry requirement for blacks into white society.[88]

Western understandings of civilization are invoked through a recurring use of two key concepts: reason and private enterprise. The "collapse, particularly of the Marxist economic system in Eastern Europe" supposedly served "as a warning to those who insist on persisting with it in Africa. Those who seek to force this failure of a system on South Africa, should engage in a total revision of their point of view." De Klerk repeatedly described as reasonable, realistic, fair, and sensible anyone who agreed with "the overall aims to which we are aspiring." Those aims were identified as "a realistic development plan" for southern Africa; a "system for the protection of the rights of individuals, minorities and national entities"; structural changes in the economy that would "give the private sector maximum opportunity for optimal performance"; and a normalization of the political process that would not "jeopardise the maintenance of the good order."

As argued in earlier chapters, the use of reason as opposed to the free play of passion and emotion, and private property relations and enterprise in contrast to communal or tribal patterns of ownership, have historically been two of the hallmarks of Western civilization. The de Klerk speech thus constituted South Africa as Western and cast anyone who might hold to such barbaric practices as those recently abandoned by Eastern Europe as radical, unrealistic, unreasonable, unfair, and not worth talking to. Lest the Western credentials were not sufficiently obvious, the president insisted that his government accepted "the principle of the recognition and protection of the fundamental individual rights which form the constitutional basis of most Western democracies." He also aligned South Africa's economic system more explicitly with that of the West by claiming that the country was forced to make structural change to its economy, "just as its major trading partners had to do a decade or so ago," and emphasized the need "to give particular attention to the supply side of the economy." In conclusion, de Klerk called on the international community to "re-evaluate its position and to adopt a positive attitude towards the dynamic evolution which is taking place in South Africa."

What the February 1990 speech did was to make the voluntarist acceptance of civilization, rather than such fixed and inherited characteristics as skin color, the criterion for entry to the conference room of anyone wishing to negotiate with the government. In this way, it signaled a break from the politics of the Botha regime, which determined whom to talk to on the basis of race (the Indians and the Coloreds) and acceptance of separate development (the homeland leaders).

Although the February 1990 address to Parliament is perhaps most remembered for its promise of Nelson Mandela's release from jail, it is not obvious that a so-called communist like Mandela was one of the reasonable people with whom the NP wanted to negotiate. In a hard-hitting document submitted to P. W. Botha in 1989,[89] Mandela ridiculed the NP notion that majority rule was "a disaster to be avoided at all costs" (a "death knell" as de Klerk called it the same year). He pointed out the hypocrisy of whites for whom "majority rule is acceptable as long as it is considered within the context of white politics." Calling majority rule and internal peace "the two sides of a coin" that white South Africa would have to accept if there were ever to be peace in the country, Mandela insisted that the ANC would not abandon majority rule as a precondition for talks with the government. This precondition demonstrated that the government did not want peace in the country and, instead of a "strong and independent ANC," wanted "a weak and servile organization playing a supportive role to white minority rule, not a nonaligned ANC, but one which is a satellite of the West, and which is ready to serve the interests of capitalism."

Mandela's suspicions about the government's intentions with regard to the ANC were confirmed in the speech by de Klerk just cited. Arguing that "the events in the Soviet Union and Eastern Europe . . . weaken the capability of organizations which were previously supported strongly from those quarters" (i.e., the ANC and the SACP), de Klerk asserted that "the activities of the organizations from which the prohibitions are now being lifted no longer entail the same degree of threat to internal security which initially necessitated the imposition of the prohibitions." This may simply have been a reference to the drying up of arms supplies to the ANC that social transformation in Eastern Europe had since entailed. But de Klerk went on to say that there had been "important shifts of emphasis in the statements and points of view of the most important of the organizations concerned, which indicate a new approach and a preference for peaceful solutions."

Evidence for a new approach was not forthcoming, but what de Klerk may have had in mind was a statement issued the previous month by the London office of the ANC. Stating that they recognized President de Klerk's "gestures of material significance," four senior members of the movement said that the ANC was prepared to make significant compromises with Pretoria and pointed out, for example, that they were offering to negotiate even though apartheid had not been abolished.[90]

The ANC may have been "reasonable" in 1990 simply because it expressed a willingness to negotiate with the government. It may also have been reasonable because, while insisting on the nonnegotiability of majority rule, it evidently remained committed to the clauses in the 1955 Freedom Charter promising equal rights to all national groups. Soon after his release from prison, for example, Mandela told newspaper editor Max du Preez that the ANC believed the culture of everyone had to be protected and that everyone must have their own schools, language, culture, and religion because the country would be enriched as a result. This sounded remarkably like the NP's traditional defense of group rights, although Mandela went on to say that the state had a duty to provide nonracial schools that everyone could attend.[91]

But the question of whether the ANC was committed to the "barbaric" clauses in the Freedom Charter which promised the nationalization of industry and its transfer "to the ownership of the people as a whole" remained unanswered. The answer may depend upon who is speaking for the ANC, when they are speaking, and to whom they are speaking. Written on behalf of the ANC by Robert Davies, for example, a position paper on the economy available in early 1991[92] expressed "little faith in the capacity of 'free market' solutions to do anything other than reproduce the existing concentrations of income and wealth." This expression is consistent with earlier stances. But the paper went on to "acknowledge that market relations will be the basis on which the economy of a democratic, non-racial country operates." The necessity for ownership of industry by the people as a whole was reiterated, but Davies mentioned state control of "major infrastructure and public utilities—like electricity, transport, telecommunications and water services" rather than, as does the Freedom Charter, "the soil, the banks, and monopoly industry."[93] By contrast, Nelson Mandela told an audience of business executives only a few months later that the ANC still wanted to nationalize mines and banks because, he said, "the majority of the population did not have access to South Africa's resources."[94]

Whatever the differences to be resolved within the ANC, major differences between the ANC and the NP remain on matters of political economy. The ANC has likened the privatization program of the government to "selling off the family silver at knock-down prices" and demanded "immediate renationalization."[95] The ANC also has insisted on the restitution of land to those dispossessed under apartheid, while the NP remains determined to protect current property owners, including those with title to land taken away from blacks.[96] The ANC describes the watchword of its policy as "affirmative action," while the NP insists it does not have the resources to eliminate gross disparities between blacks and whites.[97] These differences will be at the heart of political struggles for many years to come. But the ANC's acceptance of a private sector economy and apparent commitment "to the creation of a situation in which business people, both South African and foreign, have confidence in the security of their investments"[98] make it a less unreasonable negotiating partner than might have been expected.

While de Klerk's February 1990 speech made acceptance of civilization a prerequisite to talks with the government, thus opening the possibility for dialogue with the ANC (if not with the PAC, which refused the terms), it was not exactly clear how the new South Africa was to differ from the old. *Southern Africa Report*'s early suspicion of de Klerk's government that it had no new ideas seemed confirmed soon afterward, on the occasion of a speech by Constitutional Development and Planning Minister Gerrit Viljoen.

National party promises to scrap the pillars of apartheid—the Group Areas Act, the Population Registration Act, and the Land Acts—usually have been accompanied by some reference to "generally acceptable alternative measures." The Population Registration Act, for example, is supposed to be replaced with "mutually acceptable alternative definitions of groups or of minorities based on freedom of association."[99] The aim of such "alternative measures," Viljoen told Parliament in April 1990, was to ensure that established life-styles and "standards" would be maintained. He explained that de Klerk's acceptable alternative to the Group Areas Act related to the protection of the property investment people had in their homes. This investment was affected by the area in which the property was situated and the living standards of that area. It was important, therefore, to maintain the particular living standards in such an area.

Viljoen went on to say that the government's view was that whites opposed blacks in their living areas because of their different life-style and not because of their skin color. For example, measures had to be introduced to prevent the occurrence of slum areas, overcrowding, and unhygienic practices. "Unacceptable" life-styles also would have to be dealt with. In conclusion, Viljoen summed up the government's position by saying that in the South Africa of the future, a choice of alternative life-styles had to be allowed, even if it meant exclusive schools and living areas or a choice by a person to side with a particular "group-definition."[100]

Describing such talk as "chicanery" certain to give offense to blacks, the *Southern Africa Report* insisted that the end result of the NP's plans was "the

Group Areas Act in somewhat more modern dress—but the Group Areas Act nevertheless."[101]

The chicanery was taken a step further by de Klerk in February 1991, on the occasion of the annual opening of Parliament. Most remembered for its "apartheid to go" promises,[102] the speech by the state president committed the government to the "effective protection of standards" in respect of education, housing, health, and agriculture.[103] Concretely, this commitment has resulted in legislation permitting the parents of children in white schools to keep blacks out if they wish, enabling neighborhoods to set their own standards for the prevention of physical deterioration (and so set limits on entry of blacks through resort to such possible measures as a maximum family size to prevent "overcrowding" and "slum creation"), and protecting existing property rights and security of tenure. Along with the selling of state corporations to white business and moves such as the Private Sector Initiative to boost private enterprise, these measures have ensured that the educational, physical, and economic mobility of blacks continues to be determined ultimately by the white community.

The difference from post-1948 South Africa is that skin color is no longer a state-sanctioned basis for exclusion from white society. Those deemed civilized enough may be admitted and ultimately assimilated, but what counts as civilization is still for the white community to decide. The postulate of identity has replaced the postulate of difference, so that the new South Africa shares something in common with the old one pre-National party. The old system also was in theory nonracial and held out the prospects for possible assimilation of those who passed the civilization test, but like de Klerk's South Africa and the discourse of community rights, it devolved a good deal of discretionary power onto white civil society. Reminiscent of the current "own schools" legislation, for example, the United party in 1939 proposed that if 75 percent of property owners in a district voted for residential segregation, the government would register a servitude on their title deeds, restricting ownership or occupation in that district to one race only.[104] The UP also eroded Colored franchise rights with a series of Jim Crow laws enacted in 1945, 1946, and 1948. These measures enlarged the opportunity, provided by the 1931 Electoral Laws Act, for anyone at any time to challenge a registered voter to prove his qualifications for the franchise before a magistrate's court.[105] Those who could afford the time and money to go to court and plead their case were usually successful, but the vast majority who could not would be disenfranchised in absentia.

The big difference between the old South Africa and the one envisaged by de Klerk is that no one will be forced to pass a civilization test in order to vote. Undoubtedly, it is by appeal to the concept of universal franchise that the National party hopes to legitimize the new South Africa. Indeed, de Klerk never ceases to insist that what the government has in mind "is in line with successful democratic systems all over the free world."[106] But in this regard it is important to emphasize that a new self, rather than simply a new system of representing the existing self, is what is envisaged. Those classified since 1948 as native or black are part of that envisaged self as South Africans, not as different nations. De Klerk insisted at the beginning of his speech to Parliament in 1991 that the government had to "give impetus to our resolve to build a new South African nation," that "the time has arrived for nation-building," and that "the task of nation-building is formidable."[107] De Klerk's appeal was reminiscent of the one made by Verwoerd during the republican campaign of 1960, when he exhorted whites to vote for a republic and so cooperate in "developing a united nation."[108] But whereas Verwoerd's move was to constitute South Africa as a white nation by making the postulate of identity applicable to relations between whites only—that is, it recast blacks as foreign and unassimilable—de Klerk has brought black South Africans within the boundaries of the national self. Regardless of how much control and privilege continue to remain in white hands, it is for this move that the current National party is despised by a variety of right-wing organizations.

To summarize, the National party seems determined to enable white control over the economy, schools, neighborhoods, and hospitals through a commitment to private enterprise and the discourse of community rights and standards, while it scraps apartheid legislation and promises a universal franchise to include the black majority. While recent government initiatives shift the onus for control onto white civil society and away from the state, it remains to be considered whether some legal entrenchment of white domination is also in the cards.

This question inevitably returns the discussion to an analysis of the National party's commitment to group rights as a way to institute universal franchise without majority rule. Government officials have proposed a federal model with a devolution of power down to the town (even neighborhood) level and a two-chamber parliament, one popularly elected and the other representing political parties or groups according to cultural, linguistic, or regional interests, but not according to race. Proposals for the sharing of power between up to five parties have already drawn fire as a form of entrenched white privilege.[109] But it is also necessary to ask on what basis, if not racially, such groups or parties are to be defined. De Klerk insisted in February 1990 that "everybody's political points of view will be tested against their realism, their workability and their fairness,"[110] and statements since then have demonstrated that, for the National party, racial groups are "real." Constitutional Development and Planning Minister Gerrit Viljoen, for example, told the press in 1990 that his government "doesn't like the word non-racial. Races are part of the reality of South Africa."[111] In February 1991 de Klerk spoke of "the reality of the existence of a variety of peoples and communities" that in South Africa as elsewhere "have maintained a specific identity" and voiced the conviction that "recognition has to be given to this reality in any new dispensation."[112]

What is important to remember is that identity in South Africa has never been based solely on race, and the government's willingness to make group identification a matter of "one's own inherent will and abilities and not statutory coercion"[113] opens up political space for a whole range of different possibilities. One could imagine, for example, an Afrikaner cultural group as envisaged by Piet Muller in 1980 uniting "white and brown Afrikaans-speakers"; a Pan-Africanist group bringing together Africans, Coloreds, and Indians; or a Boer group keeping alive the traditions of the Voortrekker past. A range of groups organized around the idea of a specific Zulu, Xhosa, or other ethnic identity may also emerge. All of this is possible, but the National party's assumption that socially constituted racial differences are now real suggests that the NP at least would not consider it very likely.

The implementation of all of these plans for a new South Africa will inevitably be shaped by the process of transition itself, by the way in which blacks either resist or accept the National party's initiatives. Although the government expects a new constitution to emerge from a series of negotiations with such formal political organizations as the ANC—a process that may take years rather than months—it is well aware that political struggle is not confined to the ranks of such organizations and has threatened action to stifle popular struggle in the future.

After unbanning the formal opposition groups like the ANC in 1990, de Klerk a year later implicitly recognized the importance of schools and the workplace as sites of struggle, as well as the power of various forms of mass action. He warned that schools and pupils should not "be abused for political purposes," insisted that "unjustifiable wage increases" do not "serve the overall public interest," exhorted against "militant action in the labor or other fields," and inveighed against mass actions that "exceed the bounds of the normal democratic process," that is, those which "disrupt the public, harm individuals, and undermine the economy."[114] Yet despite the constitution of such actions as rent and consumer boycotts as undemocratic and abnormal, de Klerk is unlikely to be able to prevent various forms of mass struggle in the future, for two reasons.

First, despite the ANC's insistence that lifting sanctions would make Pretoria more intransigent, it has been unable to prevent the West from rewarding de Klerk for his willingness to scrap apartheid. In order to maintain some leverage in future talks with the government, argued Christopher Wren in April 1991, the ANC "may fall back on its strategy of 'mass action'— strikes, boycotts, and other protests—that could add to instability."[115] Only a few months later the ANC and its industrial ally, Cosatu, launched a massive national strike in protest over a proposed new sales tax.[116]

Second, the localization of white control over black lives that the privatization of the economy and community rights entail will require the localization of struggle—that is, the enactment of punitive measures against schools, neighborhoods, businesses, municipal councils, and so on that refuse to admit blacks on the grounds that their standards (of education, hygiene, job qualifications, property ownership, or whatever else) are not sufficiently high. The formation of a new Cosatu/UDF civic association mentioned earlier is just one instance of a shift to this type of strategy. Just as apartheid enabled the sort of mass action it was designed to prevent by making common oppression the stimulus to a common black identity, community rights may keep alive the mass-based struggles that de Klerk has insisted must cease.

What remains to be seen is the effect on political struggle of the National party's call to make group identification a matter of choice and not coercion. As stated already, the NP seems to expect the normality of racial identification to persist without a formal system of classification, but differences over which identity to privilege have long been at the heart of political struggles, in South Africa as elsewhere. The free play of such differences that the scrapping of the Population Registration Act promises may very well result in a proliferation of groups or parties that make particular languages, histories, religions, cultural customs, or regions the immediate point of identification. Nonetheless, it is interesting to speculate how the National party would respond if everyone took de Klerk's "nation-building" message seriously and defined the self as simply South African.

Summary

This chapter began by considering the crisis of confidence in white society that many commentators have noted since the early 1970s. It argued that the crisis has been one of confidence in the state to control African mobility and to legitimize territorial separate development. Black resistance in both cases is a more convincing explanation for reform politics than greater self-confidence among Afrikaners.

The ten-year period from 1973 to 1983 constituted the first phase in the National party's reform process. The granting of limited rights in concert with an ongoing commitment to national separation rendered this phase a study in inconsistency. Blacks were both citizens with rights and rightless aliens; only the acquisition and maintenance of employment—rather than a more normal criterion such as the place of one's birth—determined whether an individual was to be one or the other. During the course of a lifetime an African could be both citizen and foreigner, self and other.

A new constitution in 1983 brought Coloreds and Indians into a tricameral Parliament still under the ultimate control of whites. This second phase of the reform process—from 1983 to 1990—merely added new inconsistencies to the old ones. Since 1948 all of South Africa's black groups were supposedly different nations, yet after 1983 two of those groups—the Indians and the Coloreds—were to be given rights as races within a common (if structurally separated) central government. Henceforward there would be rights for some based on their identity as workers and for others based on the racial category to which they had been assigned. The majority, however, were to remain rightless altogether. Lacking any sound historical or contemporary rationale, the incorporation of a supposedly alien people like the Indians undermined any possible case for continuing to exclude the alien (i.e., nonemployed by whites) Africans. A new outbreak of mass unrest within a year of the promulgation of the new constitution was the somewhat predictable outcome.

That education remains such a predominant focus of black resistance to domination is testimony to the success of Black Consciousness as a counter-discourse or hidden transcript working to denaturalize multiracialism and national separation. The Black Consciousness movement (BCM) has been able to mobilize community action, education, and labor groups due more to the appeal of a Biko-popularized philosophy than to the attractiveness of a particular political program. Biko's invocation to blacks to "rise and attain the envisaged self" implies remaking one's identity through the reclamation of silenced histories as well as through the voluntary appropriation of a black identity that challenges constructed racial categories.

Black Consciousness has been threatening enough to the National party to warrant bannings, detentions, and even (in Biko's case) deaths in custody. But Black Consciousness philosophy has had to counter, in addition to state repression, the appeal of two different forms of identity politics ongoing within the black community. On the one hand, there is the older, more established interracial alliance politics of the ANC, which treats South Africa as a country of nationalities and the term *black* as synonymous with *African*. On the other hand, there is the recently revived Inkatha movement (now Inkatha Freedom party) of Chief Gatsha Buthelezi, which organizes political action around appeal to an exclusive Zulu nationality. The "black-on-black violence" that consumes more and more lives in South Africa is a disaster and a tragedy, but it is a phenomenon that cannot be so easily written off as either the total responsibility of the government (for its active, if covert, support of Inkatha) or the inevitable effect of tribal rivalry. The violence is rooted in fundamentally different political responses to questions about identity and resistance.

Whatever the differences among the organized black groups, the massive rejection of apartheid evident in South Africa over the past few years has forced the National party finally to abandon the postulate of difference on which its policy has been based since 1948. In scrapping apartheid legislation and promising a universal franchise to include the black majority, the NP has clearly signaled the end of its commitment to the idea of national separation and the premise of radical difference. The postulate of difference has been replaced with the postulate of identity. But it is important to remember that both identity and difference historically have been hierarchical (i.e., the self always has been envisaged as superior to the other even when the prospects for eventual assimilability of the other have not been dismissed) and implicated in the perpetuation of white domination.

What the National party's plans for a new South Africa seem to entail is the formal sharing of power among groups (which may or may not be racially defined) and regions at the central level in tandem with drastically decentralized white control over the economy, schools, neighborhoods, and hospitals. The race-neutral discourse of community rights and standards is to replace the equally race-neutral idea of separate development as a way to perpetuate white control and privilege.

But what the National party wants, the National party will not necessarily get. As in previous eras, the political direction that South Africa takes will be shaped by a range of practices of resistance to domination involving not only such formal political organizations as the ANC but also less obviously political groups such as civic associations, student movements, worker federations, and so on. The greater the attempts to decentralize white control, the more localized resistance may become, so that those who look for politics only within or against the central institutions of the state will find themselves staring, increasingly, into the wrong social spaces.

NOTES

1. de Villiers, *White Tribe Dreaming*, p. 326.
2. See Brewer, *After Soweto: An Unfinished Journey*, p. 30.
3. In 1988, I interviewed a number of prominent Afrikaners from all walks of life concerning their attitudes on a number of issues, before widely circulating an extended questionnaire designed to tap the extent to which apartheid had become naturalized among the Afrikaans-speaking elite. That change in the self-confidence of Afrikaners was related to larger societal changes was a prominent theme in the interview responses. Transvaal farmer Adriaan Scheepers (who twice stood as a candidate for the old United party), for example, suggested that change had occurred because "the Nationalists can no longer exploit the group inferiority complex among Afrikaners, which is how they got into power in the first place. The group inferiority complex is now gone, and anyway you can't keep people [i.e., blacks] down indefinitely." South African Defence Force (SADF) Colonel Chris Van Zyl made essentially the same point when he said that "the Afrikaner has undergone a change of role and attitude in so far as he had to fight for an existence—let's not call it his existence, his independence—right from the beginning. To a large extent he has achieved that aim."

Willem de Klerk (former journalist and the brother of the current state president), on the other hand, had a less Afrikaner-centered view of why change was occurring. "Apartheid," he said, "failed because blacks rejected it."

4. Harrison, *The White Tribe of Africa*, pp. 271–72.

5. de Villiers, *White Tribe Dreaming*, p. 328.

6. On this point, see Greenberg, *Legitimating the Illegitimate*.

7. Giliomee and Schlemmer, *From Apartheid to Nation-Building*, chapter 4.

8. See *Southern Africa Report*, January 12, 1990, p. 8.

9. Interview with the author, Johannesburg, South Africa, June 1988.

10. See Wren, "Apartheid Battleground Shifts to Economy," p. 7.

11. Quoted in Brewer, *After Soweto: An Unfinished Journey*, p. 29.

12. Quoted in Omond, "South African Spectre of Carnage Persists," p. 11.

13. See Margaret A. Novicki's interview with the Reverend Alan Boesak in *Africa Report* (March/April 1990), pp. 17–21.

14. See, for example, a recent speech by Constitutional Development and Planning Minister Gerrit Viljoen, reprinted in *Southern Africa Report*, April 20, 1990, pp. 1–2.

15. See Maclennan, "New South Africa Need Not Punish the 'Haves,' " p. 1.

16. The Carnegie Endowment's Pauline Baker has referred to the town council plan as "a nineteenth-century notion of representation based on wealth" aimed at the preservation of white power. See Wines, "U.S. Takes Neutral Attitude on de Klerk Plan for Universal Suffrage," p. 3. The ANC, not surprisingly, has rejected the plan for similar reasons. See Noble, "South Africa's President Outlines Plan for Universal Voting Rights," pp. 1, 9.

17. See Wren, "Pretoria's Land Plan: More for Blacks," p. 3.

18. See "Education to Keep Own Group Option," *The Star*, February 1, 1991, p. 2.

19. See Wren, "Apartheid Barrier to Land Scrapped in Pretoria Plan," p. A1.

20. See Seery and Nyaka, "Mandela Says 'No' to FW," p. 2.

21. Quoted in *The Nation*, July 1, 1991, p. 16.

22. This position recently has been laid out again in an occasional paper published by the Institute for a Democratic Alternative for South Africa. See Shabalala, "Economic Emancipation: A Pan Africanist View."

23. See, for example, the statement by van der Merwe in "Visions of Change: A Symposium," pp. 38–41.

24. See the statement by Gerrit Viljoen in ibid., pp. 41–45.

25. See the statement by Nelson Mandela in ibid., pp. 32–35.

26. See, for example, a speech he gave in Natal in 1986, quoted in Mzala, *Gatsha Buthelezi*, p. 158.

27. Quoted in *New York Times*, May 18, 1973, p. 35.

28. Quoted in SAIRR, *Annual Survey of Race Relations in South Africa, 1973* (Johannesburg, 1973), pp. 281–82.

29. Biko, *I Write What I Like*, p. 68.

30. Ibid., p. 69.

31. Ibid., pp. 69–70.

32. On the BCM in general, see Motlhabi, *The Theory and Practice of Black Resistance*, chapter 4.

33. Mzala, *Gatsha Buthelezi*, p. 87.

34. Ibid., p. 116.

35. Quoted in ibid., p. 117.

36. Ibid., p. 119.

37. See, for example, the speeches quoted in ibid., p. 120; and in Mare and Hamilton, *An Appetite for Power*, p. 15.

38. Both Mzala and Mare and Hamilton dispute the high membership figures claimed for Inkatha. See Mzala, *Gatsha Buthelezi*, pp. 128–37; and Mare and Hamilton, *An Appetite for Power*, pp. 70–73.

39. *Africa Research Bulletin* (1980), p. 5614.

40. Commission on U.S. Policy toward Southern Africa, *South Africa: Time Running Out*, p. 180.

41. For a fuller account, see Davis, *Apartheid's Rebels*, chapter 2.

42. See Brewer, *After Soweto: An Unfinished Journey*, chapter 2.

43. Hufbauer and Schott, *Economic Sanctions Reconsidered: History and Current Policy*, p. 348.

44. The best account of the boycott remains that of William Finnegan, an American who taught in a Colored high school in Cape Town in 1980. See Finnegan, *Crossing the Line: A Year in the Land of Apartheid*, especially part II.

45. Mzala, *Gatsha Buthelezi*, p. 14.

46. See "Talk Can Prevent a Bloodbath in South Africa," *Die Transvaler*, May 12, 1980.

47. See "Adaptation a Weapon against Conflict," *Beeld*, July 3, 1979.

48. See "Rhodesia and Elsewhere: Lessons for South Africa," *Die Vaderland*, February 21, 1980.

49. See "Rhodesia's Lessons for South Africa Also Written in Cillie Report," *Die Burger*, March 5, 1980.

50. See "Powersharing on This Level Will Never Work," *Die Transvaler*, September 6, 1980.

51. See "Afrikaner with 'New Eyes' toward the Future," *Beeld*, March 5, 1980.

52. Lelyveld, *Move Your Shadow*, p. 350.

53. Quoted in Greenberg, *Legitimating the Illegitimate*, p. 178.

54. *Southern Africa Report*, August 15, 1986, p. 3.

55. Wren, "South African Racial Toll Put at More Than 4,000," p. 3.

56. *Southern Africa Report*, January 29, 1988, p. 7.

57. Ibid., December 1, 1989, p. 6.

58. See Davis, *Apartheid's Rebels*, chapter 3.

59. *Southern Africa Report*, March 16, 1990, p. 1.

60. See Beresford, "ANC Sets Government an Ultimatum," p. 6.

61. See Riesenfeld, "David Webster: The Spirit Is Unbroken," pp. 27–30.

62. See *Southern Africa Report*, April 28, 1989, p. 3.

63. Ibid., December 2, 1988, p. 4 (on the Boksburg boycott); and March 3, 1989, p. 1 (on the Carletonville boycott).

64. Ibid., April 7, 1989, p. 5.

65. Mzala, *Gatsha Buthelezi*, pp. 15–16.

66. Ibid., pp. 20–21.

67. In 1983, for example, Buthelezi put the blame for the resistance to the Lamontville township's incorporation into KwaZulu on the role played by non-Zulus:

> We are sick and tired of people of Xhosa extraction here in our midst. . . . Lawyers, men of the cloth and people who penetrated our own organization, of Xhosa extraction, cannot be allowed the freedom in our midst to wreak havoc among our people and our youth. (Mzala, *Gatsha Buthelezi*, p. 120)

68. Ibid., p. 158.

69. Ibid., p. 159.

70. Ibid., p. 162.

71. Ibid.

72. Mare and Hamilton, *An Appetite for Power*, p. 77.

73. See Mzala, *Gatsha Buthelezi*, p. 122.

74. Ibid., p. 128.

75. Mufson, "A Long View from Deep Soweto," pp. 8–11.

76. Thurow, "Brothers Symbolize Split in South Africa," p. 2.

77. Harrison, *The White Tribe of Africa*, p. 276.

78. See Louw, "After a Feint to the Left, de Klerk Backs Conservative Apartheid and Blights Prospects of 'Reform,' " pp. 1–2.

79. See *Southern Africa Report*, August 11, 1989, p. 1; and August 25, 1989, p. 1.

80. Ibid., October 6, 1989, p. 4.

81. Ibid., December 1, 1989, p. 6.

82. See the editorial by Raymond Louw in *Southern Africa Report*, March 9, 1990, p. 1.

83. See ibid., March 9, 1990, p. 1.

84. See ibid., October 6, 1989, pp. 1, 7.

85. Ibid., October 20, 1989, p. 2.

86. This four-phase scenario was outlined by Constitutional Development and Planning Minister Gerrit Viljoen in April 1990. See "Chief Negotiator Gerrit Viljoen Hopes New Constitution Will Be Ready in Two Years," *Southern Africa Report*, April 20, 1990, p. 3.

87. See Omond, "South African Spectre of Carnage Persists."

88. See the transcript of the speech in *Southern Africa Report*, February 9, 1990, pp. 7–16.

89. See the transcript entitled "Mandela's Blueprint for South Africa's Future," *Guardian Weekly*, February 4, 1990, pp. 8–9.

90. See *Southern Africa Report*, January 19, 1990, p. 12.

91. See ibid., March 2, 1990, p. 12.

92. Davies, "Nationalization: A View from the ANC."

93. See Mandela, *The Struggle Is My Life*, p. 51.

94. Quoted in Wren, "Apartheid Battleground Shifts to Economy."

95. Davies, "Nationalization: A View from the ANC."

96. See Wren, "Pretoria's Land Plan: More for Blacks," p. 3.

97. See Davis, *Apartheid's Rebels*; and Wren, "Europe Drops Sanctions: A Reward, Not a Cure, for South Africa," p. E5.

98. This comment was made by Mandela before the U.S. Congress in Washington, D.C. *See Southern Africa Report*, June 29, 1990, p. 3. For a contrast, see Mandela's own earlier views on imperialism in Mandela, *The Struggle Is My Life*, pp. 72–77.

99. See the speech by Viljoen quoted in *Southern Africa Report*, April 20, 1990, p. 2.

100. Ibid., April 27, 1990, p. 2.

101. Ibid.

102. "Apartheid to go" was the headline in *The Star* (Johannesburg) on February 1, 1991, p. 1.

103. Address by State President F. W. de Klerk to the South African Parliament, February 1, 1991, p. 6. Transcript available from the South African Consulate, Beverly Hills, Calif.

104. See Lewis, *Between the Wire and the Wall*, p. 191.

105. Ibid., p. 211.

106. Quoted in Noble, "South African President Outlines Plan."

107. De Klerk's address to Parliament, 1991, pp. 1–2.

108. See Hepple, *Verwoerd*, p. 177.
109. See "Democracy and Majority Rule," *Guardian Weekly*, September 15, 1991, p. 9.
110. Quoted in *Southern Africa Report*, February 9, 1990, p. 16.
111. Quoted in *New York Times*, February 15, 1990, p. 3.
112. De Klerk's address to Parliament, 1991, p. 8.
113. Ibid.
114. Ibid., pp. 11–12, 16.
115. See Wren, "Europe Drops Sanctions."
116. See Wren, "Strike by Blacks Paralyzes South Africa," p. 3.

6

Global Power and South African Politics: To Be Continued . . .

No book on South Africa these days, it seems, can conclude without some speculation as to what the future holds for the country. Such speculation is frequently presented in the form of a number of alternative scenarios. Stephen Davis, for example, concludes his recent book on the ANC by considering four possibilities: government entrenchment, government crackdown, revolution, and negotiation. Deeming the last of the four most likely, Davis suggests that the National party, if clever, might be able to cause ruptures among blacks and forge a "reformist alliance" without the ANC, preserving, in the process, most of the privileges that whites now enjoy. To prevent this, Davis argues, the ANC needs time to win over rival constituencies and strengthen the internal underground; too rapid a move toward negotiations, presumably, would not be in the ANC's best interest.[1]

The NP's perception at the time it unbanned the ANC that the ANC was weak, the partiality of the security forces in dealing with violent conflict between Inkatha and affiliates of the ANC, the government's acknowledgment of covert funding of Inkatha, and the ANC's withdrawal on two occasions from talks with the government,[2] all lend credence to the "Davis scenario." Davis's argument that the objective of negotiations is the retention of white privilege also has been supported in this book through analysis of debates in the Afrikaans press at the time of Zimbabwean independence and of recent National party policy initiatives.

There is therefore nothing wrong per se in speculating about South Africa's future; Davis's work demonstrates the political astuteness of many such recent speculations. This book will "join the club" and conclude with a few speculations of its own. But in light of the major premise that South African politics are an effect of global power relations, this book cannot conclude, as so many recent books do, by discussing the possible effects of changing relations of power at the domestic level only—for example, the implications of a Conservative party electoral victory for future struggle and change. While not politically irrelevant and no doubt academically interesting, such an analysis would leave untouched the major issues raised in previous chapters, namely how global relations of power constitute subjects and normalize relations of domination, while at the same time disseminating ideas about what constitutes normality in dealing with the various types of resistance that domination inevitably generates. What form resistance takes, its magnitude, and struggles among the subjugated themselves over how best to resist also have been shown to be a local effect of global relations of power.

Given the theoretical (Foucaultian) attitude to power and struggle, and its emphasis on power as a global network of relations, this book will conclude by considering the possible future implications for South Africa of a number of shifting and ongoing relations of power in which South African citizens are or might be enmeshed. These implications are the decline of communism in Eastern Europe and the reassertion of American hegemony in the international system; the ongoing interventions by the West, in the name of "development," into the lives of Third World peoples; and the multiracialism of Western states during the past few years in particular. Whether the current exercise of global power enlarges or diminishes the prospects for an end to white domination in South Africa is a major concern of this chapter.

CIVILIZATION AS A GLOBAL NORM

Long considered hallmarks of barbarism, as previous chapters demonstrated, the decline of communalism and ownership of property by the people as a whole in Eastern Europe and the Soviet Union has been heralded as the final realization of freedom in the state and reason in history.[3] As such, it seems to presage the final victory of civilization over barbarism on a global scale. Whether there really is justification for such complacency is questionable. But in thinking about the implications for South Africa of the people's revolutions in Eastern Europe, there are three specific consequences of those revolutions that need to be addressed: (1) the effects on the ANC of the drying up of military support at a time when Europe is ignoring the ANC's opposition to the lifting of sanctions, (2) the effects on the entire liberation struggle of the absence of a global counter-discourse of resistance to capitalist democracy, and (3) the effects on the entire liberation struggle of the global reassertion of American hegemony. Each of these points will be discussed in turn.

The Decline of Support for the ANC

Pressure on the ANC from the West to adopt negotiation as the method of achieving its objectives—that is, the traditional Western stance against violence as a political strategy for opposition movements—was joined in 1990 by similar pressures from the still-existing Soviet Union. Although the Soviets said they would continue to support the liberation movement even to the extent of supporting its armed struggle (now suspended), they told the ANC that they wanted a negotiated settlement, and soon.[4] Embroiled in its own problems, the emergent Commonwealth of Independent States (the former Soviet Union) is simply in no position to aid the ANC.

Pressure on the ANC for a negotiated settlement has been reinforced by the revolutions in Eastern Europe, from whence a good deal of ANC support came. East Germany, once the major military supplier of Umkonto (the armed wing of the ANC), ceased supplying aid even before the reunification of East and West Germany; since then all military aid has come to a halt. That leaves the ANC with only the Scandinavian countries (particularly Sweden) as major backers and there is little prospect of these countries being able to shoulder the costs of the exiled ANC population, let alone its various training camps and other operations. Scandinavia, in addition, has a long-standing policy of supplying humanitarian aid only.

The ANC must, in addition to strengthening the movement domestically and resolving internal differences, devote time to fundraising activities overseas. Recognizing that the diminished material support could force the movement to make compromises that it would wish to avoid, Mandela called on the international community in 1990 to fund the ANC to enable it to continue its campaign for change in South Africa.[5] Thanks largely to the stature of the man, these requests generated a positive response. The Canadian government, for example, established a "Mandela Fund" and a $1 million business training fund,[6] while Mandela and the Rockefeller Foundation in the United States began plans for the creation of a South African development bank to change the country's white-dominated economy through foreign investment.[7] But at a time when South Africa is wracked by violence and many others—in Eastern Europe in particular—are competing for access to funding resources, it is not clear how much more money the South African liberation movements realistically can expect.

In addition to worrying about lack of funds for themselves, the ANC and others have expressed concern that the West not "reward" de Klerk by lifting sanctions against South Africa. The National party reacted with delight, for example, when Britain lifted its cultural boycott and announced in February 1990 that the voluntary bans on new investment also were to be lifted despite opposition from Britain's European Community partners.[8] Nelson Mandela's biographer Fatima Meer spoke for many black South Africans (certainly those affiliated with the ANC) when she argued that "this is not the time for South Africa's trading partners to talk about withdrawing sanctions or rewarding de Klerk. Any such 'reward' would be the kiss of death and may revive white delusions that they could revert to apartheid after all." The interests of all who seriously want change, she went on, "are best served by retaining sanctions, even increasing them, until the delicate transition to democracy has been made and a new government is actually, or about to be, installed."[9]

Mandela made a big impact on Western leaders during his 1990 diplomatic tours, being warmly received in Canada, France, Germany, and the United States—even in Great Britain, only a year after Margaret Thatcher refused all talks with "the terrorist organization." Yet a year later, Mandela found little support in Japan and Britain for his pleas to hold the line on sanctions and was unable to prevent the European Community from voting to lift the sanctions earlier imposed on South Africa. This defeat prompted Mandela to deplore how readily "Europe allies itself with white South Africa and has no regard for the life, the views and the needs of black South Africa." He also bemoaned "that race still plays such a significant part in decision-making even as we enter the much-heralded 21st century."[10]

The notion that Europe has reasserted its historical alliance with white South Africa was implicitly supported soon after Mandela's speech by the National party's Foreign Minister Roelof "Pik" Botha. Invoking the importance of the "psychological effect of the decision," Botha said at a news conference that "it should now make it clear to South Africans that the way the State President has chosen is the way that Europe will support."[11]

Although the ANC has proved stronger than the NP hoped in 1990, the decline of support for the ANC from both East and West clearly has tipped the balance of power in favor of the government. As Botha indicated, the psychological importance of the lifting of sanctions is not to be overlooked, because it promises Western support for the regime at a time when opposition movements insist that fundamental change has yet to occur. The necessity to devote time and energy to securing new sources of funding stretches the leadership of the ANC increasingly thin and puts pressure on Congress as a whole at a time when it is faced with a myriad of other problems. While searching for an end to black-on-black violence, the ANC must respond to charges of lack of organization, of autocratic leadership, of lack of democratic processes between branches, of internal differences, and of uncertain policies.[12] In addition to organizing strikes, the ANC has joined a "patriotic front" to press for an interim government,[13] moves which demonstrate that the option of a return to a purely armed struggle is not feasible given the current global political climate. The moves also suggest that the ANC is not by itself strong enough to overturn minority privilege. The ANC will almost certainly figure largely at the negotiating table, but unless it can harness the enormous stock of support that it still enjoys at the grassroots level, it will be forced to enter negotiations from an unenviable position—that of a junior and weak partner to the National party.

How the ANC is able to resolve its actual and potential problems seems to depend on precisely what the movement claims political violence is preventing it from doing—namely, organizing at the local level. There is, therefore, some credence to the movement's claim that elements within the government have a large stake in keeping the violence going. Given all of these constraints, the ANC seems to have had little option, in the short run, but to initiate the formation of a patriotic front. The PAC's Dikgang Moseneke may be correct in his assertion that the unity movement "has introduced a major shift in the balance of power" between the National party and its opponents.[14] But given the ongoing differences between the ANC and the PAC, as well as the refusal of the Inkatha Freedom party to join, it remains to be seen how long the patriotic front can hold together. And even if it can do so through the negotiation process, the organized opposition as a whole needs to grapple with other effects of the decline of communism in Eastern Europe and the Soviet Union.

The Absence of a Global Challenge to Capitalist Democracy

Operating in the name of Marxism, or Marxism-Leninism, the states of the Soviet Union and Eastern Europe challenged the norm of capitalist democracy on a global scale, particularly after World War II and the rise to unprecedented economic preeminence of the United States. The increasing embracement by these countries of "the market" and "elections" as the solution to their political and economic problems—that is, the seeming capitulation to the civilized principles of private enterprise, private property, individualism, and so on—has left those who would resist the negative effects of civilization without a ready-made counter-discourse to which to appeal. Mandela, for example, has stressed to Western audiences that fewer than ten corporate conglomerates control 90 percent of the shares on the Johannesburg stock exchange and that more than 80 percent of South Africa's land is in white hands. He has insisted that such "excessive concentration of wealth" on the part of a few must be redressed, while at the same time admitting that the ANC has "no blueprint" for how this is to be done.[15] Rather than appeal to such stock formulas as nationalization, as not only the ANC but many liberation movements did at the height of Soviet power, opponents of capitalism may be forced to invoke "the market" as the privileged subject around which all struggles for economic justice must orient themselves.

To a certain extent, this shift has already happened—indeed, "market relations" have been accepted as normal by all opposition groups in South Africa.[16] At the same time, there has been resistance to the idea that the market must be free; that is, to the notion that accepting market relations necessarily means accepting free enterprise.[17] Victory celebrations for liberal capitalism are not the only discernable response to the demise of so-called Marxist-Leninist systems, in South Africa or anywhere else. Trying to figure out what went wrong in Eastern Europe, people on the left have used the occasion of the demise of communism not to retreat to capitalism but to rethink the essence of socialism and what a system true to socialist values might look like.

If there is a consistent theme to the critiques of Soviet-style socialism it is that the "model" was undemocratic. C. Douglas Lummis has recently demonstrated how Lenin actually was quite frank in emphasizing that in the field of economic development—his project for the Soviet Union—there is no room for democracy,[18] while Michael Burawoy has argued that a "radical democracy" must go beyond both "bourgeois democracy"—which "systematically demobilizes subordinate classes"—and a "state socialism" which "systematically destroyed the independent power of the working class in the name of Marxism." Responding to the question of what lessons for South Africa can be drawn from the experiences of Eastern Europe, Burawoy pointed out the importance of retaining and building upon democratic practices outside of the formal institutions of the state. South Africa, he suggested, is fortunate since lengthy struggles have created autonomous realms in civil society and in the workplace; continuing to expand and consolidate those realms during and after the formal democratization process toward majority rule will remain an important political project.[19]

Enjoying an anomalous amount of strength for a communist party, according to Patrick Laurence,[20] the South African Communist party moved quickly with the events in Eastern Europe to rethink its own position on socialism. Party General Secretary Joe Slovo argued in May 1990 that socialism had proved unable to compete with world capitalism because it had been "distorted by various countries." The SACP intended to continue to cultivate support for socialism but was not blind to its failures: "the party still endorses the processes of perestroika and glasnost."[21] A month later, Slovo argued that the significant message to be drawn from Eastern Europe was that socialism could not flourish without democracy and a communist party could not constitutionally entrench its leading role; it had to earn it. No meaningful emancipation of the majority of South Africa's people was possible, the SACP believed, "without major redistribution of wealth and without affirmative social and economic programmes."[22]

Although it is not always clear from these debates whether democracy is envisaged as a prerequisite for the attainment of socialism or an outcome of socialist practices, what they represent are attempts to resist the normality of thinking that only free-market economies can bring democracy.[23] In the South African context, whereas Burawoy emphasized the importance of local democratic practices for socialism, the SACP alluded to "affirmative action." This phrase was explicitly described recently by Robert Davies for the ANC as "the watchword of our policy."[24] The appropriation of the discourse of affirmative action by various groups in South Africa is a move that may have important tactical implications for the liberation struggle.

Certainly the National party has shown little enthusiasm for the SACP since its unbanning and displays scant evidence that it listens seriously to what communists have to say. Nonetheless, the NP, as demonstrated in earlier chapters, appeals increasingly for legitimacy from the West on the grounds of what "other democracies" do in relations with their own minorities within rather than with their colonies without. Although often challenged in the United States, in particular by right-wing groups, both Britain and the United States have instituted a range of policies for blacks that fall under the umbrella of "affirmative action"—a point that will be returned to later in the chapter. By appropriating that discourse as a way to promote socialist policies, opposition groups in South Africa will not necessarily erode the government's commitment to white domination, but they will at least have a discursive weapon with which to appear reasonable in fending off the government's extreme free-market prescriptions.

Although both the National party and the Inkatha Freedom party remain wedded to free-market capitalism,[25] acceptance of at least some future role for socialism is more widespread in South Africa than might be expected in light of the global changes mentioned. Even in the business community, for example, one finds those like Ronnie Bethlehem, the group economics consultant for Johannesburg Consolidated Investments, arguing that what is vital to the interests of business is a market economy, not capitalism. "What gives hope for the future of South Africa," according to Bethlehem, "is the fact that a market system can accommodate simultaneously economic institutions which are both capitalist and socialist. It is the duality of capitalism and socialism that SA will have to incorporate in its mixed market system."[26]

The effects on South Africa of the demise of communism in the Soviet Union and Eastern Europe are a reinvigoration of the importance of democracy and acceptance of a role for the market without a concomitant abandonment of socialism as an objective. The question remains of what socialism is if it is not what communist countries had until so recently. In this regard, a 1991 article extolling the virtues of "the social democratic vision," written by the University of the Western Cape's Pieter le Roux, is worth citing at some length.[27]

Le Roux refers in the course of his article to a meeting of the Socialist International which took place in June 1989. At that meeting, Swedish Prime Minister Ingmar Carlson argued that the experience of the Eastern European countries showed that the nationalization of the means of production did not in any way guarantee fulfillment of the socialist goals of liberty, equality, and solidarity. For social democrats, "socialism is today defined in terms of the outcome of the economic process and not in terms of who owns the means of production."[28] The emphasis has shifted away from the ownership issue to the question of who controls the economic decisions which are of importance to society. Reminiscent of Burawoy's point about the importance of an autonomous power base for the working class, le Roux suggests that, indirectly, government and the trade unions exercise a tremendous influence on the type and level of investments that industrialists make.

Although he seems to be advocating some form of corporatist model as the way to achieve socialism, le Roux argues that the success of social democratic countries like Sweden can at least in part be ascribed to the investments made in human resources—education, health, and housing—at relatively early stages of their development. "It is interesting to note," he continues, "that the social democracies in the initial phases of development have channelled social investments precisely to those societal needs stressed in the Freedom Charter. Expenditure on education, housing and health do not only meet the aspirations of the people, but are also social investments which, if correctly made, will enhance the future rate of growth of the South African economy."[29] After maintaining that South Africa will have to develop its own version of social democracy appropriate to the country's special circumstances, le Roux invokes a long-standing ANC demand and argues that "land redistribution will, for example, have to be part and parcel of any system that evolves."[30]

There are a number of important points to make about the way that le Roux sets out to rethink the meaning of socialism for South Africa. First, he locates the only "true" socialism in Western, not Eastern Europe, thereby equating it with successful democratic systems rather than with failed authoritarian ones. When de Klerk insists that capitalism is consistent with "the basic values and ideals of the world's successful democracies and economies,"[31] others can claim that socialism is as well.

Second, le Roux makes a commitment to expenditure on education, housing, and health the essence of the Freedom Charter and not, as so many do, its commitment to nationalization. He not only makes investment in social welfare the key to socialism but also turns socialism into a universal value and ideal espoused by everybody, including the National party. De Klerk recently placed "effective educational, health and welfare services, as well as adequate housing and recreational facilities," on the list of basic values and ideals that belong not to any single political party but that are universal.[32]

Finally, le Roux demolished the pervasive tendency to treat social investment and economic growth as competing objectives by making the former a vital prerequisite to the latter. In this way he also disassociated socialism from stagnation and empty supermarket shelves by making it a key ingredient in a healthy growing economy.

Le Roux's article is not some sort of blueprint for South Africa's future, and its citation is not meant to imply that all questions of political economy may now be neatly resolved. What this work and the discourse of affirmative action demonstrate is the vibrancy of local efforts—in the absence of a ready-made global counter-discourse to liberal capitalist democracy of the sort that Marxist-Leninist regimes offered—to rethink creatively the meaning of socialism. Rather than privileging state ownership of the means of production, emphasis has shifted to analyses of how the state can best democratically facilitate the sort of egalitarian outcome that free market processes alone cannot ensure. There are multiple ways, other than nationalization, for states to intervene in economic procedures in order to effect certain outcomes.[33] The above analysis of the effects of the collapse of communism on South Africa suggests that struggles over what form state intervention should take are likely to join education, health, housing, and land as the major political economic struggles of the next few years.

The Reassertion of American Hegemony

Despite the claims to a "new world order" since the collapse of communism and renewed American adventurism in the Persian Gulf, the demise of the Soviet Union as a superpower seems only to have led to unmitigated enthusiasm in the United States for its self-appointed "global policeman" role. As one African scholar recently bemoaned, "the world is justly confronted with the moral dilemma of choosing between the era of duplicity, double standards, superpower arrogance and opportunism on the one hand, and naked daylight banditry and megalomania on the other."[34] Regardless of whether the world comes to accept military interventions by the United States into other people's countries, the undisputed status of the United States as sole remaining superpower is likely to have a number of effects on the liberation struggle in South Africa.

As already mentioned, the drying up of funding for the various liberation movements from Eastern Europe has forced diplomatic "begging bowl" missions by Mandela and others to Western Europe, Japan, Canada, and the United States. Although the United States has been by no means the only country willing to entertain delegations from the ANC, it promises through its vast network of international development agencies to be a much bigger market for fund-seekers to tap. Financial aid to the "victims of apartheid" was also explicitly promised in the U.S. Comprehensive Anti-Apartheid Act of 1986 through which Congress imposed sanctions on South Africa's minority government.

The problem with American aid is that, particularly since the collapse of communist regimes, it is available for use only to stimulate private enterprise and not for spending on whatever it is that the victims of apartheid might deem they need. Thus in 1989 the U.S. Agency for International Development (USAID) began to investigate the prospects for a massive investment in black business ventures in South Africa. The feasibility of a private venture capital company which would make commercially viable investments was considered, as was assistance aimed at facilitating black participation in the private economy. Also being considered was the feasibility of making the services of the Export-Import Bank available to black business. Believing that black management talent will be a catalyst for further black economic empowerment, USAID determined that the development of a successful black-controlled economy is critically dependent on the emergence of black business institutions.[35]

Whether or not USAID's assumptions are correct, the funneling of American capital to the victims of apartheid through such channels, rather than directly to various groups to determine how the money should be spent, has to constrain those groups' options. The resumption of an armed struggle, for example, is clearly not a viable financial alternative at this time.

As undisputed single superpower, the United States has manifested an ongoing desire to foster private enterprise around the world. It also has begun to reevaluate previous tendencies to support unconditionally any undemocratic regime claiming to represent an "anti-communist bastion of the free world." In December 1989, for example, the American ambassador to Tanzania, Donald K. Petterson, noted in a confidential cable to Washington that American policy in Africa had been tied closely to the geopolitical competition with the Soviet Union and China. "Now, however, with the passing of the Cold War, our need for Africa diminishes." Consequently, he said, the United States should adopt a policy that "more explicitly and broadly ties developmental aid to political reforms in Africa."[36]

As previous chapters noted, the constitution and reconstitution of South Africa as Western at the height of the Cold War was one of the strategies adopted by the National party for retaining membership in the club of civilized nations. If Africa is no longer important and anticommunist discourse no longer an automatic guarantor of American support, then the National party will have to find other means of retaining its club membership. Yet the unavailability of the anticommunist trump card is less of a liability for the NP than the drying up of funds from Eastern Europe is a hardship for its opponents. The Pretoria regime has only to free all remaining political prisoners for American sanctions to be lifted; at that point, it can expect support from the United States in the same way that it has already reclaimed the historical support of Western Europe. As for "political reform" being now a prerequisite for development aid in Africa, Assistant Secretary of State Herman Cohen has made it clear that what that phrase refers to is evolution "toward Western-style democracy."[37] In other words, as long as South Africa maintains a commitment to private enterprise and institutes a system of universal franchise for the black majority through regularly held elections, it will be a normal capitalist democracy worthy of American support, even if the situation of white domination has not been eradicated.

If South Africa is to remain a "problem," the focus of external opposition must shift from the set of practices known as apartheid to the situation of white domination that those same practices have been meant to preserve. If, as the previous chapter argued, the National party's current project is to localize domination and make its perpetuation the responsibility of communities and the (largely white) business sector, localized modes of resistance such as consumer boycotts will continue to be as vital an element in the struggle against white domination as the actions of such formal political organizations as the ANC. But because such struggles are by their very nature less visible to the outside world than more dramatic riots and demonstrations, it will be up to the various liberation movements to keep the issue of white domination alive.

THE DISCOURSE OF DEVELOPMENT

According to Lummis, it was U.S. President Harry S. Truman who introduced the term *underdevelopment* into public discourse in 1949, during the course of a speech which committed the United States to "embark on a bold new program for making the benefits of our scientific advances and industrial progress available for the improvement and growth of underdeveloped areas." Truman described the program as a splendid venture "aimed at enabling millions of people to raise themselves from the level of colonialism to self-support and ultimate prosperity," a venture "consistent with our policies of preventing the expansion of Communism." The key to the success of this venture, according to Truman, was the investment of American capital and the ability to persuade capitalists that they were working in foreign countries not to exploit them but to develop them.[38]

Contained within Truman's speech are all the elements of what Lummis calls the "ideology of development." Development is something that the West, with its scientific advances and industrial progress, already has; the concept of underdevelopment places the vast majority of the world's cultures into a single category, the sole characteristic of which is the absence of certain characteristics of the industrialized countries.[39] In this way, a developed/underdeveloped hierarchy is established, setting the "modern" Western world in opposition to other areas of the globe that remain "traditional"—that is, less cosmopolitan, less scientific, less secular, less rational, less individualist, and less democratic. They are defined solely in relation to the West, the foundational source of "development," as an inferior or derivative form.

In his emphasis on "self-support and ultimate prosperity," Truman alludes to what are normally taken to be the hallmarks of development, namely, national autonomy and economic growth. So pervasive is acceptance of the Western model of national autonomy that it informs the work even of the critics of mainstream development theory. For all of its accomplishments, the dependency school of social theory left intact the classical image of the West as *the* image or model of what it means to be developed.[40]

Finally, Truman endorses capitalist intervention and the avoidance of communism as key strategies for the development of Third World countries. Progress can be judged quantitatively by the sheer amount of foreign capitalist penetration of a country, although how exactly this is to attain the ultimate objective of a self-sustaining economy is left unstated.

The global discourse of development establishes continuities with classically colonial modes of subjugation and domination. Governance of the Third World is no longer effected by force; control is now exerted indirectly by foreign capitalists, whose confidence in stability and order is required to maintain economic growth, and by a host of "development experts" sent by such agencies as the World Bank to identify and solve problems. The continuity is in terms of how development discourse constitutes both social bodies and individuals who perceive themselves as being poor, lacking, and part of an inferior culture.[41]

In the nineteenth century, difference was defined as the "uncivilized" otherness to be conquered (the postulate of difference) or assimilated (the postulate of identity) in the name of civilization. Both colonial societies under the control of guardians and colonized peoples themselves were described as barbaric. Previous chapters demonstrated how knowledge-producing apparatuses such as missionary schools and churches normalized the civilized/uncivilized hierarchy among some colonized peoples, while global social movements such as Ethiopianism and Pan-Africanism offered subversive counter-discourses. Peculiar to South Africa, although informed by the writings of African intellectuals and others, Black Consciousness also had as its major political project the reclamation of positive self-definitions for black people through a reinvigoration of black culture and history.

The term *underdeveloped* is only the latest way of classifying the other as inferior. Although not explicitly portrayed as such, the relationship in development discourse between an individual developed subject (be it a society or a person) and a nondeveloped object implicitly contains a parent/child metaphor, as did the colonial discourse of guardianship. As Ashis Nandy has pointed out in a critique of such colonial metaphors, the child in the modern world is not seen as a physically smaller version of the adult with a somewhat different set of qualities and skills:

> To the extent adulthood itself is valued as a symbol of completeness and as an end-product of growth or development, childhood is seen as an imperfect state on the way to adulthood, normality, full socialization and humanness. This is the theory of progress as applied to the individual life-cycle. The result is the frequent use of childhood as a design of cultural and political immaturity or, it comes to the same thing, inferiority. Much of the pull of the ideology of colonialism and much of the power of the idea of modernity can be traced to the evolutionary implications of the concept of the child in the Western worldview.[42]

When the idea of certain societies and individuals as "children" is normalized within the context of development discourse, two effects are discernable. First, as with individuals, the standard measure by which a society is judged is in terms of how quickly it can grow and become autonomous; hence the emphasis on economic growth and being self-supporting in Truman's cited speech. The problem with such a standard of judgment is twofold. On the one hand, it constitutes as "successful" even those countries—such as India— that have been most destructive of man, nature, and culture in the name of development. Destruction is attributed to overpopulation or other such trappings of "underdevelopment," while "success" is attributed to "appropriate" interventions by foreign agencies such as the World Bank and multinational corporations. On the other hand, social equality and democracy tend to take a back seat to economic growth, either because they are deliberately sacrificed by developmentalist elites or because they are presumed dependent upon economic development itself. Man, nature, culture, social equality, and democracy are all sacrificed to the god of development.

Second, as Gustavo Esteva has pointed out, peoples whose cultures have for millennia taught them that the overt and unlimited pursuit of material gain is offensive and dishonorable now reject this way of thinking as ignorant and backward: "Our culturally imposed limitation of economic ends has been constantly disqualified; it was seen as apathy, conformism and, especially as a serious 'obstacle to development,' characteristic of a 'pre-modern mentality.' We ourselves came to see it like this." By teaching people to see themselves as obstacles to development, Esteva argues, the development metaphor promotes a colonization of consciousness of the deepest sort and is profoundly antidemocratic; it takes away from the hands of people the possibility of defining their own ways of life.[43]

Although Esteva and others emphasize the pervasive effects of the discourse of development, no norm is ever universal, as previous chapters argued. While still on the margins of Third World studies, there are those associated with liberation theology, feminist ecology, and even various Western development agencies who share a common concern for the physical and cultural survival of the world's poor, as well as for the "local knowledges" that are so often devalued by Western (or Western-educated) development "experts."[44] Formalized in a number of Third World countries in the 1970s into an approach called Participatory Action Research (PAR), these counter-discourses are concerned with the question of how to generate popular power (rather than economic growth) so that people may gain control over the forces that shape their lives. PAR projects combine techniques of adult education, social science research, and political activism. At root are a rejection of abstract, "top-down" development plans that attempt to universalize the Western experience; an encouragement of local grassroots initiatives; and stress on the need for economic processes that are both rooted in the needs of specific communities and appropriate for local ecosystems. Emphasis is placed on grassroots inquiry into what development means to poor and disenfranchised people in developing areas. As a consequence, it is hoped, development ceases to be something that is done to, rather than by, people and becomes instead a process in which people participate in the making of their own communities. PAR stresses diversity, plurality, and empowerment.[45]

What does all of this mean in terms of future struggle and change in South Africa? First, the normality of considering economic growth a societal objective of fundamental importance is so pervasive that no major political group has challenged it; in fact, both the NP and the ANC make significant growth the major objective of their economic policies. The privatization of the economy was justified by de Klerk in February 1991 as the most effective way to return South Africa—a "developing society"—to "a high growth path."[46] National party MP Fanus Schoeman basically summed up the government's position when he said that the promotion of private enterprise was necessary for the "successful upliftment of underdeveloped areas and communities."[47] As for the ANC, its Department of Economic Policy has said that the organization "believes that it is absolutely imperative to reverse the present trend towards stagnation and to promote economic growth. Without significant growth in our economy we will not be able to address the pressing problems of poverty and inequality confronting our people."[48]

Where government and opposition differ is not in terms of the objective of economic growth but on the question of how best to achieve it as well as on the nature of the relationship between economic growth and social welfare. The National party stresses that private enterprise is the best way to achieve economic growth and that growth, in turn, will enable the state through taxation revenue to "uplift the disadvantaged," although it resists the possibility of higher taxation of companies in order to speed that "upliftment" along. Opposing any move that would threaten the power of Anglo-American, Rembrandt, Sanlam, and other corporate conglomerates (as well as the power of white commercial agriculture), the NP wants to strengthen, rather than curtail, the current wealth-producing sector. It wants, in other words, to keep economic assets in white hands and let the market take care of redistribution.[49]

The ANC's plans are very different. Reminiscent of le Roux's argument that investment in social welfare is the best way to promote economic growth, the ANC advocates land reform; affirmative action to correct racial and gender imbalances in the economy; major new housing, education, health, and welfare programs; the provision of infrastructure to deprived areas; and cooperation with the Organization for African Unity and the Southern Africa Development Coordination Conference. Supporting small-scale enterprises, shifting the tax burden toward corporations and away from the poor, promoting environmentally sound growth, reintegrating South Africa into the world economy on a competitive basis, and harnessing mass-based organizations in planning reconstruction, are all mentioned by the ANC as the tasks of a democratic, nonracial government.[50]

These differences over the best way to achieve economic growth again mean that questions of political economy will remain at the heart of organized struggle probably for many years to come. Although it has been argued that the ANC for a variety of reasons is weak vis-à-vis the government, the ongoing debate about socialism in South Africa may facilitate more openness to the ANC's plans than the National party would like. What is troubling about the priority attached to growth is that it so often requires sacrifice; when push comes to shove, local cultures, communities, and environments are swept aside to make way for a high GNP. When this happens, equality and democracy become outcomes that are always desired, always promised, but always, ultimately, deferred.

What prospects are there that South Africa will be able to avoid what has happened in so many other developing countries? The prospects seem to depend on the extent to which people are able to retain a sense of self-worth and resist being constituted as poor, lacking, and inferior—that is, to resist the destruction of their own cultures and communities in the name of development. In this regard, the years of struggle against white domination may have given South Africa an advantage over other societies in that Black Consciousness has continued a tradition of emphasizing local autonomy, self-definition, and cultural reclamation.

Despite the marginalization of the PAC in the realm of organized politics, the Black Consciousness movement has grown steadily over the past few years. Usual indicators of this growth are a resurgence of PAC-affiliated trade unions and youth organizations since 1986.[51] But equally important is the dissemination through an indigenous BCM-inspired liberation theology, as well as through popular theater and poetry, of the idea that blacks must be proud of their own culture and resist both the negation of their humanity and the exploitative values imported into South Africa by whites.[52]

As demonstrated in previous chapters, Black Consciousness continued and expanded upon earlier traditions, such as Ethiopianism and Pan-Africanism, that resisted the discourse of the civilizing mission and its constitution of certain peoples supposedly in need of upliftment as barbaric. The continuing strength of the BCM means that it may be turned against the discourse of development and its reconstitution of people considered lacking in Western terms as underdeveloped. Major struggles in the future between a developmentalist elite—of whatever color—and the mass of the people bent on retaining control of their own lives and community practices are a distinct possibility. If this happens, there will no doubt be many people ready to argue that blacks have demonstrated once again that they cannot get along with each other, that South Africa has "gone the way of the rest of Africa," and that maybe apartheid was not so bad after all. But if equality and democracy are not evident in a new South Africa, it makes little difference to the oppressed if their ongoing subjugation is justified by reference to apartheid or to development. Resistance, in a variety of forms, will continue.

MULTIRACIALISM IN THE WEST

The final part of this chapter considers the implications for South Africa of racial struggles in Western countries—specifically, Great Britain and the United States—over the past ten to fifteen years. What Patricia Williams describes as an "increasing effort to expand racial paradigms"—that is, to allow increased differentiation and a celebration of difference—has been more frequently touted during this time as a desirable social norm.[53] Denigratingly referred to by its opponents as "political correctness" and approvingly by its adherents as "multiculturalism" or "affirmative action," the discourse of difference has had a number of effects that are relevant to a consideration of the South African case. The purpose here is not to join the fray and offer personal judgment about the merits of current racial politics. Nor is it to suggest that a South Africa without apartheid will become exactly like the United States or Great Britain. The wresting of control of the courts, the bureaucracy, the political system, the economy, and so on from whites might render comparisons to African states like Zimbabwe more appropriate than to Western ones. But until that happens (and perhaps even after it does), the examples cited here are applicable for two reasons. First, Britain and the United States demonstrate the pervasiveness of racial discrimination even in societies with racially neutral legal systems; indeed, they demonstrate how such seemingly nonracial criteria as employment qualifications can perpetuate discrimination. At a time when the National party is seeking to emulate what other democracies do and is appealing to standards to maintain certain forms of privilege, it is important to consider how such emulation might maintain discrimination even while rendering South African policies more acceptable to the West.

The second reason for analyzing race politics in Britain and the United States has more to do with racial identity than with discrimination, although the two are often linked. What these two cases demonstrate is how the very determination of people of color to fight discrimination—either through the courts or by the utilization of affirmative action programs—can serve to constitute or reinscribe particular racial identities. As organized opposition to the NP (the ANC and the SACP, at least) has made a commitment to affirmative action, the "politics of affirmation" has constituted the United States and Britain as multiracial (i.e., more like South Africa) and not as nonracial. Affirmative action in South Africa might serve progressive social purposes yet keep alive the racial identities once inscribed by the Population Registration Act, a scenario that could in turn hinder the formation of political parties and groups in anything other than racial terms.

Britain and the United States differ in terms of the actual policies they have adopted, but the effects of those policies are in some ways similar. It is in terms of those common effects that the possible implications of affirmative action policies for racial identity in South Africa will be considered.

Affirming the Multiracial Norm: The British Race Relations Act of 1976

Great Britain since the end of its imperial heyday is in some ways very similar to South Africa since 1948. Referring to what he calls "Britain's postcolonial decline and crisis," Paul Gilroy argues that the term *race* has acquired an explicitly cultural rather than a biological inflection (as it had before the rise of modern "scientific" racism in the nineteenth century) and that hand in hand with the culturalism of the new racism is a definition of race as a matter of difference rather than of hierarchy. This process is "the same process," Gilroy points out, "that marked the inauguration of the apartheid system in 1948."[54]

Gilroy also points out that nationalism and racism have become so closely identified in Britain that to speak of the nation is to speak automatically in racially exclusive terms. Blackness and Englishness are constructed as incompatible, mutually exclusive identities. To speak of the British or English people is to speak of the white people.[55] In other words, nationalist discourse constitutes Britain as white in the same way that it constituted South Africa as white at the heyday of apartheid.

But who in Britain, exactly, is black? Gilroy argues that the logic of Britain's crisis is itself a logic of cultural and political fragmentation that includes the decomposition of open, inclusive definitions of blackness that facilitated political alliances between the people of Afro-Caribbean and Asian descent. More restrictive definitions of the term *black* as referring to those of Afro-Caribbean heritage only are beginning to be articulated at a time when some vocal elements within black communities have also sought to emphasize the cultural incompatibility of black settlers with Britain and British-ness.[56] As in South Africa, historically black is a contested concept among the subordinate groups themselves, generating struggles over whether identity can be voluntarily chosen or is fixed by heritage and over appropriate relations between the self and others (in this case, the question of whether a multiracial society such as Britain can ever be a single nation). But if challenges to a common black identity are emerging from within the black community itself, the implication is that the norm of constituting Britons as black (Afro-Caribbean), white (British), and Asian is becoming more widespread.

Gilroy suggests that Britain's cultural politics are racial because culture is conceived by "the vocal ideologists of the English New Right" along ethni-cally absolute lines, not as something changing and dynamic but as a fixed property of social groups. When the communal life of those once conceived as biologically distinct races is submitted to such assumptions, culture becomes a pseudobiological property; hence "culture" does duty for the term *race*.[57] I do not disagree with this formulation, but I want to suggest that in addition to the discursive moves of a racist elite, prior struggles by the subordinate groups in Britain to overcome racial discrimination have resulted in legislation that contributes to the constitution of Britain as a multiracial society.

The legislation in question is the British Race Relations Act of 1976, which enabled people to take civil action in respect of discrimination in certain areas of life on "racial grounds." Discrimination occurs if on racial grounds persons treat someone less favorably than they treat or would treat others. According to Peter Fitzpatrick, almost all cases brought under the legislation concern employment. These cases are taken to an administrative court called an industrial tribunal. The act also constitutes and empowers a governmental Commission for Racial Equality, which is "to work towards the elimination of discrimination." Most emphasis is given to its broadest power to investigate discriminatory practices, to issue nondiscrimination notices, and to take court proceedings to have these enforced.[58]

Fitzpatrick argues that the act treats racial discrimination as an aberrant practice, a particular episode that disturbs the normal course. Legal remedies, in turn, need only reassert the normal course—that is, focus on the act of the wrongdoer and correct or compensate for it. The only significant remedy provided in the legislation is damages seen as redress, as affirming the norm. The overt purpose of the act then is to affirm Britain as a nonracist society, and the "burden of proof" is on the complainant, the person wronged, to establish that the norm has been disturbed. According to Fitzpatrick, this burden is heavy indeed, for racially based decisions can so easily be obscured or justified. The unsurpassed aptness of a rejected applicant is not evidence of racial discrimination as long as the employer can convince a tribunal that she or he was rejected on other grounds. Apparently, tribunals repeatedly uphold employers' purported rejection of applicants in such terms as demeanor, personality, ability to fit in, and even favoritism on the part of the employer.[59] In other words, it is almost impossible for the complainant to tie discrimination to race as long as the defendant insists that discrimination occurred for other reasons.

The Race Relations Act demonstrates most obviously the difficulty that victims of discrimination face in trying to prove that such discrimination was unlawful. When the National party recently introduced into Parliament a series of measures related to land and housing (the Upgrading of Land Tenure Rights Bill, the Residential Environment Bill, the Less-Formal Township Establishment Bill, and the Rural Development Bill), it was criticized for omitting to bar landlords from discriminating in private leases against potential tenants. In response, Hernus Kriel, the minister of planning and provincial affairs, said he expected this "subtler discrimination" to be challenged through the courts, as it has been in the United States.[60] What the British example of challenges to discrimination through the existing courts implies is that landlords will be overwhelmingly successful as long as they do not admit that race was the discriminating factor. They can appeal, for example, to the ready-made discourse provided by the National party and cite "different life-styles" or "unacceptable standards" as the driving consideration behind their actions. But a more subtle implication of the British legislation for South Africa, in addition to the obvious difficulty of successfully proving discrimination, is the way that it reconstitutes racial identities and maintains the norm of considering Britain a multiracial—if nonracist—society.

Other than being denied jobs, there are a host of ways that people of color are treated less favorably than whites in nonracist Britain. Attacks by the National Front and other white supremacy organizations on the homes of people of Asian descent are common, particularly in London (and other large cities) where a favorite method of intimidation is petrol bombs thrown through mailboxes. Other examples of unequal treatment which are even more common are precisely those that the National party intends to leave to the South African courts, namely, discrimination in housing. Blacks are routinely told by real estate agents that no housing is available in certain neighborhoods despite "for sale" signs, by landlords that apartments have just been rented, and by homeowners that their house has been taken off the market. Such cases of discrimination are of course very difficult to prove, which is why they are probably far more widespread than the number of reported cases suggests, but victims nonetheless routinely fight for damages through the courts.

It is in the decision of people of color to resist discrimination that the Race Relations Act enables the reconstitution of Britain as a multiracial society, for the only way to fight discrimination is to claim it as a racial incident. In other words, an Asian family may be told quite openly by a real estate agent that he cannot take them to look at houses in a certain neighborhood because "no offense; people there just don't like the smell of curry," but olfactory discrimination is not legally a ground on which to sue for damages. As Fitzpatrick's work has demonstrated, almost any reason for discrimination is accepted as legal by the courts as long as race is not one of them, so race becomes the only grounds on which discrimination can be fought. In one sense, it hardly matters to the people concerned what the reasons are for their differential treatment, but the requirement to appeal to race constitutes them as a race, even if they never thought of themselves in racial terms before. If black is coming increasingly to mean people of Afro-Caribbean descent only, those of Asian descent who protest discrimination through the courts would seem to have little option but to constitute themselves as members of "the Asian race."

In short, allowing discrimination on grounds other than race—that is, enabling those who discriminate against people of color to invoke personality, standards, or whatever—has the effect of forcing the victims continually to constitute and reconstitute themselves in racial terms if they hope to seek redress. In the absence of the Population Registration Act, then, there are other ways for South Africa to be reconstituted as a multiracial society.

Affirmative Action and Race Classification in the United States

There are some obvious similarities between Britain and the United States in terms of fighting discrimination through the courts. Victims of job discrimination have been suing for damages through the courts ever since the landmark Civil Rights Act of 1964. A bipartisan civil rights bill approved by President George Bush in October 1991 seeks to mitigate the ways that discrimination against people of color is still routinely practiced:

> What is demeaning in this era of double-speak-no-evil is going on interviews and not getting hired because someone doesn't think we'll be comfortable. It is demeaning not to get promoted because we're judged "too weak," then putting in a lot of energy the next time and being fired because we're "too strong. . . . " It is very demeaning to stand on street corners unemployed and begging. It is downright demeaning to have to explain why we haven't been employed for months and then watch the job go to someone who is "more experienced." It is outrageously demeaning that none of this can be called racism, even if it happens only to, or to large numbers of, black people; as long as it's done with a smile, a handshake and a shrug; as long as the phantom-word "race" is never used.[61]

The bill refers (among other things) to the "disparate impact" on various social groups of hiring and promotion practices, such as tests, that while fair at face value can result in the hiring, for example, of proportionately more whites than blacks or men than women. Intended to overcome the constraints imposed by a series of 1989 Supreme Court decisions, the new legislation would shift the burden of proving that the employer had no sound business necessity for disparate impact from the employee to the employer.[62] But the basic commitment of the U.S. government (like the British) is still to race neutrality in law as a successor to racial omission in the Constitution of the United States. This neutrality, Williams argues, cannot be an antidote to race bias in real life. She strongly defends affirmative action programs on the grounds that they were designed to remedy a segregationist view of equality in which positivistic categories of race reigned supreme—that is, when white by definition meant good or deserving and black was equated with bad or unworthy of inclusion. It is thus, Williams argues, that "affirmative action is an affirmation; the affirmative act of hiring—or hearing—blacks is a recognition of individuality that includes blacks as a social presence, that is profoundly linked to the fate of blacks and whites and women and men either as subgroups or as one group."[63]

Williams's defense of affirmative action as a way to affirm that blacks are worthy of inclusion in society suggests why the concept may have broad appeal in South Africa. On the one hand, the ANC's official position is that affirmative action is necessary to correct racial and gender imbalances in the workplace, but it is not clear how the organization plans to respond to the inevitable argument that affirmative action will entail a drop in standards. Black Consciousness, on the other hand, stresses the need for a new and incisive redefinition, reidentification, and reappraisal of black life through cultural reaffirmation.[64] Between the ANC's more means-ends–oriented and the BCM's more philosophical approach to the politics of affirmation, it seems likely that political struggles in South Africa in the future will pit the discourse of affirmative action in the name of racial and gender equality against that of standards in the name of maintaining civilization.

Given the evident appeal of affirmative action for black South Africans, it seems pertinent to address an effect of such action that goes unnoticed in the United States in all of the heated debates about whether it is good or bad. Such debates frequently bog down in the issue of whether the effect of affirmative action is reverse discrimination against white males; what is a more relevant effect when speculating about South Africa's future is the racial classification that affirmative action seems to require.

It seems impossible in contemporary America for anyone to fill out a form—from market-research surveys by companies to data demanded of job candidates from personnel and affirmative action offices—without having to reveal a racial identity. What is most striking about this norm of racial identification is the way that a range of minority groups within society have been constituted as races along with whites and blacks. The standard race classification scheme, for example, lists six categories: white, black, Hispanic, Asian, Native American, and Hawaiian or Pacific Islander. At what point exactly did Americans of descent other than African or European become races? It would no doubt prove impossible to pinpoint exactly the onset of the practice of classifying minorities as races, but that is not a primary concern. The point is to demonstrate the similar effects of the politics of affirmation in Britain and the United States mentioned earlier. In both cases, be it through legislation designed to punish race discrimination or through a social commitment to increasing the visibility of minorities in all walks of life, citizens are required to constitute themselves in racial terms. It is in this way that nonracial societies without apartheid are constituted and reconstituted as multiracial.

The example of the United States suggests that affirmative action requires race classification, so that there are other ways to maintain racial identities in South Africa in the absence of the Population Registration Act. The question of what sort of classification scheme might accompany affirmative action cannot be determined in advance, but it seems possible that struggles over whether to constitute everyone as black and white (consistent with a BCM orientation) or to reconstitute them in the terms of the Population Registration Act (which the ANC might not object to) will occur in the future. Classification is not bad in and of itself, and if it is done for positive reasons and in terms that make sense to the people involved it does not necessarily generate conflict. But precisely because questions of racial identity have generated struggle in the past, it is unlikely that a classification scheme can be devised, whether for affirmation purposes or for something else, on which everyone in South Africa will agree.

In conclusion, this book would like to offer a blueprint for social peace and harmony in South Africa in the future, but it cannot do so. From a Foucaultian perspective, struggle is never eradicated from social life; only the form of struggle changes. To conclude by hoping for a struggle-free South Africa would be inconsistent theoretically with the attitude to power that informed this work and would be politically utopian. The best that can be hoped for is that South Africans of whatever color will find a way to resolve their differences that at the very least preserves their physical survival and at most does not negate their dignity as human beings.

NOTES

1. Davis, *Apartheid's Rebels*, chapter 6.

2. The ANC withdrew from talks with the government in May 1991 in protest over its handling of black-on-black violence, but this was not the first time that the ANC suspended talks. The first time was in April 1990, in protest at police action in the township of Sebokeng (near Johannesburg) which left fourteen people dead and more than 400 wounded. On the first withdrawal, see *Southern Africa Report*, April 6, 1990, p. 1.

3. See, for example, the much-cited article by Fukuyama, "The End of History?" pp. 3–18.

4. *Southern Africa Report*, February 23, 1990, p. 2.

5. Ibid., March 2, 1990, p. 5.

6. Ibid., June 8, 1990, p. 4.

7. See Kifner, "Planning Is Begun on South African Aid Bank," p. 3.

8. See *Southern Africa Report*, February 23, 1990, p. 2.

9. See Meer, "Negotiating a Nonracial Democracy," pp. 345–49.

10. See Wren, "Mandela Calls West Europe Racist on Sanctions," p. 7.

11. See Wren, "Europe Drops Sanctions," p. E5.

12. See Omond, "African National Congress Is Left with a Credibility Problem," p. 11.

13. The patriotic front is comprised of the ANC, the PAC, Cosatu, the National Congress of Trade Unions, and the South African Communist party, as well as of some homeland parties and other groups. See Wren, "Anti-Apartheid Groups Seek Meeting of All Parties," p. 7.

14. Ibid.

15. See Kifner, "Planning Is Begun on South African Aid Bank."

16. The PAC, for example, is perhaps more committed than any other group to the necessity for "central economic planning by the state," yet it insists that "the state should not disallow all room for market forces to operate." See Shabalala, "Economic Emancipation: A Pan Africanist View," pp. 6–7.

17. On this point, see Davies, "Nationalization: A View from the ANC," p. 1.

18. See Lummis, "Development against Democracy," p. 39.

19. See Burawoy's interview with Eddie Webster, "The State of Socialism," pp. 33–36.

20. See Laurence, "Comrades and Capitalists," pp. 39–42.

21. See "SACP Intends to Become Mass-Based," in *Southern Africa Report*, May 18, 1990, p. 3.

22. See "The Communists Come in Out of the Cold," *Southern Africa Report*, June 22, 1990, p. 3.

23. Lummis is most explicit in rejecting this idea when he says that "today workers in socialist countries, at least some of them, hope that a return to the free market will bring them democracy. But this only takes the problem back to where it was in the nineteenth century. The free market continues to generate inequality in wealth and power, as before." See "Development against Democracy," pp. 33–34.

24. See Davis, *Apartheid's Rebels*, p. 2.

25. The National party position as elaborated by de Klerk has been well-documented in previous chapters; the IFP's contention that "only an economy based largely on free enterprise will allow our people to realize their full potential" can be found in "Visions of Change: A Symposium," pp. 25–28.

26. See Bethlehem, "Economics and Non-Racial Democracy," pp. 9–11.

27. See le Roux, "The South African Economy: The Challenge of Democracy," pp. 3–8.

28. Ibid., p. 7.

29. Ibid.

30. Ibid.

31. See de Klerk's address to Parliament, 1991, p. 3.

32. Ibid., pp. 2–3.

33. In a recent article, Thomas J. Biersteker identified six different forms of state economic intervention; these he called influence, regulation, mediation, distribution, production, and planning. See "Reducing the Role of the State in the Economy: A Conceptual Exploration of IMF and World Bank Prescriptions," pp. 477–92.

34. See Soyinka, "A Time of Transition," pp. 4–5.

35. See "U.S. Planning Massive Aid for Black Business," *Southern Africa Report*, August 19, 1989, p. 11.

36. See A Reporter at Large, "African Democracy," *New Yorker*, September 3, 1990, p. 101.

37. Ibid., p. 102.

38. See Lummis, "Development against Democracy," p. 44.

39. Ibid., p. 48.

40. See Manzo, "Modernist Discourse and the Crisis of Development Theory," pp. 3–45.

41. On this point, see also Dubois, "The Governance of the Third World: A Foucaultian Perspective on Power Relations in Development," especially pp. 25–26.

42. See Nandy, "Reconstructing Childhood: A Critique of the Ideology of Adulthood," in *Traditions, Tyranny and Utopias: Essays in the Politics of Awareness*.

43. Gustavo Esteva, quoted in Lummis, "Development against Democracy," p. 49.

44. An enormous literature associated with liberation theology exists that now spans (in addition to its native Latin America) several continents; for a good overview, see Ferm, *Third World Liberation Theologies: A Reader*. On feminist ecology, see Shiva, *Staying Alive: Women, Ecology and Development*. On the concerns of those associated with various Western development agencies, see Oxfam's (of Great Britain) Edwards, "The Irrelevance of Development Studies," pp. 116–35; and the Broederlijk Delen's (of Belgium) Verhelst, *No Life without Roots: Culture and Development*.

45. On PAR, see Escobar, "Discourse and Power in Development: Michel Foucault and the Relevance of His Work to the Third World," pp. 377–400; and Fals-Borda, *Knowledge and People's Power*.

46. See de Klerk's address to Parliament, 1991, p. 11.

47. See Schoeman, "In Quest of Co-Operation: A National Party Perspective," p. 5.

48. See African National Congress, "An African National Congress Discussion Document on Economic Policy," p. 9.

49. See Schoeman, "In Quest of Co-operation: A National Party Perspective."

50. African National Congress, "An African National Congress Discussion," pp. 9–13.

51. See "Enter the 'Purist' Pan Africanist Movement and a Resurgence of Black Consciousness," *Southern Africa Report*, December 8, 1989, pp. 1–2.

52. On liberation theology and its relationship to Black Consciousness, see, for example, Alan Boesak, who has argued that "[what] gave rise to the development of a liberation theology in South Africa, is a human consciousness that we call black consciousness. Through black consciousness black people discover that they are children of God and that they have rights to exist in God's world." Boesak, "Liberation Theology in South Africa," p. 266. On the influence of independent African churches on contemporary black theology in South Africa, see Kretzschmar, *The Voice of Black Theology in South Africa*. On the influence of the BCM on drama and poetry, see Shava, "Black Is Beautiful: Black Consciousness and the Poetry of Affirmation in the 1970s," in his book *A People's Voice: Black South African Writing in the Twentieth Century*.

53. See Williams, *The Alchemy of Race and Rights: Diary of a Law Professor*, p. 121.

54. See Gilroy, "One Nation under a Groove: The Cultural Politics of 'Race' and Racism in Britain," p. 266.

55. Ibid., p. 268.

56. Ibid., pp. 270–71.

57. Ibid., pp. 266–67.

58. Fitzpatrick, "Racism and the Innocence of Law," p. 252.

59. Ibid., pp. 252–53.

60. See Wren, "Apartheid Barrier to Land Scrapped in Pretoria Plan," p. A7.

61. Williams, *The Alchemy of Race and Rights*, pp. 48–49.

62. See "The Compromise on Civil Rights," *New York Times*, October 26, 1991, p. 7.

63. Ibid., pp. 110, 121.

64. See Shava, "Black Is Beautiful," in his *A People's Voice*.

Bibliography

BOOKS AND JOURNAL ARTICLES

Abercrombie, Nicholas, Stephen Hill, and Bryan S. Turner (1980). *The Dominant Ideology Thesis*. London: Allen and Unwin.

Adam, Heribert, and Hermann Giliomee (1979). *Ethnic Power Mobilized: Can South Africa Change?* New Haven, Conn., and London: Yale University Press.

African National Congress (1991). "An African National Congress Discussion Document on Economic Policy." In *Economy: Growth and Redistribution*. IDASA, Occasional Paper no. 34.

Akhalwaya, Ameen (1989). "Zephania Mothopeng: Free at Last." *Africa Report* (January/February): 31–33.

Ashforth, Adam (1990). *The Politics of Official Discourse in Twentieth Century South Africa*. Oxford: Clarendon Press.

Askin, Steve (1989). "The Business of Sanctions Busting." *Africa Report* (January/February): 18–20.

Ballinger, Margaret (1969). *From Union to Apartheid: A Trek to Isolation*. Cape Town: Juta and Co.

Barron, Debora B., and John Immerwahr (1979). "The Public Views South Africa: Pathways Through a Gathering Storm." *Public Opinion* (January/February): 54–59.

Beinart, William, and Colin Bundy (1987). *Hidden Struggles in Rural South Africa: Politics and Popular Movements in the Transkei and Eastern Cape, 1890–1930*. Berkeley and Los Angeles: University of California Press.

Beresford, David (1991). "ANC Sets Government an Ultimatum." *Guardian Weekly* April 14: 6.

——— (1991). "Tragi-comedies of Apartheid Bigotry." *Guardian Weekly* June 23: 11.

Bethlehem, Ronnie (1991). "Economics and Non-Racial Democracy." In *Economic Prospects after Apartheid*. IDASA, Occasional Paper no. 27.

Biersteker, Thomas J. (1990). "Reducing the Role of the State in the Economy: A Conceptual Exploration of IMF and World Bank Prescriptions." *International Studies Quarterly* (December): 477–92.

Biko, Steve (1978). *I Write What I Like*. London: Heinemann.

Bloomberg, Charles (1989). *Christian-Nationalism and the Rise of the Afrikaner Broeder-bond in South Africa, 1918–1948*. Edited by Saul Dubow. Bloomington, Ind.: Indiana University Press.

Boesak, Alan (1986). "Liberation Theology in South Africa." In *Third World Liberation Theologies: A Reader*, edited by Deane W. Ferm. Maryknoll, N.Y.: Orbis Books.

Bonner, Philip (1982). "The Transvaal Native Congress, 1917–1920." In *Industrialization and Social Change in South Africa: African Class Formation, Culture, and Consciousness, 1870–1930*, edited by Shula Marks and Richard Rathbone. London and New York: Longman.

————— (1990). "The Politics of Black Squatter Movements on the Rand, 1944–1952." *Radical History Review* 46/47: 89–115.

Botha, Jan (1967). *Verwoerd Is Dead*. Cape Town: Books of Africa.

Bozzoli, Belinda (1981). *The Political Nature of a Ruling Class: Capital and Ideology in South Africa, 1890–1933*. London and Boston: Routledge and Kegan Paul.

—————, ed. (1987). *Class, Community and Conflict: South African Perspectives*. Johannesburg: Ravan Press.

Bozzoli, Belinda, and Peter Delius (1990). "Radical History and South African Society." *Radical History Review* 46/47: 13–45.

Bradford, Helen (1987). "We Are Now the Men: Women's Beer Protests in the Natal Countryside, 1929." In *Class, Community and Conflict: South African Perspectives*, edited by Belinda Bozzoli. Johannesburg: Ravan Press.

Brewer, John (1986). *After Soweto: An Unfinished Journey*. Oxford: Clarendon Press.

Bundy, Colin (1972). "The Emergence and Decline of a South African Peasantry." *African Affairs* 71, no. 285 (October): 373–76.

————— (1979). *The Rise and Fall of the South African Peasantry*. London: Heinemann.

————— (1990). "An Image of Its Own Past? Toward a Comparison of American and South African Historiography." *Radical History Review* 46/47: 117–43.

Burawoy, Michael (1981). "The Capitalist State in South Africa: Marxist and Sociological Perspectives on Race and Class." *Political Power and Social Theory* 2: 279–335.

————— (1990). "The State of Socialism." *Work in Progress* (September): 33–36.

Buthelezi, Mangosuthu G. (1990). "Visions of Change: A Symposium." *Journal of Democracy* 1, no. 4: 25–28.

Campbell, David (1990). "Global Inscription: How Foreign Policy Constitutes the United States." *Alternatives* 15: 263–86.

————— (1992). *Writing Security: U.S. Foreign Policy and the Politics of Identity*. Minneapolis: University of Minnesota Press.

Cardoso, Fernando H. (1973). "Associated-Dependent Development: Theoretical and Practical Implications." In *Authoritarian Brazil: Origins, Policies, and Future*, edited by Alfred Stepan. New Haven, Conn., and London: Yale University Press.

Comaroff, Jean (1985). *Body of Power, Spirit of Resistance*. Chicago: University of Chicago Press.

Commission on U.S. Policy toward Southern Africa (1981). *South Africa: Time Running Out*. Berkeley and Los Angeles: University of California Press.

Cooper, Alice (1988). *International Business in South Africa, 1988*. Washington, D.C.: Investor Responsibility Research Center.

Davenport, T. R. H. (1960). "Civil Rights in South Africa, 1910–1960." *Acta Juridica* 11–28.

Davies, Robert (1991). "Nationalization: A View from the ANC." In *Economy: Growth and Redistribution*. IDASA, Occasional Paper no. 34.

Davis, Stephen (1987). *Apartheid's Rebels.* New Haven, Conn., and London: Yale University Press.

de Villiers, Marq (1987). *White Tribe Dreaming.* New York: Penguin.

Doxey, Margaret P. (1972). *Economic Sanctions and International Enforcement.* New York: Oxford University Press.

Dubois, Marc (1991). "The Governance of the Third World: A Foucaultian Perspective on Power Relations in Development." *Alternatives* 16: 1–39.

Dubow, Saul (1990). "Afrikaner Nationalism, Apartheid, and the Conceptualization of 'Race.' " Paper presented at the 33d annual meeting of the African Studies Association, Baltimore, Md., November.

du Toit, Andre (1983). "No Chosen People: The Myth of the Calvinist Origins of Afrikaner Nationalism and Racial Ideology." *American Historical Review* (October): 920–52.

du Toit, Andre, and Hermann Giliomee (1983). *Afrikaner Political Thought.* Vol. 1, *1780–1850.* Berkeley and Los Angeles: University of California Press.

Edwards, Michael (1989). "The Irrelevance of Development Studies." *Third World Quarterly* 11, no. 1 (January): 116–35.

Ehrensaft, Philip (1985). "Phases in the Development of South African Capitalism: From Settlement to Crises." In *The Political Economy of Contemporary Africa,* edited by Peter C. W. Gutkind and Immanuel Wallerstein. Beverly Hills, Calif.: Sage.

Escobar, Arturo (1984). "Discourse and Power in Development: Michel Foucault and the Relevance of His Work to the Third World." *Alternatives* 10 (Winter): 377–400.

Evans, Peter (1979). *Dependent Development: The Alliance of Multinational, State, and Local Capital in Brazil.* Princeton, N.J.: Princeton University Press.

Fals-Borda, Orlando (1988). *Knowledge and People's Power.* Delhi: Indian Social Institute.

Ferm, Deane W. (1986). *Third World Liberation Theologies: A Reader.* Maryknoll, N.Y.: Orbis Books.

Finnegan, William (1986). "Coming Apart over Apartheid: The Story behind the Republicans' Split on South Africa." *Mother Jones* (April/May): 19–23, 40–46.

——— (1986). *Crossing the Line: A Year in the Land of Apartheid.* New York: Harper & Row.

First, Ruth, Jonathan Steele, and Christabel Gurney (1972). *The South African Connection: Western Investment in Apartheid.* London: Temple Smith.

Fitzpatrick, Peter (1990). "Racism and the Innocence of Law." In *Anatomy of Racism,* edited by David Theo Goldberg. Minneapolis: University of Minnesota Press.

Foucault, Michel (1979). *Discipline and Punish.* New York: Vintage Books.

——— (1980). *Power/Knowledge: Selected Interviews and Other Writings, 1972–1977.* Edited by Colin Gordon. New York: Pantheon.

Frank, Andre Gunder (1967). *Capitalism and Underdevelopment in Latin America.* New York: Monthly Review Press.

Frankel, S. Herbert (1969). *Capital Investment in Africa.* New York: Howard Fertig.

Fukuyama, Francis (1989). "The End of History?" *National Interest* 16 (Summer): 3–18.

Gerhart, Gail (1978). *Black Power in South Africa.* Berkeley and Los Angeles: University of California Press.

Geyser, O., ed. (1977). *B. J. Vorster: Select Speeches.* Cape Town: Printpak.

Giliomee, Hermann (1975). "The Development of the Afrikaner's Self-Concept." In *Looking at the Afrikaner Today,* edited by Hendrik H. Van der Merwe. Cape Town: Tafelberg Publishers.

Giliomee, Hermann, and Lawrence Schlemmer (1989). *From Apartheid to Nation-Building*. Oxford: Oxford University Press.

Gilroy, Paul (1990). "One Nation under a Groove: The Cultural Politics of 'Race' and Racism in Britain." In *Anatomy of Racism*, edited by David Theo Goldberg. Minneapolis: University of Minnesota Press.

Greenberg, Stanley (1980). *Race and State in Capitalist Development*. New Haven, Conn., and London: Yale University Press.

—— (1981). "Economic Growth and Political Change: The South African Case." *Journal of Modern African Studies* 19, no. 4: 667–704.

—— (1987). *Legitimating the Illegitimate: State, Markets and Resistance in South Africa*. Berkeley and Los Angeles: University of California Press.

Hahlo, H. R., and Ellison Kahn (1960). *South Africa: The Development of Its Laws and Constitution*. London: Stevens and Sons.

Hanlon, Joseph (1986). *Beggar Your Neighbors: Apartheid Power in Southern Africa*. Bloomington, Ind.: Indiana University Press.

Harris, Norman (1927). *Europe and Africa*. New York: Houghton Mifflin.

Harrison, David (1981). *The White Tribe of Africa*. Berkeley and Los Angeles: University of California Press.

Hepple, Alexander (1967). *Verwoerd*. Baltimore, Md.: Penguin.

"History from South Africa." (1990). *Radical History Review* 46/47.

Hoernle, R. F. Alfred (1923–1926). "The Concept of the 'Primitive.' " *Bantu Studies: A Journal Devoted to the Scientific Study of Bantu, Hottentot, and Bushman* II: 327–32.

Houghton, D. Hobart (1967). *The South African Economy*. Cape Town: Oxford University Press.

Hufbauer, Gary C., and Jeffrey J. Schott (1985). *Economic Sanctions Reconsidered: History and Current Policy*. Washington, D.C.: Institute for International Economics.

Hugo, Pierre (1988). "Towards Darkness and Death: Racial Demonology in South Africa." *Journal of Modern African Studies* 24, no. 4: 567–90.

Johnstone, Frederick A. (1970). "White Prosperity and White Supremacy in South Africa Today." *African Affairs* 69 (April): 124–40.

Kammen, Michael (1980). *People of Paradox*. New York: Oxford University Press.

Karis, Thomas, and Gwendolen M. Carter, eds. (1972). *From Protest to Challenge: A Documentary History of African Politics in South Africa, 1822–1964*. 2 vols. Stanford, Calif.: Hoover Institution Press.

Kiernan, V. G. (1980). *America: The New Imperialism, from White Settlement to World Hegemony*. London: Zed Books.

Kifner, John (1990). "Planning Is Begun on South African Aid Bank." *New York Times*, July 5: 3.

Kretzschmar, Louise (1986). *The Voice of Black Theology in South Africa*. Johannesburg: Ravan Press.

Lauren, Paul G. (1988). *Power and Prejudice: The Politics and Diplomacy of Racial Discrimination*. Boulder, Colo., and London: Westview Press.

Laurence, Patrick (1990). "Comrades and Capitalists." *Africa Report* (September/October): 39–42.

Leatt, James, Theo Kneifel, and Klaus Nurnberger, eds. (1986). *Contending Ideologies in South Africa*. Grand Rapids, Mich.: Eerdmans.

Leftwich, Adrian (1974). "The Constitution and Continuity of South African Inequality: Some Conceptual Questions." In *South Africa: Economic Growth and Political Change*, edited by Adrian Leftwich. London: Oxford University Press.

Legassick, Martin (1975). "South Africa: Forced Labor, Industrialization, and Racial Differentiation." In *The Political Economy of Africa*, edited by R. Harris. Cambridge, Mass.: Schenkman Publishing.

Lelyveld, Joseph (1985). *Move Your Shadow*. New York: Random House.

le Roux, Pieter (1991). "The South African Economy: The Challenge of Democracy." In *Economic Prospects after Apartheid*. IDASA, Occasional Paper no. 27.

Lewis, Gavin (1987). *Between the Wire and the Wall: A History of South African "Colored" Politics*. New York: St. Martin's Press.

Lewsen, Phyllis, ed. (1988). *Voices of Protest: From Segregation to Apartheid, 1938–1948*. Craighall, South Africa: A. D. Donker.

Libby, Ronald T. (1987). "Transnational Corporations and the National Bourgeoisie: Regional Expansion and Party Realignment in South Africa." In *Studies in Power and Class in Africa*, edited by Irving L. Markovitz. New York: Oxford University Press.

Lipton, Merle (1985). *Capitalism and Apartheid: South Africa, 1910–1984*. Totowa, N.J.: Rowman and Allanheld.

Lodge, Tom (1983). *Black Politics in South Africa since 1945*. London and New York: Longman.

Loubser, Dr. J. A. (1987). *The Apartheid Bible: A Critical Review of Racial Theology in South Africa*. Cape Town: Longman.

Louw, Raymond (1989). "After a Feint to the Left, de Klerk Backs Conservative Apartheid and Blights Prospects of 'Reform.' " *Southern Africa Report* May 19: 1–2.

Lummis, C. Douglas (1991). "Development against Democracy." *Alternatives* 16, no. 1 (Winter): 31–66.

McHenry, Donald F. (1985). "The United Nations and Decolonization." *Africa Report* (September/October): 4–10.

Maclennan, John (1991). "New South Africa Need Not Punish the 'Haves.' " *Sunday Star* February 4: 1.

Magubane, Bernard M. (1979). *The Political Economy of Race and Class in South Africa*. New York: Monthly Review Press.

Malan, D. F. (1987). "Apartheid: A Divine Calling." In *The Anti-Apartheid Reader*, edited by David Mermelstein. New York: Grove Press.

Mandela, Nelson (1986). *The Struggle Is My Life*. New York: Pathfinder Press.

——— (1990). "Visions of Change: A Symposium." *Journal of Democracy* 1, no. 4: 38–41.

Manzo, Kate (1986). "U.S. South Africa Policy in the 1980s: Constructive Engagement and Beyond." *Policy Studies Review* 6, no. 2 (November): 212–21.

——— (1991). "Modernist Discourse and the Crisis of Development Theory." *Studies in Comparative International Development* 26, no. 2: 3–45.

Mare, Gerhard, and Georgina Hamilton (1987). *An Appetite for Power: Buthelezi's Inkatha and South Africa*. Bloomington, Ind.: Indiana University Press.

Marks, Shula, and Richard Rathbone, eds. (1982). *Industrialization and Social Change in South Africa: African Class Formation, Culture, and Consciousness, 1870–1930*. London and New York: Longman.

Mbeki, Govan (1973). *South Africa: The Peasants' Revolt*. Gloucester, Mass.: Peter Smith.

Meer, Fatima (1971). "African Nationalism: Some Inhibiting Facts." In *South Africa: Sociological Perspectives*, edited by Heribert Adam. New York and London: Oxford University Press.

——— (1990). "Negotiating a Nonracial Democracy." *The Nation* (March 12): 345–49.

Motlhabi, Mokgethi (1984). *The Theory and Practice of Black Resistance to Apartheid.* Johannesburg: Skotaville Publishers.

Mufson, Steven (1988). "A Long View from Deep Soweto." *Mother Jones* (February/March): 8–11.

Muller, C. F. J. (1969). *Five Hundred Years: A History of South Africa.* Pretoria and Cape Town: Academia Press.

Myers, Desaix (1980). *U.S. Business in South Africa: The Economic, Political and Moral Issues.* Bloomington, Ind., and London: Indiana University Press.

Mzala (1988). *Gatsha Buthelezi: Chief with a Double Agenda.* London: Zed Books.

Nandy, Ashis (1987). *Traditions, Tyranny and Utopias: Essays in the Politics of Awareness.* Delhi: Oxford University Press.

Nattrass, Jill (1977). "The Narrowing of Wage Differentials in South Africa." *South African Journal of Economics* 45, no. 4 (December): 408–32.

———— (1978). "Economic Development and Political Change—A Suggested Theoretical Framework." In *Change, Reform and Economic Growth in South Africa,* edited by Lawrence Schlemmer and Eddie Webster. Johannesburg: Ravan Press.

———— (1981). *The South African Economy: Its Growth and Change.* Cape Town: Oxford University Press.

Noble, Kenneth B. (1991). "South Africa's President Outlines Plan for Universal Voting Rights." *New York Times* September 5: 1, 9.

Ngubane, Jordan K. (1963). *An African Explains Apartheid.* New York: Praeger.

Nolutshungu, Sam C. (1975). *South Africa in Africa: A Study of Ideology and Foreign Policy.* New York: Africana Publishing.

Odendaal, Andre (1984). *Black Protest Politics in South Africa to 1912.* Totowa, N.J.: Barnes and Noble.

O'Meara, Dan (1983). *Volkskapitalisme: Class, Capital and Ideology in the Development of Afrikaner Nationalism, 1934–1948.* Cambridge: Cambridge University Press.

Omond, Roger (1991). "African National Congress Left with a Credibility Problem." *Guardian Weekly* April 14: 11.

———— (1991). "South African Spectre of Carnage Persists." *Guardian Weekly* April 14: 11.

Rabinow, Paul, ed. (1984). *The Foucault Reader.* New York: Pantheon Books.

Rheinallt-Jones, J. D., ed. (1923–1941). *Bantu Studies: A Journal Devoted to the Scientific Study of Bantu, Hottentot, and Bushman.* Johannesburg: University of Witwatersrand Press.

Richardson, Peter, and Jean-Jacques van Helten (1982). "Labor in the South African Gold Mining Industry, 1886–1914." In *Industrialization and Social Change in South Africa: African Class Formation, Culture, and Consciousness, 1870–1930,* edited by Shula Marks and Richard Rathbone. New York: Longman.

Riesenfeld, Daniel (1989). "David Webster: The Spirit Is Unbroken." *Africa Report* (May/June): 27–30.

Sachs, Bernard (1961). *The Road from Sharpeville.* New York: Marzani and Munsell.

Sampson, Anthony (1987). *Black and Gold: Tycoons, Revolutionaries, and Apartheid.* New York: Pantheon.

Schaeffer, M. (1977). "The History of Industrial Legislation as Applied in South Africa with Special Reference to Black Workers." *Journal of South African Law* 49–55.

Schoeman, Fanus (1991). "In Quest of Co-Operation: A National Party Perspective." In *Economy: Growth and Redistribution.* IDASA, Occasional Paper no. 34.

Scott, James C. (1990). *Domination and the Arts of Resistance: Hidden Transcripts.* New Haven, Conn., and London: Yale University Press.

Seery, Brendan, and Sefako Nyaka (1991). "Mandela Says 'No' to FW." *Sunday Star* February 3: 2.

Seidman, Ann, and Neva Seidman (1977). *South Africa and U.S. Multinational Corporations.* Westport, Conn.: Lawrence Hill and Co.

—— (1980). *Outposts of Monopoly Capitalism: Southern Africa in the Changing Global Economy.* Westport, Conn.: Lawrence Hill and Co.

Shabalala, Sipho (1991). "Economic Emancipation: A Pan Africanist View." In *Economy: Growth and Redistribution.* IDASA, Occasional Paper no. 34.

Shava, Piniel V. (1989). *A People's Voice: Black South African Writing in the Twentieth Century.* London: Zed Books.

Shillington, Kevin (1982). "The Impact of the Diamond Discoveries on the Kimberley Hinterland." In *Industrialization and Social Change in South Africa: African Class Formation, Culture, and Consciousness, 1870–1930,* edited by Shula Marks and Richard Rathbone. New York: Longman.

Shiva, Vandana (1989). *Staying Alive: Women, Ecology and Development.* London: Zed Books.

South African Native Congress (1903). "Questions Affecting the Natives and Colored People Resident in British South Africa." In *From Protest to Challenge: A Documentary History of African Politics in South Africa, 1822–1964,* edited by Thomas Karis and Gwendolen M. Carter. 1973. Stanford, Calif: Hoover Institution Press.

Soyinka, Wole (1991). "A Time of Transition." *Transition* 51: 4–5.

Sparks, Allister (1990). *The Mind of South Africa.* New York: Alfred A. Knopf.

Tambo, Oliver (1966). "Passive Resistance in South Africa." In *Southern Africa in Transition,* edited by John A. Davis and James K. Baker. New York: Praeger.

Thompson, Leonard (1985). *The Political Mythology of Apartheid.* New Haven, Conn., and London: Yale University Press.

Thurow, Roger (1989). "Brothers Symbolize Split in South Africa." *Wall Street Journal* March 3: 3.

Todorov, Tzvetan (1982). *The Conquest of America.* Translated by Richard Howard. New York: Harper & Row.

Trapido, Stanley (1979). "South Africa in a Comparative Study of Industrialization." *Journal of Development Studies* 7, no. 2 (April): 309–20.

Turrell, Rob (1982). "Kimberley: Labor and Compounds, 1871–1888." In *Industrialization and Social Change in South Africa: African Class Formation, Culture, and Consciousness, 1870–1930,* edited by Shula Marks and Richard Rathbone. New York: Longman.

Van der Horst, Sheila T. (1971). *Native Labor in South Africa.* London: Frank Cass.

Van der Merwe, J. H. (1990). "Visions of Change: A Symposium." *Journal of Democracy* 1, no. 4: 38–41.

Van Onselen, Charles (1982). *Studies in the Social and Economic History of the Witwatersrand, 1886–1914.* Vol. 1, *New Babylon.* New York: Longman.

Verhelst, Thierry G. (1990). *No Life without Roots: Culture and Development.* London: Zed Books.

Viljoen, Gerrit (1990). "Visions of Change: A Symposium." *Journal of Democracy* 1, no. 4: 41–45.

Walshe, Peter (1971). *The Rise of African Nationalism in South Africa.* Berkeley and Los Angeles: University of California Press.

Weinberg, Eli (1981). *Portrait of a People: A Personal Photographic Record of the South African Liberation Struggle.* London: International Defence and Aid Fund for Southern Africa.

Williams, Patricia J. (1991). *The Alchemy of Race and Rights: Diary of a Law Professor.* Cambridge, Mass.: Harvard University Press.

Wilson, Francis (1972). *Labor in the South African Gold Mines, 1911–1969.* Cambridge: Cambridge University Press.

Wilson, Francis, and Mamphela Ramphele (1989). *Uprooting Poverty: The South African Challenge.* New York: W. W. Norton.

Wilson, Monica, and Leonard Thompson, eds. (1969). *The Oxford History of South Africa,* vol. I. New York and London: Oxford University Press.

Wines, Michael (1991). "U.S. Takes Neutral Attitude on de Klerk Plan for Universal Suffrage." *New York Times,* September 6: 3.

Wolpe, Harold (1972). "Capitalism and Cheap Labor Power in South Africa: From Segregation to Apartheid." *Economy and Society* 1, no. 3: 425–56.

Wolpe, Howard, ed. (1980). *The Articulation of Modes of Production.* London: Routledge and Kegan Paul.

Wren, Christopher (1989). "South African Racial Toll Put at More Than 4,000." *New York Times,* March 5: 3.

––––––– (1991). "Apartheid Barrier to Land Scrapped in Pretoria Plan." *New York Times,* March 13: A1.

––––––– (1991). "Pretoria's Land Plan: More for Blacks." *New York Times,* March 16: 3.

––––––– (1991). "For a Dispossessed Tribe, a Time of Reckoning." *New York Times,* April 18: 4.

––––––– (1991). "Europe Drops Sanctions: A Reward, Not a Cure, for South Africa." *New York Times,* April 21: E5.

––––––– (1991). "Mandela Calls West Europe Racist on Sanctions." *New York Times,* April 28: 7.

––––––– (1991). "Apartheid Battleground Shifts to Economy." *New York Times,* October 13: 7.

––––––– (1991). "Seeking Respect, Pretoria Bets on Its Strong Economy." *New York Times,* October 27: 4.

––––––– (1991). "Anti-Apartheid Groups Seek Meeting of All Parties." *New York Times,* October 28: 7.

––––––– (1991). "Strike by Blacks Paralyzes South Africa." *New York Times,* November 5: 3.

NEWSPAPERS, PERIODICALS, AND ANNUALS

Africa Report (bimonthly), 1986–1990.

Africa Research Bulletin (weekly), 1980.

Africa Today (monthly), 1963.

Annual Report of the South African Institute for Race Relations, 1933–1951.

Annual Survey of Race Relations in South Africa, 1951–1973.

Beeld (daily), 1979–1980.

Die Burger (daily), 1980.

Die Transvaler (daily), 1980.

Die Vaderland (daily), 1980.

Guardian Weekly, 1990–1991.

The Nation, 1990–1991.

New Yorker (weekly), 1990.

New York Times (daily), 1960, 1973, 1989–1991.

Rapport (daily), 1980.

South Africa Yearbook, 1975, 1984.
Southern Africa Report (weekly), 1986–1990.
The Star (daily), 1991.
Sunday Star, 1991.
Wall Street Journal (daily), 1985, 1989.

Index

ABOUT THE AUTHOR

KATHRYN A. MANZO is an Assistant Professor of Political Science at Williams College.